WEBSTER'S
CONCISE
SPANISH–ENGLISH
ENGLISH–SPANISH
DICTIONARY

WEBSTER'S
CONCISE
SPANISH–ENGLISH
ENGLISH–SPANISH
DICTIONARY

**GEDDES&
GROSSET**

This edition published 2005 by Geddes & Grosset,
David Dale House, New Lanark, ML11 9DJ, Scotland

© 2004 Geddes & Grosset

First published 2004, reprinted 2005

ISBN 1 84205 453 8

Printed and bound in Poland

Abbreviations/Abreviaturas

abrev	abbreviation	abreviatura
adj	adjective	adjectivo
adv	adverb	adverbio
art	article	artículo
auto	automobile	automóvil
aux	auxiliary	auxiliar
bot	botany	botánica
chem	chemistry	química
col	colloquial term	lengua familiar
com	commerce	comercio
compd	in compounds	usada en palabras compuestas
comput	computers	informática
conj	conjunction	conjunctión
dep	sport	deporte
excl	exclamation	exclamación
f	feminine noun	sustantrivo femenino
fam	colloquial term	lengua familiar
ferro	railway	ferrocarrilero
fig	figurative use	uso figurado
gr	grammar	gramática
imp	impersonal	impersonal
inform	computers	informática
interj	interjection	interjección
invar	invariable	invariable
irr	irregular	irregular
jur	law term	jurisprudencia
law	law term	jurisprudencia
ling	linguistics	lingüística
m	masculine noun	sustantivo masculino
mar	marine term	vocablo marítimo
mat, math	mathematics	matemáticas
med	medicine	medicina
mil	military term	lo militar
mus	music	música
n	noun	sustantivo
pej	pejorative	peyorativo
pl	plural	plural
pn	pronoun	pronombre

poet	poetical term	vocablo poético
prep	preposition	preposición
quim	chemistry	química
rad	radio	radio
rail	railway	ferrocarilero
sl	slang	argot
teat	theatre	teatro
tec	technology	téchnica, tecnologia
TV	television	televisión
vb	verb	verbo
vi	intransitive verb	verbo intransitivo
vr	reflexive verb	verbo reflexivo
vt	transitive verb	verbo transitivo

Spanish–English Dictionary

A

a *prep* to; in; at; according to; on; by; for; of.

abadía *f* abbey.

abajo *adv* under, underneath; below.

abalanzarse *vr* to rush forward.

abandonado/da *adj* derelict; abandoned; neglected.

abandonar *vt* to abandon; to leave:—~**se** *vr* ~ **a** to give oneself up to.

abarcar *vt* to include; to monopolize.

abarrotado/da *adj* packed.

abarrotar *vt* to tie down; (*mar*) to stow.

abastecer *vt* to purvey.

abatido/da *adj* dejected, low-spirited; abject.

abatimiento *m* low spirits *pl*, depression.

abatir *vt* to knock down; to humble.

abdicar *vt* to abdicate.

abdomen *m* abdomen.

abdominal *adj* abdominal.

abecedario *m* alphabet; spelling book, primer.

abeja *f* bee.

aberración *f* aberration.

abertura *f* aperture, chink, opening.

abeto *m* fir tree.

abierto/ta *adj* open; sincere; frank.

abismal *adj* abysmal.

abismo *m* abyss; gulf; hell.

ablandar *vt*, *vi* to soften.

abnegado/da *adj* selfless.

abogacía *f* legal profession.

abogado/a *m/f* lawyer; barrister.

abogar *vi* to intercede:—~ **por** to advocate.

abolir *vt* to abolish.

abollar *vt* to dent.

abonado/da *adj* paid-up:—*m/f* subscriber.

abonar *vt* to settle; to fertilize.

abono *m* payment; subscription; dung, manure.

aborrecer *vt* to hate, abhor.

abortar *vi* to miscarry; to have an abortion.

aborto *m* abortion; monster.

abotonar *vt* to button.

abovedado/da *adj* vaulted.

abrasar *vt* to burn; to parch:—~**se** *vr* to burn oneself.

abrazar *vt* to embrace; to surround; to contain.

abrazo *m* embrace.

abrebotellas *m invar* bottle opener.

abrelatas *m invar* can opener.

abreviar *vt* to abridge, cut short.

abridor *m* opener.

abrigar *vt* to shelter; to protect.

abrigo *m* shelter; protection; aid.

abril *m* April.

abrillantar *vt* to polish.

abrir *vt* to open; to unlock.

abrochar *vt* to button; to do up.

abrumar *vt* to overwhelm.

absolución *f* forgiveness, absolution.

absoluto/ta *adj* absolute.

absorber *vt* to absorb.

absorción *f* absorption; takeover.

absorto *adj* engrossed.

abstemio *adj* teetotal.

abstracción *f* abstraction.

abstracto/ta *adj* abstract.

abstraer *vt* to abstract:—~**se** *vr* to be absorbed.

absuelto/ta *adj* absolved.

absurdo *adj* absurd.

abuela f grandmother.

abuelo m grandfather.

abulia f lethargy.

abultado/da adj bulky, large, massive.

abultar vt to increase, enlarge:—vi to be bulky.

abundante adj abundant, copious.

aburrido/da adj boring, bored.

aburrir vt to bore, weary.

abusar vt to abuse.

acá adv here.

acabado/da adj perfect, accomplished; old.

acabar vt to finish, complete; to achieve:—~se vr to finish, expire.

academia f academy; literary society.

acaecer vi to happen.

acallar vt to quiet, hush; to soften, appease.

acalorado/da adj heated.

acampar vt (mil) to encamp.

acanalado/da adj grooved; fluted.

acaparar vt to monopolize; to hoard.

acariciar vt to fondle, caress.

acarrear vt to transport; to occasion.

acaso m chance:—adv perhaps.

acatarrarse vr to catch cold.

acceder vi to agree:—~ a to have access to.

accesible adj attainable; accessible.

acceso m access; fit.

accidentado/da adj uneven; hilly; eventful.

accidental adj accidental; casual.

accidente m accident.

acción f action, operation; share.

accionar vt to work.

accionista m shareholder.

acebo m holly tree.

acechar vt to lie in ambush for; to spy on.

aceite m oil.

aceituna f olive.

aceitunado/da adj olive-green.

aceleración f acceleration.

aceleradamente adv swiftly, hastily.

acelerar vt to accelerate; to hurry.

acento m accent.

aceptar vt to accept, admit.

acera f sidewalk.

acerca prep about, relating to.

acercar vt to move nearer:—~se vr ~ a to approach.

acero m steel.

acertar vt to hit; to guess right.

acertijo m riddle.

achacar vt to impute.

achaque m ailment; excuse; subject, matter.

achicar vt to diminish; to humiliate; to bale (out).

achicharrar vt to scorch; to overheat.

aciago/ga adj unlucky; ominous.

ácido m acid:—~/da adj acid, sour.

acierto m success; solution; dexterity.

aclamar vt to applaud, acclaim.

aclaración f clarification.

aclarar vt to clear; to brighten; to explain; to clarify.

acobardar vt to intimidate.

acodarse vr to lean.

acoger vt to receive; to welcome; to harbor:—~se vr to take refuge.

acogida f reception; asylum.

acometida f attack, assault.

acomodar vt to accommodate, arrange:—~se vr to comply.

acompañar vt to accompany; to join; (mus) to accompany.

acompasado/da adj measured; well-proportioned.

acondicionar vt to arrange; to condition.

acongojar vt to distress.

aconsejar *vt* to advise:—**~se** *vr* to take advice.

acontecer *vi* to happen.

acontecimiento *m* event, incident.

acoplar *vt* to couple; to fit; to connect.

acordar *vt* to agree; to remind:—**~se** *vr* to agree; to remember.

acorde *adj* harmonious:—*m* chord.

acordeón *m* accordion.

acorralar *vt* to round up; to intimidate.

acortar *vt* to abridge, shorten:—**~se** *vr* to become shorter.

acostar *vt* to put to bed; to lay down:—**~se** *vr* to go to bed; to lie down.

acostumbrar *vi* to be used to:—*vt* to accustom:—**~se** *vr* ~ **a** to become used to.

acotar *vt* to set bounds to; to annotate.

ácrata *m/f* anarchist.

acreditar *vt* to guarantee; to assure; to authorize.

acreedor *m* creditor.

acribillar *vt* to riddle with bullets; to molest, torment.

acta *f* act:—**~s** *fpl* records *pl*.

actitud *f* attitude; posture.

actividad *f* activity; liveliness.

activo/va *adj* active; diligent.

acto *m* act, action; act of a play; ceremony.

actor *m* actor; plaintiff.

actriz *f* actress.

actuación *f* action; behavior; proceedings *pl*.

actual *adj* actual, present.

actualizar *vt* to update.

actuar *vt* to work; to operate:—*vi* to work; to act.

acuarela *f* watercolor.

acudir *vi* to go to; to attend; to assist.

acuerdo *m* agreement:—**de ~** OK.

acumular *vt* to accumulate, collect.

acurrucarse *vr* to squat; to huddle up.

adelantado/da *adj* advanced; fast.

adelantar *vt, vi* to advance, accelerate; to pass.

adelante *adv* forward(s):—*excl* come in!

adelanto *m* advance; progress; improvement.

adelgazar *vt* to make thin or slender; to discuss with subtlety.

además *adv* moreover, besides:—**~ de** besides.

adentro *adv* in; inside.

aderezar *vt* to dress, adorn; to prepare; to season.

adeudar *vt* to owe:—**~se** *vr* to run into debt.

adherir *vi:*—**~a** to adhere to; to espouse.

adiestrar *vt* to guide; to teach, instruct.

adiós *excl* goodbye; hello.

adivinar *vt* to foretell; to guess.

admirar *vt* to admire; to surprise:—**~se** *vr* to be surprised.

admitir *vt* to admit; to let in; to concede; to permit.

admonición *f* warning.

adobar *vt* to dress; to season.

adobe *m* adobe, sun-dried brick.

adobo *m* dressing; pickle sauce.

adolecer *vi* to suffer from.

adolescencia *f* adolescence.

adónde *adv* where.

adoptar *vt* to adopt.

adoquín *m* paving stone.

adorar *vt* to adore; to love.

adormecer *vt* to put to sleep:—**~se** *vr* to fall asleep.

adornar vt to embellish, adorn.

adosado/da adj semi-detached.

adquirir vt to acquire.

adrede adv on purpose.

aduana f customs pl.

adueñarse vr:—~ **de** to take possession of.

adular vt to flatter.

adulterio m adultery.

adulto/ta adj, m/f adult, grown-up.

advenedizo m upstart.

advenimiento m arrival; accession.

adversidad f adversity; setback.

advertencia f warning, foreword.

advertir vt to notice; to warn.

aerodeslizador m hovercraft.

aeronave f spaceship.

aeropuerto m airport.

afán m hard work; desire.

afanar vt to harass; (col) to pinch:—~se vr to strive.

afear vt to deform, misshape.

afección f affection; fondness, attachment; disease.

afectar vt to affect, feign.

afectuoso/sa adj affectionate; moving; tender.

afeitar vt:—~se vr to shave.

aferrar vt to grapple, grasp, seize.

afianzar vt to strengthen; to prop up.

aficionado/da adj keen:—m/f lover, devotee; amateur.

afilado adj sharp.

afilar vt to sharpen, grind.

afín m related; similar.

afinar vt to tune; to refine.

afincarse vr to settle.

afirmar vt to secure, fasten; to affirm, assure.

aflicción f affliction, grief.

aflictivo/va adj distressing.

aflojar vt to loosen, slacken, relax.

aflorar vi to emerge.

afluente adj flowing:—m tributary.

afónico/ca adj hoarse; voiceless.

afortunado/da adj fortunate, lucky.

afrenta f outrage; insult.

afrontar vt to confront; to bring face to face.

afuera adv out, outside.

agacharse vr to stoop, squat.

agarradero m handle.

agarrar vt to grasp, seize:—~se vr to hold on tightly.

agasajar vt to receive and treat kindly; to regale.

agenciarse vr to obtain.

agenda f diary.

agente m agent; policeman.

ágil adj agile.

agilidad f agility, nimbleness.

agitar vt to wave; to move:—~se vr to become excited; to become worried.

aglomeración f crowd; jam.

agobiar vt to weigh down; to oppress; to burden.

agolparse vr to assemble in crowds.

agonía f agony.

agorar vt to predict.

agostar vt to parch.

agosto m August.

agotado/da adj exhausted; finished; sold out.

agotar vt to exhaust; to drain; to misspend.

agradable adj pleasant; lovely.

agradar vt to please, gratify.

agradecer vt to be grateful for; to thank.

agradecido/da adj thankful.

agrandar vt to enlarge; to exaggerate.

agrario/ria adj agrarian; agricultural.

agravante f further difficulty.

agraviar vt to wrong; to offend:—**~se** vr to be aggrieved; to be piqued.

agredir vt to attack.

agregar vt to aggregate, heap together; to collate; to appoint.

agreste adj rustic, rural.

agrícola adj farming compd.

agricultor/ra m/f farmer.

agrietarse vr to crack.

agrimensor m surveyor.

agrio adj sour, acrid; rough, craggy; sharp, rude, unpleasant.

agrupar vt to group, cluster; to crowd.

agua f water.

aguacate m avocado pear.

aguacero m cloudburst, downpour.

aguado/da adj watery.

aguafuerte m etching.

aguamarina f aquamarine (gem stone).

aguanieve f sleet.

aguantar vt to bear, suffer; to hold up.

aguardar vt to wait for.

aguarrás f turpentine.

agudo/da adj sharp; keen-edged; smart; fine; acute; witty; brisk.

aguijón m sting of a bee, wasp, etc; stimulation.

águila f eagle; genius.

aguileño/ña adj aquiline; sharp-featured.

aguja f needle; spire; hand; magnetic needle; (ferro) points pl.

agujerear vt to pierce, bore.

agujero m hole.

ahí adv there.

ahijada f goddaughter.

ahijado m godson.

ahínco m earnestness; eagerness.

ahogar vt to smother; to drown; to suffocate; to oppress; to quench.

ahora adv now, at present; just now.

ahorrar vt to save; to avoid.

ahumar vt to smoke, cure (in smoke):—**~se** vr to fill with smoke.

ahuyentar vt to drive off; to dispel.

aire m air; wind; aspect; musical composition.

aislar vt to insulate; to isolate.

ajardinado/da adj landscaped.

ajedrez m chess.

ajedrezado/da adj chequered.

ajeno/na adj someone else's; foreign; ignorant; improper.

ajetreo m activity; bustling.

ajo m garlic.

ajorca f bracelet.

ajustar vt to regulate, adjust; to settle (a balance); to fit.

al = a el.

ala f wing; aisle; row, file; brim:—m/f winger.

alabar vt to praise; to applaud.

alacena f cupboard, closet.

alacrán m scorpion.

alambre m wire.

alameda f avenue; poplar grove.

álamo m poplar.

alargar vt to lengthen; to extend.

alarido m outcry, shout:—**dar ~s** to howl.

alarma f alarm.

alba f dawn.

albañil m mason, bricklayer.

albarán m invoice.

albaricoque m apricot.

albedrío m free will.

albergue m shelter:—**~ de juventud** youth hostel.

albóndiga f meatball.

albornoz m burnous:—**~ de bañio** bath robe.

alboroto m noise; disturbance, riot.

alborozo m joy.

albricias fpl good news pl.

albufera f lagoon.

álbum m album.

alcachofa f artichoke.

alcalde m mayor.

alcaldesa f mayoress.

alcantarilla m sewer; gutter.

alcanzar vt to reach; to get, obtain; to hit.

alcaparra f caper.

alcayata f hook.

alcázar m castle, fortress.

alcornoque m cork tree.

aldea f village.

aleatorio/ria adj random.

aleccionar vt to instruct; to train.

alegar vt to allege; to quote.

alegrar vt to cheer; to poke; to liven up:—~se vr to get merry.

alegre adj happy; merry, joyful; content.

alegría f happiness; merriment.

alejar vt to remove; to estrange:—~se vr to go away.

alemán/ana adj, m/f German:—m German language.

alentar vt to encourage.

alergia f allergy.

alero m gable-end; eaves pl.

alertar vt to alert.

aleta f fin; wing; flipper; fender.

alfabeto m alphabet.

alfarería f pottery.

alféizar m window sill.

alfiler m pin; clip; clothes pin.

alfombra f carpet; rug.

alga f (bot) seaweed.

algo pn something; anything:—adv somewhat.

algodón m cotton; cotton plant; cotton wool.

alguien pn someone, somebody; anyone, anybody.

alguno/na adj some; any; no:—pn someone, somebody.

alhaja f jewel.

aliado/da adj allied.

alianza f alliance, league; wedding ring.

alicates mpl pincers pl, nippers pl.

aliciente m attraction; incitement.

aliento m breath; respiration.

aligerar vt to lighten; to alleviate; to hasten; to ease.

alijo m lightening of a ship; alleviation; cache.

alimentar vt to feed, nourish:—~se vr to feed.

aliñar vt to adorn; to season.

alinear vt to arrange in line:—~se vr to line up.

alisar vt to plane; to polish; to smooth.

aliviar vt to lighten; to ease; to relieve, mollify.

allá adv there; over there; then.

allanar vt to level, flatten; to subdue; to burgle.

allí adv there, in that place.

alma f soul; human being.

almacén m warehouse, store; magazine.

almacenar vt to store (up).

almeja f clam.

almena f battlement.

almendra f almond.

almíbar m syrup.

almirez m mortar.

almizcle m musk.

almohada f pillow; cushion.

almorranas fpl hemorrhoids pl.

almuerzo m lunch.

alocado/da adj crazy; foolish; inconsiderate.

alojamiento m lodgings, rooming house; housing.

alpargata *f* rope-soled shoe.

alpinismo *m* mountaineering.

alquilar *vt* to let, rent; to hire.

alquitrán *m* tar, liquid pitch.

alrededor *adv* around.

alta *f* (*mil*) discharge from hospital.

altanero/ra *adj* haughty, arrogant, vain, proud.

altavoz *m* loudspeaker, amplifier.

alterar *vt* to alter, change; to disturb.

altercado *m* altercation, controversy; quarrel.

alterno/na *adj* alternate; alternating.

Alteza *f* Highness (title).

altibajos *mpl* ups and downs *pl*.

altitud *f* height; altitude.

altivo/va *adj* haughty, proud, highflown.

alto/ta *adj* high; tall:—*m* height; story; highland; (*mil*) halt; (*mus*) alto:—**i~!/i~ ahí!** *interj* stop!

altura *f* height; depth; mountain summit; altitude.

alubia *f* kidney bean.

alucinar *vt* to blind, deceive:—*vi* to hallucinate.

alumbrado *m* lighting; illumination.

alumbrar *vt* to light:—*vi* to give birth.

alumno/na *m/f* student, pupil.

alza *f* rise; sight.

alzar *vt* to raise, lift up:—**~se** *vr* to get up; to rise in rebellion.

ama *f* mistress; owner; housewife; foster mother.

amable *adj* kind, nice.

amagar *vt* to threaten; to shake one's fist at:—*vi* to feint.

amamantar *vt* to suckle.

amanecer *vi* to dawn:—**al ~** at daybreak.

amanerado/da *adj* affected.

amansar *vt* to tame; to soften; to subdue:—**~se** *vr* to calm down.

amante *m/f* lover.

amapola *f* (*bot*) poppy.

amar *vt* to love.

amargo/ga *adj* bitter, acrid; painful:—*m* bitterness.

amarillo/lla *adj* yellow:—*m* yellow.

amarrar *vt* to moor; to tie, fasten.

amasar *vt* to knead; (*fig*) to arrange, settle; to prepare.

ámbar *m* amber.

ambiente *m* atmosphere; environment.

ambiguo/gua *adj* ambiguous; doubtful, equivocal.

ámbito *m* circuit, circumference; field; scope.

ambos/bas *adj*, *pn* both.

ambulante *adj* traveling.

ambulatorio *m* state-run clinic.

amenazar *vt* to threaten.

ameno/na *adj* pleasant; delicious; flowery (of language).

América *f* America:—**~ del Norte/del Sur** North/South America.

amianto *m* asbestos.

amiga *f* (female) friend.

amigo *m* friend; comrade; lover:—**~/ga** *adj* friendly.

aminorar *vt* to diminish; to reduce.

amistad *f* friendship.

amistoso/sa *adj* friendly, cordial.

amo *m* owner; boss.

amoldar *vt* to mold; to adapt:—**~se** *vr* to adapt oneself.

amor *m* love; fancy; lover:—**~ mio** my love:—**por ~ de Dios** for God's sake:—**~ propio** self-love.

amortiguador *m* shock absorber.

amortizar *vt* to redeem, pay, liquidate, discharge (a debt).

amperio m amp.

ampliar vt to amplify, enlarge; to extend; to expand.

amplificador m amplifier.

amplio/lia adj ample, extensive.

ampolla f blister; ampoule.

amueblar vt to furnish.

anacoreta m anchorite, hermit.

anacronismo m anachronism.

añadir vt to add.

analfabeto/ta adj illiterate.

analgésico m painkiller.

análisis m analysis.

anaranjado/da adj orange-colored.

anarquía f anarchy.

ancho/cha adj broad, wide, large:—m breadth, width.

anchoa f anchovy.

anchura f width, breadth.

anciano/na adj old:—m/f old man/ woman.

ancla f anchor.

anclaje m anchorage.

andamiaje m scaffolding.

andar vi to go, walk; to fare; to act, proceed.

andén m sidewalk; (ferro) platform; quayside.

andrajo m rag.

anegar vt to inundate, submerge;.

añejo/ja adj old; stale, musty.

anexión f annexation.

anfibio/bia adj amphibious.

anfitrión/ona m/f host(ess).

ángel m angel.

angosto/ta adj narrow, close.

anguila f eel.

angula f elver.

angular adj angular:—**piedra ~** f cornerstone.

ángulo m angle, corner.

angustia f anguish; heartache.

anhelar vi to gasp:—vt to long for.

anidar vi to nestle, make a nest; to dwell, inhabit.

añil m indigo plant; indigo.

anillo m ring.

ánima f soul.

animación f liveliness; activity.

animado/da adj lively.

animal adj, m animal.

animar vt to animate, liven up; to comfort; to revive:—**~se** vr to cheer up.

ánimo m soul; courage; mind; intention:—excl come on!

anís m aniseed; anisette.

aniversario/ria adj annual:—m anniversary.

ano m anus.

año m year.

anoche adv last night.

anochecer vi to grow dark:—m nightfall.

anónimo/ma adj anonymous.

añoranza f longing.

anormal adj abnormal.

anotar vt to comment, note.

anquilosamiento m paralysis.

ánsar m goose.

ansiar vt to desire.

ansiedad f anxiety.

antagónico/ca adj antagonistic; opposed.

antaño adv formerly.

ante m suede:—prep before; in the presence of; faced with.

anteanoche adv the night before last.

anteayer adv the day before yesterday.

antebrazo m forearm.

antelación f:—**con ~** in advance.

antemano adv:—**de ~** beforehand.

antena f feeler, antenna; aerial.

antepasado/da *adj* passed, elapsed:— **~s** *mpl* ancestors *pl*.

anterior *adj* preceding; former.

antes *prep, adv* before:—*conj* before.

antibiótico *m* antibiotic.

anticiclón *m* anticyclone.

anticipar *vt* to anticipate; to forestall; to advance.

anticonceptivo *m* contraceptive.

anticongelante *m* antifreeze.

anticuado/da *adj* antiquated.

anticuerpo *m* antibody.

antiestético/ca *adj* unsightly.

antifaz *m* mask.

antiguamente *adv* in ancient times, of old.

antiguo/gua *adj* antique, old, ancient.

antipático/ca *adj* unpleasant.

antojo *m* whim, fancy; longing.

antorcha *f* torch; taper.

antro *m* (*poet*) cavern, den, grotto.

antropófago *m* cannibal.

antropología *f* anthropology.

anual *adj* annual.

anudar *vt* to knot; to join:—**~se** *vr* to get into knots.

anular *vt* to annul; to revoke; to cancel:—*adj* annular.

anunciar *vt* to announce; to advertise.

anuncio *m* advertisement.

anzuelo *m* hook; allurement.

apacible *adj* affable; gentle; placid, quiet.

apaciguar *vt* to appease; to pacify, calm.

apagar *vt* to put out; to turn off; to quench, extinguish.

apañar *vt* to grasp; to pick up; to patch:—**~se** *vr* to manage.

aparador *m* sideboard; store window.

aparato *m* apparatus; machine; radio or television set; ostentation, show; (*med*) bandage, dressing.

aparcamiento *m* parking lot.

aparcar *vt, vi* to park.

aparecer *vi* to appear:—**~se** *vr* to appear.

aparentar *vt* to look; to pretend; to deceive.

apariencia *f* outward appearance.

apartamento *m* flat, apartment.

apartar *vt* to separate, divide; to remove; to sort;.

aparte *m* aside; new paragraph:—*adv* apart, separately; besides; aside.

apasionado/da *adj* passionate; devoted; fond; biased.

apeadero *m* halt, stopping place; station.

apearse *vr* to dismount; to get down/out/off.

apechugar *vt* to face up to.

apego *m* attachment, fondness.

apelar *vi* (*jur*) to appeal:—**~ a** to have recourse to.

apellido *m* surname; family name; epithet.

apenar *vt* to grieve; to embarrass:— **~se** *vr* to grieve; to be embarrassed.

apenas *adv* scarcely, hardly:—*conj* as soon as.

apéndice *m* appendix, supplement.

apercibirse *vr* to notice.

aperitivo *m* aperitif; appetizer.

apero *m* agricultural implement.

apesadumbrar *vt* to sadden.

apestar *vt* to infect:—*vi* **~ a** to stink of.

apetito *m* appetite.

apiadarse *vr* to take pity.

apilar *vt* to pile up:—**~se** *vr* to pile up.

apiñado/da *adj* crowded; pyramidal; pine-shaped.

apio *m* (bot) celery.

apisonadora *f* steamroller.

aplacar *vt* to appease, pacify:—**~se** *vr* to calm down.

aplastar *vt* to flatten, crush.

aplatanarse *vr* to get weary.

aplaudir *vt* to applaud; to extol.

aplauso *m* applause; approbation, praise.

aplazar *vt* to postpone.

aplicado/da *adj* studious; industrious.

aplicar *vt* to apply; to clasp; to attribute:—**~se** *vr* ~ **a** to devote oneself to.

aplique *m* wall light.

aplomo *m* self-assurance.

apocado/da *adj* timid.

apoderado/da *adj* powerful:—*m* proxy, attorney; agent.

apodo *m* nickname, sobriquet.

apogeo *m* peak.

apósito *m* (med) external dressing.

aposta *adv* on purpose.

apostar *vt* to bet, wager; to post soldiers:—*vi* to bet.

apóstol *m* apostle.

apoteosis *f* apotheosis.

apoyar *vt* to rest; to favor, patronize, support:—**~se** *vr* to lean.

apreciar *vt* to appreciate; to estimate, value.

aprecio *m* appreciation; esteem.

apremiante *adj* urgent.

aprender *vt* to learn:—**~ de memoria** to learn by heart.

aprensión *f* apprehension.

apresar *vt* to seize, grasp.

apresurar *vt* to accelerate, hasten, expedite:—**~se** *vr* to hurry.

apretar *vt* to compress, tighten; to constrain:—*vi* to be too tight.

aprisa *adv* quickly, swiftly; promptly.

aprobar *vt* to approve; to pass:—*vi* to pass.

apropiado/da *adj* appropriate.

aprovechar *vt* to use; to exploit; to profit from; to take advantage of:—*vi* to be useful; to progress:—**~se** *vr* ~ **de** to use; to take advantage of.

aproximar *vt* to approach:—**~se** *vr* to approach.

aptitud *f* aptitude, fitness, ability.

apto/ta *adj* apt; fit, able; clever.

apuesta *f* bet, wager.

apuñalar *vt* to stab.

apuntar *vt* to aim; to level, point at; to mark:—*vi* to begin to appear or show itself; to prompt (theater):—**~se** *vr* to score; to enrol.

apurado/da *adj* poor, destitute of means; exhausted; hurried.

aquél/~ la *pn* that (one):—**~ los/~ las** *pl* those (ones).

aquel/~la *adj* that:—**~los/~las** *pl* those.

aquello *pn* that.

aquí *adv* here; now.

árabe *adj, m/f*, *m* (ling) Arab, Arabic.

arado *m* plough.

araña *f* spider; chandelier.

arañar *vt* to scratch; to scrape; to corrode.

arancel *m* tariff.

arandela *f* washer.

arar *vt* to plough.

árbitro *m* arbitrator; referee; umpire.

árbol *m* tree; (mar) mast; shaft.

arbolado/da *adj* forested; wooded:—*m* woodland.

arbusto *m* shrub.

arca *f* chest, wooden box.

arcada *f* arch; arcade:—**~s** *fpl* retching.

arce *m* maple tree.

archivar *vt* to file.

arcilla *f* clay.

arco *m* arc; arch; fiddle bow; hoop:—~iris rainbow.

arder *vi* to burn, blaze.

ardilla *f* squirrel.

área *f* area.

arena *f* sand; grit; arena.

arenque *m* herring:—~ **ahumado** red herring.

argolla *f* large ring.

argucia *f* subtlety.

argumentar *vt*, *vi* to argue, dispute; to conclude.

árido/da *adj* dry; barren.

arisco/ca *adj* fierce; rude; intractable.

arlequín *m* harlequin, buffoon.

arma *f* weapon, arms.

armado/da *adj* armed; reinforced.

armador *m* shipowner; privateer; jacket, jerkin.

armar *vt* to man; to arm; to fit:—~**la** to kick up a fuss.

armario *m* wardrobe; cupboard.

armazón *f* chassis; skeleton; frame.

armonía *f* harmony.

armonizar *vt* to harmonize; to reconcile.

arnés *m* harness:—~**eses** *mpl* gear, trappings *pl*.

aro *m* ring; earring.

aroma *m* aroma, fragrance.

arpa *f* harp.

arpía *f* (*poet*) harpy, shrew.

arpillera *f* sackcloth.

arpón *m* harpoon.

arqueado/da *adj* arched, vaulted.

arquero *m* archer.

arquitectónico/ca *adj* architectural.

arrabal *m* suburb; slum.

arraigado *adj* deep-rooted; established.

arraigar *vi* to root; to establish:—*vt* to establish;.

arrancar *vt* to pull up by the roots; to pull out:—*vi* to start; to move.

arrasar *vt* to demolish, destroy.

arrastrar *vt* to drag:—*vi* to creep, crawl; to lead a trump at cards:—~**se** *vr* to crawl; to grovel.

arrebatar *vt* to carry off, snatch; to enrapture.

arrebato *m* fury; rapture.

arrecife *m* reef.

arreglar *vt* to regulate; to tidy; to adjust:—~**se** *vr* to come to an understanding.

arrellanarse *vr* to sit at ease; to make oneself comfortable.

arrendar *vt* to rent, let out, lease.

arrendatario/ria *m/f* tenant.

arrepentirse *vr* to repent.

arrestar *vt* to arrest; to imprison.

arriate *m* flowerbed; causeway.

arriba *adv* above, over, up; high; on high, overhead; aloft.

arribista *m/f* upstart.

arriendo *m* lease; farm rent.

arriesgado *adj* risky, dangerous; daring.

arriesgar *vt* to risk, hazard; to expose to danger:—~**se** *vr* to take a chance.

arrimar *vt* to approach, draw near; (*mar*) to stow (cargo):—~**se** *vr* to sidle up; to lean.

arrinconar *vt* to put in a corner; to lay aside.

arrodillarse *vr* to kneel down.

arrogante *adj* arrogant; haughty, proud; stout.

arrojar *vt* to throw, fling; to dash; to emit; to shoot, sprout:—~**se** *vr* to hurl oneself.

arrollar *vt* to run over; to defeat heavily.

arropar *vt* to clothe, dress:—~**se** *vr* to wrap up.

arroyo *m* stream; gutter.

arroz *m* rice.

arrozal *m* ricefield.

arrugar *vt* to wrinkle; to rumple; to fold:—~ **la frente** to frown:—~**se** *vr* to shrivel.

arruinar *vt* to demolish; to ruin:—~**se** *vr* to go bankrupt.

arrullar *vt* to lull:—*vi* to coo.

artesanía *f* craftsmanship.

ártico/ca *adj* arctic, northern:—*m* **el A~** the Arctic.

articular *vt* to articulate; to joint.

artículo *m* article; clause; point; (*gr*) article; condition.

artífice *m* artisan; artist.

artificio *m* workmanship, craft; artifice, cunning trick.

artimaña *f* trap; cunning.

artista *m* artist; craftsman.

arzobispo *m* archbishop.

as *m* ace.

asa *f* handle; lever.

asado *m* roast meat; barbecue.

asaltar *vt* to assault; to storm (a position); to assail.

asamblea *f* assembly, meeting.

asar *vt* to roast.

ascender *vi* to be promoted; to rise:—*vt* to promote.

ascenso *m* promotion; ascent.

ascensor *m* elevator.

asco *m* nausea; loathing.

ascua *f* red-hot coal.

asear *vt* to clean; to tidy.

asedio *m* siege.

asegurar *vt* to secure; to insure; to affirm; to bail:—~**se** *vr* to make sure.

asentar *vt* to sit down; to affirm, assure; to note:—*vi* to suit.

asentir *vi* to acquiesce, concede.

aseo *m* cleanliness; neatness:—~**s** *mpl* rest room.

aséptico/ca *adj* germ-free.

asequible *adj* attainable; obtainable.

aserrar *vt* to saw.

aserrín *m* sawdust.

asesinar *vt* to assassinate; to murder.

asesorar *vt* to advise; to act as consultant:—~**se** *vr* to consult.

asfalto *m* asphalt.

asfixiar *vt* to suffocate:—~**se** *vr* to suffocate.

así *adv* so, thus, in this manner; like this; therefore; so that; also:—~ **que** so that; therefore:—**así/así** so-so; middling.

asiento *m* chair; bench; stool; seat; contract; entry; residence.

asignar *vt* to assign, attribute.

asignatura *f* subject; course.

asilo *m* asylum, refuge.

asimismo *adv* similarly, in the same manner.

asir *vt* to grasp, seize; to hold, grip:—*vi* to take root.

asistencia *f* audience; presence; assistance, help.

asistir *vi* to be present; to assist:—*vt* to help.

asma *f* asthma.

asno *m* ass.

asociación *f* association; partnership.

asolear *vt* to expose to the sun:—~**se** *vr* to sunbathe.

asomar *vi* to appear:—~**se** *vr* to appear, show up.

asombrar *vt* to amaze; to astonish:—~**se** *vr* to be amazed; to get a fright.

aspa *f* cross; sail.

aspecto *m* appearance; aspect.

áspero/ra *adj* rough, rugged; craggy, knotty; horrid; harsh, hard; severe, austere; gruff.

aspiración *f* breath; pause.

asqueroso/sa *adj* disgusting.

asta *f* lance; horn; handle.

astilla *f* chip (of wood), splinter.

astillero *m* dockyard.

astral *adj* astral.

astro *m* star.

astrología *m* astrology.

astronomía *f* astronomy.

astucia *f* cunning, slyness.

astuto/ta *adj* cunning, sly; astute.

asumir *vt* to assume.

asunto *m* subject, matter; affair, business.

asustar *vt* to frighten:—**~se** *vr* to be frightened.

atacar *vt* to attack.

atajo *m* short cut.

atañer *vi:*—**~ a** to concern.

atar *vt* to tie; to fasten.

atardecer *vi* to get dark:—*m* dusk; evening.

atascar *vt* to jam; to hinder:—**~se** *vr* to become bogged down.

ataúd *m* coffin.

atemorizar *vt* to frighten:—**~se** *vr* to get scared.

atención *f* attention, heedfulness; civility; observance, consideration.

atender *vi* to be attentive:—*vt* to attend to; to heed, expect, wait for; to look at.

atenerse *vr:*—**~ a** to adhere to.

atentamente *adv:*—**le saluda ~** yours faithfully.

atento/ta *adj* attentive; heedful; observing; mindful; polite, courteous, mannerly.

atenuar *vt* to diminish; to lessen.

ateo/a *adj, m/f* atheist.

aterciopelado/da *adj* velvety.

aterrar *vt* to terrify:—**~se** *vr* to be terrified.

aterrizar *vi* to land.

aterrorizar *vt* to frighten, terrify.

atesorar *vt* to treasure *or* hoard up (riches).

atestado/da *adj* packed:—*m* affidavit.

atestiguar *vt* to witness, attest.

atiborrar *vt* to stuff:—**~se** *vr* to stuff oneself.

ático *m* attic.

atinado/da *adj* wise; correct.

atizar *vt* to stir (the fire) with a poker; to stir up.

atlántico/ca *adj* atlantic.

atleta *m* athlete.

atletismo *m* athletics.

atomizador *m* spray.

átomo *m* atom.

atónito/ta *adj* astonished, amazed.

atontado/da *adj* stunned; silly.

atornillar *vt* to screw on; to screw down.

atosigar *vt* to poison; to harass; to oppress.

atracar *vt* to moor; to rob:—**~se** *vr* **~ (de)** to stuff oneself (with).

atractivo/va *adj* attractive; magnetic:—*m* charm.

atraer *vt* to attract, allure.

atragantarse *vr* to stick in the throat, choke.

atrapar *vt* to trap; to nab; to deceive.

atrás *adv* backward(s); behind; previously:—**hacia ~** backward(s).

atrasar *vi* to be slow:—*vt* to postpone:—**~ el reloj** to put back a watch:—**~se** *vr* to stay behind; to be late.

atravesado/da *adj* oblique; cross; perverse; mongrel; degenerate.

atravesar *vt* to cross; to pass over; to pierce; to go through:——**se** *vr* to get in the way; to meddle.

atreverse *vr* to dare, venture.

atribuir *vt* to attribute, ascribe; to impute.

atril *m* lectern; bookrest.

atrio *m* porch; portico.

atrocidad *f* atrocity.

atropellar *vt* to trample; to run down; to hurry; to insult:——**se** *vr* to hurry.

atroz *adj* atrocious, heinous; cruel.

atuendo *m* attire.

atún *m* tuna (fish).

aturdir *vt* to stun, confuse; to stupefy.

audaz *adj* audacious, bold.

audiencia *f* audience.

auge *m* boom; climax.

augurio *m* omen.

aula *f* lecture room.

aullar *vi* to howl.

aumentar *vt* to augment, increase; to magnify; to put up:——*vi* to increase; to grow larger.

aún *adv* even:——~ asi even so.

aunque *adv* though, although.

auricular *m* receiver:——~**es** *mpl* headphones *pl*.

aurora *f* dawn.

ausencia *f* absence.

ausente *adj* absent.

auspicio *m* auspice; prediction; protection.

austero/ra *adj* austere, severe.

auténtico/ca *adj* authentic.

autoadhesivo/va *adj* self-adhesive.

autobús *m* bus.

autocar *m* bus, coach.

autóctono/na *adj* native.

autodefensa *f* self-defense.

autodeterminación *f* self-determination.

autoescuela *f* driving school.

automovilismo *m* motoring; motor racing.

autónomo/ma *adj* autonomous.

autopista *f* motorway.

autopsia *f* post mortem, autopsy.

autor/ra *m/f* author; maker; writer.

autoridad *f* authority.

autorizar *vt* to authorize.

autorretrato *m* self-portrait.

autoservicio *m* self-service store; restaurant.

autostop *m* hitch-hiking.

autosuficiencia *f* self-sufficiency.

autovía *f* state highway.

auxiliar *vt* to aid, help, assist; to attend:——*adj* auxiliary.

aval *m* guarantee; guarantor.

avanzar *vt, vi* to advance.

avaricia *f* avarice.

avaro/ra *adj* miserly:——*m/f* miser.

ave *f* bird; fowl.

avecinarse *vr* to approach.

avellana *f* hazelnut.

avena *f* oats *pl*.

avenida *f* avenue.

aventajar *vt* to surpass, excel.

aventura *f* adventure; event, incident.

avergonzar *vt* to shame, abash:——**se** *vr* to be ashamed.

avería *f* breakdown.

averiado/da *adj* broken down; out of order.

averiguar *vt* to find out; to inquire into; to investigate.

avestruz *m* ostrich.

aviación *f* aviation; air force.

avicultura *f* poultry farming.

avidez *f* covetousness.

avinagrado/da *adj* sour.

avión *m* airplane.
avioneta *f* light aircraft.
avisar *vt* to inform; to warn; to advise.
aviso *m* notice; warning; hint.
avispa *f* wasp.
avispado/da *adj* lively, brisk; vivacious.
¡ay! *excl* alas!; ow!:—**¡~ de mi!** alas! poor me!
ayer *adv* yesterday.
ayuda *f* help, aid; support:—*m* deputy, assistant.
ayudar *vt* to help, assist; to further.
ayunar *vi* to fast, abstain from food.

ayuntamiento *m* town/city hall.
azabache *m* jet.
azafata *f* air hostess.
azafrán *m* saffron.
azahar *m* orange or lemon blossom.
azar *m* fate:—**por ~** by chance:—**al~** at random.
azotar *vt* to whip, lash.
azotea *f* flat roof of a house.
azúcar *m* sugar.
azufre *m* sulfur, brimstone.
azul *adj* blue:—**~ celeste** sky blue.
azulejo *m* tile.

B

baba *f* dribble, spittle.
babero *m* bib.
babia *f*:—**estar en ~** to be absent-minded *or* dreaming.
baca *f* (*auto*) luggage rack.
bacalao *m* cod.
bache *m* pothole.
bachillerato *m* baccalaureate.
bahía *f* bay.
bailar *vi* to dance.
bailarín/ina *m/f* dancer.
baja *f* fall; casualty.
bajada *f* descent; inclination; slope; ebb.
bajamar *f* low tide.
bajar *vt* to lower, let down; to lessen; to humble; to go/come down.
bajo/ja *adj* low; abject, despicable; common; humble:—*prep* under, underneath, below:—*adv* softly; quietly:—*m* (*mus*) bass; low place.
bala *f* bullet.
balance *m* hesitation; balance sheet; balance; rolling (of a ship).
balanza *f* scale; balance; judgement.

balar *vi* to bleat.
balcón *m* balcony.
balde *m* bucket:—**de ~** *adv* gratis, for nothing:—**en ~** in vain.
baldío/dia *adj* waste; uncultivated.
baldosa *f* floor; tile; flagstone.
ballena *f* whale; whalebone.
balneario *m* spa.
baloncesto *m* basketball.
balonmano *m* handball.
balonvolea *m* volleyball.
balsa *f* balsa wood; pool; raft, float; ferry.
bañador *m* swimsuit.
bañar *vt* to bathe; to dip; to coat (with varnish):—**~se** *vr* to bathe; to swim.
bancarrota *f* bankruptcy.
banco *m* bench; work bench; bank.
banda *f* band; sash; ribbon; troop; party; gang; touchline.
bandada *f* flock; shoal.
bandeja *f* tray, salver.
bandera *f* banner, standard; flag.
bando *m* faction, party; edict.
bandolero *m* bandit.

bañera f bath (tub).

baño m bath; dip; bathtub; varnish; crust of sugar; coating.

banqueta f three-legged stool; sidewalk.

banquete m banquet; formal dinner.

banquillo m dock.

bar m bar.

baraja f deck of cards.

barandilla f small balustrade, small railing.

barato/ta adj cheap:—**de ~** gratis:— m cheapness; bargain sale.

barba f chin; beard:—**~ a ~** face to face.

barbaridad f barbarity, barbarism; outrage.

bárbaro/ra adj barbarous; cruel; rude; rough.

barbecho m first ploughing, fallow land.

barbero m barber.

barbilampiño/ña adj clean-shaven; (fig) inexperienced.

barbilla f chin.

barca f boat.

barco m boat; ship.

barnis m varnish; glaze.

barómetro m barometer.

barquillo m wafer; cornet, cone.

barra m bar; rod; lever; French loaf; sandbank.

barraca f hut.

barranco m gully, ravine; (fig) great difficulty.

barrenar vt to drill, bore; (fig) to frustrate.

barrendero m sweeper, garbage man.

barrer vt to sweep.

barrera f barrier; turnpike; claypit.

barriga f abdomen; belly.

barril m barrel; cask.

barrio m area, district.

barro m clay, mud.

barrote m ironwork of doors, windows, tables; crosspiece.

barruntar vt to guess; to foresee; to conjecture.

bártulos mpl gear, belongings pl.

barullo m uproar.

basar vt to base:—**~se** vr **~ en** to be based on.

báscula f scales pl.

base f base, basis.

básico/ca adj basic.

bastante adj sufficient, enough:—adv quite.

bastar vi to be sufficient, be enough.

bastidor m embroidery frame:—**~es** mpl scenery (on stage).

basto/ta adj coarse, rude, unpolished.

bastón m cane, stick; nightstick; (fig) command.

bastos mpl clubs pl (one of the four suits at cards).

basura f trash, garbage.

bata f bathrobe; overall; laboratory coat.

batalla f battle, combat; fight.

batata f sweet potato.

batería m battery; percussion.

batir vt to beat; to whisk; to dash; to demolish; to defeat.

baúl m trunk.

bautisar vt to baptize, christen.

baza f card-trick.

bazo m spleen.

beato/ta adj happy; blessed; devout:— m lay brother:—m/f pious person.

bebé m/f baby.

beber vt to drink.

bebida f drink, beverage.

beca f fellowship; grant, bursary, scholarship; sash; hood.

bedel *m* head porter; uniformed employee.

belén *m* nativity scene.

bélico/ca *adj* warlike, martial.

belladona *f* (*bot*) deadly nightshade.

belleza *f* beauty.

bello/lla *adj* beautiful; handsome; lovely; fine.

bellota *f* acorn.

bemol *m* (*mus*) flat.

bendecir *vt* to bless; to consecrate; to praise.

bendito/ta *adj* saintly; blessed; simple; happy.

beneficiar *vt* to benefit; to be of benefit to.

beneficio *m* benefit, advantage; profit; benefit night.

beneficioso/sa *adj* beneficial.

beneplácito *m* consent, approbation.

benévolo/la *adj* benevolent, kindhearted.

benigno/na *adj* benign; kind; mild.

berberecho *m* cockle.

berenjena *f* eggplant.

bergantín *m* (*mar*) brig.

berrear *vi* to low, bellow.

berrinche *m* anger, rage, tantrum (applied to children).

berrinchudo/da *adj* bad-tempered.

berro *m* watercress.

berza *f* cabbage.

besar *vt* to kiss:—**~se** *vr* to kiss.

bestia *f* beast, animal; idiot.

besugo *m* sea bream.

betún *m* shoe polish.

biberón *m* feeding bottle.

bibliófilo/la *m/f* book-lover, bookworm.

bibliografía *f* bibliography.

biblioteca *f* library.

bicarbonato *m* bicarbonate.

bicho *m* small animal; bug:—**mal ~** villain.

bici *f* (*fam*) bike.

bicicleta *f* bicycle.

bidé *m* bidet.

bien *m* good, benefit; profit:—**~es** *mpl* goods *pl*, property; wealth:—*adv* well, right; very; willingly; easily:—**~ que** *conj* although:—**está ~** very well.

bienestar *m* well-being.

bienhechor/ra *m/f* benefactor.

bienvenida *f* welcome.

bifurcación *f* fork.

bigote *m* mustache; whiskers *pl*.

bilingüe *adj* bilingual.

bilis *f* bile.

billar *m* billiards *pl*.

billete *m* note, bill; ticket; (*ferro*) ticket:—**~ sencillo** single ticket:—**~ de ida y vuelta** return ticket.

biografía *f* biography.

biología *f* biology.

biombo *m* screen.

birlar *vt* to knock down at one blow; to pinch (*fam*).

bis *excl* encore.

bisabuela *f* great-grandmother.

bisabuelo *m* great-grandfather.

bisagra *f* hinge.

bisiesto *adj*:—**año ~** leap year.

bisnieto/ta *m/f* great-grandson/ daughter.

bistec *m* steak.

bisturí *m* scalpel.

bisutería *f* costume jewelry.

bisco/ca *adj* cross-eyed.

biscocho *m* sponge cake; biscuit; ship's biscuit.

blanco/ca *adj* white; blank:—*m* whiteness; white person; blank, blank space; target (to shoot at).

blando/da *adj* soft, smooth; mild, gentle; (*fam*) cowardly.

blanquear *vt* to bleach; to whitewash; to launder (money).

blasfemar *vi* to blaspheme.

bledo *m:*—**no me importa un ~** I don't give a damn (*sl*).

blindado/da *adj* armor-plated; bullet-proof.

bloc *m* writing pad.

bloque *m* block.

bloquear *vt* to block; to blockade.

blusa *f* blouse.

bobada *f* folly, foolishness.

bobina *f* bobbin.

bobo/ba *m/f* idiot, fool; clown, funny man:—*adj* stupid, silly.

boca *f* mouth; entrance, opening; mouth of a river:—**~ en ~** *adv* by word of mouth:—**a pedir de ~** to one's heart's content.

bocacalle *f* entrance to a street.

bocadillo *m* sandwich, roll.

bocado *m* mouthful.

bocazas *m invar* big-mouth.

boceto *m* sketch; design; mock-up.

bochorno *m* sultry weather, scorching heat; blush.

bocina *f* (*mus*) trumpet; (*auto*) horn.

bocinar *vi* to sound a horn, hoot.

boda *f* wedding.

bodega *f* wine cellar; warehouse; bar.

bofetada *f* slap (in the face).

boina *f* beret.

boj *m* box, box tree.

bola *f* ball; marble; globe; (*fam*) lie, fib.

bolera *f* bowling alley.

bolero *m* bolero jacket; bolero dance.

boletín *m* bulletin; journal, review.

boleto *m* ticket.

boliche *m* jack at bowls; bowls, bowling alley; dragnet.

bolígrafo *m* (ballpoint) pen.

bollo *m* bread roll; lump.

bolo *m* ninepin; (large) pill.

bolsa *f* purse; bag; pocket; sac; stock exchange.

bolsillo *m* pocket; purse.

bomba *f* pump; bomb; surprise:— **dar a la ~** to pump:—**~ de gasolina** gas pump.

bombero *m* fireman.

bombilla *f* light bulb.

bombo *m* large drum.

bombón *m* chocolate.

bondad *f* goodness, kindness; courtesy.

bondadoso/sa *adj* good, kind.

boñiga *f* cow pat.

bonito *adj* pretty, nice-looking; pretty good, passable:—*m* tuna (fish).

boquerón *m* anchovy; large hole.

boquilla *f* mouthpiece of a musical instrument; nozzle.

borde *m* border; margin; (*mar*) board.

bordear *vi* (*mar*) to tack:—*vt* to go along the edge of; to flank.

bordillo *m* curb.

bordo *m* (*mar*) board of a ship.

boreal *adj* boreal, northern.

borracho/cha *adj* drunk, intoxicated; blind with passion:—*m/f* drunk, drunkard.

borrador *m* first draft; scribbling pad; eraser.

borrar *vt* to erase, rub out; to blur; to obscure.

borrasca *f* storm; violent squall of wind; hazard; danger.

borrico/ca *m/f* donkey, ass; blockhead.

borrón *m* blot, blur.

bosque *m* forest; wood.

bosquejo *m* sketch (of a painting); unfinished work.

bostezar *vi* to yawn; to gape.

bota *f* leather wine-bag; boot.

botánica *f* botany.

bote *m* bounce; thrust; tin, can; boat.

botella *f* bottle.

botijo *m* earthenware pitcher.

botín *m* high boot, half-boot; gaiter; booty.

botiquín *m* medicine chest.

botón *m* button; knob (of a radio etc); (*bot*) bud.

bóveda *f* arch; vault, crypt.

boxeo *m* boxing.

boya *f* (*mar*) buoy.

boyante *adj* buoyant, floating; (*fig*) fortunate, successful.

bozo *m* down (on the upper lip or chin); headstall (of a horse).

braga *f* sling, rope; nappy, diaper:— ~s *fpl* breeches *pl*; panties *pl*.

bragueta *f* fly, flies *pl* (of pants/ trousers).

brasa *f* live coal:—**estar hecho una ~** to be very flushed.

bravío/vía *adj* ferocious, savage, wild; coarse.

bravo/va *adj* brave, valiant; bullying; savage, fierce; rough; sumptuous; excellent, fine:—*excl* well done!

braza *f* fathom.

brazo *m* arm; branch (of a tree); enterprise; courage:—**luchar a ~ par-tido** to fight hand-to-hand.

brea *f* pitch; tar.

brebaje *m* potion.

brecha *f* (*mil*) breach; gap, opening.

breva *f* early fig; early large acorn.

breve *m* papal brief:—*f* (*mus*) breve:— *adj* brief, short:—**en ~** shortly.

brezo *m* (*bot*) heather.

bribón/ona *adj* dishonest, rascally.

bricolaje *m* do-it-yourself.

brida *f* bridle; clamp, flange.

brigada *f* brigade; squad, gang.

brillante *adj* brilliant; bright, shining:— *m* diamond.

brillar *vi* to shine; to sparkle, glisten; to shine, be outstanding.

brincar *vi* to skip; to leap, jump; to gambol; to fly into a passion.

brindis *m invar* toast.

brío *m* spirit, dash.

brisca *f* card game.

broca *f* reel; drill; shoemaker's tack.

brocado *m* gold or silver brocade:— ~/**da** *adj* embroidered, like brocade.

brocha *f* large brush:—**~ de afeitar** shaving brush.

broche *m* clasp; brooch; cufflink.

broma *f* joke.

bromear *vi* to joke.

bronca *f* row.

bronceado/da *adj* tanned:—*m* bronzing, suntan.

brotar *vi* (*bot*) to bud, germinate; to gush, rush out; (*med*) to break out.

bruces *adv:*—**a ~/de ~** face downward(s).

bruja *f* witch.

brújula *f* compass.

bruma *f* mist; (*mar*) sea mist.

bruñir *vt* to polish; to put rouge on.

brusco/ca *adj* rude; sudden; brusque.

brutal *adj* brutal, brutish:—*m* brute.

bruto *m* brute, beast:—**~~/ ta** *adj* stupid; gross; brutish.

bucal *adj* oral.

bucear *vi* to dive.

bucle *m* curl.

buen *adj* (before *m* nouns) good.

bueno/na *adj* good, perfect; fair; fit, proper; good-looking:—**ibuenos días!** good morning!:—**ibuenas tardes!** good afternoon:—**ibuenas noches!** good night!:—**i~!** right!

buey *m* ox, bullock.

bufanda *f* scarf.

bufete *m* desk, writing-table; lawyer's office.

bufo/fa *adj* comic:—**opera ~a** *f* comic opera.

buhardilla *f* attic.

búho *m* owl; unsocial person.

buitre *m* vulture.

bujía *f* candle; spark plug.

bullicio *m* bustle; uproar.

bulto *m* bulk; tumor, swelling; bust; baggage.

buñuelo *m* doughnut; fritter.

buque *m* vessel, ship, tonnage, capacity (of a ship); hull (of a ship).

burbuja *f* bubble.

burdel *m* brothel.

burguesía *f* bourgeoisie.

burlar *vt* to hoax; to defeat; to play tricks on, deceive; to frustrate:—**~se** *vr* to joke, laugh at.

burro *m* ass, donkey; idiot; sawhorse.

bursátil *adj* stock exchange *compd.*

buscar *vt* to seek, search for; to look for; to hunt after:—*vi* to look, search, seek.

busilis *m* difficulty, snag.

busto *m* bust.

butaca *f* armchair; seat.

butano *m* butane.

butifarra *f* Catalan sausage.

butrón *m* burglary.

buzo *m* diver.

buzón *m* mailbox; conduit, canal; cover of a jar.

C

cabalgar *vi* to ride, go riding.

cabalgata *f* procession.

caballa *f* mackerel.

caballería *f* mount, steed; cavalry; cavalry horse; chivalry; knighthood.

caballero *m* knight; gentleman; rider, horseman.

caballete *m* ridge of a roof; painter's easel; trestle; bridge (of the nose).

caballo *m* horse; (at chess) knight; queen (in cards):—**a ~** on horseback.

cabecera *f* headboard; head; far end; pillow; headline; vignette.

cabecilla *m* ringleader.

cabello *m* hair.

caber *vi* to fit.

cabeza *f* head; chief, leader; main town, chief center.

cabida *f* room, capacity.

cabildo *m* chapter (of church); meeting of a chapter; corporation of a town.

cabina *f* cabin; telephone booth.

cabizbajo/ja, cabizcaido/da *adj* crestfallen; pensive, thoughtful.

cable *m* cable, lead, wire.

cabo *m* end, extremity; cape, headland; (*mar*) cable, rope.

cabra *f* goat.

cabrón *m* cuckold:—**i~!** (*fam*) bastard! (*sl*).

cacahuete *m* peanut.

cacao *m* (*bot*) cacao tree; cocoa.

cacarear *vi* to crow; to brag, boast.

cacerola f pan, saucepan; casserole.

cachalote m sperm whale.

cacharro m pot.

cachivache m pot; piece of junk.

cachondo/da adj randy; funny.

cachorro/ra m/f puppy; cub.

caco m pickpocket; coward.

cada adj invar each; every.

cadáver m corpse, cadaver.

cadena f chain; series, link; radio or TV network.

cadera f hip.

caducar vi to become senile; to expire, lapse; to deteriorate.

caer vi to fall; to tumble down; to lapse; to happen; to die:—~se vr to fall down.

café m coffee; cafe, coffee house.

cafetera f coffee pot.

cagar vi (fam) to have a shit (sl).

caimán m caiman, alligator.

caja f box, case; casket; cashbox; cash desk; supermarket check-out:—~ de ahorros savings bank:—~ de cambios gearbox.

cajón m bureau; locker.

cal f lime:—~ viva quick lime.

calabacín m small marrow, zucchini.

calabaza f pumpkin, squash.

calamar m squid.

calar vt to soak, drench; to penetrate, pierce; to see through; to lower:—~se vr to stall (of a car).

calavera f skull; madcap.

calcar vt to trace, copy.

calcetín m sock.

calcio m calcium.

calcomanía f transfer.

calculadora f calculator.

calcular vt to calculate, reckon; to compute.

caldear vt to weld; to warm, heat up.

calderada f stew.

calderilla f small change.

caldo m stock; broth.

calefacción f heating.

calendario m calendar.

calentar vt to warm up, heat up:—~se vr to grow hot; to dispute.

calidad f grade, quality, condition; kind.

cálido/da adj hot; (fig) warm.

caliente adj hot; fiery:—en ~ in the heat of the moment.

callado/da adj silent, quiet.

callar vi, ~se vr to be silent, keep quiet.

calle f street; road.

callejear vi to loiter about the streets.

callejón m alley.

callo m corn; callus:—~s mpl tripe.

calmante m (med) sedative.

calmar vt to calm, quiet, pacify:—vi to become calm.

calor m heat, warmth; ardor, passion.

calumnia f calumny, slander.

calvo/va adj bald; bare, barren.

calzado m footwear.

calzoncillos mpl underpants, shorts pl.

cama f bed:—hacer la ~ to make the bed.

cámara f hall; chamber; room; camera; cine camera.

camarada m/f comrade, companion.

camarera f waitress.

camarero m waiter.

camarón m shrimp, prawn.

camarote m berth, cabin.

cambalache m exchange, swap.

cambiar vt to exchange; to change:—vi to change, alter:—~se vr to move house.

cambio m change, exchange; rate of exchange; bureau de change.

camelar vt to flirt with.

camello m camel; drug dealer.

camilla f couch; cot; stretcher.
caminar vi to travel; to walk, go.
camino m road; way.
camión m truck.
camisa f shirt; chemise.
camisería f dry goods store.
camiseta f T-shirt; undershirt.
camisón m nightgown.
campamento m (mil) encampment.
campana f bell.
campanario m belfry.
campeón/ona m/f champion.
campesino/na, campestre adj rural.
campo m country; field; camp; ground; pitch.
caña f cane, reed; stalk; shinbone; glass of beer:—~ **dulce** sugar cane.
cañada f gully; glen; sheep-walk.
canal m channel, canal.
canalla f mob, rabble.
cáñamo m hemp.
canas fpl gray hair:—**peinar** ~ to grow old.
cañaveral m reedbed.
cancelar vt to cancel; to write off.
cancha f (tennis) court.
canción f song.
candado m padlock.
candilejas fpl footlights pl.
canela f cinnamon.
cangrejo m crab; crayfish.
canica f marble.
canilla f shinbone; arm-bone; tap of a cask; spool.
canjear vt to exchange.
cano/na adj gray-haired; whitehaired.
canoso/sa adj gray-haired; white-haired.
cansancio m tiredness, fatigue.
cansar vt to tire, tire out; to bore:— ~**se** vr to get tired, grow weary.
cantante m/f singer.

cantar m song:—vt to sing; to chant:— vi to sing; to chirp.
cántaro m pitcher; jug:—**llover a ~s** to rain heavily, pour.
cantera f quarry.
cantidad f quantity, amount; number.
cantina f buffet, refreshment room; canteen; cellar; snack bar; bar.
canto m stone; singing; song; edge.
canuto m (fam) joint (sl), marijuana cigarette.
caño m tube, pipe; sewer.
cañón m tube, pipe; barrel; gun; canyon.
caoba f mahogany.
caos m chaos; confusion.
capa f cloak; cape; layer, stratum; cover; pretext.
capacidad f capacity; extent; talent.
capataz m foreman, overseer.
capaz adj capable; capacious, spacious, roomy.
capeo m challenging of a bull with a cloak.
caperuza f hood.
capirote m hood.
capital m capital; capital sum:—f capital, capital city:—adj capital; principal.
capítulo m chapter of a cathedral; chapter (of a book).
capó m (auto) hood.
capote m greatcoat; bullfighter's cloak.
capricho m caprice, whim, fancy.
captar vt to captivate; to understand; (rad) to tune in to, receive.
capturar vt to capture.
capucha f cap, cowl, hood of a cloak.
capullo m cocoon of a silkworm; rose-bud.
cara f face; appearance:—~ **a** ~ face to face.

cárabe m amber.

caracol m snail; seashell; spiral.

carácter m character; quality; condition; hand-writing.

característico/ca adj characteristic.

caradura m/f:—**es un ~** he's got a nerve.

caramba excl well!

carámbano m icicle.

carambola f cannon (at billiards); trick.

caravana f trailer; queue; tailback (traffic).

carbón m coal; charcoal; carbon; carbon paper.

carboncillo m charcoal.

carbono m (quim) carbon.

carburador m carburettor.

carcajada f (loud) laugh.

cárcel f prison, penitentiary; jail.

carcoma f deathwatch beetle; woodworm; anxious concern.

cardenal m cardinal; cardinal bird; (med) bruise, weal.

cardo m thistle.

carecer vi:—**~ de** to want, lack.

cargar vt to load, burden; to charge:—vi to charge; to load (up); to lean.

cargo m burden, loading; employment, post; office; charge, care; obligation; accusation.

carguero m freighter.

caricia f caress.

caridad f charity.

caries f (med) tooth decay, caries.

cariño m fondness, tenderness; love.

carmesí adj, m crimson.

carmín m carmine; rouge; lipstick.

carne f flesh; meat; pulp (of fruit).

carné, carnet m driver's license:—**~ de identidad** identity card.

carnicería f butcher's (store); carnage, slaughter.

caro/ra adj dear; affectionate; dear, expensive:—adv dearly.

carpa f carp (fish); tent.

carpeta f table cover; folder, file, portfolio.

carpintero m carpenter.

carraca f carrack (ship); rattle.

carrera f career; course; race; run, running; route; journey:—**a ~ abierta,** at full speed.

carrete m reel, spool, bobbin.

carretera f highway.

carril m lane (of highway); furrow.

carrillo m cheek; pulley.

carro m cart; car.

carrocería f bodywork, coachwork.

carta f letter; map; document; playing card; menu:—**~ blanca** carte blanche:—**~ credencial** o **de creencia** credentials pl:—**~ certificada** registered letter:—**~ de crédito** credit card:—**~ verde** green card.

cartabón m square (tool).

cartel m placard; poster; wall chart; cartel.

cartera f satchel; purse, handbag; briefcase.

carterista m/f pickpocket.

cartero m mailman.

cartón m cardboard, pasteboard; cartoon.

casa f house; home; firm, company:—**~ de campo** country house:—**~ de moneda** mint:—**~ de huéspedes** boarding house, rooming house.

casar vt to marry; to couple; to abrogate; to annul:—**~se** vr to marry, get married.

cascabel m small bell; rattlesnake.

cascada f cascade, waterfall.

cascanueces *m invar* nutcracker.

cascar *vt* to crack, break into pieces; (*fam*) to beat:—**~se** *vr* to be broken open.

cáscara *f* rind, peel; husk, shell; bark.

casco *m* skull; helmet; fragment; shard; hulk (of a ship); crown (of a hat); hoof; empty bottle, returnable bottle.

cascote *m* rubble, fragment of material used in building.

caserío *m* country house; hamlet.

casero *m* landlord; janitor:—**~/ra,** *adj* domestic; household *compd*; homemade.

caset(t)e *m* cassette:—*f* casseteplayer.

casi *adv* almost, nearly:—**~ nada** next to nothing:—**~ nunca** hardly ever, almost never.

caso *m* case; occurrence, event; hap, casuality; occasion; (*gr*) case:—**en ese ~** in that case:—**en todo ~** in any case:—**~ que** in case.

caspa *f* dandruff; scurf.

castaño *m* chestnut tree:—**~/na** *adj* chestnut(-colored), brown.

castañuela *f* castanet.

castellano *m* Castilian, Spanish.

castigar *vt* to castigate, punish; to afflict.

castillo *m* castle.

castizo/za *adj* pure, thoroughbred.

casto/ta *adj* pure, chaste.

castor *m* beaver.

castrar *vt* to geld, castrate; to prune; to cut the honeycombs out of (beehives).

casualidad *f* chance, accident.

cataplasma *f* poultice.

catar *vt* to taste; to inspect, examine; to look at; to esteem.

catarata *f* (*med*) cataract; waterfall.

catarro *m* catarrh; cold.

cátedra *f* professor's chair.

categoría *f* category; rank.

católico/ca *adj, m/f* catholic.

catorce *adj, m* fourteen.

catre *m* cot.

cauce *m* riverbed; (*fig*) channel.

caucho *m* rubber; tire.

caudal *m* volume, flow; property, wealth; plenty.

causa *f* cause; motive, reason; lawsuit:—**a ~ de** considering, because of.

causar *vt* to cause; to produce; to occasion.

cautela *f* caution, cautiousness.

cautivar *vt* to take prisoner in war; to captivate, charm.

cauto/ta *adj* cautious, wary.

cavar *vt* to dig up, excavate:—*vi* to dig, delve; to think profoundly.

caverna *f* cavern, cave.

cavidad *f* cavity, hollow.

cavilar *vt* to ponder, consider carefully.

cazador/ra *m/f* hunter; *m* huntsman:—**~ furtivo** poacher.

cazar *vt* to chase, hunt; to catch.

cazo *m* saucepan; ladle.

cazuela *f* casserole; pan.

cebada *f* barley.

cebar *vt* to feed (animals), fatten.

cebo *m* feed, food; bait, lure; priming.

cebolla *f* onion; bulb.

cebra *f* zebra.

cedazo *m* sieve, strainer.

ceder *vt* to hand over; to transfer, make over; to yield, give up:—*vi* to submit, comply, give in; to diminish, grow less.

cedro *m* cedar.

cédula *f* certificate; document; slip of paper; bill:—**~ de cambio** bill of exchange.

cegar *vi* to grow blind:—*vt* to blind; to block up.

ceja *f* eyebrow.

cejar *vi* to go backward(s); to slacken, give in.

celebrar *vt* to celebrate; to praise:—**~ misa** to say mass.

célebre *adj* famous, renowned; witty, funny.

celeste *adj* heavenly; sky-blue.

celestial *adj* heavenly; delightful.

celo *m* zeal; rut (in animals):—**~s** *mpl* jealousy.

celoso/sa *adj* zealous; jealous.

célula *f* cell.

cementerio *m* graveyard.

cena *f* supper.

cenar *vt* to have for dinner:—*vi* to have supper, have dinner.

cenegal *m* quagmire.

cenicero *m* ashtray.

ceniza *f* ashes *pl*:—**miércoles de ~** Ash Wednesday.

censo *m* census; tax; ground rent:—**~ electoral** electoral roll.

censurar *vt* to review, criticize; to censure, blame.

centella *f* lightning; spark.

centenar *m* hundred.

centeno *m* rye.

centésimo/ma *adj* hundredth:—*m* hundredth.

centígrado *m* centigrade.

centímetro *m* centimeter.

céntimo *m* cent.

centinela *f* sentry, guard.

central *adj* central:—*f* head office, headquarters; (telephone) exchange.

centro *m* center:—**~ comercial** shopping center.

centuplicar *vt* to increase a hundredfold.

ceñido/da *adj* tight-fitting; sparing, frugal.

ceñudo/da *adj* frowning, grim.

cepa *f* stock (of a vine); origin (of a family).

cepillo *m* brush; plane (tool).

cepo *m* branch, bough; trap; snare; poorbox.

cera *f* wax:—**~s** *fpl* honeycomb.

cerámica *f* pottery.

cerca *f* enclosure; fence:—**~s** *mpl* objects *pl* in the foreground of a painting:—*adv* near, at hand, close by:—**~ de** close, near.

cercano/na *adj* near, close by; neighboring, adjoining.

cerciorar *vt* to assure, ascertain, affirm:—**~se** *vr* to find out.

cerdo *m* pig, hog.

cerebro *m* brain.

cereza *f* cherry.

cerilla *f* wax taper; ear wax:—**~s** *fpl* matches, safety matches *pl*.

cero *m* nothing, zero.

cerrado/da *adj* closed, shut; locked; overcast, cloudy; broad (of accent).

cerrajero *m* locksmith.

cerrar *vt* to close, shut; to block up; to lock:—**~ la cuenta** to close an account:—**~se** *vr* to close; to heal; to cloud over:—*vi* to close, shut; to lock.

cerro *m* hill; neck (of an animal); backbone; combed flax or hemp:—**en ~** bareback.

cerrojo *m* bolt (of a door).

certamen *m* competition, contest.

certero *adj* accurate; well-aimed.

certeza, certidumbre f certainty.

certificado m certificate:—**~/da** adj registered (of a letter).

cerveza m beer.

cesar vt to cease, stop; to fire (sl); to remove from office:—vi to cease, stop; to retire.

cese m suspension; dismissal.

cesión f cession; transfer.

césped m grass; lawn.

cesta f basket, pannier.

chabola f shack.

chal m shawl.

chalado/da adj crazy.

chale(t) m detached house.

chaleco m vest.

champán m champagne.

champiñón m mushroom.

champú m shampoo.

chamuscar vt to singe, scorch.

chantaje m blackmail.

chapa f metal plate; panel; (auto) license plate.

chaparrón m heavy shower (of rain).

chapuza f badly done job.

chaqueta f jacket.

charco m pool, puddle.

charcutería f store selling pork meat products.

charlar vi to chat.

charlatán/ana m/f chatterbox.

charol m varnish; patent leather.

chasco m disappointment; joke, jest.

chasis m invar (auto) chassis.

chasquido m crack; click.

chatarra f scrap.

chato/ta adj flat, flattish; snub-nosed.

chaval/la m/f lad/lass.

chicle m chewing gum.

chico/ca adj little, small:—m/f boy/girl.

chiflado/da adj crazy.

chile m chilli pepper.

chillar vi to scream, shriek; to howl; to creak.

chimenea f chimney; fireplace.

china f pebble; porcelain, chinaware; China silk.

chincheta f thumbtack.

chino/na adj, m/f Chinese:—m Chinese language.

chirriar vi to hiss; to creak; to chirp.

chisme m tale; thingummyjig.

chispa f spark; sparkle; wit; drop (of rain); drunkenness.

chiste m funny story, joke.

chivo/va m/f billy/nanny goat.

chocar vi to strike, knock; to crash:—vt to shock.

chochear vi to dodder, be senile; to dote.

chocolate m chocolate.

chófer m driver.

chopo m (bot) black poplar.

chorizo m pork sausage.

chorro m gush; jet; stream:—**a ~s** abundantly.

chuchería f trinket.

chulear vi to brag.

chuleta f chop.

chulo m rascal; pimp.

chupar vt to suck; to absorb.

churro m fritter.

ciática f sciatica.

cicatriz f scar.

cicatrizar vt to heal.

ciclista m/f cyclist.

ciclo m cycle.

cicuta f (bot) hemlock.

ciego/ga adj blind.

cielo m sky; heaven; atmosphere; climate.

ciempiés m invar centipede.

cien adj, m a hundred.

ciénaga f swamp.
ciencia f science.
cieno m mud; mire.
cierto/ta adj certain, sure; right, correct:—**por ~** certainly.
ciervo m deer, hart, stag:—**~ volante** stag beetle.
cierzo m cold northerly wind.
cifra f number, numeral; quantity; cipher; abbreviation.
cigarra f cicada.
cigarro m cigar; cigarette.
cigüeña f stork; crank (of a bell).
cilindro m cylinder.
cima f summit; peak; top.
cimiento m foundation, groundwork; basis, origin.
cinc m zinc.
cincelar vt to chisel, engrave.
cinco adj, m five.
cincuenta adj, m fifty.
cine m cinema.
cínico/ca adj cynical.
cinta f band, ribbon; reel.
cintura f waist.
cinturón m belt, girdle; (fig) zone:—**~ de seguridad** seatbelt.
ciprés m cypress tree.
circo m circus.
circuito m circuit; circumference.
circular adj circular; circulatory:—vt to circulate:—vi (auto) to drive.
círculo m circle; (fig) scope, compass.
circunspecto/ta adj circumspect, cautious.
circunstancia f circumstance.
circunvalacion f:—**carretera de ~** bypass.
cirio m wax candle.
ciruela f plum:—**~ pasa** prune.
cirugía f surgery.
cisne m swan.

citar vt to make an appointment with; to quote; (jur) to summon.
ciudad f city; town.
ciudadano/na m/f citizen:—adj civic.
clamor m clamor, outcry; peal of bells.
clandestino/na adj clandestine, secret, concealed.
clara f egg-white.
claraboya f skylight.
clarear vi to dawn:—**~se** vr to be transparent.
clarín m bugle; bugler.
clarinete m clarinet:—m/f clarinetist.
claro/ra adj clear, bright; evident, manifest:—m opening; clearing (in a wood).
clase f class; rank; order.
clasificar vt to classify.
claudicar vi to limp; to act deceitfully; to back down.
claustro m cloister; faculty (of a university).
cláusula f clause.
clavar vt to nail.
clave f key; (mus) clef:—m harpsichord.
clavel m (bot) carnation.
clavicordio m clavichord.
clavícula f clavicle, collar bone.
clavija f pin, peg.
clavo m nail; corn (on the feet); clove.
clemente adj clement, merciful.
clérigo m priest; clergyman.
cliente m/f client.
clima m climate.
climatizado/da adj air-conditioned.
clínica f clinic; private hospital.
clip m paper clip.
cloaca f sewer.
coacción f coercion, compulsion.

coagular *vt,* **~se** *vr* to coagulate; to curdle.

coartada *f (jur)* alibi.

coartar *vt* to limit, restrict, restrain.

cobalto *m* cobalt.

cobarde *adj* cowardly, timid.

cobaya *f* guinea pig.

cobertizo *m* small shed; shelter.

cobijar *vt* to cover; to shelter.

cobrar *vt* to recover:——**se** *vr (med)* to come to.

cobre *m* copper; kitchen utensils *pl;* (*mus*) brass.

cocear *vt* to kick; (*fig*) to resist.

cocer *vt* to boil; to bake (bricks):——*vi* to boil; to ferment:——**se** *vr* to suffer intense pain.

cochambroso/sa *adj* nasty; filthy, stinking.

coche *m* car; coach, carriage; pram, baby carriage:——(*ferro*) **~ cama** sleeping car:——**~ restaurante** restaurant car.

cochino/na *adj* dirty, filthy; nasty:——*m* pig, hog.

cocina *f* kitchen; stove; cookery.

cocinero/ra *m/f* cook.

coco *m* coconut; bogeyman.

cocodrilo *m* crocodile.

codazo *m* blow given with the elbow.

codear *vt, vi* to elbow:——**se** *vr* **~se con** to rub shoulders with.

codiciar *vt* to covet, desire.

código *m* code; law; set of rules.

codillo *m* knee of a four-legged animal; angle; (*tec*) elbow (joint).

codo *m* elbow.

codorniz *f* quail.

coetáneo/nea *adj* contemporary.

coexistir *vi* to coexist.

cofia *f* (nurse's) cap.

cofradía *f* brotherhood, fraternity.

cofre *m* trunk.

coger *vt* to catch, take hold of; to occupy, take up:——**se** *vr* to catch.

cogollo *m* heart of a lettuce or cabbage; shoot of a plant.

cogote *m* back of the neck.

cohecho *m* bribery.

coherencia *f* coherence.

cohete *m* rocket.

cohibido/da *adj* shy.

coincidir *vi* to coincide.

coito *m* intercourse, coitus.

cojear *vi* to limp, hobble; (*fig*) to go astray.

cojín *m* cushion.

cojo/ja *adj* lame, crippled.

col *f* cabbage.

cola *f* tail; queue; last place; glue.

colaborar *vi* to collaborate.

colada *f* wash, washing; (*quím*) bleach; sheep run.

colador *m* sieve.

colar *vt* to strain, filter:——*vi* to ooze:—— **~se en** to get into without paying.

colcha *f* bedspread, counterpane.

colchón *m* mattress.

coleccionar *vt* to collect.

colecta *f* collection (for charity).

colectivo/va *adj* collective.

colega *m/f* colleague.

colegial *m* schoolboy.

colegiala *f* schoolgirl.

colegio *m* college; school.

colegir *vt* to collect; to deduce, infer.

cólera *f* bile; anger; fury, rage; cholera.

coleta *f* pigtail.

colgar *vt* to hang; to suspend; to decorate with tapestry:——*vi* to be suspended.

colibrí *m* hummingbird.

coliflor *m* cauliflower.

colina *f* hill.

colisión f collision; friction.

colmar vt to heap up:—vi to fulfill, realize.

colmena f hive, beehive.

colmillo m eyetooth; tusk.

colmo m height, summit; extreme:—**a ~** plentifully.

colocar vt to arrange; to place; to provide with a job:—**~se** vr to get a job.

collar m necklace; (dog) collar.

colono m colonist; farmer.

coloquio m conversation; conference.

color m color, hue; dye; rouge; suit (of cards).

colorado/da adj ruddy; red.

colorete m rouge.

columna f column.

columpio m swing, seesaw.

colza f (bot) rape; rape seed.

coma f (gr) comma:—m (med) coma.

comadreja f weasel.

comandante m commander.

comarca f territory, district.

combatir vt to combat, fight; to attack:—vi to fight.

combinar vi to combine.

combustible adj combustible:—m fuel.

comedia f comedy; play, drama.

comedido/da adj moderate, restrained.

comedor/ra m/f glutton:—m dining room.

comentar vt to comment on, expound.

comentario m comment, remark; commentary.

comenzar vi to commence, begin.

comer vt to eat; to take (a piece at chess):—vi to have lunch.

comercial adj commercial.

comercio m trade, commerce; business.

comestible adj eatable:—mpl **~s** food, foodstuffs pl.

cometa m comet:—f kite.

cometer vt to commit, charge; to entrust.

cómico/ca adj comic, comical.

comida f food; eating; meal; lunch.

comillas fpl quotation marks pl.

comino m cumin (plant or seed).

comisaría f police station; commissariat.

como adv as; like; such as.

cómo adv how?; why?:—excl what?

cómoda f bureau.

cómodo/da adj convenient; comfortable.

compacto/ta adj compact; close, dense.

compadecer vt to pity:—**~se** vr to agree with each other.

compaginar vt to arrange, put in order:—**~se** vr to tally.

compañero/ra m/f companion, friend; comrade; partner.

compañía f company.

comparar vt to compare.

compartimento m compartment.

compartir vt to share.

compás m compass; pair of compasses; (mus) measure, beat.

compatible adj:—**~ con** compatible with, consistent with.

compensar vt to compensate; to recompense.

competencia f competition, rivalry; competence.

competente adj competent; adequate.

compilar vt to compile.

compinche m pal, mate (sl).

complacencia f pleasure; indulgence.

complacer vt to please:—**~se** vr to be pleased with.

complejo m complex:—**~/ja** adj complex.

complementario/ria *adj* complementary.

complemento *m* complement.

completar *vt* to complete.

completo/ta *adj* complete; perfect.

complicar *vt* to complicate.

cómplice *m/f* accomplice.

complot *m* plot.

componer *vt* to compose; to constitute; to mend, repair; to strengthen, restore; to compose, calm:—**~se** *vr* **~se de** to consist of.

comportamiento *m* behavior.

compostura *f* composition, composure; mending, repairing; discretion; modesty, demureness.

compota *f* stewed fruit.

comprar *vt* to buy, purchase.

comprender *vt* to include, contain; to comprehend, understand.

compresa *f* sanitary napkin.

comprimido *m* pill.

comprimir *vt* to compress; to repress, restrain.

comprobar *vt* to verify, confirm; to prove.

comprometer *vt* to compromise; to embarrass; to implicate; to put in danger:—**~se** *vr* to compromise oneself.

compuerta *f* hatch; sluice.

compuesto *m* compound:—**~/ta** *adj* composed; made up of.

compulsar *vt* to collate, compare; to make an authentic copy.

compungirse *vr* to feel remorseful.

comulgar *vt* to administer communion to:—*vi* to receive communion.

común *adj* common, usual, general:—*m* community; public:—**en ~** in common.

comunicar *vt* to communicate:—**~se** *vr* to communicate (with each other).

comunidad *f* community.

con *prep* with; by:—**~ que** so then, providing that.

coñac *m* brandy, cognac.

cóncavo/va *adj* concave.

concebir *vt* to conceive:—*vi* to become pregnant.

conceder *vt* to give; to grant; to concede, allow.

concejal/la *m/f* member of a council.

concentrar *vt:*—**~se** *vr* to concentrate.

concepto *m* conceit, thought; judgement, opinion.

concernir *v imp* to regard, concern.

concertar *vt* to coordinate; to settle; to adjust; to agree; to arrange, fix up:—*vi* (*mus*) to harmonize, be in tune.

concesión *f* concession.

concha *f* shell; tortoise-shell.

conciencia *f* conscience.

concienciar *vt* to make aware:—**~se** *vr* to become aware.

concierto *m* concert; agreement; concerto:—**de ~** in agreement, in concert.

conciliar *vt* to reconcile:—*adj* conciliar, council.

conciso/sa *adj* concise, brief.

concluir *vt* to conclude, end, complete; to infer, deduce:—**~se** *vr* to conclude.

concordar *vt* to reconcile, make agree:—*vi* to agree, correspond.

concordia *f* conformity, agreement.

concretar *vt* to make concrete; to specify.

concubina *f* concubine.

concurrido/da *adj* busy.

concursante *m/f* competitor.

concurso *m* crowd; competition; help, cooperation.

conde *m* earl, count.

condenable *adj* culpable.

condenar *vt* to condemn; to find guilty:——**se** *vr* to blame oneself; to confess (one's guilt).

condensar *vt* to condense.

condescender *vi* to acquiesce, comply.

condición *f* condition, state; quality; status; rank; stipulation.

condimentar *vt* to flavor, season.

condolerse *vr* to sympathize.

condón *m* condom.

conducir *vt* to convey, conduct; to drive; to manage:—*vi* to drive:——**(a)** to lead (to):——**se** *vr* to conduct oneself.

conducta *f* conduct, behavior; management.

conducto *m* conduit, pipe; drain; (*fig*) channel.

conductor/ra *m/f* conductor, guide; (*ferro*) guard; driver.

conectar *vt* to connect.

conejo *m* rabbit.

conexión *f* connection; plug; relationship.

confección *f* preparation; clothing industry.

conferencia *f* conference; telephone call.

confesar *vt* to confess; to admit.

confianza *f* trust; confidence; conceit; familiarity:——**en ~** confidential.

confiar *vt* to confide, entrust:—*vi* to trust.

configurar *vt* to shape, form.

confinar *vt* to confine:—*vi* **~ con** to border upon.

confirmar *vt* to confirm; to corroborate.

confiscar *vt* to confiscate.

confitería *f* sweet store.

confitura *f* preserve; jam.

conflicto *m* conflict.

conformar *vt* to shape; to adjust, adapt:—*vi* to agree:——**se** *vr* to conform; to resign oneself.

conforme *adj* alike, similar; agreed:—*prep* according to.

confortar *vt* to comfort; to strengthen; to console.

confundir *vt* to confound, jumble; to confuse:——**se** *vr* to make a mistake.

confusión *f* confusion.

congelado/da *adj* frozen:—*mpl* **~s** frozen food.

congelar *vt* to freeze:——**se** *vr* to congeal.

congeniar *vi* to get on well.

congoja *f* anguish, distress, grief.

congraciarse *vr* to ingratiate oneself.

congregar(se) *vt* (*vr*) to assemble, meet, collect.

conjetura *f* conjecture, guess.

conjugar *vt* (*gr*) to conjugate; to combine.

conjunto/ta *adj* united, joint:—*m* whole; (*mus*) ensemble, band; team.

conjurar *vt* to exorcize:—*vi* to conspire, plot.

conmemorar *vt* to commemorate.

conmigo *pn* with me.

conmover *vt* to move; to disturb.

conmutador *m* switch.

conmutar *vt* (*jur*) to commute; to exchange.

connotar vt to imply.

cono m cone.

conocer vt to know, understand:— ~se vr to know one another.

conocimiento m knowledge, understanding; (med) consciousness; acquaintance; (mar) bill of lading.

conquistar vt to conquer.

consabido/da adj well-known; above-mentioned.

consagrar vt to consecrate.

consanguíneo/nea adj related by blood.

consecuencia f consequence; conclusion; consistency:—por ~ therefore.

consecuente adj consistent.

conseguir vt to attain; to get, obtain.

consejo m advice; council.

consentir vt to consent to; to allow; to admit; to spoil (a child).

conserje m doorman; janitor.

conservar vt to conserve; to keep; to preserve (fruit).

conservas fpl canned food.

conservatorio m (mus) conservatoire.

consideración f consideration; respect.

considerar vt to consider.

consigna f (mil) watchword; order, instruction; (ferro) left-luggage office.

consignar vt to consign, dispatch; to assign; to record, register.

consigo pn (m) with him; (f) with her; (vd) with you; (refl) with oneself.

consiguiente adj consequent.

consistente adj consistent; firm, solid.

consistir vi:—~ **en** to consist of; to be due to.

consola f control panel.

consolar vt to console, comfort, cheer.

consolidar vt to consolidate.

consonante m rhyme:—f (gr) consonant:—adj consonant, harmonious.

consorcio m partnership.

consorte m/f consort, companion, partner; accomplice.

conspirar vi to conspire, plot.

constante adj constant; firm.

constar vi to be evident, be certain; to be composed of, consist of.

constatar vt to note; to check.

consternar vt to dismay; to shock.

constipado/da adj:—estar ~ to have a cold.

constituir vt to constitute; to establish; to appoint.

construir vt to form; to build, construct; to construe.

consuegro/gra m/f father-in-law/ mother-in-law of one's son or daughter.

consuelo m consolation, comfort.

cónsul m consul.

consultar vt to consult, ask for advice.

consultor/ra m/f adviser, consultant.

consultorio m (med) consulting room, doctor's rooms.

consumar vt to consummate, finish; to carry out.

consumir vt to consume; to burn, use; to waste, exhaust:—~se vr to waste away, be consumed.

contabilidad f accounting; bookkeeping.

contacto m contact; (auto) ignition.

contado/da adj:—~s scarce, few:— m **pagar al** ~ to pay (in) cash.

contador m meter; counter in a cafe:—~/~a m/f accountant.

contagiar vt to infect:—~se vr to get infected.

contaminar vt to contaminate; to pollute; to corrupt.

contar vt to count, reckon; to tell:—vi to count:—~ **con** to rely upon.

contemplar vt to look at; to contemplate, consider; to meditate.

contemporáneo/nea adj contemporary.

contenedor m container.

contener vt to contain, hold; to hold back; to repress:—~se vr to control oneself.

contentar vt to content, satisfy; to please:—~se vr to be pleased or satisfied.

contento/ta adj glad; pleased; content:—m contentment; (jur) release.

contestador m:—~ **automatico** answering machine.

contestar vt to answer, reply; to prove, corroborate.

contienda f contest, dispute.

contigo pn with you.

contiguo/gua adj contiguous, close.

continente m continent, mainland:—adj continent.

contingencia f risk; contingency.

continuar vt, vi to continue.

continuo/nua adj continuous.

contorno m environs pl; contour, outline:—**en** ~ round about.

contra prep against; contrary to; opposite.

contrabajo m (mus) double bass; bass guitar; low bass.

contrabando m contraband; smuggling.

contrachapado m plywood.

contradecir vt to contradict.

contraer vt to contract, shrink; to make (a bargain):—~se vr to shrink, contract.

contrahecho/cha adj deformed; hunchbacked; counterfeit, fake, false.

contralto m (mus) contralto.

contrapartida f (com) balancing entry.

contrapelo adv:—**a** ~ against the grain.

contrapeso m counterpoise; counterweight.

contraproducente adj counterproductive.

contrariar vt to contradict, oppose; to vex.

contrariedad f opposition; setback; annoyance.

contrario/ria m/f opponent:—adj contrary, opposite:—**por el** ~ on the contrary.

contrarrestar vt to return a ball; (fig) to counteract.

contraseña f countersign; (mil) watchword.

contrasentido m contradiction.

contrastar vt to resist; to contradict; to assay (metals); to verify (measures and weights):—vi to contrast.

contratar vt to contract; to hire, engage.

contratiempo m setback; accident.

contrato m contract, agreement.

contravenir vi to contravene, transgress; to violate.

contraventana f shutter.

contribución f contribution; tax.

contribuir vt, vi to contribute.

contrincante m competitor.

controlar vt to control; to check.

contumaz adj obstinate, stubborn; (jur) guilty of contempt of court.

contundente adj overwhelming; blunt.

contusión f bruise.

convalecer vi to recover from sickness, convalesce.

convencer vt to convince.

conveniencia f suitability; usefulness; agreement:—~s fpl property.

convenir vi to agree, suit.

convento *m* convent, nunnery; monastery.

conversar *vi* to talk, converse.

convicto/ta *adj* convicted (found guilty).

convidar *vt* to invite.

convocar *vt* to convoke, assemble.

convocatoria *f* summons; notice of a meeting.

conyugal *adj* conjugal, married.

cónyuge *m/f* spouse.

cooperar *vi* to cooperate.

coordinar *vt* to arrange, coordinate.

copa *f* cup; glass; top of a tree; crown of a hat:—**~s** *fpl* hearts *pl* (at cards).

copiar *vt* to copy; to imitate.

copla *f* verse; (*mus*) popular song, folk song.

copo *m* small bundle; flake of snow.

coquetear *vi* to flirt.

coraje *m* courage; anger, passion.

coral *m* coral; choir:—*adj* choral.

corazón *m* heart; core:—**de ~** willingly.

corazonada *f* inspiration; quick decision; presentiment.

corbata *f* tie.

corchete *m* clasp; hook and eye.

corcho *m* cork; float (for fishing); cork bark.

cordel *m* cord, rope; (*mar*) line.

cordero *m* lamb; lambskin; meek, gentle person.

cordial *adj* cordial, affectionate:—*m* cordial.

cordillera *f* range of mountains.

cordón *m* cord, string; lace; cordon.

cornada *f* thrust with a bull's horn.

coro *m* choir; chorus.

corona *f* crown; coronet; top of the head; crown (of a tooth); tonsure; halo.

coronilla *f* crown of the head.

corpiño *m* bodice.

corporal *adj* corporal.

corpulento/ta *adj* corpulent, bulky.

corral *m* yard; farmyard; corral; playpen.

correa *f* leather strap, thong; flexibility.

correcto/ta *adj* exact, correct.

corregir *vt* to correct, amend; to reprehend:—**~se** *vr* to reform.

correo *m* post, mail; courier; mailman:—**a vuelta de ~** by return of post:—**~s** *mpl* post office.

correr *vt* to run; to flow; to travel over; to pull (a drape):—*vi* to run, rush; to flow; to blow (applied to the wind):—**~se** *vr* to be ashamed; to slide, move; to run (of colors).

correspondencia *f* correspondence; communication; agreement.

corresponder *vi* to correspond; to answer; to be suitable; to belong; to concern:—**~se** *vr* to love one another.

corresponsal *m/f* correspondent.

corriente *f* current; course, progression; (electric) current:—*adj* current; common, ordinary, general; fluent; flowing, running.

corro *m* circle of people.

corroer *vt* to corrode, erode.

corromper *vt* to corrupt; to rot; to turn bad; to seduce; to bribe:—**~se** *vr* to rot; to become corrupted:—*vi* to stink.

cortacesped *m* lawn mower.

cortado *m* coffee with a little milk:—**~/da** *adj* cut; sour; embarrassed.

cortar *vt* to cut; to cut off, curtail; to intersect; to carve; to chop; to cut (at cards); to interrupt:—**~se** *vr* to be ashamed or embarrassed; to curdle.

corte m cutting; cut; section; length (of cloth); style:—f (royal) court; capital (city):—**C~s** fpl Spanish Parliament.

cortejo m entourage; courtship; procession; lover.

cortés/esa adj courteous, polite.

cortesía f courtesy, good manners pl.

corteza f bark; peel; crust; (fig) outward appearance.

cortina f curtain.

corto/ta adj short; scanty, small; stupid; bashful:—**a la ~a o a la larga** sooner or later.

corzo/za m/f roe deer, fallow deer.

cosa f thing; matter, affair:—**no hay tal ~** nothing of the sort!

cosecha f harvest; harvest time:—**de su ~** of one's own invention.

coser vt to sew; to join.

cosquillas fpl tickling; (fig) agitation.

costa f cost, price; charge, expense; coast, shore:—**a toda ~** at all events.

costado m side; (mil) flank; side of a ship.

costal m sack, large bag.

costar vt to cost; to need.

coste m cost, expense.

costero/ra adj coastal; (mar) coasting.

costilla f rib; cutlet:—**~s** fpl back, shoulders pl.

costra f crust; (med) scab.

costumbre f custom, habit.

cotejar vt to compare.

cotidiano/na adj daily.

cotilla m/f gossip.

cotizar vt to quote:—**~se** vr **~ a** to sell at; to be quoted at.

coto m enclosure; reserve; boundary stone.

cotorra f small parrot; (col) chatterbox.

covacha f small cave, grotto.

coyuntura f joint, articulation; juncture.

coz f kick; recoil (of a gun); ebbing (of a flood); (fig) insult.

cráneo m skull.

crear vt to create, make; to establish.

crecer vi to grow, increase; to rise.

crecida f swell (of rivers).

creciente f crescent (moon); (mar) flood tide:—adj growing; crescent.

crecimiento m increase; growth.

crédito m credit; belief, faith; reputation.

creer vt, vi to believe; to think; to consider.

crema f cream; custard.

cremallera f zipper.

crepúsculo m twilight.

cresta f crest (of birds).

creyente m/f believer.

cría f breeding; young.

criadero m (bot) nursery; breeding place.

criadilla f testicle; small loaf; truffle.

crianza f breeding, rearing.

criar vt to create, produce; to breed; to breast-feed; to bring up.

criatura f creature; child.

crimen m crime.

criminal adj, m/f criminal.

crin f mane; horsehair.

crío/a m/f (fam) kid.

cripta f crypt.

crisis f invar crisis.

crisol m crucible; melting pot.

crispar vt to set on edge; to tense up.

cristal m crystal; glass; pane; lens.

cristalino/na adj crystalline.

cristalizar vt to crystallize.

cristiano/na adj, m/f Christian.

criterio m criterion.

crítica m/f criticism.

criticar vt to criticize.

croar vi to croak.

cromo *m* chrome.

crónica *f* chronicle; news report; feature.

crónico/ca *adj* chronic.

cronista *m/f* chronicler; reporter; columnist.

cronómetro *m* stopwatch.

cruce *m* crossing; crossroads.

crucero *m* cruiser; cruise; transept; crossing.

crucifijo *m* crucifix.

crucigrama *m* crossword.

crudo/da *adj* raw; green, unripe; crude; cruel; hard to digest.

cruel *adj* cruel.

crueldad *f* cruelty.

crujiente *adj* crunchy.

crujir *vi* to crackle; to rustle.

crustáceo *m* crustacean.

cruz *f* cross; tails (of a coin).

cruzar *vt* to cross; (*mar*) to cruise:—~se *vr* to cross; to pass each other.

cuaderno *m* notebook; exercise book; logbook.

cuadra *f* block; stable.

cuadrado/da *adj*, *m* square.

cuadrante *m* quadrant; dial.

cuadrar *vt*, *vi* to square; to fit, suit, correspond.

cuadrilátero/ra *adj*, *m* quadrilateral.

cuadrilla *f* party, group; gang, crew.

cuadro *m* square; picture, painting; window frame; scene; chart.

cuadrúpedo/da *adj* quadruped.

cuajar *vt* to coagulate; to thicken; to adorn; to set:—~se *vr* to coagulate, curdle; to set; to fill up.

cual *pn* which; who; whom:—*adv* as; like:—*adj* such as.

cuál *pn* which (one).

cualidad *f* quality.

cualquier *adj* any.

cualquiera *adj* anyone, anybody; someone, somebody; whoever; whichever.

cuando *adv* when; if; even:—*conj* since:—**de ~ en ~** from time to time:—**~ más/~ mucho** at most, at best:—**~ menos** at least.

cuándo *adv* when:—¿**de cuándo acá?** since when?

cuánto *adj* what a lot of; how much?:—¿**~s?** how many?:—*pn, adv* how; how much; how many.

cuanto/ta *adj* as many as; as much as; all; whatever:—*adv* **en ~** as soon as:—**en ~ a** as regards:—**~ más** moreover, the more as.

cuarenta *adj*, *m* forty.

cuaresma *f* Lent.

cuarto *m* fourth part; quarter; room, apartment; span:—**~s** *mpl* cash, money:—**~/ta** *adj* fourth.

cuarzo *m* quartz.

cuatro *adj*, *m* four.

cuatrocientos/tas *adj* four hundred.

cuba *f* cask; tub; (*fig*) drunkard.

cubierta *f* cover; deck of a ship; (*auto*) hood; tire; pretext.

cubierto *m* cover; shelter; place at table; meal at a fixed charge:—**~s** *mpl* cutlery, silverware.

cubo *m* cube; bucket; can:—**~de la basura** garbage can.

cubrir *vt* to cover; to disguise; to protect; to roof a building:—**~se** *vr* to become overcast.

cucaracha *f* cockroach.

cuchara *f* spoon.

cucharada *f* spoonful; ladleful.

cucharadita *f* teaspoonful.

cuchichear *vi* to whisper.

cuchillo *m* knife.

cuclillas *adv*:—**en ~** squatting.

cuclillo *m* cuckoo; (*fig*) cuckold.

cuello *m* neck; collar.

cuenca *m* bowl, deep valley; hollow; socket of the eye.

cuenta *f* calculation; account; check, bill (in a restaurant); count, counting; bead; importance.

cuento *m* tale, story, narrative.

cuerda *f* rope; string; spring.

cuerdo/da *adj* sane; prudent, judicious.

cuerno *m* horn.

cuero *m* hide, skin, leather.

cuerpo *m* body; cadaver, corpse.

cuesta *f* slope, hill; incline:—**ir ~ abajo** to go downhill:—**~ arriba** uphill.

cuestión *f* question, matter; dispute; quarrel; problem.

cueva *f* cave; cellar.

cuidado *m* care, worry, concern; charge.

cuidar *vt* to care for; to mind, look after.

culebra *f* snake.

culo *m* backside; bum (*sl*); bottom.

culpa *f* fault, blame; guilt.

culpable *adj* culpable; guilty:—*m/f* culprit.

cultivar *vt* to cultivate.

culto/ta *adj* cultivated, cultured; refined, civilized:—*m* culture; worship.

cumbre *f* top, summit.

cumplir *vt* to carry out, fulfil; to serve (a prison sentence); to carry out (death penalty); to attain, reach (a certain age):—**~se** *vr* to be fulfilled; to expire, be up.

cuna *f* cradle.

cuña *f* wedge.

cuñado/da *m/f* brother/sister-inlaw.

cura *m* priest:—*f* cure; treatment.

curar *vt* to cure; to treat, dress (a wound); to salt; to dress; to tan.

curioso/sa *adj* curious:—*m/f* bystander.

currar *vi* (*fam*)to work.

curso *m* course, direction; year (at university); subject.

curtir *vt* to tan leather:—**~se** *vr* to become sunburned; to become inured.

curva *f* curve, bend.

custodia *f* custody, safekeeping, care; monstrance.

cutis *m* skin.

cutre *adj* (*fam*) mean, grotty.

cuyo/ya *pn* whose, of which, of whom.

D

dado *m* die (*pl* dice).

daga *f* dagger.

dama *f* lady, gentlewoman; mistress; queen; actress of principal parts.

damnificar *vt* to hurt, injure, damage.

dañar *vt* to hurt, injure; to damage.

dañino/na *adj* harmful; noxious; mischievous.

danza *f* dance.

dar *vt* to give; to supply, administer, afford; to deliver.

dátil *m* (*bot*) date.

dato *m* fact.

de *prep* of; from; for; by; on; to; with.

debajo *adv* under, underneath, below.

debatir *vt* to debate, argue, discuss.

debe m (com) debit:—~ **y haber** debit and credit.

deber m obligation, duty; debt:—vt to owe; to be obliged to:—vi **debe (de)** it must, it should.

debidamente adv justly, duly; exactly, perfectly.

débil adj feeble, weak; sickly; frail.

debilitar vt to debilitate, weaken.

decadencia f decay, decline.

decena f ten.

decencia f decency.

decepción f disappointment.

decidir vt to decide, determine.

décimo/ma adj, m tenth.

decir vt to say; to tell; to speak; to name.

decisión f decision; determination, resolution; sentence.

declamar vi to declaim; to harangue.

declarar vt to declare; to manifest; to expound; to explain; (jur) to decide:—~**se** vr to declare one's opinion:—vi to testify.

declinar vi to decline; to decay, degenerate:—vt (gr) to decline.

declive m slope; decline.

decorar vt to decorate, adorn; to illustrate.

decrecer vi to decrease.

decrépito/ta adj decrepit, worn out with age.

decretar vt to decree, determine.

dedal m thimble; very small drinking glass.

dedicar vt to dedicate, devote; to consecrate:—~**se** vr to apply oneself to.

dedo m finger; toe; small bit:—~ **meñique** little finger:—~ **pulgar** thumb:—~ **del corazón** middle finger:—~ **anular** ring finger.

deducir vt to deduce, infer; to allege in pleading; to subtract.

defecto m defect; defectiveness.

defectuoso/sa adj defective, imperfect, faulty.

defender vt to defend, protect; to justify, assert;to resist, oppose.

defensor/ra m/f defender, protector; lawyer, defense counsel.

deferir vi to defer; to yield (to another's opinion):—vt to communicate.

deficiente adj defective.

definir vt to define, describe, explain; to decide.

definitivo/va adj definitive; positive.

deformar vt to deform:—~**se** vr to become deformed.

deforme adj deformed; ugly.

defraudar vt to defraud, cheat; to usurp; to disturb.

defunción f death; funeral.

degenerar vi to degenerate.

degollar vt to behead; to destroy, ruin.

degradar vt to degrade:—~**se** vr to degrade or demean oneself.

degustar vt to taste.

dehesa f pasture.

dejadez f slovenliness, neglect.

dejar vt to leave, quit; to omit; to let; to permit, allow; to forsake; to bequeath; to pardon:—~ **de** to stop; to fail to:—~**se** vr to abandon oneself.

del adj of the (contraction of de and el).

delantal m apron.

delante adv in front; opposite; ahead:—~ **de** in front of; before.

delantero/ra adj front:—m forward.

delegar vt to delegate; to substitute.

deleitar vt to delight.

deletrear vt to spell; to examine; to conjecture.

delfín *m* dolphin; dauphin.

delgado/da *adj* thin; delicate, fine; light; slender, lean.

deliberadamente *adv* deliberately.

deliberar *vi* to consider, deliberate:— *vt* to debate; to consult.

delicado/da *adj* delicate, tender; faint; exquisite; delicious, dainty; slender, subtle.

delicioso/sa *adj* delicious; delightful.

delincuencia *f* delinquency.

delineante *m/f* draftsman/woman.

delirar *vi* to rave; to talk nonsense.

delito *m* offence; crime.

demacrado/da *adj* pale and drawn.

demandar *vt* to demand; to ask; to claim; to sue.

demarcar *vt* to mark out (limits).

demás *adj* other; remaining:—*pn* **los/las** ~ the others, the rest:— **estar** ~ to be over and above; to be useless or superfluous:—**por** ~ in vain.

demasiado/da *adj* too; excessive:— *adv* too, too much.

demencia *f* madness.

demoler *vt* to demolish; to destroy.

demonio *m* demon.

demorar *vt* to delay:—~se *vr* to be delayed:—*vi* to linger.

demostrar *vt* to prove, demonstrate; to manifest.

denegar *vt* to deny; to refuse.

denigrar *vt* to blacken; to insult.

denominar *vt* to name; to designate.

denotar *vt* to denote; to express.

denso/sa *adj* dense, thick; compact.

dentado/da *adj* toothed; indented.

dentadura *f* set of teeth.

dentífrico *m* toothpaste.

dentista *m/f* dentist.

dentro *adv* within:—*pn* ~ **de** in, inside.

denunciar *vt* to advise; to denounce; to report.

depender *vi:*—~ **de** to depend on, be dependent on.

dependiente *m* sales clerk:—*adj* dependent.

depilatorio *m* hair remover.

deponer *vt* to depose; to declare; to displace; to deposit.

deportar *vt* to deport.

deporte *m* sport.

deportista *m/f* sportsman/woman.

depositar *vt* to deposit; to confide; to put away for safekeeping.

depravación *f* depravity.

deprimir *vt* to depress:—~se *vr* to become depressed.

deprisa *adv* quickly.

depurar *vt* to cleanse, purify; to filter.

derecho/cha *adj* right; straight; just; perfect; certain:—*m* right, justice; law; just claim; tax, duty; fee:—*adv* straight.

derivar *vt, vi* to derive; (*mar*) to drift.

derogar *vt* to derogate, abolish; to reform.

derramar *vt* to drain off (water); to spread; to spill, scatter; to waste, shed:—~se *vr* to pour out.

derretir *vt* to melt; to consume; to thaw:—~se *vr* to melt.

derribar *vt* to demolish; to flatten.

derrochar *vt* to dissipate; to squander.

derrotar *vt* to destroy; to defeat.

derruir *vt* to demolish.

derrumbar *vt* to throw down:—~se *vr* to collapse.

desabrido/da *adj* tasteless, insipid; rude; unpleasant.

desacato *m* disrespect, incivility.

desacertado/da *adj* mistaken; unwise; inconsiderate.

desaconsejar vt to advise against.

desacostumbrado/da adj unusual.

desacuerdo m blunder; disagreement; forgetfulness.

desafiar vt to challenge; to defy.

desafinar vi to be out of tune.

desafuero m outrage; excess.

desagradable adj disagreeable, unpleasant.

desagradecido/da adj ungrateful.

desagüe m channel, drain; drainpipe; drainage.

desahogar vt to ease; to vent:—~se vr to recover; to relax.

desahuciar vt to cause to despair; to give up; to evict.

desajustar vt to make uneven; to unbalance:—~se vr to get out of order.

desalentar vt to put out of breath; to discourage.

desaliño m slovenliness; carelessness.

desalmado/da adj cruel, inhuman.

desalojar vt to eject; to move out:—vi to move out.

desamparar vt to forsake, abandon; to relinquish.

desangrar vt to bleed; to drain (a pond); (fig) to exhaust (one's means):—~se vr to lose a lot of blood.

desanimar vt to discourage:—~se vr to lose heart.

desaparecer vi to disappear.

desapercibido/da adj unnoticed.

desaprobar vt to disapprove; to condemn; to reject.

desaprovechado/da adj useless; unprofitable; backward; slack.

desaprovechar vt to waste, turn to a bad use.

desarmar vt to disarm; to disband (troops); to dismantle; (fig) to pacify.

desarraigar vt to uproot; to root out; to extirpate.

desarrollar vt to develop; to unroll; to unfold:—~se vr to develop; to be unfolded; to open.

desasosiego m restlessness; anxiety.

desastre m disaster; misfortune.

desatar vt to untie, loose; to separate; to solve:—~se vr to come undone; to break.

desatascar vt to unblock; to clear.

desatender vt to pay no attention to; to disregard.

desatinar vi to talk nonsense; to reel, stagger.

desatornillar vt to unscrew.

desayunar vt to have for breakfast:—~se vr to breakfast:—vi to have breakfast.

desazón f disgust; uneasiness; annoyance.

desbarrar vi to talk nonsense.

desbordar vt to exceed:—~se vr to overflow.

descalabrado/da adj wounded on the head; imprudent.

descalificar vt to disqualify; to discredit.

descalzo/za adj barefooted; (fig) destitute.

descaminado/da adj (fig) misguided.

descansar vt to rest:—vi to rest; to lie down.

descansillo m landing.

descapotable m convertible.

descarado/da adj cheeky, barefaced.

descargar vt to unload, discharge:—~se vr to unburden oneself.

descarriar vt to lead astray; to misdirect:—~se vr to lose one's way; to stray; to err.

descarrilar vi (ferro) to leave or run off the rails.

descartar *vt* to discard; to dismiss; to rule out.

descendencia *f* descent, offspring.

descender *vt* to take down:—*vi* to descend, walk down; to flow; to fall:—~ **de** to be derived from.

descenso *m* descent; drop.

descifrar *vt* to decipher; to unravel.

descollar *vi* to excel.

descolorido/da *adj* pale, colorless.

descomunal *adj* uncommon; huge.

desconcertar *vt* to disturb; to confound; to disconcert:—~**se** *vr* to be bewildered; to be upset.

desconectar *vt* to disconnect.

desconfiar *vi:*—~ **de** to mistrust, suspect.

descongelar *vt* to defrost.

desconocer *vt* to disown, disavow; to be totally ignorant of (a thing); not to know (a person); not to acknowledge (a favor received).

desconsuelo *m* distress; trouble; despair.

descontar *vt* to discount; to deduct.

descontento *m* dissatisfaction; disgust.

descortés/esa *adj* impolite, rude.

descoser *vt* to unseam; to separate:—~**se** *vr* to come apart at the seams.

descreído/da *adj* incredulous.

descremado/da *adj* skimmed.

describir *vt* to describe; to draw, delineate.

descuartizar *vt* to quarter; to carve.

descubrir *vt* to discover, disclose; to uncover; to reveal; to show:—~**se** *vr* to reveal oneself; to take off one's hat; to confess.

descuento *m* discount; decrease.

descuidado/da *adj* careless, negligent.

descuidar *vt* to neglect:—*vi* ~**se** *vr* to be careless.

desde *prep* since; after; from:—~ **luego** of course:—~ **entonces** since then.

desdén *m* disdain, scorn.

desdeñar *vt* to disdain, scorn:—~**se** *vr* to be disdainful.

desdentado/da *adj* toothless.

desdicha *f* misfortune, calamity; great poverty.

desdoblar *vt* to unfold, spread open.

desear *vt* to desire, wish; to require, demand.

desecar *vt* to dry up.

desechar *vt* to depreciate; to reject; to refuse; to throw away.

desecho *m* residue:—~**s** *mpl* trash.

desembarcar *vt* to unload, disembark:—*vi* to disembark, land.

desembolsar *vt* to pay out.

desempatar *vi* to hold a play-off.

desempeñar *vt* to redeem; to extricate from debt; to fulfil (any duty or promise); to acquit:—~**se** *vr* to get out of debt.

desempleo *m* unemployment.

desencadenar *vt* to unchain:—~**se** *vr* to break loose; to burst.

desencajar *vt* to disjoint; to dislocate; to disconnect.

desencanto *m* disenchantment.

desenchufar *vt* to unplug.

desenfado *m* ease; facility; calmness, relaxation.

desenfocado/da *adj* out of focus.

desenfreno *m* wildness; lack of self-control.

desengañar *vt* to disillusion:—~**se** *vr* to become disillusioned.

desenganchar *vt* to unhook; to uncouple.

desengrasar *vt* to take the grease off.

desenlace *m* climax; outcome.

desenredar *vt* to disentangle.

desenroscar *vt* to untwist; to unroll.

desentenderse *vr* to feign not to understand; to pass by without noticing.

desenterrar *vt* to exhume; to dig up.

desentonar *vi* to be out of tune; to clash.

desenvolver *vt* to unfold; to unroll; to decipher, unravel; to develop:—~se *vr* to develop; to cope.

deseo *m* desire, wish.

desequilibrado/da *adj* unbalanced.

desertar *vt* to desert; (*jur*) to abandon (a cause).

desesperar *vi*, ~se *vr* to despair:—*vt* to make desperate.

desestabilizar *vt* to destabilize.

desfachatez *f* impudence.

desfalco *m* embezzlement.

desfallecer *vi* to get weak; to faint.

desfasado/da *adj* old-fashioned.

desfavorable *adj* unfavorable.

desfiladero *m* gorge.

desfilar *vi* (*mil*) to parade.

desfogarse *vr* to give vent to one's passion or anger.

desgana *f* disgust; loss of appetite; aversion, reluctance.

desgañitarse *vr* to scream, bawl.

desgarrar *vt* to tear; to shatter.

desgaste *m* wear (and tear).

desgracia *f* misfortune; disgrace; accident; setback.

desgreñado/da *adj* disheveled.

deshabitado/da *adj* deserted, uninhabited; desolate.

deshacer *vt* to undo, destroy; to cancel, efface; to rout (an army); to solve; to melt; to break up, divide; to dissolve in a liquid; to violate (a treaty); to diminish; to disband (troops):—~se *vr* to melt; to come apart.

deshelar *vt* to thaw:—~se *vr* to thaw, melt.

desheredar *vt* to disinherit.

deshidratar *vt* to dehydrate.

deshinchar *vt* to deflate:—~se *vr* to go flat, go down.

deshonesto/ta *adj* indecent.

deshonrar *vt* to affront, insult, defame; to dishonor.

deshuesar *vt* to rid of bones; to stone.

desidia *f* idleness, indolence.

desierto/ta *adj* deserted; solitary:—*m* desert; wilderness.

designar *vt* to design; to intend; to appoint; to express, name.

desigual *adj* unequal, unlike; uneven, craggy, cliffy.

desilusionar *vt* to disappoint:—~se *vr* to become disillusioned.

desinfectar *vt* to disinfect.

desinflar *vt* to deflate.

desinteresado/da *adj* disinterested; unselfish.

desistir *vi* to desist, cease.

desleal *adj* disloyal; unfair.

desleír *vt* to dilute; to dissolve.

deslenguado/da *adj* foul-mouthed.

desligar *vt* to untie; to separate.

deslizar *vt* to slip, slide; to let slip (a comment):—~se *vr* to slip; to skid; to flow softly; to creep in.

deslumbrar *vt* to dazzle; to puzzle.

desmayar *vi* to be dispirited or fainthearted:—~se *vr* to faint.

desmedido/da *adj* disproportionate.

desmemoriado/da *adj* forgetful.

desmentir *vt* to give the lie to:—~se *vr* to contradict oneself.

desmenuzar *vt* to crumble; to chip at; to fritter away; to examine minutely.

desmesurado/da *adj* excessive; huge; immeasurable.

desmoralizar *vt* to demoralize.

desnatado/da *adj* skimmed.

desnivel *m* unevenness of the ground.

desnudar *vt* to undress; to strip; to discover, reveal:—~**se** *vr* to undress.

desnutrido/da *adj* undernourished.

desobedecer *vt, vi* to disobey.

desocupar *vt* to vacate; to empty:— ~**se** *vr* to retire from a business; to withdraw from an arrangement.

desodorante *m* deodorant.

desolado/da *adj* desolate, disconsolate.

desordenar *vt* to disorder; to untidy:— ~**se** *vr* to get out of order.

desorganizar *vt* to disorganize.

desorientar *vt* to mislead; to confuse:—~**se** *vr* to lose one's way.

desovar *vi* to spawn.

despabilado/da *adj* watchful, vigilant; wide-awake.

despacho *m* dispatch, expedition; cabinet; office; commission; warrant, patent; expedient; smart answer.

despachurrar *vt* to squash, crush; to mangle.

despacio *adv* slowly, leisurely; little by little:—**i**~**!** softly!, gently!

desparramar *vt* to disseminate, spread; to spill; to squander, lavish:—~**se** *vr* to be dissipated.

despavorido *adj* frightened.

despecho *m* indignation; displeasure; spite; dismay, despair; deceit; derision, scorn:—**a**~ **de** in spite of.

despectivo/va *adj* pejorative, derogatory.

despedir *vt* to discharge; to dismiss (from office); to see off:—~**se** *vr* ~ **de** to say goodbye to.

despegar *vt* to unglue; to take off:— ~**se** *vr* to come loose.

despegue *m* take-off.

despeinar *vt* to ruffle.

despejado/da *adj* sprightly, quick; clear.

despellejar *vt* to skin.

despensa *f* pantry, larder; provisions *pl.*

desperdiciar *vt* to squander.

desperdigar *vt* to separate; to scatter.

desperfecto *m* slight damage; flaw.

despertador *m* alarm clock.

despertar *vt* to wake up, rouse from sleep; to excite:—*vi* to wake up; to grow lively or sprightly:—~**se** *vr* to wake up.

despiadado/da *adj* heartless; merciless.

despido *m* dismissal.

despierto/ta *adj* awake; vigilant; fierce; brisk, sprightly.

despistar *vt* to mislead; to throw off the track:—~**se** *vr* to take the wrong way; to become confused.

desplazar *vt* to move; to scroll:— ~**se** *vr* to travel.

desplegar *vt* to unfold, display; to explain, elucidate; (*mar*) to unfurl:— ~**se** *vr* to open out; to travel.

desplomarse *vr* to fall to the ground; to collapse.

despoblar *vt* to depopulate; to desolate:—~**se** *vr* to become depopulated.

despojar *vt:*—~ **(de)** to strip (of); to deprive (of):—~**se** *vr* to undress.

desposar *vt* to marry, betroth:—~**se** *vr* to be betrothed or married.

desposeer *vt* to dispossess.

déspota *m* despot.

despreciar *vt* to offend; to despise.

desprender *vt* to unfasten, loosen; to separate:—~**se** *vr* to give way; to fall down; to extricate oneself.

despreocupado/da *adj* careless; unworried.

desprevenido/da *adj* unawares, unprepared.

desproporcionado/da *adj* disproportionate.

desprovisto/ta *adj* unprovided.

después *adv* after, afterwards; next.

despuntar *vt* to blunt:—*vi* to sprout; to dawn:—**al ~ del dia** at break of day.

desquiciar *vt* to upset; to discompose; to disorder.

desquite *m* recovery of a loss; revenge, retaliation.

destacamento *m* (*mil*) detachment.

destacar *vt* to emphasize; (*mil*) to detach (a body of troops):—**~se** *vr* to stand out.

destajo *m* piecework.

destapar *vt* to uncover; to open:—**~se** *vr* to be uncovered.

destartalado/da *adj* untidy.

destello *m* signal light; sparkle.

desteñir *vt* to discolor:—**~se** *vr* to fade.

desternillarse *vr:*—**~ de risa** to roar with laughter.

desterrar *vt* to banish; to expel, drive away.

destetar *vt* to wean.

destilar *vt, vi* to distil.

destinar *vt* to destine for, intend for.

destinatario/a *m/f* addressee.

destino *m* destiny; fate, doom; destination; office.

destornillador *m* screwdriver.

destreza *f* dexterity, cleverness, cunning, expertness, skill.

destrozar *vt* to destroy, break into pieces; (*mil*) to defeat.

destruir *vt* to destroy.

desvalido/da *adj* helpless; destitute.

desvalijar *vt* to rob; to burgle.

desván *m* garret.

desvanecer *vt* to dispel:—**~se** *vr* to grow vapid, become insipid; to vanish; to be affected with giddiness.

desvarío *m* delirium; giddiness; inconstancy, caprice; extravagance.

desvelar *vt* to keep awake:—**~se** *vr* to stay awake.

desventaja *f* disadvantage; damage.

desventura *f* misfortune; calamity.

desvergüenza *f* impudence; shamelessness.

desvestir *vt:*—**~se** *vr* to undress.

desviar *vt* to divert; to dissuade; to parry (at fencing):—**~se** *vr* to go off course.

detallar *vt* to detail, relate minutely.

detener *vt* to stop, detain; to arrest; to keep back; to reserve; to with-hold:—**~se** *vr* to stop; to stay.

detenidamente *adv* carefully.

detergente *m* detergent.

deteriorar *vt* to damage.

determinar *vt* to determine:—**~se** *vr* to decide.

detestar *vt* to detest, abhor.

detonar *vi* to detonate.

detrás *adv* behind; at the back, in the back.

deuda *f* debt; fault; offence.

devanar *vt* to reel; to wrap up.

devastar *vt* to devastate.

devengar *vt* to accrue.

devoción *f* devotion, piety; strong affection; ardent love.

devolver *vt* to return; to send back; to refund:—*vi* to be sick.

devorar *vt* to devour, swallow up.

día *m* day.

diablo *m* devil.

diablura *f* prank.

diana *f* (*mil*) reveille; bull's-eye.

diapositiva *f* transparency, slide.

diario m journal, diary; daily newspaper; daily expenses pl:—~/ **ria** adj daily.

diarrea f diarrhea.

dibujar vt to draw, design.

diccionario m dictionary.

dicha f happiness, good fortune:— **por~** by chance.

diciembre m December.

dictamen m opinion, notion; suggestion; judgement.

dictar vt to dictate.

diecinueve adj, m nineteen.

dieciocho adj, m eighteen.

dieciséis adj, m sixteen.

diecisiete adj, m seventeen.

diente m tooth; fang; tusk.

diestro/tra adj right; dexterous, skillful, clever; sagacious, prudent; sly, cunning:—m skillful fencer; halter; bridle.

dieta f diet, regimen; diet, assembly; daily salary of judges.

diez adj, m ten.

diezmar vt to decimate.

difamar vt to defame, libel.

diferencia f difference.

diferenciar vt to differentiate, distinguish:—~se vr to differ, distinguish oneself.

diferente adj different, unlike.

diferido/da adj recorded.

difícil adj difficult.

dificultad f difficulty.

difundir vt to diffuse, spread; to divulge:—~se vr to spread (out).

difunto/ta adj dead, deceased; late.

digerir vt to digest; to bear with patience; to adjust, arrange.

dignarse vr to condescend, deign.

digno/na adj worthy; suitable.

dilatado/da adj large; numerous; prolix; spacious, extensive.

dilatar vt to dilate, expand; to spread out; to defer, protract.

dilema m dilemma.

diligencia f diligence; affair, business; call of nature; stage coach.

dilucidar vt to elucidate, explain.

diluir vt to dilute.

diluviar vi to rain in torrents.

diminuto/ta adj minute, small.

dimitir vt to give up:—vi to resign.

dinamita f dynamite.

dinamo f dynamo.

dineral m large sum of money.

dinero m money.

dios m god.

diosa f goddess.

diplomado/da adj qualified.

dique m dam.

dirección f direction, guidance; administration; steering.

directo/ta adj direct, straight; apparent, evident; live.

director/ra m/f director; conductor; president; manager.

dirigir vt to direct; to conduct; to regulate, govern:—~se vr to go towards; to address oneself to.

discernir vt to discern, distinguish.

discípulo m disciple; scholar.

disco m disc; record; discus; light; face (of the sun or moon); lens (of a telescope).

díscolo/la adj ungovernable; peevish.

discordante adj dissonant, discordant.

discreción f discretion; acuteness of mind.

discrepar vi to differ.

discreto/ta adj discreet; ingenious; witty, eloquent.

disculpar vt to exculpate, excuse; to acquit, absolve:—~se vr to apologize; to excuse oneself.

discurrir *vi* to ramble about; to run to and fro; to discourse (on a subject):— *vt* to invent, contrive; to meditate.

discurso *m* speech; conversation; dissertation; space of time.

discutir *vt, vi* to discuss.

disecar *vt* to dissect; to stuff.

diseminar *vt* to scatter; to disseminate, propagate.

diseñar *vt* to draw; to design.

disentir *vi* to dissent, disagree.

disfrazar *vt* to disguise, conceal; to cloak, dissemble:——**~se** *vr* to disguise oneself as.

disfrutar *vt* to enjoy:——**~se** *vr* to enjoy oneself.

disgustar *vt* to disgust; to offend:— **~se** *vr* to be displeased; to fall out.

disidente *adj* dissident:—*m/f* dissident, dissenter.

disimular *vt* to hide; to tolerate.

disipar *vt* to dissipate, disperse, scatter; to lavish.

dislocarse *vr* to be dislocated or out of joint.

disminuir *vt* to diminish; to decrease.

disolver *vt* to loosen, untie; to dissolve; to disunite; to melt, liquefy; to interrupt.

disparar *vt* to shoot, discharge, fire; to let off; to throw with violence:— *vi* to shoot, fire.

disparate *m* nonsense, absurdity, extravagance.

displicencia *f* displeasure; dislike.

disponer *vt* to arrange, prepare; to dispose.

disponible *adj* available; disposable.

dispositivo *m* device.

disputar *vt* to dispute, controvert, question:—*vi* to debate, argue.

disquete *m* floppy disk.

distancia *f* distance; interval; difference.

distante *adj* distant, far off.

distinguido/da *adj* distinguished, conspicuous.

distinguir *vt* to distinguish; to discern: ——**~se** *vr* to distinguish oneself.

distinto/ta *adj* distinct, different; clear.

distraer *vt* to distract:—**~se** *vr* to be absent-minded, be inattentive.

distraído/da *adj* absent-minded, inattentive.

distribuir *vt* to distribute.

distrito *m* district; territory.

disturbio *m* riot; disturbance, interruption.

disuadir *vt* to dissuade.

diurno/na *adj* daily.

diva *f* prima donna.

divagar *vt* to digress.

divergencia *f* divergence.

diversidad *f* diversity; variety of things.

diversificar *vt* to diversify; to vary.

diversión *f* diversion; sport; amusement; (*mil*) diversion.

divertir *vt* to divert (the attention); to amuse, entertain; (*mil*) to draw off: ——**~se** *vr* to amuse oneself.

dividir *vt* to divide; to disunite; to separate; to share out.

divieso *m* (*med*) boil.

divino/na *adj* divine, heavenly; excellent.

divorcio *m* divorce; separation, disunion.

divulgar *vt* to publish, divulge.

dobladillo *m* hem; turn-up.

doblar *vt* to double; to fold; to bend:—*vi* to turn; to toll:——**~se** *vr* to bend, bow, submit.

doble *adj* double; dual; deceitful:— **al~** doubly:—*m* double.

doblegar vt to bend:——**se** vr to yield.

doblez m crease; fold; turn-up:—f duplicity.

doce adj, m twelve.

docena f dozen.

dócil adj docile, tractable.

doctor/ra m/f doctor.

documento m document; record.

dogma m dogma.

dólar m dollar.

doler vt, vi to feel pain; to ache:——**se** vr to feel for the sufferings of others; to complain.

dolor m pain; aching, ache; affliction.

domar vt to tame; to subdue, master.

domesticar vt to domesticate.

domicilio m domicile; home, abode.

dominar vt to dominate; to be fluent in:——**se** vr to moderate one's passions.

domingo m Sunday; (Christian) Sabbath.

donar vt to donate; to bestow.

donativo m contribution.

doncella f virgin, maiden; lady's maid.

donde relative adv where

¿dónde? interrogative adv where?:— **¿de dónde?** from where?

dondequiera adv wherever.

dorado/da adj gilt compd; golden:— m gilding.

dormir vi to sleep:——**se** vr to fall asleep.

dos adj, m two.

doscientos/tas adj pl two hundred.

dosis f invar dose.

dotado/da adj gifted.

drama m drama.

dramatizar vt to dramatize.

droga f drug; stratagem; artifice, deceit.

droguería f hardware store.

ducha f shower; (med) douche.

ducho/cha adj skilled, experienced.

dudar vt to doubt.

duelo m grief, affliction; mourning.

duende m elf, hobgoblin.

dueño/ña m/f owner; landlord/lady; employer.

dulce adj sweet; mild, gentle, meek; soft:—m sweet, candy.

dúo m (mus) duo, duet.

duodécimo/ma adj twelfth.

duplicar vt to duplicate; to repeat.

duradero/ra adj lasting, durable.

durante adv during.

durar vi to last, continue.

durazno m peach; peach tree.

dureza f hardness; harshness:——~ **de oido** hardness of hearing.

duro/ra adj hard; cruel; harsh, rough: —m five peseta coin:—adv hard.

E

e conj and (before words starting with i and hi).

ébano m ebony.

ebrio/ia adj drunk.

ebullición f boiling.

echar vt to throw; to add; to pour out; to mail:——**se** vr to lie down.

eco m echo.

económico/ca adj economic; cheap; thrifty; financial; avaricious.

ecuánime *adj* level-headed.

ecuménico/ca *adj* ecumenical; universal.

edad *f* age.

edición *f* edition; publication.

edificar *vt* to build, construct; to edify.

edificio *m* building; structure.

editar *vt* to edit; to publish.

educación *f* education; upbringing; (good) manners *pl*.

educar *vt* to educate, instruct; to bring up.

efectivamente *adv* exactly; really; in fact.

efecto *m* effect; consequence; purpose:—**~s** *mpl* effects *pl*, goods *pl*: —**en~** in fact, really.

efectuar *vt* to effect, carry out.

eficaz *adj* efficient; effective.

eficiente *adj* efficient.

egoísta *m/f* self-seeker:—*adj* selfish.

eje *m* axle; axis.

ejecutar *vt* to execute, perform; to put to death; (*jur*) to distrain, seize.

ejecutivo/va *adj* executive:—*m/f* executive.

ejemplar *m* specimen; copy; example:—*adj* exemplary.

ejemplo *m* example:—**por~** for example, for instance.

ejercer *vt* to exercise; *vi* to apply oneself to the functions of an office.

ejercicio *m* exercise.

ejercitar *vt* to exercise.

ejército *m* army.

el *art*, *m* the.

él *pn* he, it.

elaborar *vt* to elaborate.

elástico/ca *adj* elastic.

elección *f* election; choice.

eléctrico/ca *adj* electric, electrical.

electrocutar *vt* to electrocute.

electrodomesticos *mpl* (electrical) household appliances *pl*.

electrotecnia *f* electrical engineering.

elefante *m* elephant.

elegante *adj* elegant, fine.

elegir *vt* to choose, elect.

elemento *m* element:—**~s** *mpl* elements, rudiments, first principles *pl*.

elevar *vt* to raise; to elevate:—**~se** *vr* to rise; to be enraptured; to be conceited.

eliminar *vt* to eliminate, remove.

eliminatoria *f* preliminary (round).

ella *pn* she; it.

ello *pn* it.

elogiar *vt* to praise, eulogize.

eludir *vt* to elude, escape.

emanar *vi* to emanate.

embadurnar *vt* to smear, bedaub.

embalaje *m* packing, package.

embaldosar *vt* to pave with tiles.

embalse *m* reservoir.

embarazada *f* pregnant woman:—*adj* pregnant.

embarazoso/sa *adj* difficult; intricate, entangled.

embarcación *f* embarkation; any vessel or ship.

embarcar *vt* to embark:—**~se** *vr* to go on board; (*fig*) to get involved (in a matter).

embargo *m* embargo:—**sin~** still, however.

embarque *m* embarkation.

embaucar *vt* to deceive; to trick.

embeber *vt* to soak; to saturate:—*vi* to shrink:—**~se** *vr* to be enraptured; to be absorbed.

embeleso *m* amazement, enchantment.

embellecer *vt* to embellish, beautify.

embestir *vt* to assault, attack.

emblanquecer vt to whiten:—~**se** vr to grow white; to bleach.

embobado/da adj amazed; fascinated.

émbolo m plunger; piston.

embolsar vt to put money into (a purse); to pocket.

emborrachar vt to intoxicate, inebriate:—~**se** vr to get drunk.

emboscada f (mil) ambush.

embotar vt to blunt:—~**se** vr to go numb.

embotellamiento m traffic jam.

embotellar vt to bottle (wine).

embozar vt to muffle (the face); (fig) to cloak, conceal.

embrague m clutch.

embriagar vt to intoxicate, inebriate; to transport, enrapture.

embrión m embryo.

embrollo m muddle.

embromar vt to tease; to cajole, wheedle.

embrujar vt to bewitch.

embrutecer vt to brutalize:—~**se** vr to become depraved.

embudo m funnel.

embustero/ra m/f impostor, cheat; liar:—adj deceitful.

embutido m sausage; inlay.

emerger vi to emerge, appear.

emigrar vi to emigrate.

eminente adj eminent, high; excellent, conspicuous.

emisora f broadcasting station.

emitir vt to emit; to issue; to broadcast.

emoción f emotion; feeling; excitement.

emocionar vt to excite; to move, touch.

emotivo/va adj emotional.

empacho m (med) indigestion.

empalagoso/sa adj cloying; tiresome.

empalmar vt to join.

empanada f (meat) pie.

empanar vt to cover with breadcrumbs.

empantanarse vr to get swamped; to get bogged down.

empapar vt to soak; to soak up:—~**se** vr to soak.

empapelar vt to paper.

empaquetar vt to pack, parcel up.

emparedado m sandwich.

emparrado m vine arbor.

empastar vt to paste; to fill (a tooth).

empatar vi to draw.

empedernido/da adj inveterate; heartless.

empedrado m paving.

empeine m instep.

empellón m push; heavy blow.

empeñar vt to pawn, pledge:—~**se** vr to pledge oneself to pay debts; to get into debt:—~**se en algo** to insist on something.

empeorar vt to make worse:—vi ~**se** vr to grow worse.

empequeñecer vt to dwarf; (fig) to belittle.

empezar vt to begin, start.

emplazamiento m summons; location.

empleado/da m/f official; employee.

emplear vt to employ; to occupy; to commission.

empobrecer vt to reduce to poverty:—vi to become poor.

empollar vt to incubate; to hatch; (fam) to swot (up).

empolvar vt to powder; to sprinkle powder upon.

empotrado/da adj built-in.

emprender vt to embark on; to tackle; to undertake.

empresa f (com) company; enterprise, undertaking.

empujar vt to push; to press forward.

empujón m push; impulse:—**a~ones** in fits and starts.

emular vt to emulate, rival.

en prep in; for; on, upon.

enaguas fpl petticoat.

enamorado/da adj in love, lovesick.

enamorar vt to inspire love in:—**~se** vr to fall in love.

enano/na adj dwarfish:—m dwarf.

enardecer vt to fire with passion, inflame.

enarenar vt to fill with sand.

encabezar vt to head; to put a heading to; to lead.

encadenar vt to chain, link together; to connect, unite.

encajar vt to insert; to drive in; to encase; to intrude:—vi to fit (well).

encaje m lace.

encalar vt to whitewash.

encallar vi (mar) to run aground.

encaminar vt to guide, show the way:—**~se** vr **~ a** to take the road to.

encandilar vt to dazzle.

encanecer vi to grow gray; to grow old.

encantado/da adj bewitched; delighted; pleased.

encantador/ra adj charming:—m/f magician.

encantar vt to enchant, charm; (fig) to delight.

encarcelar vt to imprison.

encarecimiento m price increase:—**con~** insistently.

encargado/da adj in charge:—m/f representative; person in charge.

encargar vt to charge; to commission.

encariñarse vr:—**~ con** to grow fond of.

encarnar vt to embody, personify.

encasillar vt to pigeonhole; to typecast.

encastillarse vr to refuse to yield.

encausar vt to prosecute.

encauzar vt to channel.

encebollado m casseroled beef or lamb and onions, seasoned with spice.

encenagado/da adj muddy, mudstained.

encendedor m lighter.

encender vt to kindle, light, set on fire; to inflame, incite; to switch on, to turn on:—**~se** vr to catch fire; to flare up.

encerado m blackboard.

encerar vt to wax; to polish.

encerrar vt to shut up, confine; to contain:—**~se** vr to withdraw from the world.

enchufar vt to plug in; to connect.

enchufe m plug; outlet, socket; connection; (fam) contact, connection.

encía f gum (of the teeth).

encierro m confinement; enclosure; prison, penitentiary; bull-pen; penning (of bulls).

encima adv above; over; at the top; besides:—**~ de** prep above; over; at the top of; besides.

encina f evergreen oak.

encinta adj pregnant.

enclenque adj weak, sickly:—m weakling.

encoger vt to contract, shorten; to shrink; to discourage:—**~se** vr to shrink; (fig) to cringe.

encolar vt to glue.

encolerizar vt to provoke, irritate:—
~**se** vr to get angry.

encomendar vt to recommend; to
entrust:—~**se** vr ~ **a** to entrust oneself to; to put one's trust in.

encontrar vt to meet, encounter:—vr
~**se con** to run into:—vi to assemble, come together.

encrucijada f four way stop, intersection; junction.

encuadernar vt to bind (books).

encubierto/ta adj hidden, concealed.

encubrir vt to hide, conceal.

encuesta f inquiry; opinion poll.

encurtir vt to pickle.

endeble adj feeble, weak.

endemoniado/da adj possessed with
the devil; devilish.

enderezar vt to straighten out; to set
right:—~**se** vr to stand upright.

endeudarse vr to get into debt.

endosar vt to endorse.

endrino m blackthorn, sloe.

endulzar vt to sweeten; to soften.

endurecer vt to harden, toughen:—
~**se** vr to become cruel; to grow
hard.

enebro m (bot) juniper.

enemistar vt to make an enemy:—
~**se** vr to become enemies; to fall
out.

energía f energy, power, drive; strength
of will.

energúmeno/na m/f (fam) madman/
woman.

enero m January.

enfadar vt to anger, irritate; to trouble:—~**se** vr to become angry.

énfasis m emphasis.

enfermar vi to fall ill:—vt to make
sick; to weaken.

enfermedad f illness.

enfermero/ra m/f nurse.

enfermo/ma adj sick, ill:—m/f
invalid, sick person; patient.

enfocar vt to focus; to consider (a
problem).

enfoque m focus.

enfrentar vt to confront; to put face
to face:—~**se** vr to face each other;
to meet (two teams).

enfrente adv over against, opposite;
in front.

enfriar vt to cool; to refrigerate:—
~**se** vr to cool down; (med) to catch
a cold.

enfurecer vt to madden, enrage:—
~**se** vr to get rough (of the wind and
sea); to become furious or enraged.

enfurruñarse vr to get sulky; to
frown.

engañar vt to deceive, cheat:—~**se**
vr to be deceived; to make a mistake.

enganchar vt to hook, hang up; to
hitch up; to couple, connect; to
recruit into military service:—~**se**
vr (mil) to enlist.

engañoso/sa adj deceitful, artful,
false.

engastar vt to set, mount.

engatusar vt to coax.

engendrar vt to beget, engender; to
produce.

englobar vt to include.

engordar vt to fatten:—vi to grow fat;
to put on weight.

engorroso/sa adj troublesome, cumbersome.

engranaje m gear; gearing.

engrasar vt to grease, lubricate.

engreído/da adj conceited, vain.

engullir vt to swallow; to gobble,
devour.

enharinar vt to cover or sprinkle with flour.

enhebrar vt to thread.

enhorabuena f congratulations pl:—adv all right; well and good.

enhoramala interj good riddance!

enjalbegar vt to whitewash.

enjambre m swarm of bees; crowd, multitude.

enjuagar vt to rinse out; to wash out.

enjuiciar vt to prosecute, try; to pass judgement on, judge.

enlace m connection, link; relationship.

enladrillar vt to pave with bricks.

enlazar vt to join, unite; to tie.

enlodar vt to cover in mud; (fig) to stain.

enloquecer vt to madden, drive crazy:—vi to go mad.

enmarañar vt to entangle; to complicate; to confuse:—~se vr to become entangled; to get confused.

enmendar vt to correct; to reform; to repair, compensate for; to amend:—~se vr to mend one's ways.

enmohecer vt to make moldy; to rust:—~se vr to grow moldy or musty; to rust.

enmudecer(se) vt to silence:—~se vr to grow dumb; to be silent.

ennegrecer vt to blacken; to darken; to obscure.

enojar vt to irritate, make angry; to annoy; to upset; to offend:—~se vr to get angry.

enorgullecerse vr:—~ (de) to be proud (of).

enorme adj enormous, vast, huge; horrible.

enredadera f climbing plant; bindweed.

enredar vt to entangle, ensnare, confound, perplex; to puzzle; to sow discord among:—~se vr to get entangled; to get complicated; to get embroiled.

enrejado m trelliswork.

enrevesado/da adj complicated.

enriquecer vt to enrich; to adorn:—~se vr to grow rich.

enrojecer vt to redden:—vi to blush.

enrolar vt to recruit:—~se vr (mil) to join up.

enrollar vt to roll (up).

enroscar vt to twist:—~se vr to curl or roll up.

ensalada f salad.

ensalmo m enchantment, spell.

ensalzar vt to exalt, aggrandize; to exaggerate.

ensamblar vt to assemble.

ensañar vt to irritate, enrage:—~se con vr to treat brutally.

ensanchar vt to widen; to extend; to enlarge:—~se vr to expand; to assume an air of importance.

ensangrentar vt to stain with blood.

ensartar vt to string (beads, etc).

ensayar vt to test; to rehearse.

ensayo m test, trial; rehearsal of a play; essay.

enseñar vt to teach, instruct; to show.

ensimismarse vr to be or become lost in thought.

ensordecer vt to deafen:—vi to grow deaf.

ensuciar vt to stain, soil; to defile:—~se vr to wet oneself; to dirty oneself.

ensueño m fantasy; daydream; illusion.

entablar vt to board (up); to strike up (conversation).

entablillar vt (med) to put in a splint.

entallar vt to tailor (a suit):—vi to fit.

ente m organization; entity, being; (fam) odd character.

entender vt, vi to understand, comprehend; to remark, take notice (of); to reason, think:—**a mi ~** in my opinion:—**~se** vr to understand each other.

enterar vt to inform; to instruct:—**~se** vr to find out.

enternecer vt to soften; to move (to pity):—**~se** vr to be moved.

entero/ra adj entire, complete; perfect; honest; resolute:—**por ~** entirely, completely.

enterrar vt to inter, bury.

entidad f entity; company; body; society.

entierro m burial; funeral.

entonar vt to tune, intonate; to intone; to tone:—vi to be in tune:—**~se** vr to give oneself airs.

entonces adv then, at that time.

entornar vt to half close.

entorpecer vt to dull; to make lethargic; to hinder; to delay.

entrada f entrance, entry; (com) receipts pl; entree; ticket (for cinema, theater, etc).

entrampar vt to trap, snare; to mess up; to burden with debts:—**~se** vr get into debt.

entrañable adj intimate; affectionate.

entrañas fpl entrails pl, intestines pl.

entrar vi to enter, go in; to commence.

entre prep between; among(st); in:—**~ manos** in hand.

entrecejo m space between the eyebrows; frown.

entredicho m (jur) injunction:—**estar en ~** to be banned:—**poner en ~** to cast doubt on.

entregar vt to deliver; to hand over:—**~se** vr to surrender; to devote oneself.

entremeses mpl hors d'oeuvres.

entrenarse vr to train.

entrepierna f crotch.

entresuelo m entresol; mezzanine.

entretanto adv meanwhile.

entretejer vt to interweave.

entretela f interfacing, stiffening, interlining.

entretener vt to amuse; to entertain, divert; to hold up; to maintain:—**~se** vr to amuse oneself; to linger.

entrever vt to have a glimpse of.

entrevistar vt to interview:—**~se** vr to have an interview.

entristecer vt to sadden.

entrometer vt to put (one thing) between (others):—**~se** vr to interfere.

entumecido/da adj numb, stiff.

enturbiar vt to make cloudy; to obscure, confound:—**~se** vr to become cloudy; (fig) to get confused.

entusiasmar vt to excite, fill with enthusiasm; to delight.

enumerar vt to enumerate.

envalentonar vt to give courage to:—**~se** vr to boast.

envanecer vt to make vain; to swell with pride:—**~se** vr to become proud.

envaramiento m stiffness; numbness.

envasar vt to pack; to bottle; to can.

envase m packing; bottling; canning; container; package; bottle; can.

envejecer vt to make old:—vi **~se** vr to grow old.

envenenar vt to poison; to embitter.

envés m wrong side (of material).

enviar vt to send, transmit, convey; dispatch.

enviciar vt to vitiate, corrupt:—~se vr to get corrupted.

envidia f envy; jealousy.

envidiar vt to envy; to grudge; to be jealous of.

envilecer vt to vilify, debase:—~se vr to degrade oneself.

envío m (com) dispatch, remittance of goods; consignment.

enviudar vi to become a widower or widow.

envolver vt to involve; to wrap up.

enyesar vt to plaster; (med) to put in a plaster cast.

enzarzarse vr to get involved in a dispute; to get oneself into trouble.

épico/ca adj epic.

epígrafe f epigraph, inscription; motto; headline.

episodio m episode, installment.

época f epoch; period, time.

epopeya f epic.

equidad f equity, honesty; impartiality, justice.

equilibrar vt to balance; to poise.

equilibrio m balance, equilibrium.

equipaje m luggage; equipment.

equipar vt to fit out, equip, furnish.

equipararse vr:—~ con to be on a level with.

equipo m equipment; team; shift.

equitación f horsemanship; riding.

equitativo/va adj equitable; just.

equivaler vi to be of equal value.

equivocación f mistake, error; misunderstanding.

equivocar vt to mistake:—~se vr to make a mistake, be wrong.

equívoco/ca adj equivocal, ambiguous:—m equivocation; quibble.

era f era, age; threshing floor.

erario m treasury, public funds pl.

erguir vt to erect, raise up straight:—~se vr to straighten up.

erial m fallow land.

erigir vt to erect, raise, build; to establish.

erizarse vr to bristle; to stand on end.

erizo m hedgehog:—~ de mar sea urchin.

ermita f hermitage.

erotismo m eroticism.

errar vi to be mistaken; to wander.

errata f misprint.

erre:—~ que ~ adv obstinately.

error m error, mistake, fault.

eructar vi to belch, burp.

esbelto/ta adj slim, slender.

esbirro m bailiff; henchman; killer.

esbozo m outline.

escabeche m pickle; pickled fish.

escabroso/sa adj rough, uneven; craggy; rude, risqué, blue.

escabullirse vr to escape, evade; to slip through one's fingers.

escafandra f diving suit; space suit.

escala f ladder; (mus) scale; stopover.

escalar vt to climb.

escalera f staircase; ladder.

escalfar vt to poach (eggs).

escalofriante adj chilling.

escalón m step of a stair; rung.

escama f (fish) scale.

escamar vt to scale, take off scales:—~se vr to flake off; to become suspicious.

escamotear vt to swipe; to make disappear.

escampar vi to stop raining.

escándalo m scandal; uproar.

escaño m bench with a back; seat (parliament).

escapar *vi* to escape:—**~se** *vr* to get away; to leak (water, etc).

escaparate *m* store window; wardrobe.

escape *m* escape, flight; leak; exhaust (of motor).

escarabajo *m* beetle.

escaramuza *f* skirmish; dispute, quarrel.

escarbar *vt* to scratch (the earth as hens do); to inquire into.

escarcha *f* white frost.

escarlata *adj* scarlet.

escarlatina *f* scarlet fever.

escarmentar *vi* to learn one's lesson:—*vt* to punish severely.

escarola *f* (*bot*) endive.

escarpado/da *adj* sloped; craggy.

escaso/sa *adj* small, short, little; sparing; scarce; scanty.

escenario *m* stage; set.

escéptico/ca *adj* sceptic, sceptical.

esclarecer *vt* to lighten; to illuminate; to illustrate; to shed light on (problem, etc).

esclavo/va *m/f* slave; captive.

esclusa *f* sluice, floodgate.

escoba *f* broom, brush.

escocer *vt* to sting; to burn:—**~se** *vr* to chafe.

escoger *vt* to choose, select.

escolar *m/f* schoolboy/girl:—*adj* scholastic.

escollo *m* reef, rock.

escoltar *vt* to escort.

escombros *mpl* trash; debris.

esconder *vt* to hide, conceal:—**~se** *vr* to be hidden.

escondite *m* hiding place:—**juego de ~** hide-and-seek.

escoplo *m* chisel.

escorbuto *m* scurvy.

escote *m* low neck (of a dress).

escribir *vt* to write; to spell.

escrito *m* document; manuscript, text.

escritor/ra *m/f* writer, author.

escritorio *m* writing desk; office, study.

escrúpulo *m* doubt, scruple, scrupulousness.

escuchar *vt* to listen to, heed.

escudilla *f* bowl.

escudo *m* shield.

escudriñar *vt* to search, examine; to pry into.

escuela *f* school.

esculpir *vt* to sculpt.

escupir *vt* to spit.

escurreplatos *m invar* plate rack.

escurrir *vt* to drain; to drip:—**~se** *vr* to slip away; to slip, slide:—*vi* to wring out.

ese/esa *adj* that:—**esos/as** *pl* those.

ése/ésa *pn* that (one):—**ésos/as** *pl* those (ones).

esencial *adj* essential; principal.

esfera *f* sphere; globe.

esforzarse *vr* to exert oneself, make an effort.

esfuerzo *m* effort.

esfumarse *vr* to fade away.

esgrima *f* fencing.

esguince *m* (*med*) sprain.

eslabón *m* link of a chain; steel; shackle.

esmalte *m* enamel.

esmerado/da *adj* careful, neat.

esmeralda *m* emerald.

esmero *m* careful attention, great care.

eso *pn* that.

esos/as; ésos/as *pl* of **ese/a; ése/a.**

espabilar *vt* to wake up:—**~se** *vr* to wake up; (*fig*) to get a move on.

espaciar vt to spread out; to space (out).

espacio m space; (radio or TV) program.

espada f sword; ace of spades.

espalda f back, back-part:—**~s** fpl shoulders pl.

español/la adj Spanish:—m/f Spaniard:—m Spanish language.

espantajo m scarecrow; bogeyman.

espantar vt to frighten; to chase or drive away.

esparadrapo m adhesive tape.

esparcir vt to scatter; to divulge:—**~se** vr to amuse oneself.

espárrago m asparagus.

espátula f spatula.

especia f spice.

especial adj special; particular:—**en ~** especially.

especie f species; kind, sort; matter.

especificar vt to specify.

espectáculo m spectacle; show.

espectador/ra m/f spectator.

especular vt to speculate.

espejismo m mirage.

espejo m mirror.

espeluznante adj horrifying.

esperanza f hope.

esperar vt to hope; to expect, wait for.

esperma f sperm.

espeso/sa adj thick, dense.

espesor m thickness.

espía m/f spy.

espiga f ear (of corn).

espigón m ear of corn; sting; (mar) breakwater.

espina f thorn; fishbone.

espinaca f (bot) spinach.

espinilla f shinbone.

espino m hawthorn.

espiral adj, f spiral.

espirar vt to exhale.

espíritu m spirit, soul; mind; intelligence:—**el E~ Santo** the Holy Ghost:—**~s** pl demons, hobgoblins pl.

espléndido/da adj splendid.

espliego m (bot) lavender.

espolón m spur (of a cock); spur (of a mountain range); sea wall; jetty; (mar) buttress.

espolvorear vt to sprinkle.

esponja f sponge.

espontáneo/nea adj spontaneous.

esposa f wife.

esposas fpl handcuffs pl.

esposo m husband.

espuma f froth, foam.

espumar vt to skim, take the scum off.

espumoso/sa adj frothy, foamy; sparkling (wine).

esputo m spit, saliva.

esqueje m cutting (of plant).

esquela f note, slip of paper.

esqueleto m skeleton.

esquema m scheme; diagram; plan.

esquí m ski; skiing.

esquina f corner, angle.

esquirol m blackleg.

esquivar vt to shun, avoid, evade.

esta adj f this:—**~s** pl these.

ésta pn f this:—**~s** pl these.

estable adj stable.

establecer vt to establish.

establo m stable.

estaca f stake; stick; post.

estación f season (of the year); station; railroad station, terminus:—**~ de autobuses** bus station:—**~ de servicio** service station.

estacionar vt to park; (mil) to station.

estadio m phase; stadium.

estado *m* state, condition.

Estados Unidos *mpl* United States (of America).

estafar *vt* to deceive, defraud.

estallar *vi* to crack; to burst; to break out.

estambre *m* stamen.

estamento *m* estate; body; layer; class.

estampa *f* print; engraving; appearance.

estampar *vt* to print.

estancar *vt* to check (a current); to monopolize; to prohibit, suspend:—~se *vr* to stagnate.

estancia *f* stay; bedroom; ranch; (*poet*) stanza.

estanco *m* tobacconist's (store):—~/ca *adj* watertight.

estándar *adj*, *m* standard.

estaño *m* tin.

estanque *m* pond, pool; reservoir.

estantería *f* shelves *pl*, shelving.

estar *vi* to be; to be (in a place).

estatua *f* statue.

este¹ *m* east.

este²/ta *adj* this:—**estos/tas** *pl* these.

estera *f* mat.

estéreo *adj invar*, *m* stereo.

estereotipo *m* stereotype.

estéril *adj* sterile, infertile.

esterlina *adj*:—**libra** ~ pound sterling.

estético/ca *adj* esthetic:—*f* esthetics.

estiércol *m* dung; manure.

estilo *m* style; fashion; stroke (swimming).

estima *f* esteem.

estimar *vt* to estimate, value; to esteem; to judge; to think.

estimular *vt* to stimulate, excite; to goad.

estío *m* summer.

estipular *vt* to stipulate.

estirar *vt* to stretch out.

esto *pn* this.

estofado *m* stew.

estómago *m* stomach.

estopa *f* tow.

estorbar *vt* to hinder; (*fig*) to bother:— *vi* to be in the way.

estornudar *vi* to sneeze.

estos/as, éstos/tas *pl* of **este/ta, éste/ta.**

estrado *m* drawing room; stage, platform.

estrafalario/ria *adj* slovenly; eccentric.

estrago *m* ruin, destruction; havoc.

estrangular *vt* to strangle; (*med*) to strangulate.

estraperlo *m* black market.

estratagema *f* stratagem, trick.

estrato *m* stratum, layer.

estraza *f* rag:—**papel de** ~ brown paper.

estrechar *vt* to tighten; to contract, constrain; to compress:—~se *vr* to grow narrow; to embrace:—~ **la mano** to shake hands.

estrecho *m* straits *pl*:—~/cha *adj* narrow, close; tight; intimate; rigid, austere; short (of money).

estrella *f* star.

estrellar *vt* to dash to pieces:—~se *vr* to smash; to crash; to fail.

estremecer *vt* to shake, make tremble:—~se *vr* to shake, tremble.

estrenar *vt* to wear for the first time; to move into (a house); to show (a movie) for the first time:—~se *vr* to make one's debut.

estreñido/da *adj* constipated.

estrépito *m* noise, racket; fuss.

estribillo *m* chorus.

estribo *m* buttress; stirrup; running board:—**perder los** ~**s** to fly off the handle (*fam*).

estribor m (mar) starboard.
estricto/ta adj strict; severe.
estrofa f (poet) verse, strophe.
estropajo m scourer.
estropear vt to spoil; to damage:—
~**se** vr to get damaged.
estructura f structure.
estruendo m clamor, noise; confusion, uproar; pomp, ostentation.
estuche m case (for scissors, etc); sheath.
estudiar vt to study.
estufa f heater, fire.
estupefaciente m narcotic.
estupefacto adj speechless; thunderstruck.
estupendo/da adj terrific, marvelous.
estúpido adj stupid.
etapa f stage; stopping place; (fig) phase.
etcétera adv etcetera, and so on.
eterno/na adj eternal.
ético/ca adj ethical, moral.
etiqueta f etiquette; label.
evacuar vt to evacuate, empty.
evadir vt to evade, escape.
evaluar vt to evaluate.
evaporar vt to evaporate:—~**se** vr to vanish.
eventual adj possible; temporary, casual (worker).
evidente adj evident, clear.
evitar vt to avoid.
evolucionar vi to evolve.
ex adj ex.
ex profeso adv on purpose.
exacerbar vt to exacerbate; to irritate.
exacto/ta adj exact; punctual; accurate.
exagerar vt to exaggerate.
exaltar vt to exalt, elevate; to praise, extol:—~**se** vr to get excited.

examen m exam, examination, test, inquiry.
examinar vt to examine.
exasperar vt to exasperate, irritate.
excavar vt to excavate, dig out.
exceder vt to exceed, surpass, excel, outdo.
excelente adj excellent.
excéntrico/ca adj eccentric.
excepto adv excepting, except (for).
exceso m excess.
excitar vt to excite:—~**se** vr to get excited.
exclamar vt to exclaim, cry out.
excluir vt to exclude.
excremento m excrement.
excursión f excursion, trip.
excusa f excuse, apology.
excusado m bathroom.
excusar vt to excuse; to avoid:—~
de to exempt from:—~**se** vr to apologize.
exento/ta adj exempt, free.
exhalar vt to exhale; to give off; to heave (a sigh).
exhausto/ta adj exhausted.
exhibir vt to exhibit.
exhortar vt to exhort.
exhumar vt to disinter, exhume.
exigir vt to demand, require.
exiliado/da adj exiled:—m/f exile.
existir vi to exist, be.
éxito m outcome; success; (mus,etc) hit:—**tener** ~ to be successful.
exorbitante adj exhorbitant, excessive.
exótico/ca adj exotic.
expandir vt to expand.
expatriarse vr to emigrate; to go into exile.
expectativa f expectation; prospect.
expedición f expedition.

expediente *m* expedient; means; (*jur*) proceedings *pl*; dossier, file.

expedir *vt* to send, forward, dispatch.

expensas *fpl*:—**a ~ de** at the expense of.

experimentar *vt* to experience:—*vi* **~ con** to experiment with.

experto/ta *adj* expert; experienced.

expiar *vt* to atone for; to purify.

expirar *vi* to expire.

explayarse *vr* to speak at length.

explicar *vt* to explain, expound:— **~se** *vr* to explain oneself.

explorar *vt* to explore.

explotar *vt* to exploit; to run:—*vi* to explode.

exponer *vt* to expose; to explain.

exportar *vt* to export.

exposición *f* exposure; exhibition; explanation; account.

expresar *vt* to express.

expreso/sa *adj* express, clear, specific; fast (train).

exprimir *vt* to squeeze out.

expropriar *vt* to expropriate.

expulsar *vt* to expel, drive out.

éxtasis *m* ecstasy, enthusiasm.

extender *vt* to extend, stretch out:— **~se** *vr* to extend; to spread.

extenso/sa *adj* extensive.

extenuar *vt* to exhaust, debilitate.

exterior *adj* exterior, external:—*m* exterior, outward appearance.

exterminar *vt* to exterminate.

externo/na *adj* external, outer:—*m/f* day pupil.

extinguir *vt* to wipe out; to extinguish.

extintor *m* (fire) extinguisher.

extra *adj invar* extra; good quality:— *m/f* extra:—*m* bonus.

extraer *vt* to extract.

extrañar *vt* to find strange; to miss:— **~se** *vr* to be surprised; to grow apart.

extranjero/ra *m/f* stranger; foreigner:— *adj* foreign, alien.

extraño/ña *adj* foreign; rare; singular, strange, odd.

extraviar *vt* to mislead:—**~se** *vr* to lose one's way.

extremidad *f* extremity; brim; tip:— **~es** *fpl* extremities *pl*.

extremo/ma *adj* extreme, last:—*m* extreme, highest degree:—**en ~/por ~** extremely.

extrovertido/da *adj*, *m/f* extrovert.

exuberancia *f* exuberance; luxuriance.

F

fábrica *f* factory.

fabricar *vt* to build, construct; to manufacture; (*fig*) to fabricate.

fábula *f* fable; fiction; rumor, common talk.

fabuloso/sa *adj* fabulous, fictitious.

facción *f* (political) faction; feature.

fachada *f* facade, face, front.

fácil *adj* facile, easy.

facilitar *vt* to facilitate.

fácilmente *adv* easily.

factor *m* (*mat*) factor; (*com*) factor, agent.

factura *f* invoice.

facultativo/va *adj* optional:—*m/f* doctor, practitioner.

faena f task, job; hard work.

faisán m pheasant.

fajo m bundle; wad.

falaz adj deceitful, fraudulent; fallacious.

falda f skirt; lap; flap; train; slope, hillside.

fallar vt (jur) to pronounce sentence on, judge:—vi to fail.

fallecer vi to die.

falso/sa adj false, untrue; deceitful; fake.

falta f fault, defect; want; flaw, mistake;(dep) foul.

faltar vi to be wanting; to fail; not to fulfil one's promise; to need; to be missing.

fama f fame; reputation, name.

familia f family.

familiar adj familiar; homely, domestic:—m/f relative, relation.

famoso/sa adj famous.

fanfarrón m bully, braggart.

fango m mire, mud.

fantasía f fancy; fantasy; caprice; presumption.

fantasma f phantom, ghost.

fardo m bale, parcel.

farmacia f drugstore.

faro m (mar) lighthouse; (auto) headlamp; floodlight.

farola f street light.

fascículo m part, installment.

fascinar vt to fascinate; to enchant.

fase f phase.

fastidiar vt to annoy; to offend; to spoil.

fatal adj fatal; mortal; awful.

fatiga f weariness, fatigue.

fatuo/tua adj fatuous, stupid, foolish; conceited.

fauces fpl jaws pl, gullet.

favor m favor; protection; good turn.

favorecer vt to favor, protect.

fe f faith, belief.

febrero m February.

fecha f date (of a letter etc).

fecundar vt to fertilize.

felicitar vt to congratulate.

feliz adj happy, fortunate.

felpa f plush; toweling.

felpudo m doormat.

femenino/na adj feminine; female.

feo/ea adj ugly; bad, nasty.

feria f fair, rest day; village market.

fermentar vi to ferment.

feroz adj ferocious, savage; cruel.

ferretería f hardware store.

ferrocarril m railway.

fértil adj fertile, fruitful.

festejo m courtship; feast.

festivo/va adj festive, merry; witty:—**dia ~** holiday.

feto m fetus.

fiable adj trustworthy; reliable.

fiambre m cold meat.

fianza f (jur) surety.

fiar vt to entrust, confide; to bail; to sell on credit:—**~se** vr to trust.

fibra f fibre.

ficha f token, counter (at games); (index) card.

fidelidad f fidelity; loyalty.

fideos mpl noodles pl.

fiebre f fever.

fiel adj faithful, loyal:—mpl **los ~es** the faithful pl.

fieltro m felt.

fiera f wild beast.

fiesta f party; festivity:—**~s** fpl vacations pl.

figura f figure, shape.

figurar vt to figure:—**~se** vr to fancy, imagine.

fijar vt to fix, fasten:—**~se** vr to become fixed:—**~se en** to notice.

fijo/ja adj fixed, firm; settled, permanent.

fila f row, line; (mil) rank:—**en ~** in a line, in a row.

filete m fillet; fillet steak.

filmar vt to film.

filo m edge, blade.

filosofía f philosophy.

filtro m filter.

fin m end; termination, conclusion; aim, purpose:—**al ~** at last:—**en ~** (fig) well then:—**por ~** finally, lastly.

finalmente adv finally, at last.

financiar vt to finance.

finca f land, property, real estate; country house; farm.

fingir vt to feign, fake:—**~se** vr to pretend to be:—vi to pretend.

fino/na adj fine, pure; slender; polite; acute; dry (of sherry).

firma f signature; (com) company.

firmamento m firmament, sky, heaven.

firme adj firm, stable, strong, secure; constant; resolute:—m road surface.

fiscal adj fiscal:—m/f district attorney.

fisco m treasury, exchequer.

fisgar vt to pry into.

física f physics.

flaco/ca adj lean, skinny; feeble.

flan m crème caramel.

flauta f (mus) flute.

flecha f arrow.

flequillo m fringe (of hair).

flete m (mar) freight; charter.

flexible adj flexible; compliant; docile.

flojo/ja adj loose; flexible; slack; lazy.

flor f flower.

florecer vi to blossom.

florero m vase.

flotador m float; rubber ring.

flotar vi to float.

fluctuar vi to fluctuate; to waver.

fluir vi to flow.

foco m focus; center; source; floodlight; (light)bulb.

fogón m stove; hearth.

fogoso/sa adj fiery; ardent, fervent; impetuous, boisterous.

folleto m pamphlet; folder, brochure.

follón m (fam) mess; fuss.

fomentar vt to encourage; to promote.

fondo m bottom; back; background; space:—**~s** mpl stock, funds pl, capital:—**a ~** perfectly, completely.

fontanero/ra m/f plumber.

forjar vt to forge; to frame; to invent.

forma f form, shape; pattern; (med) fitness; (dep) form; means, method:—**de ~ que** in such a manner that.

formación f formation; form, figure; education; training.

formar vt to form, shape.

fornido/da adj well-built.

forro m lining; book jacket.

fortuna f fortune; wealth.

forzar vt to force.

forzoso/sa adj indispensable, necessary.

fosa f grave; pit.

fósforo m phosphorus:—**~s** mpl matches pl.

fotocopia f photocopy.

fotografía f photography; photograph.

fracasar vi to fail.

frágil adj fragile, frail.

fraguar vt to forge; to contrive:—vi to solidify, harden.

fraile m friar, monk.

frambuesa f raspberry.

francés/sa adj French:—m French language:—m/f Frenchman/woman.

frasco m flask.

frase f phrase.

fraternal adj fraternal, brotherly.

fraude m fraud, deceit; cheat.

frazada f blanket.

frecuencia f frequency.

fregar vt to scrub; to wash up.

freír vt to fry.

frenar vt to brake; (fig) to check.

frenesí m frenzy.

freno m bit; brake; (fig) check.

frente f front; face:—~ **a** ~ face to face:—**en** ~ opposite; (mil) front:— m forehead.

fresa f strawberry.

fresco/ca adj fresh; cool; new; ruddy: —m fresh air:—m/f (fam) shameless or impudent person.

fresno m ash tree.

frigorífico m fridge.

frijol m kidney bean.

frío/fría adj cold; indifferent:—m cold; indifference.

friso m frieze; wainscot.

frito/ta adj fried.

frívolo/la adj frivolous.

frondoso/sa adj leafy.

frontera f frontier.

frontón m (dep) pelota court; pelota.

frotar vt to rub.

fructificar vi to bear fruit; to come to fruition.

frugal adj frugal, sparing.

fruncir vt to pleat; to knit; to contract:—~ **las cejas** to knit the eyebrows.

frustrar vt to frustrate.

fruta f fruit:—~ **del tiempo** seasonal fruit.

frutal m fruit tree.

frutilla f strawberry.

fuego m fire.

fuente f fountain; spring; source; large dish.

fuera adv out(side); away:—~ **de** prep outside:—¡~! out of the way!

fuerte m (mil) fortification, fort; forte:—adj vigorous, tough; strong; loud; heavy:—adv strongly; hard.

fuerza f force, strength; (elec) power; violence:—**a** ~ **de** by dint of:—~**s** mpl troops pl.

fugarse vr to escape, flee.

fugaz adj fleeting.

fullero m cardsharper, cheat.

fumar vt, vi to smoke.

función f function; duties pl; show; performance.

funcionar vi to function; to work (of a machine).

funcionario/ria m/f official; civil servant.

funda f case, sheath:—~ **de almohada** pillowcase.

fundar vt to found; to establish; to ground.

fundir vt to fuse; to melt; to smelt; (com) to merge; to bankrupt; (elec) to fuse, blow.

fúnebre adj mournful, sad; funereal.

furgoneta f pick-up (truck).

furioso/sa adj furious.

furtivo/va adj furtive.

fusible m fuse.

fusión f fusion; (com) merger.

fútbol m soccer.

futuro/ra adj, m future.

G

gabardina *f* gabardine; raincoat.

gabinete *m* (*pol*) cabinet, study; office (of solicitors, etc).

gafas *fpl* glasses *pl*, spectacles *pl*.

gafe *m* jinx.

gai (*fam*) *adj invar, m* gay (*sl*), homosexual.

gajo *m* segment (of orange).

galápago *m* tortoise.

galardón *m* reward, prize.

galbana *f* laziness, idleness.

galera *f* (*mar*) galley; wagon; galley (of type).

galería *f* gallery.

galgo *m* grayhound.

gallardo/da *adj* graceful, elegant; brave, daring.

galleta *f* biscuit.

gallina *f* hen:—*m/f* (*fig*) coward:—~ **ciega** blindman's buff.

gallo *m* cock.

gama *f* (*mus*) scale; (*fig*) range, gamut; doe.

gamba *f* shrimp.

gamberro/rra *m/f* hooligan.

gamuza *f* chamois.

gana *f* desire, wish; appetite; will, longing:—**de buena** ~ with pleasure, voluntarily:—**de mala** ~ unwillingly, with reluctance.

ganado *m* livestock, cattle *pl*:—~ **mayor** horses and mules *pl*:—~ **menor** sheep, goats and hogs *pl*.

ganar *vt* to gain; to win; to earn:—*vi* to win.

gancho *m* hook; crook.

gandul *adj, m/f* layabout.

ganga *f* bargain.

ganso/sa *m/f* gander; goose; (*fam*) idiot.

garabatear *vi, vt* to scrawl, scribble.

garaje *m* garage.

garantía *f* warranty, guarantee.

garbanzo *m* chickpea, garbanzo.

garbo *m* gracefulness, elegance; stylishness; generosity.

garganta *f* throat, gullet; instep; neck (of a bottle); narrow pass between mountains or rivers.

gárgara *f* gargling, gargle.

garra *f* claw; talon; paw.

garrafa *f* carafe; (gas) cylinder.

garrafal *adj* great, vast, huge.

garrotillo *m* (*med*) croup.

garrucha *f* pulley.

garza *f* heron.

gasa *f* gauze.

gaseoso/sa *adj* fizzy:—*f* lemonade.

gasoil *m* diesel (oil).

gasolina *f* gas.

gasolinera *f* gas station.

gastar *vt* to spend; to expend; to waste; to wear away; to use up:—~**se** *vr* to wear out; to waste.

gata *f* she-cat:—**a** ~**s** on all fours.

gato *m* cat; jack.

gavilán *m* sparrow hawk.

gavilla *f* sheaf of corn.

gaviota *f* seagull.

gazpacho *m* Spanish cold tomato soup.

gelatina *f* jelly; gelatine.

gemelo/la *m/f* twin.

gemir *vi* to groan, moan.

generación *f* generation; progeny; race.

general *m* general:—*adj* general:—**en** ~ generally, in general.

género *m* genus; kind, type; gender; cloth, material:—~**s** *mpl* goods, commodities *pl*.

generoso/sa *adj* noble, generous.

genio *m* nature, character; genius.

genital *adj* genital:—*mpl* ~**es** genitals *pl.*

gente *f* people; nation; family.

gentileza *f* grace; charm; politeness.

genuino/na *adj* genuine; pure.

geografía *f* geography.

geología *f* geology.

geometría *f* geometry.

geranio *m* (*bot*) geranium.

gerente *m/f* manager; director.

germinar *vi* to germinate, bud.

gestión *f* management; negotiation.

gesto *m* face; grimace; gesture.

gigante *m* giant:—*adj* gigantic.

gilipollas *adj invar* (*fam*) stupid:—*m/f invar* wimp (*sl*).

gimnasia *f* gymnastics.

ginebra *f* gin.

ginecólogo/ga *m/f* gynecologist.

gira *f* trip, tour.

girar *vt* to turn around; to swivel:—*vi* to go round, revolve.

girasol *m* sunflower.

gitano/na *m/f* Gipsy.

glacial *adj* icy.

glándula *f* gland.

globo *m* globe; sphere; orb; balloon:—~ **aerostatico** air balloon.

glorieta *f* bower, arbor; traffic circle.

glosar *vt* to gloss; to comment on.

glotón/ona *m/f* glutton.

gobierno *m* government.

goce *m* enjoyment.

gol *m* goal.

golondrina *f* swallow.

golosina *f* dainty, titbit; sweet.

golpe *m* blow, stroke, hit; knock; clash; coup:—**de** ~ suddenly.

goma *f* gum; rubber; elastic.

gordo/da *adj* fat, plump, big-bellied; first, main; (*fam*) enormous.

gorjear *vi* to twitter, chirp.

gorrión *m* sparrow.

gorro *m* cap; bonnet.

gorrón/ona *m/f* scrounger.

gota *f* drop; (*med*) gout.

gotera *f* leak.

gozar *vt* to enjoy, have, possess:—~**se** *vr* to enjoy oneself, rejoice.

gozne *m* hinge.

gozo *m* joy, pleasure.

grabado *m* engraving.

grabar *vt* to engrave; to record.

gracia *f* grace, gracefulness; wit:—**i(muchas)** ~**s!** thanks (very much):—**tener** ~ to be funny.

gracioso/sa *adj* graceful; beautiful; funny; pleasing:—*m* comic character.

grada *f* step of a staircase; tier, row:—~**s** *fpl* seats *pl* of stadium or theater.

grado *m* step; degree:—**de buen** ~ willingly.

gráfico/ca *adj* graphic:—*m* diagram:—*f* graph.

grajo *m* rook.

gramo *m* gram(me).

gran *adj* = **grande**.

granada *f* pomegranate.

granate *m* garnet (precious stone).

grande *adj* great; big; tall; grand:—*m/f* adult.

grandioso/sa *adj* grand, magnificent.

granel *adv:*—**a** ~ in bulk.

granizado *m* iced drink.

granizo *m* hail.

granja *f* farm.

grano *m* grain.

granuja *m/f* rogue; urchin.

grapa f staple; clamp.
grasa f suet, fat; grease.
gratis adj free.
grato/ta adj pleasant, agreeable.
gravamen m charge, obligation; nuisance; tax.
grave adj weighty, heavy; grave, important; serious.
gravilla f gravel.
gravoso/sa adj onerous, burdensome; costly.
graznar vi to croak; to cackle; to quack.
gremio m union, guild; society; company, corporation.
greña f tangle; shock of hair.
gresca f clatter; outcry; confusion; wrangle, quarrel.
grieta f crevice, crack, chink.
grifo m faucet, tap; gas station.
grillo m cricket; bud, shoot.
gripe f flu, influenza.
gris adj gray.
gritar vi to cry out, shout, yell.
grosella f redcurrant:—~ **negra** blackcurrant.
grosero/ra adj coarse; rude, badmannered.
grúa f crane (machine); derrick.
grueso/sa adj thick; bulky; large; coarse:—m bulk.
grulla f crane (bird).
gruñir vi to grunt; to grumble; to creak (of hinges, etc).
grupo m group.
gruta f grotto.
guadaña f scythe.

guante m glove.
guapo/pa adj good-looking; handsome; smart.
guardabosque m gamekeeper; ranger.
guardacostas m invar coastguard vessel.
guardaespaldas m/f invar bodyguard.
guardar vt to keep, preserve; to save (money); to guard:—~se vr to be on one's guard:—~se de to avoid, abstain from.
guardarropa f wardrobe; cloakroom.
guardia f guard; (mar) watch; care, custody:—m/f guard; police officer:—m (mil) guardsman.
guarecer vt to protect; to shelter:—~se vr to take refuge.
guarnecer vt to provide, equip; to reinforce; to garnish, set (in gold, etc); to adorn.
guasa f joke.
gubernativo/va adj governmental.
guía m/f guide:—f guidebook.
guiar vt to guide; (auto) to steer.
guijarro m pebble.
guiñar vt to wink.
guinda f cherry.
guindilla f chilli pepper.
guión m hyphen; script (of movie).
guisante m (bot) pea.
guisar vt to cook.
guitarra f guitar.
gula f gluttony.
gusano m maggot, worm.
gustar vt to taste; to sample:—vi to please, be pleasing:—**me gusta...**I like...

H

haba f bean.

haber vt to get, lay hands on; to occur:
—v imp **hay** there is, there are:—v
aux to have:——**se** vr **habérselas
con uno** to have it out with somebody:—m income, salary; assets pl;
(com) credit.

hábil adj able, clever, skillful, dexterous, apt.

habitación f habitation, abode, rooming house, dwelling, residence; room.

habitar vt to inhabit, live in.

hábito m dress; habit, custom.

habitual adj habitual, customary.

hablar vt, vi to speak; to talk.

hacendoso/sa adj industrious.

hacer vt to make; to do; to put into
practice; to perform; to effect; to
prepare; to imagine; to force; (mat)
to amount to, make:—vi to act,
behave:——**se** vr to become.

hacha f torch; ax, hatchet.

hacia adv toward(s); about:—— **arriba/
abajo** up(wards)/ down(wards).

hada f fairy.

halagar vt to cajole, flatter.

halcón m falcon.

hallar vt to find; to meet with; to
discover:——**se** vr to find oneself;
to be.

hambre f hunger; famine; longing.

harina f flour.

harto/ta adj full; fed up:—adv enough.

hasta prep up to; down to; until, as
far as:—adv even.

haya f beech tree.

hazaña f exploit, achievement.

hebilla f buckle.

hebra f thread, vein of minerals or
metals; grain of wood.

hebreo/ea m/f, adj Hebrew; Israeli:—
m Hebrew language.

hechizar vt to bewitch, enchant; to
charm.

hecho/cha adj made; done; mature;
ready-to-wear; cooked:—m action;
act; fact; matter; event.

hectárea f hectare.

helado/da adj frozen; glacial, icy;
astonished; astounded:—m ice
cream.

helar vt to freeze; to congeal; to astonish, amaze:——**se** vr to be frozen; to
turn into ice; to congeal: —vi to
freeze; to congeal.

helecho m fern.

hélice f helix; propeller.

hembra f female.

heno m hay.

heredar vt to inherit.

hereje m/f heretic.

herir vt to wound, hurt; to beat, strike;
to affect, touch, move; to offend.

hermana f sister.

hermano m brother:——**/na** adj
matched; resembling.

hermético/ca adj hermetic, airtight.

hermoso/sa adj beautiful, handsome,
lovely; large, robust.

héroe m hero.

herradura f horseshoe.

herrero m smith.

hervir vt to boil; to cook:—vi to boil;
to bubble; to seethe.

hiedra f ivy.

hiel f gall, bile.

hielo m frost; ice.

hierba f grass; herb.

hierro m iron.

hígado m liver; (fig) courage, pluck.

higiene f hygiene.

higo m fig.

hijo/ja m/f son/daughter; child; offspring.

hilera f row, line, file.

hilo m thread; wire.

hincar vt to thrust in, drive in.

hinchar vt to swell; to inflate; (fig) to exaggerate:—**se** vr to swell; to become vain.

hinojo m (bot) fennel.

hipo m hiccups pl.

hipócrita adj hypocritical:—m/f hypocrite.

hipódromo m racetrack.

hipoteca f mortgage.

historia f history; tale, story.

historieta f short story; short novel; comic strip.

hocico m snout:—**meter el ~ en todo** to meddle in everything.

hogar m hearth, fireplace; (fig) house, home; family life.

hogaza f large loaf of bread.

hoguera f bonfire; blaze.

hoja f leaf; petal; sheet of paper; blade.

hojalata f tin (plate).

hojaldre f puff pastry.

hojear vt to turn the pages of.

hola excl hello!

holgado/da adj loose, wide, baggy; at leisure; idle, unoccupied; well-off.

hollín m soot.

hombre m man; human being.

hombro m shoulder.

homenaje m homage.

homicidio m murder.

hondo/da adj deep, profound.

honesto/ta adj honest; modest.

hongo m mushroom; fungus.

honor m honor.

honorario/ria adj honorary:—~s mpl fees pl.

honra f honor, reverence; selfesteem; reputation; integrity:—~s funebres pl funeral honors pl.

hora f hour; time.

horario/ria adj hourly, hour compd:—m schedule.

horchata f tiger-nut milk.

horma f mold, form.

hormiga f ant.

hormigón m concrete.

horno m oven; furnace.

horquilla f pitchfork; hairpin.

hórreo m granary.

horrible adj horrid, horrible.

horror m horror, fright; atrocity.

hortaliza f vegetable.

hospedar vt to put up, lodge; to entertain.

hospicio m orphanage; hospice.

hospital m hospital.

hostal m small hotel.

hostelería f hotel business or trade.

hostia f host; wafer; (fam) whack (sl), punch.

hostil adj hostile; adverse.

hotel m hotel.

hoy adv today; now, nowadays:—**de~ en adelante** from now on, henceforward.

hoyo m hole, pit; excavation.

hoz f sickle; gorge.

hucha f money-box.

hueco/ca adj hollow, concave; empty; vain, ostentatious:—m interval; gap, hole; vacancy.

huelga f strike.

huella f track, footstep.

huérfano/na adj, m/f orphan.

huerta f market garden; irrigated region.

hueso *m* bone; stone, core.

huésped/da *m/f* guest, lodger, roomer; inn-keeper.

huevo *m* egg.

huir *vi* to flee, escape.

humano/na *adj* human; humane, kind.

húmedo/da *adj* humid; wet; damp.

humilde *adj* humble.

humillar *vt* to humble; to subdue:— ~se *vr* to humble oneself.

humo *m* smoke; fumes *pl.*

humor *m* mood, temper; humor.

hundir *vt* to submerge; to sink; to ruin:—~se *vr* to sink, go to the bottom; to collapse; to be ruined.

huraño/ña *adj* shy; unsociable.

hurtadillas *adv:*—a ~ by stealth.

hurtar *vt* to steal, rob.

husmear *vt* to scent; to pry into.

I

ictericia *f* jaundice.

ida *f* departure, going:—(viaje de) ~ outward journey:—~ y vuelta round trip:—~s y venidas comings and goings *pl.*

idea *f* idea; scheme.

ídem *pn* ditto.

idéntico/ca *adj* identical.

idioma *m* language.

idiota *m/f* idiot.

idóneo/nea *adj* suitable, fit.

iglesia *f* church.

ignorar *vt* to be ignorant of, not to know.

igual *adj* equal; similar; the same:— al ~ equally.

ilegal *adj* illegal, unlawful.

ileso/sa *adj* unhurt.

ilimitado/da *adj* unlimited.

iluminar *vt* to illumine, illuminate, enlighten.

ilusión *f* illusion; hope:—hacerse ~ones to build up one's hopes.

ilustre *adj* illustrious, famous.

imagen *f* image.

imaginar *vt* to imagine; to think up: —*vi* ~se *vr* to imagine.

imán *m* magnet.

imitar *vt* to imitate, copy; to counterfeit.

impaciente *adj* impatient.

impar *adj* odd.

imparcial *adj* impartial.

impedir *vt* to impede, hinder; to prevent.

impeler *vt* to drive, propel; to impel; to incite, stimulate.

impenetrable *adj* impenetrable, impervious; incomprehensible.

impenitente *adj* impenitent.

imperdible *m* safety pin.

imperdonable *adj* unforgivable.

imperfecto/ta *adj* imperfect.

impermeable *adj* waterproof:—*m* raincoat.

imperturbable *adj* imperturbable; unruffled.

implacable *adj* implacable, inexorable.

implicar *vt* to implicate, involve.

imponer *vt* to impose; to command:— ~se *vr* to assert oneself; to prevail.

impopular *adj* unpopular.

importante *adj* important, considerable.

importar *vi* to be important, matter:— *vt* to import; to be worth.

importe *m* amount, cost.

importunar vt to bother, pester.

imposible adj impossible; extremely difficult; slovenly.

impostor/ra m/f impostor, fraud.

impotencia f impotence.

impracticable adj impracticable, unworkable.

impreciso/sa adj imprecise, vague.

imprenta f printing; press; printing office.

imprescindible adj essential.

impresión f impression; stamp; print; edition.

impresionar vt to move; to impress:—~se vr to be impressed; to be moved.

imprevisto/ta adj unforeseen, unexpected.

imprimir vt to print; to imprint; to stamp.

improbable adj improbable, unlikely.

improvisar vt to extemporize; to improvise.

improviso/sa adj:—de ~ unexpectedly.

imprudente adj imprudent; indiscreet; unwise.

impúdico/ca adj shameless; lecherous.

impuesto/ta adj imposed:—m tax, duty.

impulso m impulse; thrust; (fig) impulse.

impune adj unpunished.

impuro/ra adj impure; foul.

inaccesible adj inaccessible.

inadvertido/da adj unnoticed.

inagotable adj inexhaustible.

inaguantable adj unbearable, intolerable.

inalterable adj unalterable.

inapreciable adj imperceptible; invaluable.

inaudito/ta adj unheard-of.

inaugurar vt to inaugurate.

incalculable adj incalculable.

incansable adj untiring, tireless.

incapaz adj incapable, unable.

incauto/ta adj incautious, unwary.

incendio m fire.

incentivo m incentive.

incertidumbre f doubt, uncertainty.

incierto/ta adj uncertain, doubtful.

incineración f incineration; cremation.

incitar vt to incite, excite.

inclemencia f inclemency, severity; inclemency (of the weather).

inclinar vt to incline; to nod, bow (the head):—~se vr to bow; to stoop.

incluir vt to include, comprise; to incorporate; to enclose.

incluso/sa adj included:—adv inclusively; even.

incógnito/ta adj unknown:—de ~ incognito.

incombustible adj incombustible, fireproof.

incómodo/da adj uncomfortable; annoying; inconvenient.

incomparable adj incomparable, matchless.

incompasivo adj unsympathetic.

incompleto/ta adj incomplete.

incomunicado/da adj isolated, cut off; in solitary confinement.

inconcebible adj inconceivable.

incondicional adj unconditional; whole-hearted; staunch.

inconfundible adj unmistakable.

inconsciente adj unconscious; thoughtless.

inconstante adj inconstant, variable, fickle.

incorporar vt to incorporate:—~se vr to sit up; to join (an organization), become incorporated.

incorrecto/ta *adj* incorrect.
incrédulo/la *adj* incredulous.
increíble *adj* incredible.
incremento *m* increment, increase; growth; rise.
inculcar *vt* to inculcate.
inculto/ta *adj* uncultivated; uneducated; uncouth.
incumbencia *f* obligation; duty.
incurable *adj* incurable; irremediable.
indagar *vt* to inquire into.
indebido/da *adj* undue; illegal, unlawful.
indeciso/sa *adj* hesitant; undecided.
indefenso/sa *adj* defenseless.
indemnizar *vt* to indemnify, compensate.
independiente *adj* independent.
indeterminado/da *adj* indeterminate; indefinite.
indicador *m* indicator; gage.
indicar *vt* to indicate.
índice *m* ratio, rate; hand (of a watch or clock); index, table of contents; catalog; forefinger, index finger.
indicio *m* indication, mark; sign, token; clue.
indiferencia *f* indifference, apathy.
indígena *adj* indigenous, native:—*m/f* native.
indignar *vt* to irritate; to provoke, tease:—**~se** *vr* **~ por** to get indignant about.
indigno/na *adj* unworthy, contemptible, low.
indirecta *f* innuendo, hint.
indiscreción *f* indiscretion, tactlessness; gaffe.
individual *adj* individual; single (of a room):—*m* (*dep*) singles.
individuo *m* individual.

índole *f* disposition, nature, character; soft, kind.
indolente *adj* indolent, lazy.
indómito/ta *adj* untamed, ungoverned.
inducir *vt* to induce, persuade.
indudable *adj* undoubted; unquestionable.
indultar *vt* to pardon; to exempt.
industria *f* industry; skill.
inédito/ta *adj* unpublished; (*fig*) new.
ineficaz *adj* ineffective; inefficient.
inepto/ta *adj* inept, unfit, useless.
inercia *f* inertia, inactivity.
inerte *adj* inert; dull; sluggish, motionless.
inesperado/da *adj* unexpected, unforeseen.
inevitable *adj* unavoidable.
inexacto/ta *adj* inaccurate, untrue.
inexperto/ta *adj* inexperienced.
infame *adj* infamous.
infancia *f* infancy, childhood.
infantil *adj* infantile; childlike; children's.
infarto *m* heart attack.
infatigable *adj* tireless, untiring.
infectar *vt* to infect.
infeliz *adj* unhappy, unfortunate.
inferior *adj* inferior.
infernal *adj* infernal, hellish.
infiel *adj* unfaithful; disloyal; inaccurate.
infierno *m* hell.
infiltrarse *vr* to infiltrate.
ínfimo/ma *adj* lowest; of very poor quality.
infinidad *f* infinity; immensity.
infinito/ta *adj* infinite; immense.
inflamable *adj* inflammable.
inflar *vt* to inflate, blow up; (*fig*) to exaggerate.
inflexible *adj* inflexible.

influir vt to influence.

información f information; news; (mil) intelligence; investigation, judicial inquiry.

informal adj irregular, incorrect; untrustworthy; informal.

informar vt to inform; to reveal, make known:—**se** vr to find out:—vi to report; (jur) to plead; to inform.

informática f computer science, information technology.

informe m report, statement; piece of information, account:—adj shapeless, formless.

infortunio m misfortune, ill luck.

infracción f infraction; breach, infringement.

infructuoso/sa adj fruitless, unproductive, unprofitable.

infundado/da adj groundless.

ingeniero/ra m/f engineer.

ingenio m talent; wit; ingenuity; engine:—**~ de azúcar** sugar mill.

ingenuo/nua adj naive.

ingerir vt to ingest; to swallow; to consume.

ingle f groin.

inglés/esa adj English:—m English language:—m/f Englishman/woman.

ingrato/ta adj ungrateful, thankless; disagreeable.

ingresar vt to deposit:—vi to come in.

inhabilitar vt to disqualify, disable.

inhabitable adj uninhabitable.

inhibir vt to inhibit; to restrain.

iniciar vt to initiate; to begin.

ininteligible adj unintelligible.

injertar vt to graft.

injuriar vt to insult, wrong.

injusto/ta adj unjust.

inmediaciones fpl neighborhood.

inmediatamente adv immediately, at once.

inmobiliario/ria adj real-estate compd: —f estate agency.

inmortal adj immortal.

inmóvil adj immovable, still.

inmueble m property:—adj **bienes ~s** real estate.

inmundo/da adj filthy, dirty; nasty.

inmune adj (med) immune; free, exempt.

innato/ta adj inborn, innate.

innecesario/ria adj unnecessary.

innegable adj undeniable.

innumerable adj innumerable, countless.

inocente adj innocent.

inodoro m washroom:—**~/ra** adj odorless, without smell.

inofensivo/va adj harmless.

inolvidable adj unforgettable.

inoxidable adj:—**acero ~** stainless steel.

inquietar vt to worry, disturb:—**~se** vr to worry, get worried.

inquilino/na m/f tenant; roomer, lodger.

inquirir vt to inquire into, investigate.

inscribir vt to inscribe; to list, register.

insecto m insect.

insensato/ta adj senseless, stupid; mad.

insensible adj insensitive; imperceptible; numb.

inseparable adj inseparable.

insertar vt to insert.

inservible adj useless.

insignia f badge:—**~s** fpl insignia pl.

insinuar vt to insinuate:—**~se** vr **~ en** to worm one's way into.

insípido/da adj insipid.

insistir vi to insist.

insolación f (*med*) sunstroke.

insolencia f insolence, rudeness, effrontery.

insólito/ta *adj* unusual.

insolvente *adj* insolvent.

insomnio m insomnia.

insondable *adj* unfathomable; inscrutable.

insoportable *adj* unbearable.

inspeccionar *vt* to inspect; to supervize.

inspector/ra m/f inspector; superintendent.

inspirar *vt* to inspire; (*med*) to inhale.

instalar *vt* to install.

instantáneo/nea *adj* instantaneous:— f snap(shot):—**café ~** instant coffee.

instante m instant:—**al ~** immediately, instantly.

instigar *vt* to instigate.

instinto m instinct.

instructivo/va *adj* instructive; educational.

instrumento m instrument; tool, implement.

insuficiente *adj* insufficient, inadequate.

insulso/sa *adj* insipid; dull.

insultar *vt* to insult.

insuperable *adj* insuperable, insurmountable.

intacto/ta *adj* untouched; entire; intact.

integral *adj* integral, whole:—**pan ~** wholewheat bread.

intemperie f:—**a la ~** out in the open.

intencionado/da *adj* meaningful; deliberate.

intenso/sa *adj* intense, strong; deep.

intentar *vt* to try, attempt.

intercalar *vt* to insert.

intercambio m exchange, swap.

interés m interest; share, part; concern, advantage; profit.

interesar *vt* to be of interest to, interest:—**~se** *vr* **~ en** o **por** to take an interest in:—*vi* to be of interest.

interferir *vt* to interfere with; to jam (a telephone):—*vi* to interfere.

interfono m intercom.

interino/na *adj* provisional, temporary: —m/f temporary holder of a post; stand-in.

interior *adj* interior, internal:—m interior, inside.

intermedio/dia *adj* intermediate:—m interval.

interminable *adj* interminable, endless.

intermitente *adj* intermittent; m (*auto*) indicator.

internado m boarding school.

interno/na *adj* interior, internal:—m/f boarder.

interpretar *vt* to interpret, explain; (*teat*) to perform; to translate.

interrogación f interrogation; question mark.

interrogatorio m questioning; (*jur*) examination; questionnaire.

interrumpir *vt* to interrupt.

interruptor m switch.

intervenir *vt* to control, supervise; (*com*) to audit; (*med*) to operate on:—*vi* to participate; to intervene.

intestino/na *adj* internal, interior:—m intestine.

íntimo/ma *adj* internal, innermost; intimate, private.

intranquilo/la *adj* worried.

intransitable *adj* impassable.

intrépido/da *adj* intrepid, daring.

intrigar *vt, vi* to intrigue.

introducir *vt* to introduce; to insert.

introvertido/da adj, m/f introvert.
intruso/sa adj intrusive:—m/f intruder.
inundar vt to inundate, overflow; to flood.
inusitado/da adj unusual.
inútil adj useless.
inválido/da adj invalid, null and void: —m/f invalid.
invencible adj invincible.
invernadero m greenhouse.
inverosímil adj unlikely, improbable.
inverso/sa adj inverse; inverted; contrary.
invertir vt (com) to invest; to invert.
investigar vt to investigate; to do research into.
invierno m winter.
invitar vt to invite; to entice; to pay for.
invocar vt to invoke.
ir vi to go; to walk; to travel:—~se vr to go away, depart.

ira f anger, wrath.
iris m iris (eye):—**arco** ~ rainbow.
ironía f irony.
irracional adj irrational.
irreal adj unreal.
irreflexión f rashness, thoughtlessness.
irregular adj irregular; abnormal.
irremediable adj irremediable; incurable.
irresistible adj irresistible.
irreverente adj irreverent; disrespectful.
irrisorio/ria adj derisory, ridiculous.
irritar vt to irritate, exasperate; to stir up; to inflame.
isla f island, isle.
istmo m isthmus.
italiano/na adj Italian:—m Italian language:—m/f Italian.
itinerario m itinerary.
izquierdo/da adj left; left-handed:—f left; left(-wing).

J

jabalí m wild boar.
jabón m soap.
jaca f pony.
jacinto m hyacinth.
jadear vi to pant.
jaleo m racket, uproar.
jamás adv never:—**para siempre ~** for ever.
jamón m ham:—~ **de York** cooked ham:—~ **serrano** cured ham.
jaque m check (at game of chess):— ~ **mate** checkmate.
jaqueca f migraine.
jarabe m syrup.

jardín m garden.
jarra f jug, jar, pitcher:—**en ~s, de ~s** with hands to the sides.
jaula f cage; cell for mad people.
jazmín m jasmin.
jefe m chief, head, leader:—(ferro) ~ **de tren** guard, conductor.
jerarquía f hierarchy.
jerigonza f jargon, gibberish.
jeringa f syringe.
jeroglífico/ca adj hieroglyphic:—m hieroglyph, hieroglyphic.
jersey m sweater, pullover.
jilguero m goldfinch.

jinete/ta *m/f* horseman/woman, rider.
jipijapa *m* straw hat.
jirón *m* rag, shred.
jornada *f* journey; day's journey; working day.
jornal *m* day's wage.
jornalero *m* (day) laborer.
joroba *f* hump:—*m/f* hunchback.
jota *f* jot, iota; Spanish dance.
joven *adj* young:—*m/f* youth; young woman.
jovial *adj* jovial, cheerful.
joya *f* jewel:—~s *fpl* jewelry.
juanete *m* (*med*) bunion.
jubilar *vt* to pension off; to superannuate; to discard:—~se *vr* to retire.
júbilo *m* joy, rejoicing.
judía *f* bean:—~ **verde** French bean.
judicial *adj* judicial.
judío/día *adj* Jewish:—*m/f* Jewish man/woman.
juego *m* play; amusement; sport; game; gambling.
jueves *m invar* Thursday.
juez *m/f* judge.

jugar *vt, vi* to play, sport, gamble.
jugo *m* sap, juice.
juguete *m* toy, plaything.
juicio *m* judgement, reason; sanity; opinion.
julio *m* July.
junco *m* (*bot*) rush; junk (Chinese ship).
junio *m* June.
junta *f* meeting; assembly; congress; council.
juntar *vt* to join; to unite:—~se *vr* to meet, assemble; to draw closer.
junto/ta *adj* joined; united; near; adjacent:—~s together:—*adv* **todo** ~ all at once.
jurar *vt, vi* to swear.
jurídico/ca *adj* lawful, legal; juridical.
justicia *f* justice; equity.
justificante *m* voucher; receipt.
justo/ta *adj* just; fair, right; exact, correct; tight:—*adv* exactly, precisely; just in time.
juventud *f* youthfulness, youth; young people *pl*.
juzgado *m* tribunal; court.

K

kilogramo *m* kilogram(me).
kilómetro *m* kilometer.

kiosco *m* kiosk.

L

la *art f* the:—*pn* her; you; it.
labio *m* lip; edge.
labor *f* labor, task; needlework; farmwork; ploughing.

laborioso/sa *adj* laborious; hardworking.
labrar *vt* to work; to carve; to farm; (*fig*) to bring about.

laca f lacquer; hairspray.

lacio/cia adj faded, withered; languid; lank (hair).

lacrar vt to seal (with sealing wax).

lactancia f lactation; breast-feeding.

lácteo/tea adj:—**productos ~s** dairy products.

ladera f slope.

ladino/na adj cunning, crafty.

lado m side; faction, party; favor, protection; (mil) flank:—**al ~ de** beside:—**poner a un ~** to put aside:—**por todos ~s** on all sides.

ladrar vt to bark.

ladrillo m brick.

ladrón/ona m/f thief, robber.

lagar m wine press.

lagartija f (small) lizard.

lagarto m lizard.

lago m lake.

lágrima f tear.

laguna f lake; lagoon; gap.

laico/ca adj lay.

lamentar vt to be sorry about; to lament, regret:—vi ~**se** vr to lament, complain; to mourn.

lamer vt to lick, lap.

lámina f plate, sheet of metal; engraving.

lámpara f lamp.

lana f wool.

lancha f barge, lighter; launch.

langosta f locust; lobster.

lanzar vt to throw; (dep) to bowl, pitch; to launch, fling; (jur) to evict.

lápida f flat stone, tablet.

lápiz m pencil; mechanical pencil.

largamente adv for a long time.

largo/ga adj long; lengthy, generous; copious:—**a la ~a** in the end, eventually.

las art fpl the:—pn them; you.

lascivo/va adj lascivious; lewd.

láser m laser.

lástima f compassion, pity; shame.

lastimar vt to hurt; to wound; to feel pity for:—~**se** vr to hurt oneself.

lastre m ballast.

lata f tin; tin can; (fam) nuisance.

latido m (heart)beat.

latifundio m large estate.

latir vi to beat, palpitate.

latitud f latitude.

latón m brass.

latoso/sa adj annoying; boring.

laúd f lute (musical instrument).

laudable adj laudable, praiseworthy.

laurel m (bot) laurel; reward.

lavabo m washbasin; washroom.

lavadora f washing machine.

lavanda f lavender.

lavar vt to wash; to wipe away:—~**se** vr to wash oneself.

laxante m (med) laxative.

lazarillo m:—**perro ~** guide dog.

lazo m knot; bow; snare, trap; tie; bond.

le pn him; you; (dativo) to him; to her; to it; to you.

leal adj loyal; faithful.

lebrel m greyhound.

lección f reading; lesson; lecture; class.

leche f milk.

lecho m bed; layer.

lechón m sucking pig.

lechuga f lettuce.

lechuza f owl.

leer vt, vi to read.

legado m bequest, legacy; legate.

legal adj legal; trustworthy.

legaña f sleep (in eyes).

legislar vt to legislate.

legítimo/ma adj legitimate, lawful; authentic.

legumbres *fpl* pulses *pl*.

lejano/na *adj* distant, remote; far.

lejía *f* bleach.

lejos *adv* at a great distance, far off.

lelo/la *adj* stupid, ignorant:—*m/f* idiot.

lema *m* motto; slogan.

leña *f* firewood, kindling.

lencería *f* linen, drapery.

lengua *f* tongue; language.

lenguado *m* sole.

lenguaje *m* language.

lente *m/f* lens.

lenteja *f* lentil.

lentilla *f* contact lens.

lento/ta *adj* slow.

león *m* lion.

leopardo *m* leopard.

leotardos *mpl* tights, pantihose.

lesión *f* wound; injury; damage.

letal *adj* mortal, deadly.

letanía *f* litany.

letargo *m* lethargy.

letra *f* letter; handwriting; printing type; draft of a song; bill, draft:—**~s** *fpl* letters *pl*, learning.

letrero *m* sign; label.

leucemia *f* leukemia.

levadura *f* yeast; brewer's yeast.

levantar *vt* to raise, lift up; to build; to elevate; to hearten, cheer up:—**~se** *vr* to get up; to stand up.

levante *m* Levant; east; east wind.

levantisco *adj* turbulent, restless.

leve *adj* light; trivial.

léxico *m* vocabulary.

ley *f* law; standard (for metal).

leyenda *f* legend.

liar *vt* to tie, bind; to confuse.

libélula *f* dragonfly.

liberal *adj* liberal, generous:—*m/f* liberal.

libertad *f* liberty, freedom.

libra *f* pound:—**~ esterlina** pound sterling.

libre *adj* free; exempt; vacant.

librería *f* book store.

libreta *f* notebook:—**~ de ahorros** savings book.

libro *m* book.

licencia *f* license; licentiousness.

licenciado/da *adj* licensed:—*m/f* graduate.

lícito/ta *adj* lawful, fair; permissible.

líder *m/f* leader.

liebre *f* hare.

lienzo *f* linen; canvas; face or front of a building.

liga *f* suspender; birdlime; league; coalition; alloy.

ligar *vt* to tie, bind, fasten:—**~se** *vr* to commit oneself:—*vi* to mix, blend; (*fam*) to pick up.

ligero/ra *adj* light, swift; agile; superficial.

liguero *m* suspender belt.

lijar *vt* to smooth, sandpaper.

lima *f* file.

límite *m* limit, boundary.

limón *m* lemon.

limosna *f* alms *pl*, charity.

limpiar *vt* to clean; to cleanse; to purify; to polish; (*fig*) to clean up.

linaza *f* linseed.

lince *m* lynx.

lindar *vi* to be adjacent.

lindo/da *adj* pretty; lovely.

línea *f* line; cable; outline.

lino *m* flax.

linterna *f* lantern, lamp; torch.

lío *m* bundle, parcel; (*fam*) muddle, mess.

liquidar *vt* to liquidate; to settle (accounts).

líquido/da *adj* liquid.

lirio m (bot) iris.

lirón m dormouse; (fig) sleepyhead.

liso/sa adj plain, even, flat, smooth.

lisonja f adulation, flattery.

lista f list; register; catalog; menu.

listo/ta adj ready; smart, clever.

litera f berth; bunk, bunk bed.

litigio m lawsuit.

litoral adj coastal:—m coast.

litro m liter (measure).

liviano/na adj light; fickle; trivial.

llama f flame; llama (animal).

llamar vt to call; to name; to summon; to ring up, telephone:—vi to knock at the door; to ring up, telephone:—~se vr to be named.

llano/na adj plain; even, level, smooth; clear, evident:—m plain.

llanta f (wheel) rim; tire; inner (tube).

llanura f evenness, flatness; plain, prairie.

llave f key:—~ **maestra** master key.

llegar vi to arrive:—~ **a** to reach:—~se vr to come near, approach.

llenar vt to fill; to cover; to fill out (a form); to satisfy, fulfil:—~se vr to gorge oneself.

llevar vt to take; to wear; to carry; to convey, transport; to drive; to lead; to bear:—~se vr to carry off, take away.

llorar vt, vi to weep, cry.

llover vi to rain.

lluvia f rain.

lo pn it; him; you:—art the.

lobo m wolf.

lóbulo m lobe.

local adj local:—m place, site.

loco/ca adj mad:—m/f mad person.

locutor/ra m/f (rad) announcer; (TV) newsreader.

lodo m mud, mire.

lograr vt to achieve; to gain, obtain.

lombarda f red cabbage.

lombriz f worm.

lomo m loin; back (of an animal); spine (of a book):—**llevar** o **traer a** ~ to carry on the back.

lona f canvas.

loncha f slice; rasher.

longaniza f pork sausage.

longitud f length; longitude.

loro m parrot.

los art mpl the:—pn them; you.

losa f flagstone.

lote m lot; portion.

loza f crockery.

lucero m morning star, bright star.

luchar vi to struggle; to wrestle.

luciérnaga f glowworm.

lucir vt to light (up); to show off:—vi to shine:—~se vr to make a fool of oneself.

luego adv next; afterward(s):—**desde** ~ of course.

lugar m place, spot; village; reason:—**en** ~ **de** instead of, in lieu of.

lúgubre adj lugubrious; sad, gloomy.

lujo m luxury; abundance.

lujuria f lust.

lumbre f fire; light.

luna f moon; glass plate for mirrors; lens.

lunar m mole, spot:—adj lunar.

lunes m invar Monday.

lupa f magnifying glass.

lupanar m brothel.

luto m mourning (dress); grief.

luz f light.

M

maceta f flowerpot.

machacar vt to pound, crush:—vi to insist, go on.

macho adj male; (fig) virile:—m male; (fig) he-man.

macizo/za adj massive; solid:—m mass, chunk.

madera f wood; lumber.

madrastra f stepmother.

madre f mother; womb.

madreselva f honeysuckle.

madriguera f burrow; den.

madrugar vi to get up early; to get ahead.

maduro/ra adj ripe, mature.

maestro m master; teacher:—~/ tra adj masterly, skilled; principal.

magia f magic.

magisterio m teaching; teaching profession; teachers pl.

magnetofón, magnetófono m tape recorder.

magnífico/ca adj magnificent, splendid.

mago/ga m/f magician.

magullar vt to bruise; to damage; to bash (sl).

mahometano/na m/f, adj Muslim.

maíz m maize, Indian corn.

majadero/ra adj dull; silly, stupid:—m idiot.

majo/ja adj nice; attractive; smart.

majuelo m vine newly planted; hawthorn.

mal m evil; hurt; harm, damage; misfortune; illness:—adj (before masculine nouns) bad.

malcriado/da adj rude, ill-behaved; naughty; spoiled.

maldad f wickedness.

maldecir vt to curse.

maldito/ta adj wicked; damned, cursed.

malecón m pier.

maleducado/da adj bad-mannered, rude.

malestar m discomfort; (fig) uneasiness; unrest.

maleta f suitcase; (auto) trunk.

maleza f weeds pl; thicket.

malgastar vt to waste, ruin.

malhablado/da adj foul-mouthed.

malhechor/ra m/f malefactor; criminal.

malhumorado/da adj cross, badtempered.

malla f mesh, network:—~s fpl leotard.

malo/la adj bad; ill; wicked:—m/f villain.

maltratar vt to ill-treat, abuse, mistreat.

malva f (bot) mallow.

malvado/da adj wicked, villainous.

mama f teat; breast.

mamá f (fam) mum, mummy.

mamar vt, vi to suck.

mamífero m mammal.

manada f flock, herd; pack; crowd.

manantial m source, spring; origin.

manchar vt to stain, soil.

manco/ca adj one-armed; onehanded; maimed; faulty.

mancomunidad f union, fellowship; community; (jur) joint responsibility.

mandar vt to command, order; to bequeath; to send.

mandarina f tangerine.

mandíbula f jaw.

mandil m apron.

manera f manner, way; fashion; kind.

manga f sleeve; hose.

mango m handle; mango.

manguera f hose; pipe.

maní m peanut.

manifestación f manifestation; show; demonstration; mass meeting.

manifestar vt to manifest, declare.

maniobrar vt to maneuvre; to handle.

manipular vt to manipulate.

maniquí m dummy:—m/f model.

manivela f crank.

mano f hand; hand (of clock, etc); foot, paw (of animal); coat (of paint); lot, series; hand (at game):—**a ~ by hand**:—**a ~s llenas** liberally, generously.

manojo m handful, bunch.

manopla f wash cloth; mitten; gauntlet.

manosear vt to handle; to mess up.

manso/sa adj tame; gentle, soft.

manta f blanket.

manteca f fat:—**~ de cerdo** lard.

mantel m tablecloth.

mantener vt to maintain, support; to nourish; to keep:—**~se** vr to hold one's ground; to support oneself.

mantequilla f butter.

manzana f apple.

manzanilla f camomile; camomile tea; manzanilla sherry.

maña f handiness, dexterity, cleverness, cunning; habit, custom; trick.

mañana f morning:—adv tomorrow.

mapa m map.

maquillar vt to make up:—**~se** vr to put on make-up.

máquina f machine; (ferro) engine; camera; (fig) machinery; plan, project.

maquinilla f:—**~ de afeitar** razor.

maquinista m (ferro) train driver; operator; (mar) engineer.

mar m/f sea.

maravilla f wonder.

marca f mark; stamp; make, brand.

marcar vt to mark; to dial; to score; to record; to set (hair):—vi to score; to dial.

marchar vi to go; to work:—**~se** vr to go away.

marco m frame; framework; (dep) goalposts pl.

marea f tide.

marear vt (mar) to sail, navigate; to annoy, upset:—**~se** vr to feel sick; to feel faint; to feel dizzy.

marfil m ivory.

margarita f daisy.

margen m margin; border:—f bank (of river).

marido m husband.

marinero/ra adj sea compd; seaworthy:—m sailor.

marioneta f puppet.

mariposa f butterfly.

mariquita f ladybird.

marisco m shellfish pl.

mármol m marble.

marrano m hog, boar.

marrón adj brown.

martes m invar Tuesday.

martillo m hammer.

marzo m March.

mas adv but, yet.

más adv more; most; besides, moreover:—**a ~ tardar** at latest:—**sin ~ ni ~** without more ado.

masa f dough, paste; mortar; mass.

mascar vt to chew.

máscara m/f masked person:—f mask.

mascullar vt to mumble, mutter.

mástil m (mar) mast.

mastín m mastiff.

mata f shrub; sprig, blade; grove, group of trees; mop of hair.

matadero m slaughterhouse.

matar vt to kill; to execute; to murder:—~**se** vr to kill oneself, commit suicide.

matasellos m invar postmark.

mate m checkmate:—adj matt.

material adj material, physical:—m equipment, materials pl.

maternidad f motherhood.

matinal adj morning compd.

matiz m shade of color; shading.

matrícula f register, list; (auto) registration number; license plate.

matrimonio m marriage, matrimony.

matriz f matrix; womb; mold, form.

maullar vi to mew.

mayo m May.

mayor adj main, chief; (mus) major; biggest; eldest; greater, larger; elderly:—m chief, boss; adult:—**al por ~** wholesale:—~**es** mpl forefathers.

mayoría f majority, greater part:—~ **de edad** coming of age.

mayúsculo/la adj (fig) tremendous:—f capital letter.

mazo m bunch; club, mallet; bat.

mazorca f ear of corn.

me pn me; to me.

mear vi (fam) to pee, piss (sl).

mecanógrafo/fa m/f typist.

mecer vt to rock; to dandle (a child).

mechar vt to lard; to stuff.

mechón m lock of hair; large bundle of threads or fibres.

media f stocking; sock; average.

medianoche f midnight.

mediante prep by means of.

mediar vi to intervene; to mediate.

medicamento m medicine.

médico/ca adj medical:—m/f doctor.

medida f measure.

medio/dia adj half:—**a medias** partly:—m middle; average; way, means; medium.

mediodía m noon, midday.

medir vt to measure:—~**se** vr to be moderate.

medrar vi to grow, thrive, prosper; to improve.

médula f marrow; essence, substance; pith.

medusa f jellyfish.

mejilla f cheek.

mejillón m mussel.

mejor adj, adv better; best.

mejorar vt to improve, ameliorate; to enhance:—vi to improve; (med) to recover, get better:—~**se** vr to improve, get better.

melenudo/da adj long-haired.

melindroso/sa adj prudish, finicky.

mella f notch in edged tools; gap.

mellizo/za adj, m/f twin.

melocotón m peach.

meloso/sa adj honeyed; mellow.

membrete m letter head.

membrillo m quince; quince tree.

memoria f memory; report; record:—~**s** fpl memoirs pl.

mendigar vt to beg.

menear vt to move from place to place; (fig) to handle:—~**se** vr to move; to shake; to sway.

menguante f waning.

meñique m little finger.

menor m/f young person, juvenile:—adj less; smaller; minor:—**al por ~** retail.

menos adv less; least:—**a lo ~** o **por lo ~** at least:—prep except; minus.

menospreciar vt to undervalue; to despise, scorn.

mensaje m message.

mensual *adj* monthly.

menta *f* mint.

mente *f* mind; understanding.

mentecato/ta *adj* silly, stupid:—*m/f* idiot.

mentir *vt* to feign; to pretend:—*vi* to lie.

mentira *f* lie, falsehood.

menudo/da *adj* small; minute; petty, insignificant:—**a ~** frequently, often.

mercader *m* dealer, trader.

mercado *m* market; marketplace.

mercancía *f* commodity:—**~s** *fpl* goods *pl*, merchandise.

mercurio *m* mercury.

merecer *vt* to deserve, merit.

meridional *adj* southern.

merienda *f* (light) tea; afternoon snack; picnic.

merluza *f* hake.

mermelada *f* jam.

mero *m* pollack (fish):—**~/ra** *adj* mere, pure.

mes *m* month.

mesa *f* table; desk; plateau:—**~ redonda** round table.

mestizo/za *adj* of mixed race; crossbred:—*m/f* half-caste.

meta *f* goal; finish.

metal *m* metal; (*mus*) brass; timbre (of voice).

meter *vt* to place, put; to insert, put in; to involve; to make, cause:—**~se** *vr* to meddle, interfere.

método *m* method.

metro *m* meter; subway.

mezclar *vt* to mix:—**~se** *vr* to mix; to mingle.

mezquino/na *adj* mean; smallminded, petty; wretched.

mezquita *f* mosque.

mi *adj* my.

mí *pn* me; myself.

miedo *m* fear, dread.

miel *f* honey.

miembro *m* member.

mientras *adv* meanwhile:—*conj* while; as long as.

miércoles *m invar* Wednesday.

mierda *f* (*fam*) shit (*sl*).

miga *f* crumb:—**~s** *fpl* fried breadcrumbs *pl*.

mijo *m* (*bot*) millet.

mil *m* one thousand.

milagro *m* miracle, wonder.

milésimo/ma *adj*, *m* thousandth.

milímetro *m* millimeter.

milla *f* mile.

millión *m* million.

mimar *vt* to spoil, pamper.

mimbre *m* wicker.

mimo *m* caress; spoiling; mime.

mina *f* mine; underground passage.

minero/ra *m/f* miner.

minifalda *f* miniskirt.

mínimo/ma *adj* minimum.

minoría *f* minority.

minucioso/sa *adj* meticulous; very detailed.

minúsculo/la *adj* minute:—*f* small letter.

minusválido/da *adj* (physically) handicapped:—*m/f* (physically) handicapped person.

minuto *m* minute.

mío/mía *adj* mine.

miope *adj* short-sighted.

mirar *vt* to look at; to observe; to consider:—*vi* to look:—**~se** *vr* to look at oneself; to look at one another.

mirlo *m* blackbird.

misa *f* mass:—**~ del gallo** midnight mass.

miserable adj miserable; mean; squalid (place); (fam) despicable:— m/f rotter.

misericordia f mercy.

mismo/ma adj same; very.

mitad f half; middle.

mitin m (political) rally.

mixto/ta adj mixed.

mobiliario m furniture.

mochila f backpack.

mochuelo m red owl.

moco m snot (sl), mucus.

moda f fashion, style.

modales mpl manners pl.

modelo m model, pattern.

módico/ca adj moderate.

modificar vt to modify.

modisto/ta m/f dressmaker.

modo m mode, method, manner.

modorra f drowsiness.

mofarse vr:—~ de to mock, scoff at.

moflete m fat cheek.

moho m rust; mold, mildew.

mojar vt to wet, moisten:—~se vr to get wet.

mojón m landmark.

molde m mold; pattern; model.

moler vt to grind, pound; to tire out; to annoy, bore.

molestar vt to annoy, bother; to trouble:—vi to be a nuisance.

molino m mill.

momentáneo/nea adj momentary.

momento m moment.

momia f mummy.

mondadientes m invar toothpick.

mondar vt to clean; to cleanse; to peel:—~se vr ~ de risa (fam) to split one's sides laughing.

mondo/da adj clean; pure:—~ y lirondo bare, plain; pure and simple.

moneda f money; currency; coin.

monja f nun.

mono/na adj lovely; pretty; nice:— m/f monkey; ape:—mpl dungarees pl; overalls pl.

monstruo m monster.

montaje m assembly; decor (of theater); montage.

montaña f mountain.

montar vt to mount, get on (a bicycle, horse, etc); to assemble, put together; to overlap; to set up (a business); to beat, whip (in cooking): —vi to mount; to ride:—~ a to amount to.

monte m mountain; woodland:—~ alto forest:—~ bajo scrub.

montón m heap, pile; mass:—a ~ones, abundantly, by the score.

montura f mount; saddle.

monzón m monsoon.

mora f blackberry.

morado/da adj violet, purple.

morcilla f blood sausage.

mordaz adj biting, scathing; pungent.

mordaza f gag; clamp.

morder vt to bite; to nibble; to corrode, eat away.

moreno/na adj brown; swarthy; dark-skinned.

morir vi to die; to expire; to die down:—~se vr to die; (fig) to be dying.

morisco/ca adj Moorish.

moroso/sa adj slow, sluggish; (com) slow to pay up.

morral m haversack.

morro m snout; nose (of plane, etc).

morsa f walrus.

mortal adj mortal; fatal, deadly.

mosca f fly.

mosquearse vr (fam) to get cross; (fam) to take offence.

mosquitero m mosquito net.

mosquito m gnat, mosquito.

mostaza f mustard.

mosto m must, grape juice.

mostrador m counter.

mostrar vt to show, exhibit; to explain:—**~se** vr to appear, show oneself.

mote m nickname.

motivo m motive, cause, reason.

moto (fam), **motocicleta** f motorcycle.

motor m engine, motor.

mover vt to move; to shake; to drive; (fig) to cause:—**~se** vr to move; (fig) to get a move on.

móvil adj mobile, movable; moving:— m motive.

mozo/za adj young:—m/f youth, young man/girl; waiter/waitress.

muchacho/a m/f boy/girl:—f maid, maidservant.

mucho/cha adj a lot of, much:—adv much, a lot; long.

mudar vt to change; to shed:—**~se** vr to change one's clothes; to change house:—vi to change.

mudo/da adj dumb; silent, mute.

mueble m piece of furniture:—**~s** mpl furniture.

mueca f grimace, funny face.

muela f tooth, molar.

muelle m spring; regulator; quay.

muérdago m (bot) mistletoe.

muerte f death.

mujer f woman.

mulato adj mulatto.

muleta f crutch.

mullido/da adj soft; springy.

mulo/la m/f mule.

multa f fine, penalty.

mundial adj worldwide; world compd.

mundo m world.

muñeca f wrist; child's doll.

municipio m town council; municipality.

murciélago m bat.

murmullo m murmur, mutter.

murmurar vi to murmur; to gossip.

muro m wall.

músculo m muscle.

museo m museum.

musgo m moss.

música f music.

muslo m thigh.

mustio/tia adj parched, withered; sad, sorrowful.

mutuo/tua adj mutual, reciprocal.

muy adv very; too; greatly:—**~ ilustre** most illustrious.

N

nabo m turnip.

nácar m mother-of-pearl, nacre.

nacer vi to be born; to bud, shoot (of plants); to rise; to grow.

nacimiento m birth; nativity.

nada f nothing:—adv no way, not at all, by no means.

nadar vi to swim.

nadie pn nobody, no one.

nafta f gas.

nalgas fpl buttocks pl.

naranja f orange.

nariz f nose.

narrar vt to narrate, tell.

nata f cream.

natillas fpl custard.

naturaleza f nature.

naufragar vi to be shipwrecked; to suffer ruin in one's affairs.

náutica f navigation.

navaja f penknife; razor.

nave f ship; nave; warehouse.

navegar vt, vi to navigate; to sail; to fly.

Navidad f Christmas.

nebuloso/sa adj misty; cloudy; nebulous; foggy; hazy; drizzling:—f nebula.

neceser m toilet bag; holdall.

necesitar vt to need:—vi to want, to need.

necio/cia adj ignorant; stupid, foolish; imprudent.

nefasto/ta adj unlucky.

negado/da adj incapable, unfit.

negar vt to deny; to refuse:—~se vr ~ a hacer to refuse to do.

negocio m business, affair; transaction; firm; place of business.

negro/gra adj black:—m black:—m/f Black.

nene m, **nena** f baby.

neto/ta adj neat, pure; net.

neumático/ca adj pneumatic:—m tire.

neutro/tra adj neutral; neuter.

nevar vi to snow.

nevera f icebox.

ni conj neither, nor.

nido m nest; hiding place.

niebla f fog; mist.

nieta f granddaughter.

nieto m grandson.

nieve f snow.

niña f little girl; pupil, (of eye).

ningún, **ninguno/na** adj no:—pn nobody; none; not one; neither.

niño/ña adj childish:—m/f child; infant:—**desde** ~ from infancy, from a child:—m boy.

nitidez f clarity; brightness; sharpness.

nivel m level; standard; height:—**a** ~ perfectly level.

no adv no; not:—excl no!

no obstante adv nevertheless, notwithstanding.

noche f night; evening; darkness:— ~ **buena** Christmas Eve:—~ **vieja** New Year's Eve:—**¡buenas** ~**s!** good night!

noción f notion, idea.

nocivo/va adj harmful.

nogal m walnut tree.

nombrar vt to name; to nominate; to appoint.

nombre m name; title; reputation.

nómina f list; (com) payroll.

non adj odd, uneven:—m odd number.

nor(d)este adj northeast, northeastern:—m northeast.

nórdico/ca adj northern; Nordic.

noria f water wheel; big wheel.

noroeste adj northwest, northwestern:—m northwest.

norte adj north, northern:—m north; (fig) rule, guide.

nos pn us; to us; for us; from us; to ourselves.

nosotros/tras pn we; us.

nostalgia f homesickness.

notar vt to note; to mark; to remark:—~se vr to be obvious.

noticia f information; note:—~s fpl news.

noticiario m newsreel; news bulletin.

notificar vt to notify, inform.

novato/ta adj inexperienced:—m/f beginner.

novecientos/tas adj nine hundred.

novedad f novelty; modernness; newness; piece of news; change.

noveno/na adj ninth.

noventa *adj, m* ninety.
novia *f* bride; girlfriend; fiancée.
noviembre *m* November.
novio *m* bridegroom; boyfriend; fiancé.
nube *f* cloud.
nublado/da *adj* cloudy:—*m* storm cloud.
nuca *f* nape (of the neck); scruff of the neck.
nudillo *m* knuckle.
nudo *m* knot.

nuera *f* daughter-in-law.
nuestro/tra *adj* our:—*pn* ours.
nueve *m, adj* nine.
nuevo/va *adj* new; modern; fresh:—*f* piece of news:—**¿que hay de ~?** is there any news?, what's new?
nuez *f* nut; walnut; Adam's apple:— **~ moscada** nutmeg.
número *m* number; cipher.
nunca *adv* never.
nutria *f* otter.
nutrir *vt* to nourish; to feed.

Ñ

ñato/ta *adj* snub-nosed.
ñoño/ña *adj* insipid; spineless; silly.

ñoñeria *f* insipidness.

O

o *conj* or; either.
obedecer *vt* to obey.
obeso/sa *adj* obese, fat.
objetar *vi* to object.
objeto *m* object; aim.
obligar *vt* to force:—**~se** *vr* to bind oneself.
obra *f* work; building, construction; play:—**por ~ de** thanks to.
obrero/ra *adj* working; labor *compd:* —*m/f* worker; laborer.
obsequiar *vt* to lavish attention on:— **~con** to present with.
observar *vt* to observe; to notice.
obstáculo *m* obstacle, impediment.
obstinarse *vr* to be obstinate:—**~ en** to persist in.
obstruir *vt* to obstruct:—**~se** *vr* to be blocked up, be obstructed.
obtener *vt* to obtain; to gain.
ocasión *f* occasion, opportunity.

ocasionar *vt* to cause, occasion.
occidente *m* occident, west.
océano *m* ocean.
ochenta *m, adj* eighty.
ocho *m, adj* eight.
ochocientos *m, adj* eight hundred.
ocio *m* leisure; pastime.
octavilla *f* pamphlet.
octavo/va *adj* eighth.
octubre *m* October.
ocultar *vt* to hide, conceal.
ocupar *vt* to occupy; to hold (office):—**~se** *vr* **~ de**, **~ en** to concern oneself with; to look after.
ocurrencia *f* event; bright idea.
ocurrir *vi* to occur, happen.
odiar *vt* to hate:—**~se** *vr* to hate one another.
oeste *adj* west, western:—*m* west.
ofender *vt* to offend; to injure:—**~se** *vr* to be vexed; to take offence.

oficina f office.

oficio m employment, occupation; ministry; function; trade, business.

ofrecer vt to offer; to present; to exhibit:—~**se** vr to offer oneself; to occur, present itself.

oído m hearing; ear.

oír vt, vi to hear; to listen (to).

ojal m buttonhole.

ojalá conj if only!, would that!

ojear vt to eye, view; to glance.

ojera f bag under the eyes.

ojo m eye; sight; eye of a needle; arch of a bridge.

ola f wave.

oler vt to smell, scent:—vi to smell:—~ **a** to smack of.

olfato m sense of smell.

olivo m olive tree.

olla f pan; stew:—~ **exprés, ~ a presion** pressure cooker.

olmo m elm tree.

olor m smell, odor; scent.

olvidar vt to forget.

ombligo m navel.

once m, adj eleven.

onda f wave.

opaco/ca adj opaque; dark.

opinar vt to think:—vi to give one's opinion.

oponer vt to oppose:—~**se** vr to be opposed:—~ **a** to oppose.

oposición f opposition:—~**ones** fpl public examinations pl.

oprimir vt to oppress; to crush; to press; to squeeze.

optar vt to choose, elect.

optativo/va adj optional.

óptimo/ma adj best.

opuesto/ta adj opposite; contrary; adverse.

orar vi to pray.

ordenado/da adj methodical; tidy.

ordenador m computer.

ordenanza f order; statute, ordinance; ordination.

ordenar vt to arrange; to order; to ordain:—~**se** vr to take holy orders.

ordeñar vt to milk.

oreja f ear.

orgullo m pride, haughtiness.

oriental adj oriental, eastern.

orientar vt to orient; to point; to direct; to guide:—~**se** vr to get one's bearings; to decide on a course of action.

orificio m orifice; mouth; aperture.

orilla f limit, border, margin; edge (of cloth); shore.

orín m rust.

orina f urine.

orinal m chamber pot.

oro m gold; ~**s** mpl diamonds pl (cards).

ortiga f (bot) nettle.

oruga f (bot) caterpillar.

orzuelo m (med) stye.

os pn you; to you.

osa f she-bear:—**O~ Mayor/Menor** Great/Little Bear.

osar vi to dare, venture.

oscuro/ra adj obscure; dark.

oso m bear:—~ **blanco** polar bear.

ostentar vt to show:—vi to boast, brag.

ostra f oyster.

otoño m fall, autumn.

otorgar vt to concede; to grant.

otorrino/na, otorrinolaringólogo/ ga m/f ear, nose and throat specialist.

otro/tra adj another; other.

oveja f sheep.

ovillo m ball of wool.

óvulo m ovum.

oxidar vt to rust:—~**se** vr to go rusty.

oyente m/f listener, hearer.

P

pacificar *vt* to pacify, appease.

pacotilla *f*:—**de** ~ third-rate; cheap.

pactar *vt* to covenant; to contract; to stipulate.

padecer *vt* to suffer; to sustain (an injury); to put up with.

padrastro *m* stepfather.

padre *m* father:—~s *mpl* parents *pl*.

pagar *vt* to pay; to pay for; (*fig*) to repay:—*vi* to pay.

página *f* page.

pago *m* payment; reward.

país *m* country; region.

paisaje *m* landscape.

paisano/na *adj* of the same country:—*m/f* fellow countryman/ woman.

paja *f* straw; (*fig*) trash.

pájaro *m* bird; sly, acute fellow.

pajita *f* (drinking) straw.

pala *f* spade, shovel.

palabra *f* word:—**de** ~ by word of mouth.

paladar *m* palate; taste, relish.

palanca *f* lever.

palangana *f* basin.

palco *m* box (in a theater).

paleto/ta *m/f* rustic.

pálido/da *adj* pallid, pale.

palillo *m* small stick; toothpick:—~s *mpl* chopsticks *pl*.

paliza *f* beating, thrashing.

palma *f* palm tree; palm of the hand; palm leaf.

palmada *f* slap, clap:—~s *fpl* clapping of hands, applause.

palmera *f* palm tree.

palo *m* stick; cudgel; blow given with a stick; post; mast; bat; suit (at cards):—~s *mpl* masting.

paloma *f* pigeon, dove:—~ **torcaz** ring dove:—~ **zorita** wood pigeon.

palomilla *f* moth; wing nut; angle iron.

palpar *vt* to feel, touch.

palta *f* avocado (pear).

pámpano *m* vine branch.

pan *m* bread; loaf; food in general.

pana *f* corduroy.

pañal *m* diaper, nappy.

pandereta *f* tambourine.

pandilla *f* group; gang; clique.

paño *m* cloth; piece of cloth; duster, rag.

pantalla *f* screen; lampshade.

pantalón *m*, **pantalones** *mpl* trousers, pants *pl*.

pantano *m* marsh; reservoir; obstacle, difficulty.

pantorrilla *f* calf (of the leg).

pañuelo *m* handkerchief.

panza *f* belly, paunch.

papá *m* (*fam*) dad, pop.

papada *f* double chin.

papel *m* paper; writing; part, role (in a play):—~ **de estraza** brown paper:—~ **sellado** stamped paper.

papeleo *m* red tape.

paperas *fpl* mumps.

paquete *m* packet; parcel; package tour.

par *adj* equal; alike; even:—*m* pair; couple; peer:—**sin** ~ matchless.

para *prep* for; to, in order to; towards.

parabrisas *m invar* windshield.

paracaídas *m invar* parachute.

parada *f* halt; suspension; pause; stop; shutdown; stopping place:—~ **de autobús** bus stop.

parado/da adj motionless; at a standstill; stopped; standing (up); unemployed.

paraguas m invar umbrella.

parar vi to stop, halt:—vt to stop, detain:—**sin** ~ instantly, without delay:——**se** vr to stop, halt; to stand up.

parecer m opinion, advice, counsel; countenance, air, mien:—vi to appear; to seem:——**se** vr ~ **a** to resemble.

parecido/da adj resembling, like.

pared f wall:—~ **medianera** party wall.

pareja f pair, couple, brace.

pariente/ta m/f relative, relation.

parir vt to give birth to:—vi to give birth.

paro m strike; unemployment.

párpado m eyelid.

parra f vine raised on stakes or nailed to a wall.

párrafo m paragraph.

parrilla f grill; grille.

parte m message; report:—f part; side; party:—**de ocho días a esta** ~ within these last eight days:—**de** ~ **a** ~ from side to side, through and through.

partera f midwife.

particular adj particular, special:—m private individual; particular matter or subject treated upon.

partida f departure; party; item in an account; parcel; game.

partido m party; match; team.

partir vt to part; to divide, separate; to cut; to break:—vi to depart:——**se** vr to break (in two, etc).

parvulario m nursery school.

pasa f raisin.

pasadizo m narrow passage; narrow, covered way.

pasado/da adj past; bad; overdone; out of date:—~ **mañana** the day after tomorrow:—**la semana pasada** last week:—m past.

pasaje m passage; fare; passengers pl.

pasajero/ra adj transient; transitory; fugitive:—m/f traveler; passenger.

pasamanos m invar (hand)rail; bannister.

pasar vt to pass; to surpass; to suffer; to strain; to dissemble:—vi to pass; to happen:——**se** vr to go over (to another party); to go bad or off.

pasarela f footbridge; gangway.

pasatiempo m pastime, amusement.

Pascua f Passover; Easter.

pasear vt to walk:—vi ~**se** vr to walk; to walk about.

pasmar vt to amaze; to numb; to chill:——**se** vr to be astonished.

paso m pace, step; passage; manner of walking; flight of steps; accident:— (ferro) ~ **a nivel** grade crossing:—**al** ~ on the way, in passing.

pasta f paste; dough; pastry; (fam) dough:——**s** fpl pastries pl; pasta: —~ **de dientes** toothpaste.

pastel m cake; pie; crayon (for drawing).

pastilla f bar (of soap); tablet, pill.

pastor m shepherd; pastor.

pata f leg (of animal or furniture); foot: —**meter la** ~ to put one's foot in it.

patata f potato.

patear vt to kick; to stamp on.

patillas fpl sideburns pl.

patín m skate; runner.

patinar vi to skate; to skid; (fam) to blunder.

patio *m* courtyard; playground.

pato *m* duck.

patoso/sa *adj (fam)* clumsy.

patraña *f* lie.

patrocinar *vt* to sponsor; to back, support.

patrón/ona *m/f* boss, master/mistress; landlord/lady; patron saint:—*m* pattern.

patronal *adj*:—**la clase ~** management.

patrulla *f* patrol.

paulatino/na *adj* gradual, slow.

pausar *vi* to pause.

pauta *f* guideline.

pavo *m* turkey:—**~ real** peacock.

pavor *m* dread, terror.

payaso/sa *m/f* clown.

payo/ya *m/f* non-Gipsy (for a Gipsy).

paz *f* peace; tranquillity, ease.

peaje *m* toll.

peana *f* pedestal; footstool.

peatón *m* pedestrian.

peca *f* freckle; spot.

pecado *m* sin.

pecho *m* chest; breast(s) *(pl)*; teat; *(fig)* courage, valor:—**dar el ~ a** to suckle:—**tomar a ~** to take to heart.

pechuga *f* breast of a fowl; *(fam)* bosom.

pedazo *m* piece, bit.

pedernal *m* flint.

pediatra *m/f* pediatrician.

pedicuro/ra *m/f* chiropodist.

pedir *vt* to ask for; to petition; to beg; to order; to need; to solicit:—*vi* to ask.

pedo *m (fam)* fart *(sl)*:—**tirarse un ~** to fart *(sl)*.

pegamento *m* glue.

pegar *vt* to cement; to join, unite; to beat:—**~ fuego a** to set fire to:—*vi*

to stick; to match:—**~se** *vr* to intrude; to steal in.

pegatina *f* sticker.

peinar *vt* to comb; to style.

peine *m* comb.

pelar *vt* to cut (hair); to strip off (feathers); to peel:—**~se** *vr* to peel off; to have one's hair cut.

peldaño *m* step (of a flight of stairs).

pelear *vt* to fight, combat:—**~se** *vr* to scuffle.

pelele *m* dummy; man of straw.

película *f* film, thin covering; movie.

peligro *m* danger, peril; risk.

pelirrojo/ja *m/f* redhead:—*adj* redhaired.

pellejo *m* skin; hide, pelt; peel; wine skin; oilskin; drunkard.

pellizcar *vt* to pinch.

pelo *m* hair; pile; flaw (in precious stones).

pelota *f* ball.

peluca *f* wig.

peluquería *f* hairdresser's/barber's premises.

pelusa *f* bloom (on fruit); fluff.

pena *f* punishment, pain:—**a duras ~s** with great difficulty or trouble.

pendiente *f* slope, declivity:—*m* earring:—*adj* pending; unsettled.

pene *m* penis.

penetrante *adj* deep; sharp; piercing; searching; biting.

penique *m* penny.

penoso/sa *adj* painful.

pensar *vi* to think.

pensativo/va *adj* pensive, thoughtful.

pensión *f* guest-house; pension.

penúltimo/ma *adj* penultimate, last but one.

penumbra *f* half-light.

penuria f penury, poverty, neediness, extreme want.

peña f rock, large stone.

peón m (day) laborer; foot soldier; pawn (at chess).

peor adj, adv worse:—~ **que** ~ worse and worse.

pepino m cucumber.

pepita f kernel; pip.

pequeño/ña adj little, small; young.

pera f pear.

percatarse vr:—~ **de** to notice.

percha f coat hook; coat hanger; perch.

percibir vt to receive; to perceive, comprehend.

perder vt to lose; to waste; to miss:— ~**se** vr to go astray; to be lost; to be spoiled.

perdiz f partridge.

perdón m pardon; mercy:—**i**~! sorry!

perdonar vt to pardon, forgive; to excuse.

perdurar vi to last; to still exist.

perecedero/ra adj perishable.

peregrino/na adj (fig) strange:—m pilgrim.

perejil m parsley.

pereza f laziness, idleness.

perfil m profile.

perforar vt to perforate; to drill; to punch a hole in:—vi to drill.

perfume m perfume.

pergamino m parchment.

periódico/ca adj periodical:—m newspaper.

periodista m/f journalist.

peripecia f vicissitude; sudden change.

periquito m budgie.

perito/ta adj skillful, experienced: —m/f expert; skilled worker; technician.

perjudicar vt to prejudice, damage; to injure, hurt.

perjurar vi to perjure, swear falsely; to swear.

perla f pearl:—**de** ~**s** fine.

permanecer vi to stay; to continue to be.

permiso m permission, leave, license.

permitir vt to permit, allow.

permutar vt to exchange, permute.

pernera f trouser leg.

perno m bolt.

pernoctar vi to spend the night.

pero m kind of apple:—conj but, yet.

perogrullada f truism, platitude.

perol m large metal pan.

perro m dog.

perseguir vt to pursue; to persecute; to chase after.

perseverar vi to persevere, persist.

persiana f (Venetian) blind.

persistir vi to persist.

persona f person:—**de** ~ **a** ~ from person to person.

personaje m celebrity; character.

persuadir vt to persuade:—~**se** vr to be persuaded.

pertenecer vi:—~ **a** to belong to; to appertain, concern.

pértiga f long pole or rod.

pertinaz adj pertinacious; obstinate.

pertinente adj relevant; appropriate.

perturbar vt to perturb, disturb.

pervertir vt to pervert; to corrupt.

pesa f weight.

pesadez f heaviness, weight; gravity; slowness; peevishness, fretfulness; trouble; fatigue.

pesadilla f nightmare.

pesado/da adj peevish; troublesome; cumbersome; tedious; heavy, weighty.

pesar m sorrow, grief; repentance:—
a ~ de in spite of, not withstanding:—vi to weigh; to repent:—vt to weigh.

pescado m fish (in general).

pescar vt to fish for, catch (fish):—vi to fish.

pescuezo m neck.

pésimo/ma adj very bad.

peso m weight, heaviness; balance scales pl.

pesquisa f inquiry, examination.

pestaña f eyelash.

pestañear vi to blink.

pestillo m bolt.

petróleo m crude oil, petroleum.

pez m fish:—f pitch.

pezón m nipple.

pezuña f hoof.

piadoso/sa adj pious; mild; merciful; moderate.

piar vi to squeak; to chirp.

pibe/ba m/f boy/girl.

picado/da adj pricked; minced, chopped; bad (tooth); cross.

picante adj hot, spicy; racy.

picaporte m doorhandle; latch.

picar vt to prick; to sting; to mince; to nibble:—vi to prick; to sting; to itch:——**se** vr to be piqued; to take offence; to be moth-eaten; to begin to rot.

pícaro/ra adj roguish; mischievous, malicious; sly:—m/f rogue, knave.

pico m beak; bill, nib; peak; pick-ax.

pie m foot; leg; basis; trunk (of trees); foundation; occasion:—**a ~** on foot.

piedad f piety; mercy, pity.

piedra f stone.

piel f skin; hide; peel.

pienso m fodder.

pierna f leg (human).

pieza f piece; room.

pila f battery; trough; font; sink; pile, heap:—**nombre de ~** first name.

píldora f pill.

pileta f basin; swimming pool.

pimentón m paprika.

pimienta f pepper.

pimiento m pepper, pimiento.

piña f pineapple; fir cone; group.

pincel m paintbrush.

pinchar vt to prick; to puncture.

pincho m thorn; snack.

ping-pong m table tennis.

pino m (bot) pine.

piñón m pine nut; pinion.

pintar vt to paint; to picture; to describe; to exaggerate:—vi to paint; (fam) to count, to be important:—
~se vr to put on make-up.

pintura f painting.

pinza f claw; clothes pin; pincers pl:
——**s** fpl tweezers pl.

piojo m louse; troublesome hangeron.

pipa f pipe; sunflower seed.

pipí m (fam):—**hacer ~** to have to go (wee-wee).

piquete m prick, jab; hole; (mil) squad.

piragua f canoe.

piropo m compliment; flattery.

pisar vt to tread, trample; to stamp on (the ground); to hammer down:
—vi to tread, walk.

piscina f swimming pool.

piso m apartment; tread, trampling; floor, sidewalk; floor, story.

pisotear vt to trample, tread under foot.

pista f trace, footprint; clue.

pita f (bot) agave.

pitar vt to blow; to whistle at:—vi to whistle; to toot one's horn; to smoke.

pito m whistle; horn.

pizarra f slate.

pizca f mite; pinch.

placa f plate; badge.

placer m pleasure; delight:—vt to please.

plan m plan; design; plot; scheme.

plancha f plate; iron; gangway.

planear vt to plan:—vi to glide.

planicie f plain.

planificación f planning:—~ **familiar** family planning.

plano/na adj plain, level, flat:—m plan; ground plot, map:—~ **inclinado** (ferro) dead level.

plantación f plantation.

plantar vt to plant; to fix upright; to strike or hit (a blow); to found; to establish:—~se vr to stand upright.

plantilla f personnel; insole of a shoe.

plata f silver; plate (wrought silver); cash:—**en** ~ briefly.

plátano m banana; plane tree.

plateado/da adj silvered; plated.

platicar vi to converse.

platillo m saucer:—~s mpl cymbals pl: —~ **volador/~ volante** flying saucer.

platino m platinum:—~s mpl contact points pl.

plato m dish; plate.

playa f beach.

playera f T-shirt:—~s fpl sneakers pl.

plaza f square; place; office, employment; room; seat.

plazo m term; installment; expiry date.

plegar vt to fold; to crease.

pleito m contract, bargain; dispute, controversy, debate; lawsuit.

plenilunio m full moon.

pleno/na adj full; complete:—m plenum.

pliego m sheet of paper.

pliegue m fold; pleat.

plisado/da adj pleated:—m pleating.

plomero m plumber.

plomo m lead:—**a** ~ perpendicularly.

pluma f feather, plume.

población f population; town.

pobre adj poor.

poco/ca adj little, scanty; (pl) few:— adv little:—~ **a** ~ gently; little by little:—m small part; little.

podar vt to prune.

poder m power, authority; command; force:—vi to be able to; to possess the power of doing or performing.

podrido/da adj rotten, bad; (fig) rotten.

poesía f poetry.

polea f pulley; (mar) tackle-block.

polideportivo m sports center.

polilla f moth.

pollera f skirt.

pollo m chicken.

polo m pole; ice lolly; polo; polo neck.

polvo m powder, dust.

pólvora f gunpowder.

pomada f cream, ointment.

pomelo m grapefruit.

pómez f:—**piedra** ~ pumice stone.

pompa f pomp; bubble.

pómulo m cheekbone.

poner vt to put, place; to put on; to impose; to lay (eggs):—~se vr to oppose; to set (of stars); to become.

poniente m west; west wind.

ponzoña f poison.

popa f (mar) poop, stern.

por prep for; by; about; by means of; through; on account of.

porción f part, portion; lot.

porfiar vt to dispute obstinately; to persist in a pursuit.

pormenor f detail.

poro m pore.

porque *conj* because; since; so that.

porquería *f* nastiness, foulness; brutishness, rudeness; trifle; dirty action.

porrón *m* spouted wine jar.

portada *f* portal, porch; frontispiece.

portaequipajes *m invar* trunk (in car); baggage rack.

portarse *vr* to behave.

portátil *adj* portable.

portavoz *m/f* spokesman/woman.

porte *m* transportation (charges *pl*); deportment, demeanor, conduct.

portero *m* porter, gatekeeper.

porvenir *m* future.

posar *vi* to sit, pose:—*vt* to lay down (a burden):—**~se** *vr* to settle; to perch; to land.

posdata *f* postscript.

poseer *vt* to hold, possess.

posesivo/va *adj* possessive.

posibilitar *vt* to make possible; to make feasible.

poso *m* sediment, dregs *pl*.

posponer *vt* to postpone.

postal *adj* postal:—*f* postcard.

poste *m* post, pillar.

postergar *vt* to leave behind; to postpone.

posterioridad *f*:—**con ~** subsequently, later.

postigo *m* wicket; postern; shutter.

postizo/za *adj* artificial (not natural):—*m* wig.

postrar *vt* to humble, humiliate:—**~se** *vr* to prostrate oneself.

postre *m* dessert.

postura *f* posture, position; attitude; bet, wager; agreement, convention.

potable *adj* drinkable.

potaje *m* pottage; drink made up of several ingredients; medley of various useless things.

potro/ra *m/f* colt; foal.

pozo *m* well.

practicar *vt* to practice.

práctico/ca *adj* practical; skillful, experienced.

prado *m* lawn; meadow.

precaver *vt* to prevent; to guard against.

preceder *vt* to precede, go before.

preciado/da *adj* esteemed, valued.

precinto *m* seal.

precio *m* price; value.

precioso/sa *adj* precious; (*fam*) beautiful.

precisamente *adv* precisely; exactly.

precisar *vt* to compel, oblige; to need.

preciso/sa *adj* necessary, requisite; precise, accurate; abstracted.

precoz *adj* precocious.

precursor/ra *m/f* harbinger, forerunner.

predecir *vt* to foretell.

predicar *vt* to preach.

predilecto/ta *adj* darling, favorite.

predisponer *vt* to predispose; to prejudice.

predominar *vi* to predominate, prevail.

preferir *vt* to prefer.

pregón *m* proclamation; hue and cry.

preguntar *vt* to ask; to question; to demand; to inquire.

prejuicio *m* prejudgement; preconception; prejudice.

premiar *vt* to reward, remunerate.

premura *f* pressure, haste, hurry.

preñada *adj* pregnant.

prenda *f* pledge; garment; sweetheart; person or thing dearly loved:—**~s** *fpl* accomplishments, talents *pl*.

prender *vt* to seize, catch, lay hold of; to imprison:—**~se** *vr* to catch fire:—*vi* to take root.

prensar vt to press.
preocupar(se) vt (vr) to worry.
preparar vt to prepare:——**se** vr to be prepared.
prepucio m foreskin.
presa f capture, seizure; dike, dam.
presagio m omen.
prescindir vi:——**de** to do without; to dispense with.
presenciar vt to attend; to be present at; to witness.
presentar vt to present; to introduce; to offer; to show:——**se** vr to present oneself; to appear; to run (as candidate); to apply.
presentir vt to have a premonition of.
preservativo m condom, sheath.
presidiario m convict.
presilla f clip; loop (in clothes).
presión f pressure, pressing.
presionar vt to press; (fig) to put pressure on.
preso/sa m/f prisoner.
prestar vt to lend.
presto/ta adj quick; prompt; ready:—adv soon; quickly.
presumir vt to presume, conjecture:—vi to be conceited.
presunto/ta adj supposed; socalled.
presupuesto m presumed cost; budget.
pretender vt to claim; to try, attempt.
pretendiente m pretender; suitor.
pretexto m pretext; pretence, excuse.
prevalacer vi to prevail; to triumph; to take root.
prevenir vt to prepare; to foresee, know in advance; to prevent; to warn:——**se** vr to be prepared; to be predisposed.

prever vt to foresee, forecast.
previo/via adj previous.
previsión f foresight, prevision; forecast.
prima f bonus; (female) cousin.
primario/ria adj primary.
primavera f spring (the season).
primer(o)/ra adj first; prior; former:—adv first; rather, sooner.
primicias f first fruits pl.
primo/ma m cousin.
primogénito/ta adj, m/f first-born.
príncipe m prince.
principiante m beginner, learner.
principio m beginning, commencement; principle.
pringoso/sa adj greasy; sticky.
prisa f speed; hurry; urgency; promptness.
prismáticos mpl binoculars pl.
privación f deprivation, want.
privado/da adj private; particular.
proa f (mar) prow.
probador m fitting room.
probar vt to try; to prove; to taste:—vi to try.
probeta f test tube.
procedente adj reasonable; proper:—**~ de** coming from.
procesador m:——**~ de textos** word processor.
procesar vt to put on trial.
procurar vt to try; to obtain; to produce.
prodigar vt to waste, lavish.
producir vt to produce; (jur) to produce as evidence:——**se** vr to come about; to arise; to be made; to break out.
proeza f prowess, valor, bravery.
profanar vt to profane, desecrate.

profesor/ra *m/f* teacher.
prófugo *m* fugitive.
profundo/da *adj* profound.
programa *m* program(me).
prohibir *vt* to prohibit, forbid; to hinder.
prójimo *m* fellow creature; neighbor.
prole *f* offspring, progeny; race.
prolijidad *f* prolixity; minute attention to detail.
prólogo *m* prolog.
promedio *m* average; middle.
prometer *vt* to promise; to assure:— **~se** *vr* to become engaged.
promiscuo/cua *adj* promiscuous; confusedly mingled.
promover *vt* to promote, advance; to stir up.
promulgar *vt* to promulgate, publish.
pronosticar *vt* to predict, foretell; to conjecture.
pronto/ta *adj* prompt; ready:—*adv* promptly.
pronunciamiento *m* (*jur*) publication; insurrection, sedition.
pronunciar *vt* to pronounce; to deliver:—**~se** *vr* to rebel.
propaganda *f* propaganda; advertising.
propagar *vt* to propagate.
propasar *vt* to go beyond, exceed.
propenso/sa *adj* prone, inclined.
propiamente *adv* properly; really.
propiciar *vt* to favor; to cause.
propiedad *f* property, possessions *pl*; right of property; propriety.
propina *f* tip.
propio/pia *adj* proper; own; typical; very.
proponer *vt* to propose.
proporcionar *vt* to provide.

propósito *m* aim, purpose:—**a ~** on purpose.
propuesta *f* proposal, offer; representation.
propulsar *vt* to propel; (*fig*) to promote.
prórroga *f* prolongation; extension; extra time.
prorrumpir *vi* to break forth, burst forth.
prosa *f* prose.
proscrito/ta *adj* banned.
proseguir *vt* to continue:—*vi* to continue, go on.
prospección *f* exploration; prospecting.
prosperar *vi* to prosper, thrive.
proteger *vt* protector.
protestar *vt* to protest; to make public declaration (of faith):—*vi* to protest.
provecho *m* profit; advantage.
proveedor/ra *m/f* purveyor, supplier.
provenir *vi* to arise, originate; to issue.
provocar *vt* to provoke; to lead to; to excite.
próximamente *adv* soon.
próximo/ma *adj* next; neighboring; close, nearby.
proyectar *vt* to throw; to cast; to screen; to plan.
prueba *f* proof; reason; argument; token; experiment; essay; attempt; relish, taste.
púa *f* sharp point, prickle; shoot; pick.
pubertad *f* puberty.
publicar *vt* to publish; to make public.
publicidad *f* publicity; advertising.
público/ca *adj* public:—*m* public; audience; crowd.

puchero *m* pot; stew.

púdico/ca *adj* chaste, pure.

pudiente *adj* rich, opulent.

pudor *m* bashfulness.

pudrir *vt* to rot, putrefy:—**~se** *vr* to decay, rot.

pueblo *m* people *pl*; town, village; population; populace.

puente *m* bridge.

puerco/ca *adj* nasty; filthy, dirty; rude, coarse:—*m* pig, hog:—**~ espín** porcupine.

pueril *adj* childish; puerile.

puerro *m* leek.

puerta *f* door; doorway; gateway:—**~ trasera** back door.

puerto *m* port, harbor; haven; pass.

pues *adv* then; therefore; well:—**i~!** well, then.

puesto *m* place; particular spot; post, employment; barracks *pl*; stand.

púgil *m* boxer.

pujante *adj* powerful, strong; robust; stout, strapping.

Pulga*f* flea:—**tener malas ~s** to be easily piqued; to be ill-tempered.

pulgada *f* inch.

pulgar *m* thumb.

pulir *vt* to polish; to put the last touches to.

pulmón *m* lung.

pulpa *f* pulp; soft part (of fruit).

pulpería *f* small grocery store.

pulpo *m* octopus.

pulsar *vt* to touch; to play; to press.

pulsera *f* bracelet.

pulso *m* pulse; wrist; firmness or steadiness of the hand.

pulular *vi* to swarm.

pulverizador *m* spray gun.

puna *f* (*med*) mountain sickness.

puñado *m* handful.

puñal *m* dagger.

puño *m* fist; handful; wrist-band; cuff; handle.

punta *f* point; end; trace.

puntada *f* stitch.

puntal *m* prop, stay; buttress.

puntapié *m* kick.

puntería *f* aiming.

puntiagudo/da *adj* sharp-pointed.

puntilla *f* narrow lace edging:—**de ~s** on tiptoe.

punto *m* point; end; spot; stitch; full stop.

puntual *adj* punctual; exact; reliable.

punzada *f* prick; sting; pain; compunction.

punzante *adj* sharp.

pupila *f* pupil (of eye).

puro/ra *adj* pure; mere; clear; genuine.

púrpura *f* purple.

purulento/ta *adj* purulent.

puta *f* whore.

Q

que *pn* that; who; which; what:—*conj* that; than.

¿qué? *adj* what?; which?:—*pn* what?; which?.

quebrantar *vt* to break; to crack; to burst; to pound, grind; to violate; to fatigue; to weaken.

quedar *vi* to stay:—**~se** *vr* to remain.

quedo/da adj quiet, still:—adv softly, gently.

quejarse vr to complain of.

quemar vt to burn; to kindle:—~se vr to be parched with heat; to burn oneself:—vi to be too hot.

querella f charge; dispute; complaint.

querer vt to want; to desire; to will; to love:—m will, desire.

querido/da adj dear, beloved:—m/f darling; lover:—~ mio, ~da mia my dear, my love, my darling.

queso m cheese.

quicio m hook, hinge (of a door).

quien pn who; whom.

¿quién? pn who?; whom?.

quienquiera adj whoever.

quieto/ta adj still, peaceable.

quilla f keel.

química f chemistry.

quina f Peruvian bark, quinine.

quince adj, m fifteen; fifteenth.

quincena f fortnight.

quinientos/tas adj five hundred.

quinta f country house; levy, drafting of soldiers.

quinto adj fifth:—m fifth; drafted soldier.

quiosco m bandstand; news stand.

quirúrgico/ca adj surgical.

quiste m cyst.

quitamanchas m invar stain remover.

quitanieves m invar snowplough.

quitar vt to take away, remove; to take off; to relieve; to annul:—~se vr to take off (clothes, etc); to withdraw.

quitasol m parasol.

quizá/quizás adv perhaps.

R

rábano m radish.

rabia f rage, fury.

rabo m tail.

racha f gust of wind:—**buena/mala** ~ spell of good/bad luck.

racimo m bunch of grapes.

radiografía f x-ray.

ráfaga f gust; flash; burst.

raído/da adj scraped; worn-out; impudent.

raíz f root; base, basis; origin:—**bienes raices** mpl landed property.

raja f splinter, chip (of wood); chink, fissure.

rajatabla f:—**a** ~ adv strictly.

rallar vt to grate.

rama f branch (of tree, of family).

ramo m branch (of tree).

rampa f ramp.

rana f frog.

rancho m grub; ranch; small farm.

rancio/cia adj rank; rancid.

ranura f groove; slot.

rapar vt to shave; to plunder.

rapaz/za adj rapacious:—m/f young boy/girl.

rápido/da adj quick, rapid, swift.

rapiña f robbery.

raptar vt to kidnap.

raquítico/ca adj stunted; (fig) inadequate.

raro/ra adj rare, scarce; extraordinary.

ras m:—**a** ~ **de** level with:—**a** ~ **de tierra** at ground level.

rascacielos m invar skyscraper.

rascar vt to scratch, scrape.

rasgar vt to tear, rip.

rasgo m dash, stroke; grand or magnanimous action:—~s mpl features pl.

rasguño m scratch.

raso m satin; glade:—~/**sa** adj plain; flat:—**al** ~ in the open air.

raspa f beard (of an ear of corn); backbone (of fish); stalk (of grapes); rasp.

raspar vt to scrape, rasp.

rastrear vt to trace; to inquire into:— vi to skim along close to the ground (of birds).

rastrillo m rake.

rastro m track; rake; trace.

rata f rat.

ratificar vt to ratify, confirm.

rato m moment:—**a ~s perdidos** in leisure time.

ratón m mouse.

raya f stroke; line; part; frontier; ray (fish); roach (fish).

rayar vt to draw lines on; to cross out; to underline; to cross; to rifle.

rayo m ray, beam (of light).

raza f race, lineage; quality; crack, fissure.

razonar vi to reason; to discourse, talk.

reaccionar vi to react.

real adj real, actual; royal:—m (mil) camp.

realidad f reality; sincerity.

realizador/ra m/f producer (in TV, etc.).

realzar vt to raise, elevate; to emboss; to heighten.

reanimar vt to cheer, encourage; to reanimate.

reanudar vt to resume.

rebaja f abatement; deduction:—~s fpl sale.

rebanada f slice.

rebaño m flock (of sheep), herd (of cattle).

rebasar vt to exceed.

rebatir vt to resist; to parry, ward off; to refute; to repress.

rebeca f cardigan.

rebelarse vr to revolt; to rebel; to resist.

rebosar vi to run over, overflow; to abound.

rebotar vt to bounce; to clinch; to repel:—vi to rebound.

rebozar vt to wrap up; to fry in batter or breadcrumbs.

rebuznar vi to bray.

recado m message; errand.

recaída f relapse.

recalcar vt to stress, emphasize.

recalentar vt to heat again; to overheat.

recambio m spare; refill.

recapacitar vt to reflect.

recargar vt to overload; to recharge; to charge again.

recatado/da adj prudent; circumspect; modest.

recaudar vt to gather; to obtain; to recover.

recelo m dread; suspicion, mistrust.

receta f recipe; prescription.

rechazar vt to refuse; to repulse; to contradict.

recibir vt to receive, accept; to let in; to go to meet:—~**se** vr ~ **de** to qualify as.

recibo m receipt.

recién adv recently, lately.

reciente adj recent; new, fresh; modern.

recio/cia adj stout; strong, robust; coarse, thick; rude; arduous, rigid:—

adv strongly, stoutly:—**hablar ~** to talk loud.

recipiente *m* container.

reclamación *f* claim; reclamation; protest.

recluir *vt* to shut up.

reclutar *vt* to recruit.

recobrar *vt* to recover:—**~se** *vr* to recover (from sickness).

recodo *m* corner or angle jutting out.

recoger *vt* to collect; to take back; to get; to gather; to shelter; to compile:—**~se** *vr* to take shelter or refuge; to retire; to withdraw from the world.

recompensa *f* compensation; recompense, reward.

reconfortar *vt* to comfort.

reconocer *vt* to recognize; to examine closely; to acknowledge; to consider; (*mil*) to reconnoiter.

reconstituyente *m* tonic.

reconversión *f*:—**~ industrial** industrial rationalization.

recopilar *vt* to compile.

recordar *vt* to remember; to remind:—*vi* to remember.

recorrer *vt* to run over, peruse; to cover.

recortar *vt* to cut out.

recostar *vt* to lean, recline:—**~se** *vr* to lie down.

recoveco *m* cubby hole; bend.

recreo *m* recreation; playtime (school).

recta *f* straight line.

rectángulo/la *adj* rectangular:—*m* rectangle.

rectitud *f* straightness; rectitude; justness, honesty; exactitude.

recto/ta *adj* straight; right; just, honest:—*m* rectum.

rector/ra *m/f* superior of a community or establishment; rector (of a university); curate, rector:—*adj* governing.

recuadro *m* box; inset.

recuento *m* inventory.

recuerdo *m* souvenir; memory.

recuperar *vt* to recover:—**~se** *vr* to recover (from sickness).

recurrir *vi*:—**~ a** to resort to.

red *f* net; network; snare.

redactar *vt* to draft; to edit.

redada *f*:—**~ policial** police raid.

redimir *vt* to redeem; to ransom.

redoblar *vt* to redouble; to rivet.

redondo/da *adj* round; complete.

reducir *adj* to reduce; to limit:—**~se** *vr* to diminish.

redundancia *f* superfluity, redundancy, excess.

reembolso *m* reimbursement; refund:—**contra ~** C.O.D.

referir *vt* to refer, relate, report:—**~se** *vr* to refer or relate to.

refinado/da *adj* refined; subtle, artful.

reflejar *vt* to reflect.

reflejo *m* reflex; reflection.

reflujo *m* reflux, ebb:—**flujo y ~** the tides *pl*.

reformar *vt* to reform; to correct; to restore:—**~se** *vr* to mend; to have one's manners reformed or corrected.

reforzar *vt* to strengthen, fortify; to encourage.

refrán *m* proverb.

refrescar *vt* to refresh:—**~se** *vr* to get cooler; to go out for a breath of fresh air:—*vi* to cool down.

refriega *f* affray, skirmish, fray.

refrigerador *m*, **refrigeradora** *f* refrigerator, fridge.

refuerzo *m* reinforcement.

refugiar *vt* to shelter:——**se** *vr* to take refuge.

refunfuñar *vi* to snarl; to growl; to grumble.

regadera *f* watering can.

regalar *vt* to give (as present); to give away; to pamper; to caress.

regaliz *m* licorice.

regalo *m* present, gift; pleasure; comfort.

regañadientes:—a ~ *adv* reluctantly.

regañar *vt* to scold:—*vi* to growl; to grumble; to quarrel.

regar *vt* to water, irrigate.

regata *f* irrigation ditch; regatta.

regatear *vt* (*com*) to bargain over; to be mean with:—*vi* to haggle; to dribble (in sport).

regazo *m* lap.

regentar *vt* to rule; to govern.

régimen *m* regime, management; diet; (*gr*) rules *pl* of verbs.

registrar *vt* to survey; to inspect, examine; to record, enter in a register:——**se** *vr* to register; to happen.

regla *f* rule, ruler; period.

reglamentar *vt* to regulate.

regocijar *vt* to gladden:——**se** *vr* to rejoice.

regordete *adj* chubby, plump.

regresar *vi* to return, go back.

reguero *m* small rivulet; trickle of spilt liquid; drain, gutter.

regular *vt* to regulate, adjust:—*adj* regular; ordinary.

rehén *m* hostage.

rehuir *vt* to avoid.

rehusar *vt* to refuse, decline.

reimpresión *f* reprint.

reina *f* queen.

reincidir *vi:——* **en** to relapse into, fall back into.

reino *m* kingdom, reign.

reintegrar *vt* to reintegrate, restore: ——**se** *vr* to be reinstated or restored.

reír(se) *vi* (*vr*) to laugh.

reiterar *vt* to reiterate, repeat.

reivindicar *vt* to claim.

reja *f* ploughshare; lattice, grating.

rejoneador *m* mounted bullfighter.

relación *f* relation; relationship; report; account.

relajar *vt* to relax, slacken:——**se** *vr* to relax.

relamerse *vr* to lick one's lips; to relish.

relámpago *m* flash of lightning.

relatar *vt* to relate, tell.

relato *m* story; recital.

relegar *vt* to relegate; to banish, exile.

relente *m* evening dew.

relieve *m* relief; (*fig*) prominence.

relinchar *vi* to neigh.

reliquia *f* residue, remains *pl;* (saintly) relic.

rellano *m* landing (of stairs).

rellenar *vt* to fill up; to stuff.

reloj *m* clock; watch.

relucir *vi* to shine, glitter; to excel, be brilliant.

relumbrar *vi* to sparkle, shine.

remachar *vt* to rivet; (*fig*) to drive home.

remache *m* rivet; clinch; obstinacy.

remanente *m* remainder; (*com*) balance; surplus.

remanso *m* stagnant water; quiet place.

remar *vi* to row.

rematar *vt* to terminate, finish; to sell off cheaply:—*vi* to end.

remedar *vt* to copy, imitate; to mimic.

remediar vt to remedy; to assist, help; to free from danger; to avoid.

remesa f shipment; remittance.

remilgado/da adj prim; affected.

remitente m sender.

remojar vt to steep; to dunk.

remolacha f beet.

remolcar vt to tow.

remordimiento m remorse.

remoto/ta adj remote, distant; far.

remover vt to stir; to move around.

remozar vt to rejuvenate; to renovate.

renacer vi to be born again; to revive.

renacuajo m tadpole.

rendija f crevice, crack, cleft.

rendir vt to subject, subdue:—~se vr to yield; to surrender; to be tired out.

renegar vt to deny; to disown; to detest, abhor:—vi to apostatize; to blaspheme, curse.

renglón m line; item.

reñir vt, vi to wrangle, quarrel; to scold, chide.

renombre m renown.

renovar vt to renew; to renovate; to reform.

renta f income; rent; profit.

reo m offender, criminal.

reparar vt to repair; to consider, observe; to parry:—vi ~ **en** to notice; to pass (at cards).

repartir vt to distribute; to deliver.

repasar vt to revise; to check; to mend.

repente:—de ~ adv suddenly.

repercutir vi to reverberate; to rebound.

repetir vt, vi to repeat.

repiquetear vt to ring merrily.

repisa f pedestal, stand; shelf; windowsill.

repleto/ta adj replete, very full.

replicar vi to reply.

repoblar vt to repopulate; to reafforest.

repollo m cabbage.

reponer vt to replace; to restore:—~se vr to recover lost health or property.

reportaje m report, article.

reposar vi to rest, repose.

repostería f confectioner's (store).

reprender vt to reprimand.

represa f dam; lake.

representar vt to represent; to play on the stage; to look (age).

reprimir vt to repress; to check; to contain.

reprobable adj reprehensible.

reprochar vt to reproach.

repuesto m supply; spare part.

repugnancia f reluctance; repugnance; disgust.

requerir vt to intimate, notify; to request; to require, need; to summon.

requesón m cottage cheese.

requiebro m endearing expression.

res f head of cattle.

resabio m (unpleasant) aftertaste; vicious habit, bad custom.

resaca f surge, surf; (fig) backlash; (fam) hangover.

resaltar vi to rebound; to jut out; to be evident; to stand out.

resbaladizo/za adj slippery.

resbalar(se) vi (vr) to slip, slide.

rescindir vt to rescind, annul.

rescoldo m embers pl, cinders pl.

resecarse vr to dry up.

reseña f review; account.

resentirse vr:—~ **de** to suffer:—~ **con** to resent.

reservar vt to keep; to reserve:—~se vr to preserve oneself; to keep to oneself.

resfriado m cold.

resguardar vt to preserve, defend:—~**se** vr to be on one's guard.

residir vi to reside, dwell.

residuo m residue, remainder.

resistir vt to resist, oppose; to put up with:—vi to resist; to hold out.

resol m glare (of the sun).

resollar vi to wheeze; to take breath.

resolver vt to resolve, decide; to analyse:—~**se** vr to resolve, determine.

resoplar vi to snore; to snort.

resorte m spring.

respaldo m backing; endorsement; back of a seat.

respetar vt to respect; to revere.

respingo m start; jump.

respiradero m vent, breathing hole; rest, repose.

respirar vi to breathe.

resplandecer vi to shine; to glisten.

resplandor m splendor, brilliance.

responder vt to answer:—vi to answer; to correspond:—~ **de** to be responsible for.

responso m prayer for the dead.

respuesta f answer, reply.

resquemor m resentment.

restablecer vt to re-establish:—~**se** vr to recover.

restallar vi to crack; to click.

restar vt to subtract, take away:—vi to be left.

restaurar vt to restore.

restituir vt to restore; to return.

resto m remainder, rest.

restregar vt to scrub, rub.

restringir vt to restrict, limit; to restrain.

resuelto/ta adj resolute, determined; prompt.

resultar vi to be; to turn out; to amount to.

resumir vt to abridge; to summarize.

retahíla f range, series.

retal m remnant.

retar vt to challenge.

retener vt to retain, keep back.

retentiva f memory.

retirar vt to withdraw, retire; to remove:—~**se** vr to retire, retreat; to go to bed.

reto m challenge; threat, menace.

retocar vt to retouch; to mend; to finish off (work).

retoñar vi to sprout.

retorcer vt to twist; to wring.

retozar vi to frisk, skip.

retraído/da adj shy.

retransmitir vt to broadcast; to relay; to retransmit.

retraso m delay; slowness; backwardness; lateness:—(ferro) **el tren ha tenido** ~ the train is overdue or late.

retrato m portrait, effigy.

retrete m lavatory.

retribuir vt to repay.

retroceder vi to go backwards, fly back; to back down.

retrovisor m rear-view mirror.

retumbar vi to resound, jingle.

reúma f rheumatism.

reunir vt to reunite; to unite:—~**se** vr to gather, meet.

revancha f revenge.

revelar vt to reveal; to develop (photographs).

reventar *vi* to burst, crack; to explode; to toil, drudge.

reverdecer *vi* to grow green again; to revive.

revés *m* back; wrong side; disappointment, setback.

revisar *vt* to revise, review.

revisor *m* inspector; ticket collector.

revista *f* review, revision; magazine.

revolcarse *vr* to wallow.

revolotear *vi* to flutter.

revoltijo *m* confusion, disorder.

revoltoso/sa *adj* rebellious, unruly.

revolver *vt* to move about; to turn around; to mess up; to revolve; ~**se** *vr* to turn round; to change (of the weather).

revuelta *f* turn; disturbance, revolt.

rey *m* king; king (in cards or chess).

rezagar *vt* to leave behind; to defer:—~**se** *vr* to remain behind.

rezar *vi* to pray, say one's prayers.

rezumar *vt* to ooze, leak.

ría *f* estuary.

riada *f* flood.

ribera *f* shore, bank.

rico/ca *adj* rich; delicious; lovely; cute.

riego *m* irrigation.

rienda *f* rein of a bridle:—**dar ~ suelta** to give free rein to.

riesgo *m* risk, danger.

rifa *f* raffle, lottery.

rígido/da *adj* rigid, inflexible; severe.

riguroso/sa *adj* rigorous.

rimar *vi* to rhyme.

rímel, rimmel *m* mascara.

riña *f* quarrel, dispute.

rincón *m* (inside) corner.

rinoceronte *m* rhinoceros.

riñón *m* kidney.

río *m* river, stream.

riqueza *f* riches *pl*, wealth.

risa *f* laugh, laughter.

risco *m* steep rock.

ritmo *m* rhythm.

rizo *m* curl; ripple (on water).

robar *vt* to rob; to steal; to break into.

roble *m* oak tree.

robusto/ta *adj* robust, strong.

roca *f* rock.

rociar *vt* to sprinkle; to spray.

rocío *m* dew.

rodaja *f* slice.

rodaje *m* filming:—**en ~** (*auto*) running in.

rodear *vi* to make a detour:—*vt* to surround, enclose.

rodilla *f* knee:—**de ~s** on one's knees.

rodillo *m* roller; rolling pin.

roer *vt* to gnaw; to corrode.

rogar *vt, vi* to ask for; to beg, entreat; to pray.

rojizo/za *adj* reddish.

rojo/ja *adj* red; ruddy.

rol *m* list, roll, catalog; role.

rollo *m* roll; coil.

romería *f* pilgrimage.

romero *m* (*bot*) rosemary.

rompecabezas *m invar* riddle; jigsaw.

romper *vt* to break; to tear up; to wear out; to break up (land):—*vi* to break (of waves); to break through.

ron *m* rum.

roña *f* scab, mange; grime; rust.

roncar *vi* to snore; to roar.

ronco/ca adj hoarse; husky; raucous.
ronda f night patrol; round (of drinks, cards, etc).
ronronear vi to purr.
ropa f clothes pl; clothing; dress.
rosa f rose; birthmark.
rosado/da adj pink; rosy.
rosca f thread (of a screw); coil, spiral.
rosquilla f doughnut.
rostro m face.
roto/ta adj broken, destroyed; debauched.
rótula f kneecap; ball-and-socket joint.
rotulador m felt-tip pen.
rótulo m inscription; label, ticket; placard, poster.
rotundo/da adj round; emphatic.
rozar vt to rub; to chafe; to nibble (the grass); to scrape; to touch lightly.
rubio/bia adj fair-haired, blond(e):—m/f blond/blonde.
rudimento m principle; beginning:—~s mpl rudiments pl.

rudo/da adj rough, coarse; plain, simple; stupid.
rueda f wheel; circle; slice, round.
ruedo m rotation; border, selvage; arena, bullring.
ruego m request, entreaty.
rufián m pimp, pander; lout.
rugir vi to roar, bellow.
rugoso/sa adj wrinkled.
ruido m noise, sound; din, row; fuss.
ruin adj mean, despicable; stingy.
ruina f ruin, collapse; downfall, destruction:—~s fpl ruins pl.
ruiseñor m nightingale.
rulo m curler.
rumbo m (mar) course, bearing; road, route, way; course of events, pomp, ostentation.
rumboso/sa adj generous, lavish.
rústico/ca adj rustic:—m/f peasant.
ruta f route, itinerary.
rutina f routine; habit.

S

sábado m Saturday; (jewish) Sabbath.
sábana f sheet; altar cloth.
sabañón m chilblain.
sabelotodo m/f invar know-all.
saber vt to know; to be able to; to find out, learn; to experience:—vi ~ a to taste of:—m learning, knowledge.
sabiduría f learning, knowledge; wisdom.
sabio/bia adj sage, wise:—m/f sage, wise person.
sablazo m sword wound; (fam) sponging, scrounging.

sabor m taste, savor, flavor.
sabroso/sa adj tasty, delicious; pleasant; salted.
sabueso m bloodhound.
sacacorchos m invar corkscrew.
sacapuntas m invar pencil sharpener.
sacar vt to take out, extract; to get out; to bring out (a book etc); to take off (clothes); to receive, get; (dep) to serve.
sacerdote m priest.
saco m bag, sack; jacket.
sacudir vt to shake, jerk; to beat, hit.
sagaz adj shrewd, clever, sagacious.

sagrado/da adj sacred, holy.

sal f salt.

sala f large room; (teat) house, auditorium; public hall; (jur) court; (med) ward.

salado/da adj salted; witty, amusing.

salario m salary.

salchicha f sausage.

salchichón m (salami-type) sausage.

saldo m settlement; balance; remainder:——**s** mpl sale.

salida f exit, way out; leaving, departure; production, output; (com) sale; sales outlet.

saliente adj projecting; rising; (fig) outstanding.

salir vi to go out, leave; to depart, set out; to appear; to turn out, prove:——**se** vr to escape, leak.

salmo m psalm.

salmonete m red mullet.

salmuera f brine.

salón m living room, lounge; public hall.

salpicadero m dashboard.

salpicar vt to sprinkle, splash, spatter.

salsa f sauce.

saltamontes m invar grasshopper.

saltar vt to jump, leap; to skip, miss out:——vi to leap, jump; to bounce; (fig) to explode, blow up.

saltimbanqui m/f acrobat.

salubre adj healthy.

salud f health.

saludar vt to greet; (mil) to salute.

salvado m bran.

salvaguardar vt to safeguard.

salvaje adj savage.

salvar vt to save; to rescue; to overcome; to cross, jump across; to cover, travel; to exclude:——**se** vr to escape from danger.

salvavidas adj invar:——**bote/chaleco/cinturón** ~ lifeboat/life preserver/life belt.

salvia f (bot) sage.

salvo/va adj safe:——adv save, except (for).

San adj Saint (as title).

saña f anger, passion.

sanar vt, vi to heal.

sandalia f sandal.

sandez f folly, stupidity.

sandía f watermelon.

sangre f blood:——**a** ~ **fria** in cold blood:——**a** ~ **y fuego** without mercy.

sangriento/ta adj bloody, bloodstained, gory; cruel.

sano/na adj healthy, fit; intact, sound.

sapo m toad.

saquear vt to ransack, plunder.

sarampión m measles.

sarna f itch; mange; (med) scabies.

sarpullido m (med) rash.

sarro m (med) tartar.

sarta f string of beads, etc; string, row.

sartén f frying pan.

sastre m tailor.

satisfacer vt to satisfy; to pay (a debt):——**se** vr to satisfy oneself; to take revenge.

sauce m (bot) willow.

saúco m (bot) elder.

savia f sap.

sazonar vt to ripen; to season.

se pn reflexivo himself; herself; itself; yourself; themselves; yourselves; each other; one another; oneself.

se(p)tiembre m September.

sebo m fat, grease.

secano m dry, arable land which is not irrigated.

secar vt to dry:—**~se** vr to dry up; to dry oneself.

seco/ca adj dry; dried up; skinny; cold (of character); brusque, sharp; bare.

secuestrar vt to kidnap; to confiscate.

sed f thirst:—**tener ~** to be thirsty.

seda f silk.

sedal m fishing line.

sede f see; seat; headquarters.

sediento/ta adj thirsty; eager.

seducir vt to seduce; to bribe; to charm, attract.

segar vt to reap, harvest; to mow.

seguido/da adj continuous; successive; long-lasting:—adv straight (on); after; often.

seguir vt to follow, pursue; to continue:—vi to follow; to carry on:—**~se** vr to follow, ensue.

según prep according to.

segundo/da adj second:—m second (of time).

seguro/ra adj safe, secure; sure, certain; firm, constant:—adv for sure:—m safety device; insurance; safety, certainty.

seis adj, m six; sixth.

seiscientos/tas adj six hundred.

seísmo m earthquake.

sello m seal; stamp.

seleccionar vt to select, chose, pick.

selectivo adj selective.

selva f forest.

semáforo m traffic lights pl; signal.

semana f week.

sembrar vt to sow; to sprinkle, scatter.

semejante adj similar, like:—m fellow man.

semestral adj half-yearly.

semilla f seed.

sémola f semolina.

sempiterno/na adj everlasting.

seña f sign, mark, token; signal; (mil) password:—**~s** fpl address.

señal f sign, token; symptom; signal; landmark; (com) deposit.

señalar vt to stamp, mark; to signpost; to point out; to fix, settle:—**~se** vr to distinguish oneself, excel.

sencillo/lla adj simple; natural; unaffected; single.

senda f, **sendero** m path, trail.

seno m bosom; lap; womb; hole, cavity; sinus:—**~s** mpl breasts pl.

señor m man; gentleman; master; Mr; sir.

señora f lady; Mrs; madam; wife.

señorita f Miss; young lady.

señorito m young gentleman; rich kid.

sensación f sensation, feeling; sense.

sensato/ta adj sensible.

sensible adj sensitive; perceptible, appreciable; regrettable.

sentado/da adj sitting, seated; sedate; settled.

sentar vt to seat; (fig) to establish:—vi to suit:—**~se** vr to sit down.

sentido m sense; feeling; meaning:—**~/da** adj regrettable; sensitive.

sentir vt to feel; to hear; to perceive; to sense; to suffer from; to regret, be sorry for:—**~se** vr to feel; to feel pain; to crack (of walls, etc):—m opinion, judgement.

separar vt to separate:—**~se** vr to separate; to come away, come apart; to withdraw.

septentrional adj north, northern.

séptimo/ma adj seventh.

sepultar vt to bury, inter.

sequía f dryness; thirst; drought.

séquito m retinue, suite; group of supporters; aftermath.

ser *vi* to be; to exist:—**~ de** to come from; to be made of; to belong to:—*m* being.

serenata *f* (*mus*) serenade.

sereno *m* night watchman:—**~/na** *adj* serene, calm, quiet.

serie *f* series; sequence.

serio/ria *adj* serious; grave; reliable.

serpentear *vi* to wriggle; to wind, snake.

serpiente *f* snake.

serranía *f* range of mountains; mountainous country.

serrar *vt* to saw.

serrín *m* sawdust.

servicial *adj* helpful, obliging.

servilleta *f* napkin, serviette.

servir *vt* to serve; to wait on:—*vi* to serve; to be of use; to be in service:—**~se** *vr* to serve oneself, help oneself; to deign, please; to make use of.

sesenta *m, adj* sixty; sixtieth.

seso *m* brain.

sestear *vi* to take a nap.

seta *f* mushroom.

setecientos/tas *adj* seven hundred.

setenta *adj, m* seventy.

setiembre *m* September.

seto *m* fence; enclosure; hedge.

severo/ra *adj* severe, strict; grave, serious.

sexto/ta *adj, m* sixth.

si *conj* whether; if.

sí *adv* yes; certainly; indeed:—*pn* oneself; himself; herself; itself; yourself; themselves; yourselves; each other; one another.

siderúrgico/ca *adj* iron and steel *compd*:—*f* **la siderúrgica** the iron and steel industry.

sidra *f* cider.

siempre *adv* always; all the time; ever; still:—**~ jamás** for ever and ever.

sien *f* temple (of the head).

sierra *f* saw; range of mountains.

siete *adj, m* seven.

sigilo *m* secrecy.

sigla *f* acronym; abbreviation.

siglo *m* century.

significado *m* significance, meaning.

significativo/va *adj* significant.

signo *m* sign, mark.

siguiente *adj* following, successive, next.

silbar *vt, vi* to hiss; to whistle.

silencio *m* silence:—**¡~!** silence! quiet!

silla *f* chair; saddle; seat:—**~ de ruedas** wheelchair.

silo *m* silo; underground wheat store.

silueta *f* silhouette; outline; figure.

silvestre *adj* wild, uncultivated; rustic.

símbolo *m* symbol.

simio *m* ape.

simpático/ca *adj* pleasant; kind.

simpatizar *vi*:—**~ con** to get on well with.

simular *vt* to simulate.

sin *prep* without.

sindicato *m* trade(s) union; syndicate.

sinfín *m*:—**un ~ de** a great many.

singular *adj* singular; exceptional; peculiar, odd.

siniestro/tra *adj* left; (*fig*) sinister:—*m* accident.

sino *conj* but; except; save; only:—*m* fate.

sinsabor *m* unpleasantness; disgust.

sinuoso/sa *adj* sinuous; wavy; winding.

sinvergüenza *m/f* rogue.

siquiera *conj* even if, even though:—*adv* at least.

sitio *m* place; spot; site, location; room, space; job, post; (*mil*) siege, blockade.

situar *vt* to place, situate; to invest:—**~se** *vr* to be established in place or business.

smoking *m* tuxedo.

sobaco *m* armpit, armhole.

sobar *vt* to handle, soften; to knead; to massage, rub hard; to rumple (clothes); to fondle.

soberbia *f* pride, haughtiness; magnificence.

sobornar *vt* to suborn, bribe.

sobrante *adj* remaining:—*m* surplus, remainder.

sobrar *vt* to exceed, surpass:—*vi* to be more than enough; to remain, be left.

sobre *prep* on; on top of; above, over; more than; besides:—*m* envelope.

sobrecargar *vt* to overload; (*com*) to surcharge.

sobredosis *f* overdose.

sobreentender *vt* to deduce:—**~se** *vr* **se sobreentiende que** . . . it is implied that.

sobrellevar *vt* to carry; to tolerate.

sobremesa *f*:—**de ~** immediately after dinner.

sobrenombre *m* nickname.

sobrepasar *vt* to surpass.

sobresalto *m* start, scare; sudden shock.

sobrevenir *vi* to happen, come unexpectedly; to supervene.

sobrevivir *vi* to survive.

sobrevolar *vt* to fly over.

sobrino/na *m/f* nephew/niece.

sobrio/ria *adj* sober, frugal.

socarrón/ona *adj* sarcastic; ironic(al).

socavar *vt* to undermine.

socio/cia *m/f* associate, member.

socorrista *m/f* first aider; lifeguard.

socorro *m* help, aid, assistance, relief.

soez *adj* dirty, obscene.

sofá *m* sofa.

soga *f* rope.

soja *f* soya.

sol *m* sun; sunshine, sunlight.

solamente *adv* only, solely.

solapa *f* lapel.

solar *m* building site; piece of land; ancestral home of a family:—*adj* solar.

soldado *m/f* soldier:—**~ raso** private.

soldar *vt* to solder; to weld; to unite.

soledad *f* solitude; loneliness.

soler *vi* to be accustomed to, be in the habit of.

solicitar *vt* to ask for, seek; to apply for (a job); to canvass for; to chase after, pursue.

solidario/ria *adj* joint; mutually binding.

soliloquio *m* soliloquy, monologue.

solista *m/f* soloist.

solitario/ria *adj* solitary:—*m* solitaire:—*m/f* hermit.

sollozar *vi* to sob.

solo *m* (*mus*) solo:—**~la** *adj* alone, single:—**a solas** alone, unaided.

sólo *adv* only.

solomillo *m* sirloin.

soltar *vt* to untie, loosen; to set free, let out:—**~se** *vr* to get loose; to come undone.

soltero/ra *m/f* bachelor/single woman:—*adj* single, unmarried.

soltura *f* looseness, slackness; agility, activity; fluency.

solucionar vt to solve; to resolve.

sombra f shade; shadow.

sombrero m hat.

sombrilla f parasol.

sombrío/bría adj shady, gloomy; sad.

somero/ra adj superficial.

someter vt to conquer (a country); to subject to one's will; to submit; to subdue:—**~se** vr to give in, submit.

somnífero m sleeping pill.

sonar vt to ring:—vi to sound; to make a noise; to be pronounced; to be talked of; to sound familiar:—**~se** vr to blow one's nose.

soñar vt, vi to dream.

sondeo m sounding; boring; (fig) poll.

soneto m sonnet.

sonido m sound.

sonreír(se) vi (vr) to smile.

sonrisa f smile.

sonrojarse vr to blush.

sonsacar vt to wheedle; to cajole; to obtain by cunning.

sopa f soup; sop.

sopetón m:—**de ~** suddenly.

soplar vt to blow away, blow off; to blow up, inflate:—vi to blow, puff.

soplón/ona m/f telltale.

soportal m portico.

soportar vt to suffer, tolerate; to support.

sorber vt to sip; to inhale; to swallow; to absorb.

sorbete m sherbet; iced fruit drink.

sordo/da adj deaf; silent, quiet:—m/f deaf person.

sorprender vt to surprise.

sorteo m draw; raffle.

sortija f ring; ringlet, curl.

sortilegio m sorcery.

sosegar vt to appease, calm:—vi to rest.

soso/sa adj insipid, tasteless; dull.

sospechar vt to suspect.

sostén m support; bra; sustenance.

sostener vt to sustain, maintain:— **~se** vr to support or maintain oneself; to contrive, remain.

sota f knave (at cards).

sótano m basement, cellar.

su pn his, her, its, one's; their; your.

suave adj smooth, soft; delicate; gentle; mild, meek.

subalterno/na adj secondary; auxiliary.

subasta f auction.

subcampeón/ona m/f runner-up.

subestimar vt to underestimate.

subir vt, vi to raise, lift up; to go up; to climb, ascend, mount; to increase, swell; to get in, get on, board; to rise (in price).

súbito/ta adj sudden, hasty; unforeseen.

sublevar vt to excite (a rebellion); to incite (a revolt):—**~se** vr to revolt.

submarino/na adj underwater:—m submarine.

subrayar vt to underline.

subsanar vt to excuse; to mend, repair; to overcome.

subsidio m subsidy, aid; benefit, allowance.

su(b)stancia f substance.

su(b)straer vt to remove; (mat) to subtract:—**~se** vr to avoid; to withdraw.

subterráneo/nea adj subterranean; underground:—m underground passage; (ferro) underground (railway).

suburbio m slum quarter; suburbs pl.

subvencionar vt to subsidize.

sucedáneo/nea adj substitute:—m substitute (food).

suceder vt to succeed, inherit:—vi to happen.

suceso m event; incident.

sucesor/ra m/f successor; heir.

sucio/cia adj dirty, filthy; obscene; dishonest.

sucursal f branch (office).

sudar vt, vi to sweat.

sudeste adj southeast, southeastern:—m southeast.

sudoeste adj southwest, southwestern:—m southwest.

suegra f mother-in-law.

suegro m father-in-law.

suela f sole of the shoe.

sueldo m wages pl, salary.

suelo m ground; floor; soil, surface.

suelto/ta adj loose; free; detached; swift:—m loose change.

sueño m sleep; dream.

suero m (med) serum; whey.

suerte f fate, destiny, chance, lot, fortune, good luck; kind, sort.

sufrir vt to suffer; to bear, put up with; to support.

sugerir vt to suggest.

sujetador m fastener; bra.

sujetar vt to fasten, hold down; to subdue; to subject:—~se vr to subject oneself.

sujeto/ta adj fastened, secure; subject, liable:—m subject; individual.

sumamente adv extremely.

sumar vt to add, add up; to collect, gather:—vi to add up.

sumergir vt to submerge, sink; to immerse.

sumidero m sewer, drain.

suministrar vt to supply, furnish.

sumiso/sa adj submissive, docile.

sumo/ma adj great, extreme; highest, greatest:—**a lo ~** at most.

súper f four-star (gas).

superar vt to surpass; to overcome; to exceed, go beyond.

superficial adj superficial; shallow.

superficie f surface; area.

superintendente m/f superintendent, supervisor; floorwalker.

superior adj superior; upper; higher; better:—m/f superior.

supermercado m supermarket.

superviviente m/f survivor:—adj surviving.

suplente m/f substitute.

suplicar vt to beg (for), plead (for); to beg; to plead with.

suplicio m torture.

suplir vt to supply; to make good, make up for; to replace.

suponer vt to suppose:—vi to have authority.

suprimir vt to suppress; to abolish; to remove; to delete.

supuesto m assumption:—~/ta adj supposed:—~ **que** conj since, granted that.

sur adj south, southern:—m south; south wind.

surco m furrow; groove.

surgir vi to emerge; to crop up.

surtido m assortment, supply.

surtir vt to supply, furnish, provide:—vi to spout, spurt.

suscitar vt to excite, stir up.

susodicho/cha adj above-mentioned.

suspender vt to suspend, hang up; to stop; to fail (an exam etc).

suspicaz adj suspicious, mistrustful.

suspirar vi to sigh.

sustentar vt to sustain; to support, nourish.

susto m fright, scare.

sustraer vt to take away; to subtract.

susurrar vi to whisper; to murmur; to rustle:—**~se** vr to be whispered about.

sutil adj subtle; thin; delicate; very soft; keen, observant.

suyo/ya adj his; hers; theirs; one's; his; her; its own; one's own; their own:—**de ~** per se:—**los ~s** mpl his own, near friends, relations, family, supporters.

T

tabaco m tobacco; (fam) cigarettes pl.

tabique m thin wall; partition wall.

tabla f board; shelf; plank; slab; index of a book; bed of earth in a garden.

tablero m plank, board; chessboard; dashboard; bulletin board; gambling den.

taburete m stool.

tacaño/ña adj mean, stingy; crafty.

tachar vt to find fault with; to erase.

tachuela f tack, nail.

tácito/ta adj tacit, silent; implied.

taco m stopper, plug; heel (of a shoe); wad; book of coupons; billiard cue.

tacón m heel.

tacto m touch, feeling; tact.

tahona f bakery.

taimado/da adj sly, cunning, crafty.

tajo m cut, incision; cleft, sheer drop; working area; chopping block.

tal adj such:—**con ~ que** provided that:—**no hay ~** no such thing.

taladro m drill; borer, gimlet.

talante m mood; appearance; aspect; will.

talar vt to fell (trees); to desolate.

talega f, **talego** m bag; bagful.

talla f raised work; sculpture; stature, size; measure (of anything); hand, draw, turn (at cards).

tallar vt to cut, chop; to carve in wood; to engrave; to measure.

taller m workshop, laboratory.

tallo m shoot, sprout.

talón m heel; receipt; cheque.

tamaño m size, shape, bulk.

tambalearse vr to stagger, waver.

también adv also, as well; likewise; besides.

tambor m drum; drummer; eardrum.

tamiz m fine sieve.

tampoco adv neither, nor.

tan adv so.

tanto m certain sum or quantity; point; goal:—**~/ta** adj so much, as much; very great:—adv so much, as much; so long, as long.

tapar vt to stop up, cover; to conceal, hide.

tapia f wall.

tapicería f tapestry; upholstery; upholsterer's (store).

tapiz m tapestry; carpet.

tapón m cork, plug, bung.

taquigrafía f shorthand.

taquilla f booking office; takings pl.

tardar vi to delay; to take a long time; to be late.

tarde f afternoon; evening:—adv late.

tarea f task.

tarima f platform; step.

tarjeta f card; visiting card:—**~ postal** postcard.

tarro *m* pot.

tarta *f* cake.

tartamudear *vi* to stutter, stammer.

tarugo *m* wooden peg or pin.

tasar *vt* to appraise, value.

tatarabuelo/la *m/f* great-great-grand-father/mother.

tataranieto/ta *m/f* great-great-grand-son/daughter.

tatuaje *m* tattoo; tattooing.

taurino/na *adj* bullfighting *compd*.

taza *f* cup; basin of a fountain.

te *pn* you.

té *m* (*bot*) tea.

teatro *m* theater, playhouse.

tebeo *m* comic.

techo *m* roof; ceiling.

tecla *f* key (of an organ, piano, etc).

técnico/ca *adj* technical.

tedio *m* boredom; dislike, abhor-rence.

tejado *m* roof covered with tiles.

tejer *vt* to weave.

tejo *m* quoit; yew tree.

tejón *m* badger.

tela *f* cloth; material.

telaraña *f* cobweb.

telefax *m invar* fax; fax (machine).

televisor *m* television set.

telón *m* curtain, drape.

tema *m* theme.

temblar *vi* to tremble.

temer *vt* to fear, doubt:—*vi* to be afraid.

temerario/ria *adj* rash.

temible *adj* dreadful, terrible.

témpano *m* ice-floe.

templado/da *adj* temperate, tem-pered.

templar *vt* to temper, moderate, cool; to tune:—**~se** *vr* to be mod-erate.

temple *m* temperature; tempera; tem-perament; tuning:—**al ~** painted in distemper.

temporada *f* time, season; epoch, period.

temprano/na *adj* early, anticipated:—*adv* early; very early, prematurely.

tenaz *adj* tenacious; stubborn.

tenaza(s) *f* (*pl*) tongs *pl*, pincers *pl*.

tender *vt* to stretch out; to expand; to extend; to hang out; to lay:—**~se** *vr* to stretch oneself out.

tendero/ra *m/f* shop-keeper.

tendón *m* tendon, sinew.

tenebroso/sa *adj* dark, obscure.

tenedor *m* holder, keeper, tenant; fork.

tener *vt* to have; to take; to hold; to possess:—**~se** *vr* to stand upright; to stop, halt; to resist; to adhere.

tenia *f* tapeworm.

teñir *vt* to tinge, dye.

tensar *vt* to tauten; to draw.

tentar *vt* to touch; to try; to tempt; to attempt.

tentempié *m* (*fam*) snack.

tenue *adj* thin; tenuous, slender.

terapia *f* therapy.

tercer(o)/ra *adj* third:—*m* (*jur*) third party.

tercio/cia *adj* third:—*m* third part.

terciopelo *m* velvet.

terco/ca *adj* obstinate.

tergiversar *vt* to distort.

terminante *adj* decisive; categorical.

terminar *vt* to finish; to end; to ter-minate:—*vi* to end; to stop.

termo *m* flask.

ternero/ra *m/f* calf; veal; heifer.

ternilla *f* gristle.

ternura *f* tenderness.

terrado *m* terrace.

terrateniente *m/f* landowner.

terraza *f* balcony; (flat) roof; terrace (in fields).

terremoto *m* earthquake.

terreno/na *adj* earthly, terrestrial:—*m* land, ground, field.

terrón *m* clod of earth; lump:—**~ones** *mpl* landed property.

terror *m* terror, dread.

terso/sa *adj* smooth, glossy.

tertulia *f* club, assembly, circle.

tesorero *m* treasurer.

tesoro *m* treasure; exchequer.

testamento *m* will, testament.

testar *vt*, *vi* to make one's will.

testarudo/da *adj* obstinate.

testificar *vt* to attest, witness.

testigo *m* witness, deponent.

teta *f* breast.

tetera *f* teapot.

tetilla *f* nipple; teat (of a bottle).

tétrico/ca *adj* gloomy, sullen, surly.

tez *f* complexion, hue.

ti *pn* you; yourself.

tía *f* aunt; (fam) bird.

tibio/bia *adj* lukewarm.

tiburón *m* shark.

tiempo *m* time; term; weather; (gr) tense; occasion, opportunity; season.

tienda *f* tent; awning; tilt; shop.

tierno/na *adj* tender.

tierra *f* earth; land, ground; native country.

tieso/sa *adj* stiff, hard, firm; robust; valiant; stubborn.

tiesto *m* earthen pot.

tigre *m* tiger.

tijeras *fpl* scissors *pl*.

tilde *f* tilde (ñ).

tilo *m* lime tree.

timar *vt* to con; to swindle.

timbre *m* stamp; bell; timbre; stamp duty.

tímido/da *adj* timid; cowardly.

timón *m* helm, rudder.

tímpano *m* ear-drum; small drum.

tina *f* tub; bath (tub).

tinieblas *fpl* darkness; shadows *pl*.

tino *m* skill; judgement, prudence.

tinta *f* ink; tint, dye; color.

tinte *m* tint, dye; dry cleaner's.

tinto/ta *adj* dyed:—*m* red wine.

tío *m* uncle; (fam) guy.

tiovivo *m* merry-go-round.

tipico/ca *adj* typical; characteristic; picturesque; traditional; regional.

tipo *m* type; norm; pattern; guy.

tiquismiquis *m invar* fussy person.

tira *f* abundance; strip.

tirachinas *m invar* slingshot.

tirado/da *adj* dirt-cheap; (fam) very easy:—*f* cast; distance; series; edition.

tirano/na *m/f* tyrant.

tirante *m* joist; stay; strap; brace:—*adj* taut, extended, drawn.

tirar *vt* to throw; to pull; to draw; to drop; to tend, aim at:—*vi* to shoot; to pull; to go; to tend to.

tirita *f* (sticking) plaster.

tiritar *vi* to shiver.

títere *m* puppet; ridiculous little fellow.

titubear *vi* to stammer; to stagger; to hesitate.

titular *adj* titular:—*m/f* occupant:—*m* headline:—*vt* to title:—**~se** *vr* to obtain a title.

tiza *f* chalk.

tiznar *vt* to stain; to tarnish.

tizón *m* half-burnt wood.

toalla *f* towel.

tobillo *m* ankle.

tobogán *m* toboggan; roller-coaster; slide.

tocadiscos *m invar* record player.

tocado *m* headdress, headgear.

tocar *vt* to touch; to strike; (*mus*) to play; to ring (a bell):—*vi* to belong; to concern; to knock; to call; to be a duty or obligation.

tocino *m* bacon.

todavía *adv* even; yet, still.

todo/da *adj* all, entire; every:—*pn* everything, all:—*m* whole.

todopoderoso/sa *adj* almighty.

toldo *m* awning; parasol.

tomar *vt* to take; to seize, grasp; to understand; to interpret, perceive; to drink; to acquire:—*vi* to drink; to take.

tomavistas *m invar* cine-camera.

tomillo *m* thyme.

tomo *m* bulk; tome; volume.

tonada *f* tune, melody.

tonel *m* cask, barrel.

tonelada *f* ton; (*mar*) tonnage duty.

tónico/ca *adj* tonic, strengthening:— *m* tonic (water); (*mus*) tonic; (*fig*) keynote.

tontería *f* foolery, nonsense.

tonto/ta *adj* stupid, foolish.

topar *vt* to run into; to find.

topo *m* mole; stumbler.

toquilla *f* head-scarf; shawl.

tórax *m* thorax.

torbellino *m* whirlwind.

torcer *vt* to twist, curve; to turn; to sprain:—**~se** *vr* to bend; to go wrong:—*vi* to turn off.

torcido/da *adj* oblique; crooked.

tordo *m* thrush:—**~/da** *adj* speckled black and white.

torear *vt* to avoid; to tease:—*vi* to fight bulls.

tormenta *f* storm, tempest.

tornar *vt* to return; to restore:—**~se** *vr* to become:—*vi* to return:—**~ a hacer** to do again.

tornasolado *adj* iridescent; shimmering.

torneo *m* tournament.

tornillo *m* screw.

torno *m* winch; revolution.

toro *m* bull.

toronja *f* grapefruit.

torpe *adj* dull, heavy; stupid.

torre *f* tower; turret; steeple.

torrefacto/ta *adj* roasted.

torta *f* cake; (*fam*) slap.

tortilla *f* omelet; pancake.

tortuga *f* tortoise; turtle.

tos *f* cough.

tosco/ca *adj* coarse, ill-bred, clumsy.

toser *vi* to cough.

tostado/da *adj* parched; sunburnt; light-yellow; light-brown.

tostar *vt* to toast, roast.

total *m* whole, totality:—*adj* total, entire:—*adv* in short.

tóxico/ca *adj* toxic:—*m* poison.

trabajar *vt* to work, labor; to persuade; to push:—*vi* to strive.

trabalenguas *m invar* tongue twister.

trabar *vt* to join, unite; to take hold of; to fetter, shackle.

tracción *f* traction:—**~ delantera/ trasera** front-wheel/rear-wheel drive.

traducir *vt* to translate.

traer *vt* to bring, carry; to attract; to persuade; to wear; to cause.

traficar *vi* to trade, do business, deal.

tragaluz *m* skylight.

tragaperras *m* o *f invar* slot machine.

tragar *vt* to swallow; to swallow up.

trago *m* drink; gulp; adversity, misfortune.

traicionar *vt* to betray.

traje *m* suit; dress; costume.

trajinar *vt* to carry:—*vi* to bustle about; to travel around.

trama *f* plot; weft, woof.

tramitar *vt* to transact; to negotiate; to handle.

tramo *m* section; piece of ground; flight of stairs.

tramoya *f* scene, theatrical decoration; trick.

trampa *f* trap, snare; trapdoor; fraud.

trampolín *m* trampoline; diving board.

tramposo/sa *adj* deceitful, swindling.

tranca *f* bar, crossbeam.

trance *m* danger; last stage of life; trance.

tranquilizar *vt* to calm; to reassure.

tranquilo/la *adj* tranquil, calm, quiet.

transbordador *m* ferry.

transbordo *m* transfer:—**hacer ~** to change (trains).

transcurrir *vi* to pass; to turn out.

transeúnte *adj* transitory:—*m* passerby.

transigir *vi* to compromise.

tránsito *m* passage; transition; road, way; change; removal; death of holy or virtuous persons.

transmitir *vt* to transmit; to broadcast.

transparente *adj* transparent; seethrough.

transpirar *vt* to perspire; to transpire.

tranvía *m* tram.

trapo *m* rag, tatter.

tráquea *f* windpipe.

tras *prep* after, behind.

trascender *vi* to smell; to come out:— **~ de** to go beyond.

trasegar *vt* to move about; to decant.

trasero/ra *adj* back:—*m* bottom.

trasfondo *m* background.

trasgredir *vt* to contravene.

trashumante *adj* migrating.

trasladar *vt* to transport; to transfer; to postpone; to transcribe, copy:— **~se** *vr* to move.

trasnochar *vi* to watch, sit up the whole night.

traspasar *vt* to remove, transport; to transfix, pierce; to return; to exceed (the proper bounds); to transfer.

traste *m* fret (of a guitar):—**dar al ~ con algo** to ruin something.

trastero *m* lumber room.

trastienda *f* back room behind a shop.

trasto *m* piece of junk; useless person.

trastornar *vt* to overthrow, overturn; to confuse:—**~se** *vr* to go crazy.

trastrocar *vt* to invert (the order of).

tratar *vt* to traffic, trade; to use; to treat; to handle; to address; **~se** *vr* to treat each other.

trato *m* treatment; manner, address; trade, traffic; conversation; (*com*) agreement.

través *m* (*fig*) reverse:—**de** *o* **al ~** across, crossways:—**a ~ de** *prep* across; over; through.

travesía *f* crossing; cross-street; trajectory; (*mar*) side wind.

travieso/sa *adj* restless, uneasy, fidgety; lively; naughty.

trayecto *m* road; journey, stretch; course.

trazar vt to plan out; to project; to trace.

trébedes fpl trivet, tripod.

trébol m trefoil, clover.

trece adj, m thirteen; thirteenth.

trecho m space, distance of time or place:—**a ~s** at intervals.

tregua f truce, cessation of hostilities.

treinta adj, m thirty.

tremendo/da adj terrible, formidable; awful, grand.

tren m train, retinue; show, ostentation; (ferro) train:—~ **de gran velocidad** fast or express train:—~ **de mercancias** freight train.

trenza f braid (in hair), plaited silk.

trepar vi to climb; to crawl.

tres adj, m three.

tresillo m three-piece suite; (mus) triplet.

tricotar vi to knit.

trigésimo/ma adj, m thirtieth.

trigo m wheat.

trillado/da adj beaten; trite, hackneyed:—**camino ~** common routine.

trinar vi to trill, quaver; to be angry.

trinchar vt to carve, divide (meat).

trineo m sled.

trino m trill.

tripa f gut, intestine:—~**s** fpl guts; tripe.

tripulación f crew.

tripular vt to man; to drive.

tris m invar:—**estar en un ~ de** to be on the point of.

triste adj sad, mournful, melancholy.

triturar vt to reduce to powder; to grind, pound.

triza f:—**hacer ~s** to smash to bits; to tear to shreds.

trocar vt to exchange.

trompa f trumpet; proboscis; large top.

trompazo m heavy blow; accident.

trompeta f trumpet:—m trumpeter.

tronar vi to thunder; to rage.

tronco m trunk; log of wood; stock.

tropel m confused noise; hurry; bustle, confusion; heap; crowd:—**en ~** in a tumultuous and confused way.

tropezar vi to stumble:—vt to meet accidentally.

trotamundos m invar globetrotter.

trotar vi to trot.

trozo m piece.

trucha f trout.

truco m knack; trick.

trueno m thunderclap.

trueque m exchange.

truncar vt to truncate, maim.

tu adj your.

tú pn you.

tubería f pipe; pipeline.

tubo m tube.

tuerca f nut.

tumba f tomb.

tumbar vt to knock down:—vi to fall down:—~**se** vr to lie down to sleep.

tumbona f easy chair; beach chair.

tunda f beating.

tupido/da adj dense.

turbar vt to disturb, trouble:—~**se** vr to be disturbed.

turbio/bia adj muddy; troubled.

turno m turn; shift; opportunity.

turrón m nougat (almond cake).

tutear vt to address as 'tu'.

tutor m guardian, tutor.

tuyo/ya adj yours:—~**s** pl friends and relations of the party addressed.

U

u *conj* or (instead of o before an o or ho).

ubicar *vt* to place:—**~se** to be located.

ufanarse *vr* to boast.

últimamente *adv* lately.

ultimar *vt* to finalize; to finish.

último/ma *adj* last; latest; bottom; top.

ultrajar *vt* to outrage; to despise; to abuse.

ultramar *adj, m* overseas.

ultramarinos *mpl* groceries.

umbral *m* threshold.

un/una *art* a, an:—*adj, m* one (for **uno**).

uña *f* nail; hoof; claw, talon.

ungir *vt* to anoint.

ungüento *m* ointment.

únicamente *adv* only, simply.

único/ca *adj* only; singular, unique.

unidad *f* unity; unit; conformity; union.

unificar *vt* to unite.

unir *vt* to join, unite; to mingle; to bind, tie:—**~se** *vr* to associate.

uno *m* one:—**~/una** *adj* one; sole, only:—**~ a otro** one another:—**~ a ~** one by one:—**a una** jointly together.

untar *vt* to anoint; to grease; (*fam*) to bribe.

urbanidad *f* urbanity, politeness.

urbanismo *m* town planning.

urbanización *f* housing estate.

urdir *vt* to warp; to contrive.

urgencia *f* urgency; emergency; need, necessity.

urinario/ria *adj* urinary:—*m* urinal.

urna *f* urn; ballot box.

urraca *f* magpie.

usado/da *adj* used; experienced; worn.

usar *vt* to use, make use of; to wear:— **~se** *vr* to be used.

usted *pn* you.

usuario *m* user.

útero *m* uterus, womb.

util *adj* useful, profitable:—*m* utility.

utilizar *vt* to use; to make useful.

uva *f* grape.

V

vaca *f* cow; beef.

vacaciones *fpl* vacation; holidays *pl.*

vacante *adj* vacant:—*f* vacancy.

vaciar *vt* to empty, clear; to mold:—*vi* to fall, decrease (of waters):—**~se** *vr* to empty.

vacilar *vi* to hesitate; to falter; to fail.

vacío/cía *adj* void, empty; unoccupied; concave; vain; presumptuous:—*m* vacuum; emptiness.

vacuna *f* vaccine.

vacuno/na *adj* bovine, cow *compd.*

vagar *vi* to rove or loiter about; to wander.

vago/ga *adj* vagrant; restless; vague.

vagón *m* (*ferro*) wagon; carriage:—**~ de mercancias** goods wagon.

vaho *m* steam, vapor.

vaina *f* pod, husk.

vaivén *m* fluctuation, instability; giddiness.

vajilla *f* crockery.

vale *m* OK; promissory note, IOU.

valer *vi* to be valuable; to be deserving; to cost; to be valid; to be worth; to produce; to be current:—*vt* to protect, favor; to be worth; to be equivalent to:—**~se** *vr* to employ, make use of; to have recourse to.

valiente *adj* robust, vigorous; valiant, brave; boasting.

valija *f* suitcase.

valioso/sa *adj* valuable.

valla *f* fence; hurdle; barricade.

valle *m* valley.

valor *m* value; price; validity; force; power; courage, valor.

valorar *vt* to value; to evaluate.

vals *m invar* waltz.

valsar *vi* to waltz

válvula *f* valve.

vanidoso/sa *adj* vain, showy; haughty; conceited.

vano/na *adj* vain; useless, frivolous; arrogant; futile:—**en ~** in vain.

vapor *m* vapor, steam; breath.

vaquero *m* cow-herd:—**~/ra** *adj* belonging to a cowman:—**~s** *mpl* jeans *pl*.

vara *f* rod; pole, staff; stick.

variar *vt* to vary; to modify; to change:—*vi* to vary.

varices *fpl* varicose veins *pl*.

varilla *f* small rod; curtain rod; spindle, pivot.

vario/ria *adj* varied, different; vague; variegated:—**~s** *pl* some; several.

varón *m* man, male.

vasco/ca *adj*, *m/f* Basque.

vasija *f* vessel.

vaso *m* glass; vessel; vase.

vástago *m* bud, shoot; offspring.

vasto/ta *adj* vast, huge.

vaticinar *vt* to divine, foretell.

vatio *m* watt.

vecindad *f* inhabitants of a place; neighborhood.

vecino/na *adj* neighboring; near:—*m* neighbor, inhabitant.

veinte *adj*, *m* twenty.

veintena *f* twentieth part; score.

vejar *vt* to vex; to humiliate.

vejez *f* old age.

vejiga *f* bladder.

vela *f* watch; watchfulness; nightguard; candle; sail:—**hacerse a la ~** to set sail.

velar *vi* to stay awake; to be attentive: —*vt* to guard, watch.

velero/ra *adj* swift-sailing.

veleta *f* weather cock.

vello *m* down; gossamer; short downy hair.

velo *m* veil; pretext.

velocidad *f* speed; velocity.

vena *f* vein.

venado *m* deer; venison.

vencer *vt* to defeat; to conquer, vanquish:—*vi* to win; to expire.

vendaje *m* bandage, dressing for wounds.

vendaval *m* gale.

vender *vt* to sell.

vendimia *f* grape harvest; vintage.

vendimiar *vt* to harvest, gather; to profit from (something).

veneno *m* poison, venom.

venerar *vt* to venerate, worship.

vengar *vt* to revenge, avenge:—**~se** *vr* to take revenge.

venida *f* arrival; return; overflow of a river.

venidero/ra *adj* future:—**~s** *mpl* posterity.

venir vi to come, arrive; to follow, succeed; to happen; to spring from:—**~se** vr to ferment.

venta f sale.

ventaja f advantage.

ventana f window; window shutter; nostril.

ventilar vt to ventilate; to fan; to discuss.

ventisca f, **ventisco** m snowstorm.

ventosidad f flatulence.

ventura f happiness; luck, chance, fortune:—**por ~** by chance.

ver vt to see, look at; to observe; to visit:—vi to understand; to see:—**~se** vr to be seen; to be conspicuous; to find oneself:—**~se con uno** to have a bone to pick with someone:—m sense of sight; appearance.

veraneo m summer vacation.

verano m summer.

veras fpl truth, sincerity:—**de ~** in truth, really.

veraz adj truthful.

verbena f fair; dance.

verdad f truth, veracity; reality; reliability.

verdadero/ra adj true; real; sincere.

verde m, adj green.

verdura f verdure; vegetables pl, greens pl.

vereda f path, trail; sidewalk.

vergüenza f shame; bashfulness; confusion.

verificar vt to check, verify:—**~se** vr to happen.

verruga f wart.

vertedero m sewer, drain; tip.

verter vt to pour; to spill; to empty:—vi to flow.

vértice m vertex, zenith; crown (head).

vertiente f slope; waterfall, cascade.

vertiginoso/sa adj giddy.

vespertino/na adj evening compd.

vestíbulo m vestibule, lobby.

vestido m dress; clothes pl.

vestir vt to put on; to wear; to dress; to adorn; to cloak, disguise:—vi to dress:—**~se** to get dressed.

vestuario m clothes pl; uniform; vestry; changing room.

veta f vein (in mines, wood, etc); streak; grain.

veteado/da adj veined; striped:—m veining; streaks.

veterano/na adj experienced, practiced:—m veteran, old soldier.

veterinaría f veterinary medicine.

veterinario/ria m/f veterinary surgeon.

vez f time; turn; return:—**cada ~** each time:—**una ~** once:—**a veces** sometimes, by turns.

veza f (bot) vetch.

vía f way; road, route; mode, manner, method; (ferro) railway line.

viajante m sales representative.

viajar vi to travel.

víbora f viper.

vibrar vt, vi to vibrate.

vicio m vice.

vid f (bot) vine.

vida f life.

vídeo m video.

vidriera f stained-glass window; shop window.

vidrio m glass.

vieira f scallop.

viejo/ja adj old; ancient, antiquated.

viento m wind; air.

vientre m belly.

viernes m invar Friday:—**V ~ Santo** Good Friday.

viga f beam; girder.

vigente adj in force.

vigésimo/ma *adj, m* twentieth.

vigía *f* (*mar*) lookout:—*m* watchman.

vigilar *vt* to watch over:—*vi* to keep watch.

vil *adj* mean, sordid, low; worthless; infamous; ungrateful.

vilipendiar *vt* to despise, revile.

villancico *m* Christmas carol.

vilo:—**en ~** *adv* in the air; in suspense.

vinagre *m* vinegar.

vincular *vt* to link.

viñedo *m* vineyard.

vino *m* wine:—**~ tinto** red wine.

violar *vt* to rape; to violate; to profane.

violentar *vt* to force.

violento/ta *adj* violent; forced; absurd; embarrassing.

violeta *f* violet.

violón *m* double bass.

virar *vi* to swerve.

viril *adj* virile, manly.

virtud *f* virtue.

viruela *f* smallpox.

visa *f*, **visado** *m* visa.

viscoso/sa *adj* viscous, glutinous.

visillos *mpl* net curtains *pl*.

visión *f* sight, vision; fantasy.

visitar *vt* to visit.

vislumbrar *vt* to catch a glimpse of; to perceive indistinctly.

visón *m* mink.

víspera *f* eve; evening before:—**~s** *pl* vespers.

vista *f* sight, view; vision; eyesight; appearance; looks *pl*; prospect; intention; (*jur*) trial:—*m* customs officer.

vistazo *m* glance.

vistoso/sa *adj* colorful, attractive, lively.

vitalicio/cia *adj* for life.

vitorear *vt* to shout, applaud.

vitrina *f* showcase.

viudo/a *f* widower, widow.

vivaz *adj* lively.

víveres *mpl* provisions.

vivero *m* nursery (for plants); fish farm.

vivienda *f* housing; flat, apartment.

viviente *adj* living.

vivir *vt* to live through; to go through:—*vi* to live; to last.

vivo/va *adj* alive; lively:—**al ~** to the life; very realistically.

vocablo *m* word, term.

vocal *f* vowel:—*m/f* member (of a committee):—*adj* vocal, oral.

vociferar *vt* to shout; to proclaim in a loud voice:—*vi* to yell.

volante *adj* flying:—*m* (*auto*) steering wheel; note; pamphlet; shuttlecock.

volar *vi* to fly; to pass swiftly (of time); to rush, hurry:—*vt* to blow up, explode.

volcán *m* volcano.

volcar *vt* to upset, overturn; to make giddy; to empty out; to exasperate:—**~se** *vr* to tip over.

volquete *m* tipcart; dump truck.

voltear *vt* to turn over; to overturn:—*vi* to roll over, tumble.

voltereta *f* tumble; somersault.

voluble *adj* unpredictable; fickle.

volumen *m* volume; size.

voluntad *f* will, willpower; wish, desire.

volver *vt* to turn (over); to turn upside down; to turn inside out:—*vi* to return, go back:—**~se** *vr* to turn around.

vórtice *m* whirlpool.

vos *pn* you.

vosotros/tras *pn pl* you.

votar *vi* to vow; to vote.

voz *f* voice; shout; rumor; word, term.

vuelo *m* flight; wing; projection of a building; ruffle, frill:—**cazar al ~ to** catch in flight:—**~ chárter** charter flight.

vuelta *f* turn; circuit; return; row of stitches; cuff; change; bend, curve; reverse, other side; return journey.

vuestro/tra *adj* your:—*pn* yours.

WXYZ

xenofobia *f* xenophobia.

xilófono *m* xylophone.

y *conj* and.

ya *adv* already; now; immediately; at once; soon:—*conj* ~ **que** since, seeing that:—**i~!** of course!, sure!

yacimiento *m* deposit.

yate *m* yacht, sailing boat.

yedra *f* ivy.

yegua *f* mare.

yema *f* bud; leaf; yolk:—**~ del dedo** tip of the finger.

yerno *m* son-in-law.

yeso *m* gypsum; plaster:—**~ mate** plaster of Paris.

yo *pn* I:—**~ mismo** I myself.

yodo *m* iodine.

yogur *m* yogurt.

yunque *m* anvil.

yute *m* jute.

zafiro *m* sapphire.

zaguán *m* porch, hall.

zalamero/ra *adj* flattering:—*m/f* wheedler.

zamarra *f* sheepskin (jacket).

zambullirse *vr* to plunge into water, dive.

zampar *vt* to gobble down; to put away hurriedly:—**~se** *vr* to thrust oneself suddenly into any place; to crash, hurtle.

zanahoria *f* carrot.

zancada *f* stride.

zancudo/da *adj* long legged:—*m* mosquito.

zángano *m* drone; idler, slacker.

zanja *f* ditch, trench.

zapata *f* boot:—**~ de freno** (*auto*) brake shoe.

zapatilla *f* slipper; pump (shoe); (*dep*) trainer, training shoe.

zapato *m* shoe.

zarandear *vt* to shake vigorously.

zarcillo *m* earring; tendril.

zarpar *vi* to weigh anchor.

zarza *f* bramble.

zarzuela *f* Spanish light opera.

zócalo *m* plinth, base; baseboard.

zona *f* zone; area, belt.

zopenco/ca *adj* dull, very stupid.

zoquete *m* block; crust of bread; (*fam*) blockhead.

zorro/a *m* fox; cunning person.

zozobrar *vi* (*mar*) to founder; to capsize; (*fig*) to fail; to be anxious.

zueco *m* wooden shoe; clog.

zumbar *vt* to hit:—**~se** *vr* to hit each other:—*vi* to buzz.

zumo *m* juice.

zurcir *vt* to darn; (*fig*) to join, unite; to hatch (lies).

zurdo/da *adj* left; left-handed.

zurrar *vt* (*fam*) to flog, lay into; (*fig*) to criticize harshly.

English–Spanish Dictionary

A

a *art* un, uno, una:—*prep* a, al, en.

abandon *vt* abandonar, dejar.

abash *vt* avergonzar, causar confusión,

abbey *n* abadía *f.*

abbot *n* abad *m.*

abbreviate *vt* abreviar, acortar.

abbreviation *n* abreviatura *f.*

abdicate *vt* abdicar; renunciar.

abdication *n* abdicación *f;* renuncia *f.*

abdomen *n* abdomen, bajo vientre *m.*

abduct *vt* secuestrar.

aberration *n* error *m;* aberración *f.*

abet *vt:*—**to aid and ~** ser cómplice de.

abide *vt* soportar, sufrir.

ability *n* habilidad, capacidad.

ablaze *adj* en llamas.

able *adj* capaz, hábil.

able-bodied *adj* robusto/ta, vigoroso/sa.

ably *adv* con habilidad.

abnormal *adj* anormal.

abnormality *n* anormalidad *f.*

aboard *adv* a bordo.

abode *n* domicilio *m.*

abolish *vt* abolir, anular.

abolition *n* abolición, anulación *f.*

abominable *adj* abominable.

abomination *n* abominación *f.*

aboriginal *adj* aborigen.

abort *vi* abortar.

abortion *n* aborto *m.*

abound *vi* abundar.

about *prep* acerca de, acerca.

above *prep* encima.

aboveboard *adj* legitimo/ma.

abrasion *n* abrasión *f.*

abrasive *adj* abrasivo/va.

abroad *adv* en el extranjero.

abrupt *adj* brusco/ca.

abscess *n* absceso *m.*

abscond *vi* esconderse; huirse.

absence *n* ausencia *f.*

absent *adj* ausente.

absentee *n* ausente *m.*

absent-minded *adj* distraído/da.

absolute *adj* absoluto/ta.

absorb *vt* absorber.

abstain *vi* abstenerse.

abstinence *n* abstinencia *f.*

abstinent *adj* abstinente.

abstract *adj* abstracto/ta:—*n* extracto *m.*

abstraction *n* abstracción *f.*

absurd *adj* absurdo/da.

abundance *n* abundancia *f.*

abundant *adj* abundante.

abuse *vt* abusar; maltratar.

abusive *adj* abusivo/va, ofensivo/va.

abysmal *adj* abismal.

abyss *n* abismo *m.*

acacia *n* acacia *f.*

academic *adj* académico/ca.

academy *n* academia *f.*

accede *vi* acceder.

accelerate *vt* acelerar.

accelerator *n* acelerador *m.*

accent *n* acento *m;* tono *m.*

accentuate *vt* acentuar.

accept *vt* aceptar; admitir.

acceptable *adj* aceptable.

acceptance *n* aceptación *f.*

access *n* acceso *m;* entrada *f.*

accessible *adj* accesible.

accession *n* aumento.

accessory *n* accesorio *m.*

accident n accidente m; casualidad f.
acclaim vt aclamar, aplaudir.
accommodate vt alojar; complacer.
accommodation n alojamiento m.
accompany vt acompañar.
accomplice n cómplice m.
accomplish vt efectuar, completar.
accord n acuerdo, convenio m.
accordance n:—**in ~ with** de acuerdo con.
according prep segun, conforme.
accordion n (mus) acordeón m.
account n cuenta f.
accountability n responsabilidad f.
accountancy n contabilidad f.
accountant n contable, contador m.
accrue vi resultar, provenir.
accumulate vt acumular; amontonar.
accuracy n exactitud f.
accurate adj exacto/ta.
accursed adj maldito/ta.
accuse vt acusar; culpar.
accustom vt acostumbrar.
ache n dolor m:—vi doler.
achieve vt realizar; obtener.
achievement n realización f.
acid adj ácido/da; agrio/ria:—n ácido m.
acknowledge vt reconocer, confesar.
acne n acne m.
acorn n bellota f.
acoustics n acústica f.
acquaint vt informar, avisar.
acquaintance n conocimiento m; conocido m.
acquire vt adquirir.
acquisition n adquisición
acquit vt absolver.
acquittal n absolución f.
acre n acre m.
acrid adj acre.
acrimony n acrimonio m.

across adv de través.
action n acción f.
activate vt activar.
active adj activo/va.
activity n actividad f.
actor n actor m.
actress n actriz f.
actual adj real; efectivo/va.
actuary n actuario de seguros m.
acumen n agudeza f.
acute adj agudo/da; ingenioso/sa.
ad n aviso m.
adage n proverbio m.
adamant adj inflexible.
adapt vt adaptar.
adaptor n adaptador m.
add vt añadir, agregar:—**to ~ up** sumar.
adder n culebra f; víbora f.
addict n drogadicto m.
addiction n dependencia f.
addition n adición f.
additional adj adicional.
additive n aditivo m.
address vt dirigir:—n dirección f.
adenoids npl vegetaciones adenoideas fpl.
adept adj hábil.
adequacy n suficiencia f.
adequate adj adecuado/da; suficiente.
adhere vi adherir.
adhesion n adhesión f.
adhesive adj pegajoso/sa.
adhesiveness n adhesividad f.
adieu adv adiós:—n despedida f.
adjacent adj adyacente, contiguo/gua.
adjective n adjetivo m.
adjoining adj contiguo/gua.
adjournment n prorroga f.
adjudicate vt adjudicar.

adjust *vt* ajustar, acomodar.
adjustable *adj* ajustable.
adjustment *n* ajustamiento *m*.
ad lib *vt* improvisar.
administer *vt* administrar.
administration *n* administración *f*.
administrative *adj* administrativo/va.
admirable *adj* admirable.
admiral *n* almirante *m*.
admire *vt* admirar.
admirer *n* admira/a *m/f*.
admission *adj* entrada *f*.
admit *vt* admitir.
admittance *n* entrada *f*.
admittedly *adj* de acuerdo que.
admonish *vt* amonestar.
ad nauseam *adv* hasta el cansancio.
adolescence *n* adolescencia *f*.
adopt *vt* adoptar.
adorable *adj* adorable.
adore *vt* adorar.
adorn *vt* adornar.
adrift *adv* a la deriva.
adult *adj* adulto/ta.
adulterate *vt* adulterar, corromper.
adulterer *n* adultero *m*.
adultery *n* adulterio *m*.
advance *vt* avanzar; promover.
advantage *n* ventaja *f*.
advantageous *adj* ventajoso/sa.
adventure *n* aventura *f*.
adventurous *adj* intrépido/da.
adverb *n* adverbio *m*.
adversary *n* adversario enemigo *m*.
adversity *n* calamidad *f*; infortunio *m*.
advertise *vt* anunciar.
advertisement *n* aviso *m*.
advice *n* consejo *m*; aviso *m*.
advisability *n* prudencia *f*.
advise *vt* aconsejar; avisar.
advocacy *n* defensa *f*.

advocate *n* abogado *m*; protector *m*.
aerial *n* antena *f*.
aerobics *npl* aerobic *m*.
aerometer *n* areómetro *m*.
aerosol *n* aerosol *m*.
afar *adv* lejos, distante.
affair *n* asunto *m*; negocio *m*.
affect *vt* conmover; afectar.
affection *n* cariño *m*.
affidavit *n* declaración jurada *f*.
affiliate *vt* afiliar.
affiliation *n* afiliación *f*.
affinity *n* afinidad *f*.
affirm *vt* afirmar, declarar.
affirmation *n* afirmación *f*.
affirmative *adj* afirmativo/va.
affix *vt* pegar:—*n* (*gr*) afijo *m*.
afflict *vt* afligir.
affliction *n* aflicción *f*; dolor *m*.
affluence *n* opulencia *f*.
affluent *adj* opulento/ta.
affray *n* asalto *m*; tumulto *m*.
aflame *adv* en llamas.
afloat *adv* flotante, a flote.
afore *prep* antes:—*adv* primero.
afraid *adj* espantado/da.
afresh *adv* de nuevo, otra vez.
after *prep* después.
afterbirth *n* secundinas *fpl*.
after-effects *npl* consecuencias *fpl*.
afterlife *n* vida venidera *f*.
aftermath *n* consecuencias *fpl*.
afternoon *n* tarde *f*.
aftershave *n* aftershave *m*.
aftertaste *n* resabio *m*.
afterwards *adv* después.
again *adv* otra vez.
against *prep* contra.
agate *n* ágata *f*.
age *n* edad *f*; vejez *f*.
agency *n* agencia *f*.
agenda *n* orden del día *m*.

agent n agente m.

aggrandizement n engrandecimiento m.

aggravate vt agravar, exagerar.

aggregate n agregado m.

aggregation n agregación f.

aggression n agresión f.

aggressor n agresor m.

aggrieved adj ofendido/da.

aghast adj horrorizado/da.

agile adj ágil; diestro/tra.

agitate vt agitar.

ago adv pasado.

agonizing adj atngustioso.

agony n agonía f.

agree vt convenir:—vi estar de acuerdo/da.

agreeable adj agradable; amable.

agreement n acuerdo m.

agriculture n agricultura f.

ah! excl ¡ah! ¡ay!

ahead adv más allá, delante de otro.

aid vt ayudar, socorrer.

AIDS n SIDA m.

ail vt afligir, molestar.

ailment n dolencia, indisposición f.

aim vt apuntar aspirar a; intentar.

air n aire m:—vt airear; ventilar.

air balloon n globo aerostático m.

airborne adj aerotransportado/da.

air-conditioning n climatización f.

aircraft n avión m.

air force n fuerzas aéreas fpl.

airline n línea aérea f.

airmail n:—by ~ por avión,

airplane n avión m.

airport n aeropuerto m.

airstrip n pista de aterrizaje f.

airy adj bien ventilado/da.

aisle n nave de una iglesia f.

akin adj parecido/da.

alabaster n alabastro m.

alarm n alarma f:—vt alarmar; inquietar.

alas adv desgraciadamente.

albeit conj aunque.

album n album m.

alchemy n alquimia f.

alcohol n alcohol m.

alcoholic adj alcohólico/ca:—n alcoholizado m.

alcove n nicho m.

alder n aliso m.

ale n cerveza f.

alert adj vigilante; alerto/ta.

algae npl alga f.

algebra n álgebra f.

alias adj alias.

alibi n (law) coartada f.

alien adj ajeno/na.

alienate vt enajenar.

alight vi apearse.

align vt alinear.

alike adj semejante, igual.

alive adj vivo/va, viviente; activo/va.

alkali n álcali m.

alkaline adj alcalino/na.

all adj todo/da.

allay vt aliviar.

allegation n alegación f.

allege vt alegar; declarar.

allegiance n lealtad, fidelidad f.

allegorical adj alegórico/ca.

allegory n alegoría f.

allergy n alergia f.

alley n callejuela f.

alliance n alianza f.

allied adj aliado/da.

alligator n caimán m.

allocate vt repartir.

allot vt asignar.

allow vt conceder; permitir; dar.

allowance n concesión f.

alloy n liga, mezcla f.

allspice n pimienta de Jamaica f.
allude vt aludir.
allure n fascinación f.
allusion n alusión f.
allusive adj alusivo/va.
alluvial adj aluvial.
ally n aliado m:—vt aliar.
almanac n almanaque m.
almighty adj omnipotente, todopoderoso/sa.
almond n almendra f.
almost adv casi; cerca de.
aloft prep arriba.
alone adj solo.
along adv a lo largo.
aloof adv lejos.
alphabet n alfabeto m.
alphabetical adj alfabético/ca.
alpine adj alpino/na.
already adv ya.
also adv también, además.
altar n altar m.
altarpiece n retablo m.
alter vt modificar.
alteration n alteración f.
alternate adj alterno/na:—vt alternar, variar.
alternator n alternador m.
alternative n alternativa f.
although conj aunque, no obstante.
altitude n altitud, altura f.
altogether adv del todo.
aluminum n aluminio m.
always adv siempre, constantemente.
a.m. adv de la mañana.
amalgam n amalgama f.
amalgamate vt vi amalgamar(se).
amaryllis n (bot) amarillas f.
amass vt acumular, amontonar.
amateur n aficionado m.
amateurish adj torpe.
amaze vt asombrar.

amazon n amazona f.
ambassador n embajador m.
amber n ámbar m.
ambidextrous adj ambidextro/tra.
ambiguity n ambigüedad, duda f.
ambiguous adj ambiguo:—~ly adv ambiguamente.
ambition n ambición f.
amble vi andar sin prisa.
ambulance n ambulancia f.
ambush n emboscada f.
amenable adj sensible.
amend vt enmendar.
amendment n enmienda f.
amends npl compensación f.
amenities npl comodidades fpl.
America n América f.
amethyst n amatista f.
amiable adj amable.
amiableness n amabilidad f.
amiably adv amablemente.
amicable adj amigable.
amid(st) prep entre, en medio de.
amiss adv:—**something's** ~ pasa algo malo.
ammonia n amoníaco m.
ammunition n municiones fpl.
amnesia n amnesia f.
amnesty n amnistía f.
amoral adv amoral.
amorous adj amoroso/sa.
amount n importe m; cantidad f.
amp(ere) n amperio m.
amphibian n anfibio m.
amphibious adj anfibio/bia.
amphitheater n anfiteatro m.
ample adj amplio/lia.
ampleness n amplitud, abundancia f.
amplifier n amplificador m
amplify vt ampliar, extender.
amplitude n amplitud, extensión f.
amputate vt amputar.

amuse vt entretener, divertir.
amusement n diversión f.
amusing adj divertido/da.
an art un, uno, una.
anachronism n anacronismo m.
anemia n anemia f.
anesthetic n anestesia f.
analogy n analogía f.
analyse vt analizar.
anarchy n anarquía f.
anatomical adj anatómico/ca.
anatomy n anatomía f
ancestor n:—~s pl antepasados mpl.
ancestral adj hereditario/ria.
ancestry n raza, alcurnia f.
anchor n ancla f:—vi anclar.
anchovy n anchoa f.
ancient adj antiguo.
and conj y, e.
anecdote n anécdota f
anemone n (bot) anémona f
angel n ángel m
anger n cólera f:—vt enojar, irritar.
angle n ángulo m:—vt pescar concana.
anglicism n anglicismo m.
angry adj enojado/da.
anguish n ansia, angustia f
angular adj angular.
animal n adj animal m.
animation n animación f
aniseed n anís m **ankle** n tobillo m.
annals n anales mpl.
annex vt anejar:—n anejo m.
annihilate vt aniquilar.
annihilation n aniquilación f.
anniversary n aniversario m.
annotate vi anotar.
announce vt anunciar, publicar.
announcement n anuncio m.
annoy vt molestar.
annual adj anual.

annunciation n anunciación f
anoint vt untar, ungir.
anomaly n anomalía, irregularidad f.
anon adv más tarde.
anonymity n anonimato m.
anonymous adj anónimo/ma.
anorexia n anorexia f.
another adj otro/tra.
answer vt responder.
answering machine n contestador
    automático m.
ant n hormiga f.
antagonize vt provocar.
antarctic adj antártico/ca.
antelope n antílope m.
antenna npl antena f.
anterior adj anterior, precedente.
anthem n himno m.
anthology n antología f.
anthropology n antropología f
antibiotic n antibiótico m.
antibody n anticuerpo m.
Antichrist n Anticristo m.
anticipate vt anticipar, prevenir.
anticipation n anticipación f.
antidote n antídoto m.
antipodes npl antípodas fpl
antiquarian n anticuario m.
antiquated adj antiguo/gua.
antiquity n antigüedad f.
antiseptic adj antiséptico/ca.
antler n cuerna f.
anvil n yunque m.
anxiety n ansiedad, ansia f.
anxious adj ansioso/sa.
any adj pn cualquier, cualquiera;
    alguno, alguna
apart adv aparte, separadamente.
apartment n departamento m.
apathy n apatía f.
ape n mono m.

apologize vt disculpar.
apology n apología, defensa f.
apostrophe n apóstrofe m.
appall vt espantar, aterrar.
apparatus n aparato m.
apparent adj evidente, aparente.
apparition n aparición, visión f.
appeal vi apelar.
appear vi aparecer.
appease vt aplacar.
append vt anejar.
appendicitis n apendicitis f.
appendix n apéndice m.
appetite n apetito m.
applaud vi aplaudir.
apple n manzana f.
appliance n aparato m.
applicable adj aplicable.
applicant n aspirante, candidato m.
application n aplicación f; solicitud f.
applied adj aplicado/da.
apply vt aplicar.
appoint vt nombrar.
appointment n cita f; nombramiento m.
apportion vt repartir.
appraisal n estimación f.
appraise vt tasar; estimar.
appreciate vt apreciar; agradecer.
apprehend vt arrestar.
apprehension n aprensión f.
apprehensive adj aprensivo/va.
apprentice n aprendiz m.
approach vt vi aproximar(se).
appropriate vt apropiarse de:—adj apropiado/da.
approve (of) vt aprobar.
April n abril m.
apron n delantal m.
apse n ábside m.
apt adj apto/ta, idóneo/nea.

aptitude n aptitud f.
aquarium n acuario m.
Aquarius n Acuario m.
aqueduct n acueducto m.
arable adj labrantío/tía.
arbitrate vt arbitrar.
arcade n galería f.
arch n arco m.
archeology n arqueología f.
archaic adj arcaico/ca.
archbishop n arzobispo m.
archer n arquero m.
architect n arquitecto/ta m/f.
architecture n arquitectura f.
archives npl archivos mpl.
arctic adj ártico/ca.
area n área f; espacio m.
arena n arena f.
arguably adv posiblemente.
argue vi discutir.
argument n argumento m, controversia f.
arid adj árido/da, estéril.
aridity n sequedad f.
Aries n Aries m.
arise vi levantarse.
aristocracy n aristocracia f.
arithmetic n aritmética f.
ark n arca f.
arm n brazo m; arma f.
armament n armamento m.
armchair n sillón m.
armor n armadura f.
armpit n sobaco m.
army n ejercito m.
aroma n aroma m.
around prep alrededor de.
arouse vt despertar; excitar.
arraign vt acusar.
arraignment n acusación f; proceso criminal m.

arrange vt organizar.
arrangement n colocación f; arreglo.
arrant adj consumado/da.
array n serie f.
arrears npl resto de una deuda m; atraso m.
arrest n arresto m:—vt detener, arrestar.
arrival n llegada f.
arrive vi llegar.
arrogance n arrogancia, presunción f.
arrogant adj arrogante, presuntuoso/sa:—~ly adv arrogantemente.
arrogate vt arrogarse.
arrogation n arrogación f.
arrow n flecha f.
arsenal n (mil) arsenal m; (mar) atarazana, armería f.
arsenic n arsénico m.
art n arte m.
arterial adj arterial.
artery n arteria f.
artful adj ingenioso/sa.
art gallery n pinacoteca f.
arthritis n artritis f.
artichoke n alcachofa f.
article n artículo m.
articulate vt articular.
artifice n artificio m.
artillery n artillería f.
artisan n artesano/na m/f.
artist n artista m.
artistry n habilidad f.
artless adj sencillo, simple.
artlessness n sencillez f.
as conj como; mientras.
asbestos n asbesto m.
ascend vi ascender, subir.
ascribe vt atribuir.
ash n (bot) fresno m; ceniza f
ashamed adj avergonzado/da.

ashtray n cenicero m.
Ash Wednesday n miércoles de ceniza m.
ask vt pedir, rogar, preguntar por.
askew adv de lado.
asleep adj dormido/da.
asparagus n espárrago m.
aspect n aspecto m.
aspen n álamo temblón m.
asphalt n asfalto m.
asphyxia n (med) asfixia f.
asphyxiate vt asfixiar.
asphyxiation n asfixia f.
aspiration n aspiración f.
aspire vi aspirar, desear.
aspirin n aspirina f.
ass n asno m:—**she** ~ burra f.
assassin n asesino m.
assassinate vt asesinar.
assault n asalto m.
assemble vt reunir, convocar.
assembly n asamblea f.
assert vt sostener, mantener.
assess vt valorar.
assessment n valoración f.
assets npl bienes mpl.
assign vt asignar.
assimilate vt asimilar.
assist vt asistir, ayudar.
assistance n asistencia f.
assistant n asistente, ayudante m.
associate vt asociar.
association n asociación, sociedad f.
assortment n surtido m.
assume vt asumir; suponer.
assurance n seguro m.
assure vt asegurar.
asterisk n asterisco m.
asthma n asma f.
asthmatic adj asmático/ca.
astonish vt pasmar, sorprender.

astringent adj astringente.
astrologer n astrólogo/ga m/f.
astrology n astrología f.
astronaut n astronauta m/f.
astronomer n astrónomo m.
astronomy n astronomía f.
astute adj astuto/ta.
asylum n asilo, refugio m.
at prep a; en.
atheism n ateísmo m.
atheist n ateo m, atea f.
athlete n atleta m/f.
atlas n atlas m.
atmosphere n atmósfera f.
atom n átomo m.
atomic adj atómico/ca.
atrocious adj atroz.
atrocity n atrocidad, enormidad f.
attach vt adjuntar.
attaché n agregado m.
attack vt atacar; acometer.
attempt vt intentar; probar, experimentar.
attend vt servir; asistir.
attendant n sirviente m.
attention n atención f; cuidado m.
attentive adj atento/ta; cuidadoso/sa.
attest vt atestiguar.
attic n desván m; guardilla f.
attorney n abogado m.
attract vt atraer.
attraction n atracción f; atractivo m.
auburn adj moreno/na, castaño/ña.
auction n subasta f.
auctioneer n subastador/a.
audacious adj audaz.
audible adj perceptible al oído.
audience n audiencia f.
audit n auditoría f.
augment vt aumentar, acrecentar.
August n agosto m.

august adj augusto/a.
aunt n tía f.
au pair n au pair f.
aura n aura f.
auspicious adj propicio/cia.
austere adj austero/ra, severo/ra;
authentic adj auténtico/ca.
authenticate vt autenticar.
authenticity n autenticidad f.
author n autor m; escritor m.
authorization n autorización f.
authorize vt autorizar.
authority n autoridad f.
auto n carro, coche m.
autograph n autógrafo m.
automatic adj automático/ca.
autonomy n autonomía f.
autopsy n autopsia f.
auxiliary adj auxiliar, asistente.
available adj disponible.
avalanche n alud m.
avarice n avaricia f.
avenue n avenida f.
avert vt desviar, apartar.
aviary n pajarera f.
avoid vt evitar, escapar.
await vt aguardar.
awake vt despertar.
award vt otorgar:—n premio m.
aware adj consciente; vigilante.
away adv ausente, fuera.
awe n miedo, temor m.
awful adj tremendo/da; horroroso/sa.
awhile adv un rato, algún tiempo.
awkward adj torpe, rudo/da.
awning n (mar) toldo m.
awry adv oblicuamente, torcidamente.
axe n hacha f.
axiom n axioma m.
axis n eje m.
axle n eje m.

B

baboon n cinocéfalo m.

baby n niño pequeño m.

bachelor n soltero m; bachiller m.

back n dorso m.

backbone n hueso dorsal, espinazo m.

backer n partidario/ria m.

backgammon n juego de chaquete o tablas m.

background n fondo m.

backlash n reacción f.

backpack n mochila f.

backside n trasero m.

backward adj tardo/da, lento/ta.

bacon n tocino m.

bad adj mal, malo.

badge n señal f; símbolo m.

badger n tejón m.

badminton n bádminton m.

baffle vt confundir.

bag n saco m; bolsa f.

baggage n bagaje, equipaje m.

bail n fianza, caución (juratoria) f.

bailiff n alguacil m.

bake vt cocer en horno.

bakery n panadería f.

baking powder n levadura f.

balance n balanza f; equilibrio m.

balcony n balcón m.

bald adj calvo/va.

ball n bola f; pelota f; baile m.

ballad n balada f.

ballerina n bailarina f.

ballet n ballet m.

balloon n globo m.

ballpoint (pen) n bolígrafo m.

balm, balsam n bálsamo m.

balustrade n balaustrada f.

bamboo n bambú m.

ban n prohibición f.

banal adj vulgar.

banana n plátano m.

band n faja f; cuadrilla f.

bandage n venda f.

bandit n bandido/da m/f.

bang n golpe m.

bangle n brazalete m.

banister(s) n(pl) pasamanos m.

banjo n banjo m.

bank n orilla (de rió) f; montón de tierra m; banco m.

bank account n cuenta de banco f.

bankrupt adj insolvente.

banner n bandera f.

banquet n banquete m.

baptize vt bautizar.

bar n bar m; barra f.

barbecue n barbacoa f.

barber n peluquero m.

bare adj desnudo/da, descubierto/ta.

barely adv apenas.

bargain n ganga f.

barge n barcaza f.

bark n corteza f.

barley n cebada f.

barn n granero.

barometer n barómetro m.

baron n barón m.

barracks npl cuartel m.

barrel n barril m.

barren adj estéril, infructuoso/sa.

barrier n barrera f; obstáculo m.

barter vi baratar.

base n fondo m; base f; basa f.

baseball n béisbol m.

basement n sótano m.

basic adj básico/ca.

basin n jofaina, bacía f.

basis n base f; fundamento m.

basket n cesta, canasta f.

basketball n baloncesto m.
bastard n, adj bastardo/da m/f.
bat n murciélago m.
batch n serie f.
bath n baño m.
bathe vt (vi) bañar(se).
bathing suit n traje de baño m.
bathroom n (cuarto de) baño m.
baths npl piscina f.
battery n batería f.
battle n combate m.
bawdy adj indecente.
bay n bahía f; laurel.
bazaar n bazar m.
be vi ser; estar.
beach n playa, orilla f.
beacon n almenara f.
beagle n sabueso m.
beak n pico m.
beam n rayo de luz m; travesaño m.
bean n haba f.
beansprouts npl brotes de soja mpl.
bear vt llevar alguna cosa como carga; sostener; soportar.
bear n oso m.
beard n barba f.
bearer n portador/a m/f.
beast n bestia f.
beat vt golpear; tocar (un tambor).
beatify vt beatificar, santificar.
beautiful adj hermoso/sa, bello.
beauty n hermosura, belleza f.
because conj porque, a causa de.
bed n cama f.
bedroom n dormitorio m.
bee n abeja f.
beech n haya f.
beef n carne de vaca f.
beefburger n hamburguesa f.
beefsteak n bistec m.
beeline n línea recta f.
beer n cerveza f.

beetle n escarabajo m.
befall vi suceder, acontecer.
before adv, prep antes de; delante.
beg vt mendigar.
beggar n mendigo/ga m/f.
begin vt vi comenzar, empezar.
beginning n principio m.
begrudge vt envidiar.
behave vi comportarse.
behind prep detrás; atrás.
beige adj color beige.
belch vi eructar.
belief n fe, creencia f.
believe vt creer.
believer n creyente, fiel.
bell n campana f.
bellows npl fuelle m.
belly n vientre m; panza f.
belong vi pertenecer.
beloved adj querido/da, amado/da.
below adv, prep debajo, inferior; abajo.
belt n cinturón, cinto m.
bench n banco m.
bend vt encorvar, inclinar, plegar.
beneath adv, prep debajo, abajo.
benefit n beneficio m; utilidad f; provecho m.
benevolence n benevolencia f.
benevolent adj benévolo.
benign adj benigno/na.
bent n inclinación f.
bereave vt privar.
bereavement n perdida f.
beret n boina f.
berry n baya f.
beset vt acosar.
beside(s) prep al lado de; excepto.
best adj mejor.
bestial adj bestial, brutal.
bestow vt dar, conferir.
bestseller n bestseller m.

bet n apuesta f.
betray vt traicionar.
betroth vt contraer esponsales.
betting n juego m.
between prep entre, en medio de.
beverage n bebida f.
beware vi guardarse.
bewitch vt encantar, hechizar.
beyond prep más allá.
bias n propensión.
bib n babador m.
Bible n Biblia f.
bibliography n bibliografía f.
bicycle n bicicleta f.
bid vt mandar, ordenar; ofrecer.
biennial adj bienal.
bifocals npl anteojos bifocales mpl.
big adj grande, lleno/na.
bigamist n bígamo/ma m/f.
bigamy n bigamia f.
bigot n fanático/ca m/f.
bike n bici f.
bikini n bikini m.
bile n bilis f.
bilingual adj bilingüe.
bill n pico de ave m; billete.
billboard n cartelera f.
billet n alojamiento m.
billfold n cartera.
billiards npl billar m.
billion n billón f.
bin n cubo de la basura m.
binder n encuadernador/a m/f.
bingo n bingo m.
binoculars npl prismáticos mpl.
biographer n biógrafo/fa m/f.
biography n biografía f.
biological adj biológico/ca.
biology n biología f.
birch n abedul m.
bird n ave f; pájaro m.
birth n nacimiento m.

birthday n cumpleaños m invar.
biscuit n bizcocho m.
bishop n obispo m.
bit n bocado m; pedacito m.
bitch n perra f.
bite vt morder; picar.
bitter adj amargo/ga.
bitumen n betún m.
bizarre adj raro/ra.
blab vi chismear.
black adj negro/gra, oscuro/ra.
blackberry n zarzamora f.
blackbird n mirlo m.
blackboard n pizarra f.
blackmail n chantaje m:—vt chantajear.
blacksmith n herrero m.
bladder n vejiga f.
blade n hoja f; filo m.
blame vt culpar.
blameless adj inocente.
blank adj blanco/ca.
blanket n manta f.
blaspheme vt blasfemar, jurar.
blasphemy n blasfemia f.
blatant adj obvio.
blaze n llama f.
bleed vi, vt sangrar.
blemish vt manchar.
bless vt bendecir.
blessing n bendición f.
blight vt arruinar.
blind adj ciego/ga.
blink vi parpadear.
bliss n felicidad (eterna) f.
blister n ampolla f.
blitz n bombardeo aéreo m.
blizzard n huracán m.
bloated adj hinchado/da.
blob n gota f.
bloc n bloque m.
block n bloque m; obstáculo m.

blockade n bloqueo m:—vt bloquear.
blond adj rubio/bia.
blood n sangre f.
blood group n grupo sanguíneo m.
blood poisoning n envenenamiento de la sangre. m.
blood pressure n presión de sangre f.
blood sausage n morcilla f.
blood test n análisis de sangre m.
blood transfusion n transfusion de sangre f.
bloom n flor f; (also fig):—vi florecer.
blossom n flor f.
blot vt manchar.
blotchy adj muy manchado/da.
blouse n blusa f.
blow vi soplar; sonar.
blubber n grasa de ballena f.
blue adj azul.
bluebell n campanilla f.
blueprint n (fig) anteproyecto m.
blunder n desatino m.
blunt adj obtuso/sa; grosero/ra.
blush n rubor m; sonrojo m.
boar n verraco m:—**wild ~** jabalí m.
board n tabla f; mesa f.
boarder n pensionista m.
boarding card n tarjeta de embarque f.
boast vi jactarse.
boat n barco m.
bobsleigh n bob m.
bodice n corsé m.
body n cuerpo m; individuo m; gremio m.
body-building n culturismo m.
bodyguard n guardaespaldas m.
boil vi hervir; bullir.
bold adj ardiente, valiente; audaz.
bolt n cerrojo m.
bomb n bomba f.
bond n ligadura f; vinculo m.

bondage n esclavitud, servidumbre f.
bone n hueso m.
bonfire n hoguera f.
bonny adj bonito/ta.
bonus n cuota, prima f.
book n libro m.
bookcase n armario para libros m.
bookmarker n registro m.
bookstore n librería f.
boom n trueno m.
boon n presente, regalo m.
booth n barraca, cabaña f.
booty n botín m; presa f; saqueo m.
border n orilla f; borde m.
borderline n frontera f.
bore vt taladrar; barrenar; fastidiar.
boredom n aburrimiento m.
borrow vt pedir prestado/da.
bosom n seno, pecho m.
boss n jefe m; patrón/ona m/f.
botany n botánica f.
botch vt chapuzar.
both adj ambos.
bother vt preocupar; fastidiar.
bottle n botella f.
bottom n fondo m.
bough n brazo del árbol m; ramo m.
boulder n canto rodado m.
bounce vi rebotar.
bound n limite m; salto m.
boundary n limite m; frontera f.
bouquet n ramillete de flores m.
bourgeois adj burgués.
bout n ataque m.
bow vt encorvar, doblar.
bow n arco m.
bowels npl intestinos mpl.
bowl n taza; bola f.
bow tie n pajarita f.
box n caja, cajita f.
boxer n boxeador m.
boxing n boxeo m.

box office n taquilla f.
boy n muchacho m; niño m.
boycott vt boicotear:—n boicot m.
boyfriend n novio m.
bra n sujetador m.
bracelet n brazalete m.
bracket n puntal m; paréntesis m.
brag n jactancia f:—vi jactarse.
braid n pliegue m, trenza f:—vt trenzar.
brain n cerebro m.
brake n freno m:—vt vi frenar.
bran n salvado m.
branch n ramo m; rama f.
brand n marca f.
brandy n coñac m.
brass n latón m.
brassiere n sujetador m.
brave adj bravo/va, valiente.
bravery n valor m.
brawl n pelea f.
brazier n brasero m.
breach n rotura f.
bread n pan m.
breadth n anchura f.
break vt romper; quebrantar.
breakage n rotura f.
breakfast n desayuno m:—vi desayunar.
breast n pecho, seno m.
breastbone n esternón m.
breath n aliento m, respiración f; soplo
de aire m.
breathe vt vi respirar; exhalar.
breathtaking adj pasmoso/sa.
breed n casta, raza f.
breeze n brisa f.
brevity n brevedad, concisión f.
brew vt hacer; tramar, mezclar.
bribe n cohecho, soborno m.
bribery n cohecho, soborno m.
bric-a-brac n baratijas fpl.

brick n ladrillo m.
bricklayer n albañil m.
bride n novia f.
bridegroom n novio m.
bridesmaid n madrina de boda f.
bridge n puente m/f.
brief adj breve, conciso/sa, sucinto/ta.
briefcase n cartera f.
brigade n (mil) brigada f.
bright adj claro/ra, luciente, brillante.
brighten vt pulir, dar lustre.
brilliant adj brillante.
bring vt llevar, traer.
brisk adj vivo/va, alegre, jovial;
fresco/ca.
brisket n pecho (de un animal) m.
briskly adj vigorosamente.
bristle n cerda, seta f:—vi erizarse.
bristly adj cerdoso/sa, lleno/na de
cerdas.
brittle adj quebradizo, frágil.
broach vt comenzar a hablar de.
broad adj ancho.
broadcast n emisión f.
broadcasting n radiodifusión f.
broaden vt vi ensanchar(se).
broadly adv anchamente.
broad-minded adj tolerante.
brocade n brocado m.
broccoli n brécol m.
brochure n folleto m.
broil vt asar a la parrilla.
broken adj roto/ta.
broker n corredor/a m/f.
bronchial adj bronquial.
bronchitis n bronquitis f.
bronze n bronce m.
brooch n broche m.
brook n arroyo m.
broom n hiniesta f; escoba f.
broth n caldo m.
brothel n burdel m.

brother n hermano m.
brother-in-law n cuñado m.
brow n caja f; frente f; cima f.
browbeat vt intimidar.
brown adj moreno/na; castaño/ña.
browse vt ramonear.
bruise vt magullar.
brunette n morena f.
brunt n choque m.
brush n cepillo m; escobilla f.
brusque adj brusco/ca.
Brussels sprout n col de Bruselas f.
brutal adj brutal.
brutality n brutalidad f.
brute n bruto m.
bubble n burbuja f.
bubblegum n chicle m.
bucket n cubo, pozal m.
buckle n hebilla f.
bucolic adj bucólico/ca.
bud n pimpollo, botón m:—vi brotar.
Buddhism n Budismo m.
buddy n compañero m.
budge vi moverse.
budgerigar n periquito m.
budget n presupuesto m.
buff n entusiasta m.
buffalo n búfalo m.
buffet n buffet m.
buffoon n bufón, chocarrero m.
bug n chinche m.
bugle(horn) n trompa de caza f.
build vt edificar; construir.
building n edificio m; construcción f.
bulb n bulbo m; cebolla f.
bulge vi combarse:—n bombeo m.
bulk n masa f; volumen m.
bulky adj grueso/sa, grande.
bull n toro m.
bulldog n dogo m.
bulldozer n aplanadora f.

bullet n bala f.
bullfight n corrida de toros f.
bullfighter n toreo m.
bullfighting n los toros mpl.
bullion n oro o plata en barras m o f.
bullock n novillo capado m.
bullring n plaza de toros f.
bully n valentón m:—vt tiranizar.
bumblebee n abejorro m.
bump n hinchazón f.
bun n bollo m; mono m.
bunch n ramo m.
bundle n fardo m, haz m.
bung n tapón m.
bungalow n bungalow m.
bunk n litera f.
bunker n refugio m; bunker m.
burden n carga f:—vt cargar.
bureau n armario m; escritorio m.
bureaucracy n burocracia f.
burglar n ladrón m.
burial n enterramiento m; exequias fpl.
burial place n cementerio m.
burly adj corpulento/ta, fornido/da.
burn vt quemar, abrasar, incendiar:—vi arder:—n quema dura f.
burner n quemador m; mechero m.
burning adj ardiente.
burrow n conejera f.
bursar n tesorero m.
burse n bolsa, lonja f.
burst vi reventar; abrirse.
bury vt enterrar, sepultar; esconder.
bus n autobús m.
bush n arbusto, espinal m.
busily adv diligentemente, apresuradamente.
business n asunto m; negocios mpl.
businessman n hombre de negocios m.
bust n busto m.

bus-stop n parada de autobuses f.
bustle vi hacer ruido.
busy adj ocupado/da; entrometido/da.
busybody n entrometido m.
but conj pero; mas.
butcher n carnicero m.
butcher's (shop) n carnicería f.
butler n mayordomo m.
butter n mantequilla f.
buttercup n (bot) ranúnculo m.
butterfly n mariposa f.
buttocks npl posaderas fpl.
button n botón m.
buttonhole n ojal m.

buttress n estribo m; apoyo m.
buxom adj frescachona.
buy vt comprar.
buzz n susurro, zumbido m:—vi zumbar.
buzzard n ratonero común m.
buzzer n timbre m.
by prep por; a, en; de; cerca, al lado de.
bypass n carretera de circunvalación f.
by-product n derivado m.
bystander n mirador m.
byte n (comput) byte m.
byword n proverbio, refrán m.

C

cab n taxi m.
cabbage n berza, col f.
cabin n cabaña.
cabinet n consejo á ministros m; gabinete m.
cable n (mar) cable m.
cable car n teleférico m.
cactus n cacto m.
cadaver n cadáver m.
cadet n cadete m.
cadge vt mangar.
cafeteria n cantina f.
cage n jaula f.
cake n bollo m; tortita f.
calculate vt calcular.
calculator n calculadora f.
calendar n calendario m.
calf n ternero m.
call vt llamar, nombrar.
calligraphy n caligrafía f.
callous adj calloso/sa.
calm n calma, tranquilidad.

calorie n caloría f.
Calvinist n calvinista m.
camel n camello m.
cameo n camafeo m.
camera n máquina fotográfica f.
camomile n manzanilla f.
camouflage n camuflaje m.
camp n campo m.
campaign n campana f.
camping n camping m.
campsite n camping m.
can vi poder:—n lata f.
canal n estanque m; canal m.
cancel vt cancelar; anular.
cancer n cáncer m.
Cancer n Cáncer m (signo del zodiaco).
candid adj cándido/da, sencillo/lla.
candle n candela f; vela f.
candlestick n candelero m.
candy n caramelo m.
cane n cana f; bastón m.

cannabis n canabis f.
cannibal n caníbal m.
cannibalism n canibalismo m.
cannon n cañón m.
canoe n canoa f.
canon n canon m; regla f.
can opener n abrelatas m invar.
canopy n dosel, pabellón m.
canter n medio galope m.
canvas n cañamazo m.
canyon n cañón m.
cap n gorra f.
capability n capacidad f.
capable adj capaz.
cape n cabo, promontorio m.
capital adj capital; principal.
capitalism n capitalismo m.
Capitol n Capitolio m.
capitulate vi capitular.
Capricorn n Capricornio m (signo del zodiaco).
capsule n cápsula f.
captain n capitán m.
captivate vt cautivar.
capture n captura f; presa f.
car n coche, carro m; vagón m.
carafe n garrafa f.
caramel n caramelo m.
carat n quilate m.
carbohydrates npl hidratos de carbono mpl.
carcass n cadáver m.
card n naipe m; carta f.
cardboard n cartón m.
cardinal adj cardinal, principal.
care n cuidado m; solicitud f.
career n carrera f.
caress n caricia f.
caretaker n portero m.
cargo n cargamento de navío m.
caricature n caricatura f.
carnal adj carnal; sensual.

carnation n clavel m.
carnival n carnaval m.
carpenter n carpintero m.
carpentry n carpintería f.
carpet n alfombra f.
carrier n portador m.
carrot n zanahoria f.
carry vt llevar, conducir.
cart n carro m; carreta f.
cartilage n cartílago m.
carton n caja f.
cartoon n dibujo animado m.
carve vt cincelar.
carving n escultura f.
case n caja f; maleta f.
cash n dinero contante m.
cashmere n cachemira f.
cask n barril, tonel m.
casserole n cazuela f.
cassette n cassette m.
cassock n sotana f.
castanets npl castañetas fpl.
castaway n réprobo m.
caste n casta f.
castigate vt castigar.
castle n castillo m.
castrate vt castrar.
castration n capadura f.
casual adj casual.
cat n gato m; gata f.
catalog(ue) n catalogo m.
cataract n cascada f; catarata f.
catarrh n catarro m; reuma m.
catastrophe n catástrofe f.
catch vt coger.
catchphrase n lema m.
catechism n catecismo m.
categorize vt clasificar.
category n categoría f.
caterpillar n oruga f.
cathedral n catedral f.
catholic adj, n católico m.

Catholicism n catolicismo m.

cattle n ganado m.

cauliflower n coliflor f.

cause n causa f; razón f; motivo m.

causeway n arrecife m.

caustic adj, n cáustico m.

cauterize vt cauterizar.

caution n prudencia.

cavalry n caballería f.

cave n caverna f.

caviar n caviar m.

cease vt parar, suspender.

cedar n cedro m.

cede vt ceder.

ceiling n techo m.

celebrate vt celebrar.

celery n apio m.

celibacy n celibato m.

cell n celdilla f; célula f; cueva f.

cellar n sótano m.

cellophane n celofán m.

cement n cemento.

cemetery n cementerio m.

cenotaph n cenotafio m.

censor n censor m.

census n censo m.

cent n centavo m.

center n centro m.

centigrade n centígrado m.

centiliter n centilitro m.

centimeter n centímetro m.

centipede n escolopendra f.

central adj central.

centralize vt centralizar.

century n siglo m.

ceramic adj cerámico/ca.

ceremony n ceremonia f.

certain adj cierto/ta, evidente.

certificate n certificado, testimonio m.

certify vt certificar, afirmar.

cervical adj cervical.

chaffinch n pinzón m.

chain n cadena f.

chair n silla f.

chamber n cámara f.

chameleon n camaleón m.

champagne n champaña m.

championship n campeonato m.

chance n ventura, suerte f; oportunidad f.

chancellor n canciller m.

change vt cambiar.

channel n canal m.

chant n canto (llano) m.

chaos n caos m.

chapel n capilla f.

chaplain n capellán m.

chapter n capitulo m.

character n carácter m.

charcoal n carbón de leña m.

charge vt cargar; acusar, imputar.

charity n caridad.

charlatan n charlatán/tana m/f.

charm n encanto m.

charter flight n vuelo charter m.

chauffeur n chófer m.

chauvinist n machista m.

cheap adj barato/ta.

cheat vt engañar, defraudar.

check n cheque m.

checkmate n mate m.

checkout n caja f.

cheek n mejilla f.

cheese n queso m.

chef n jefe de cocina m.

chemical adj químico/ca.

chemist n químico m.

cheroot n puro m.

cherry n cereza f.

cherub n querubín m.

chess n ajedrez m.

chest n pecho m.

chestnut n castaña f.

chew vt mascar, masticar.

chewing gum n chicle m.

chicken n pollo m.

chickenpox n varicela f.

chickpea n garbanzo m.

chief adj principal.

chilblain n sabañón m.

child n niño m; niña f.

childhood n infancia, niñez f.

children npl de **child** niños mpl.

chimney n chimenea f.

chimpanzee n chimpancé m.

chin n barbilla f.

chiropodist n pedicuro m.

chirp vi chirriar.

chlorine n cloro m.

chloroform n cloroformo m.

chocolate n chocolate m.

choice n elección, preferencia f.

choir n coro m.

choke vt sofocar.

cholera n cólera m.

choose vt escoger, elegir.

chop vt tajar, cortar:—n chuleta f.

chore n faena f.

Christ n Cristo m.

christen vt bautizar.

Christianity n cristianismo m; cristiandad f.

Christmas n Navidad f.

chrome n cromo m.

chronicle n crónica f. .

chronological adj cronológico/ca.

chubby adj gordo/da.

chunk n trozo m.

church n iglesia f.

churchyard n cementerio m.

cider n sidra f.

cigar n cigarro m.

cigarette n cigarrillo m.

cinder n carbonilla f.

cinema n cine m.

cinnamon n canela f.

circle n circulo m.

circumcize vt circuncidar.

circumcision n circuncisión f.

circumference n circunferencia f; circuito m.

circumflex n acento circunflejo m.

circumstance n circunstancia.

circus n circo m.

cistern n cisterna f.

cite vt citar.

citizen n ciudadano m.

city n ciudad f.

civic adj cívico/ca.

civil adj civil, cortés.

civilization n civilización f.

clairvoyant n clarividente m/f.

clam n almeja f.

clammy adj viscoso/sa.

clamor n clamor m.

clan n familia, tribu, raza f.

clandestine adj clandestino/na.

clap vt aplaudir.

claret n clarete m.

clarify vt clarificar, aclarar.

clarinet n clarinete m.

clarity n claridad f.

class n clase f; orden f.

classic(al) adj clásico/ca:—n autor clásico m.

classify vt clasificar.

classmate n compañero de clase m.

classroom n aula f.

clause n cláusula f.

claw n garra f.

clay n arcilla f.

clean adj limpio/pia; casto/ta:—vt limpiar.

cleanse vt limpiar, purificar; purgar.

clear adj claro/ra.

clemency n clemencia f.

clement adj clemente, benigno/na.

clergy n clero m.
clerical adj clerical, eclesiástico/ca.
clerk n dependiente m; oficinista m.
clever adj listo/ta; hábil.
client n cliente m/f.
cliff n acantilado m.
climate n clima m.
climax n clímax m.
climb vt escalar, trepar.
cling vi colgar, adherirse.
clinic n clínica f.
clip vt cortar.
clique n camarilla f.
cloak n capa f.
cloakroom n guardarropa m.
clock n reloj m.
clog n zueco m.
cloister n claustro, monasterio m.
close vt cerrar; concluir, terminar.
closet n armario m.
close-up n primer plano m.
clot n grumo m; embolia f.
cloth n paño m.
clothe vt vestir.
clothes npl ropa f.
clothes pin n pinza f.
cloud n nube f.
clout n tortazo m.
clove n clavo m.
clover n trébol m.
clown n payaso m.
coach n autocar, autobús m.
coagulate vt coagular, cuajar.
coal n carbón m.
coalition n coalición, confederación f.
coarse adj basto/ta; grosero/ra.
coast n costa f.
coastguard n guardacostas m invar.
coat n chaqueta f; abrigo m.
coat hanger n percha f.
cobbler n zapatero m.

cobweb n telaraña f.
cocaine n cocaína f.
cock n gallo m; macho m.
cockle n caracol de mar m.
cockpit n cabina f.
cockroach n cucaracha f.
cocktail n cóctel m.
cocoa n coco m; cacao m.
coconut n coco m.
cod n bacalao m.
code n código m.
cod-liver oil n aceite de hígado de bacalao m.
coffee n café m.
coffer n cofre m; caja f.
coffin n ataúd m.
cog n diente (de rueda) m.
cognac n coñac m.
cogwheel n rueda dentada f.
cohabit vi cohabitar.
coherence n coherencia f.
cohesion n coherencia f.
cohesive adj cohesivo.
coil n rollo m.
coin n moneda f.
coincide vi coincidir.
coke n coque m.
colander n colador, pasador m.
cold adj frío/ría.
cold sore n herpes labial m.
coleslaw n ensalada de col f.
colic n cólico m.
collaborate vt cooperar.
collapse vi hundirse.
collapsible adj plegable.
collar n cuello m.
collarbone n clavícula f.
collate vt comparar.
collateral adj colateral.
colleague n colega m.
collect vt recoger; coleccionar.
collection n colección f; compilación f.

college n colegio m.
collide vi chocar.
colloquial adj familiar.
collusion n colusión f.
colon n dos puntos mpl; (med) colon m.
colonel n (mil) coronel m.
colonial adj colonial.
colonize vt colonizar.
colony n colonia f.
color n color m.
colossal adj colosal.
colt n potro m.
column n columna f.
columnist n columnista m.
coma n coma f.
comatose adj comatoso/sa.
comb n peine m:—vt peinar.
combat n combate m.
combination n combinación f.
combine vt combinar.
combustion n combustión f.
come vi venir.
comedy n comedia f.
comet n cometa f.
comfort n confort m.
comfortable adj cómodo/da.
comma n (gr) coma f.
command vt comandar.
commemorate vt conmemorar; celebrar.
commence vt, vi comenzar.
commencement n principio m.
commend vt encomendar.
commensurate adj proporcionado/da.
comment n comentario m.
commentator n comentador m.
commerce n comercio m.
commercial adj comercial.
commiserate vt compadecer.
commission n comisión f.

commit vt cometer.
committee n comité m.
commodity n comodidad f.
common adj común.
commotion n tumulto m.
communicate vt comunicar.
communion n comunión f.
communism n comunismo m.
community n comunidad f.
commute vt conmutar.
compact adj compacto/ta.
compact disc n disco compacto m.
companion n compañero/ra.
company n compañía, sociedad f.
compare vt comparar.
compartment n compartimiento m.
compass n brújula f.
compassion n compasión f.
compatriot n compatriota m.
compensate vt compensar.
compensation n compensación f.
compère n presentador m.
compete vi concurrir.
competent adj competente.
competition n competencia f.
competitor n competidor, rival m.
compilation n compilación f.
complain vi quejarse, lamentarse.
complement n complemento m.
complex adj complejo/ja.
complexion n tez f; aspecto m.
complicate vt complicar.
component adj componente.
compose vt componer.
composer n autor m.
composite adj compuesto/ta.
composition n composición f.
comprehend vt comprender, contener; entender.
compress vt comprimir.
comprise vt comprender.
compromise n compromiso m.

compulsive adj compulsivo/va.
computer n ordenador m.
comrade n camarada.
con vt estafar:—n estafa f.
concave adj cóncavo/va.
conceal vt ocultar, esconder.
concede vt conceder.
conceit n concepto m, capricho m.
conceive vt concebir, comprender.
concentrate vt concentrar.
concept n concepto m.
conception n concepción f.
concern vt concernir, importar.
concert n concierto m.
concession n concesión f; privilegio m.
concise adj conciso/sa.
conclude vt concluir.
conclusion n conclusión.
concord n concordia, armonía f.
concrete n concreto m.
concussion n concusión f.
condemn vt condenar.
condensation n condensación f.
condiment n condimento m; salsa f.
condition vt condicionar.
conditional adj condicional.
condom n condón m.
conduct n conducta f.
conductor n conductor m.
conduit n conducto m.
cone n cono m.
confection n confitura f.
confectioner's (shop) n pastelería f.
conference n conferencia f.
confess vt, vi confesar(se).
confession n confesión f.
confessional n confesionario m.
confetti n confeti m.
confidant n confidente.
confide vt, vi confiar; fiarse.
confidence n confianza, seguridad f.

confident adj cierto/ta, seguro/ra; confiado/da.
confine vt limitar; aprisionar.
confirm vt confirmar; ratificar.
confiscate vt confiscar.
conflagration n conflagración f.
conflict n conflicto m; combate m; pelea f.
conflicting adj contradictorio/ria.
confluence n confluencia f.
conform vt, vi conformar(se).
conformity n conformidad.
confound vt turbar, confundir.
confront vt afrontar; confrontar.
confrontation n enfrentamiento m.
confuse vt confundir.
congeal vt, vi helar, congelar(se).
congenial adj congenial.
congenital adj congénito/ta.
congested adj atestado/da.
congestion n congestión f; acumulación f.
congratulate vt congratular, felicitar.
congratulations npl felicidades fpl.
congratulatory adj congratulatorio/ria.
congregate vt congregar.
congress n congreso m; conferencia f.
congruity n congruencia f.
coniferous adj (bot) conífero/ra.
conjecture n conjetura.
conjugal adj conyugal.
conjugate vt (gr) conjugar.
conjunction n conjunción f.
conjuncture n coyuntura f.
conjure vi conjurar.
con man n timador m.
connect vt juntar, unir.
connection n conexión f.
connivance n connivencia f.
connive vi tolerar.

connoisseur n conocedor/a m/f.
conquer vt conquistar; vencer.
conqueror n vencedor/a, conquistador/a m/f.
conquest n conquista f.
conscience n conciencia f.
consciousness n conciencia f.
conscript n conscripto m.
conscription n reclutamiento m.
consecrate vt consagrar.
consecration n consagración f.
consecutive adj consecutivo/va.
consensus n consenso m.
consent n consentimiento m; aprobación f.
consequence n consecuencia f.
consequent adj consecutivo/va.
conservation n conservación f.
conservative adj conservativo/va.
conservatory n conservatorio m.
conserve vt conservar.
consider vt considerar.
considerable adj considerable.
considerate adj considerado/da.
consideration n consideración f.
consign vt consignar.
consignment n consignación f.
consist vi consistir.
consistency n consistencia f.
consistent adj consistente.
consolation n consolación f; consuelo m.
console vt consolar.
consolidate vt, vi consolidar(se).
consolidation n consolidación f.
consonant adj consonante.
consort n consorte, socio m.
conspicuous adj conspicuo/cua.
conspiracy n conspiración f.
conspirator n conspirador/a m/f.
conspire vi conspirar.
constancy n constancia.

constant adj constante.
constellation n constelación f.
constipated adj estreñido/da.
constituency n junta electoral f.
constituent n constitutivo m.
constitute vt constituir.
constitution n constitución f.
constitutional adj constitucional.
constrict vt constreñir, estrechar.
construct vt construir, edificar.
construction n construcción f.
consul n cónsul m.
consulate, consulship n consulado m.
consult vt, vi consultar(se).
consultation n consulta f.
consume vt consumir.
consumer n consumidor/a m/f.
consumption n consumo m.
contact n contacto m.
contact lenses npl lentes de contacto mpl.
contagious adj contagioso/sa.
contain vt contener.
container n recipiente m.
contaminate vt contaminar.
contamination n contaminación f.
contemplate vt contemplar.
contemplation n contemplación f.
contempt n desprecio, desdén m.
contend vi contender.
content adj contento/ta, satisfecho/cha.
contention n contención, altercación f.
contest vt contestar, disputar, litigar.
contestant n concursante/ta m/f.
context n contexto m.
continent adj continente.
contingency n contingencia f.
contingent n contingente m; cuota f.
continue vt continuar.

contort vt torcer.

contortion n contorsión f.

contour n contorno m.

contraband n contrabando m.

contraception n contracepción f.

contraceptive n anticonceptivo m.

contract vt contraer; abreviar; contratar.

contraction n contracción f; abreviatura f.

contradict vt contradecir.

contradiction n contradicción, oposición f.

contraption n artilugio m.

contrary adj contrario/ria, opuesto/ta.

contrast n contraste m.

contrasting adj opuesto/ta.

contributary adj contributario/ria.

contribute vt contribuir, ayudar.

contrive vt inventar, trazar.

control n control m; inspección f:—vt controlar; manejar; restringir; gobernar.

controversial adj polémico/ca.

controversy n controversia f.

conurbation n urbanización f.

convalesce vi convalecer.

convalescence n convalecencia f.

convene vt convocar; juntar, unir.

convenient adj conveniente.

convent n convento m.

convention n convención f.

converge vi converger.

conversation n conversación f.

converse vi conversar; platicar.

conversely adv mutuamente, recíprocamente.

convert vt, vi convertir(se).

convertible adj convertible.

convex adj convexo/xa.

convey vt transportar; transmitir, transferir.

conveyance n transporte m.

conveyancer n notario m.

conviction n convicción f.

convince vt convencer.

convivial adj sociable; hospitalario/ria.

convoke vt convocar, reunir.

convoy n convoy m.

convulse vt conmover, convulsionar.

convulsion n convulsión f.

convulsive adj convulsivo/va.

cook n cocinero m; cocinera f:—vt cocinar.

cool adj fresco/ca; indiferente.

cooperate vi cooperar.

cooperation n cooperación f.

coordinate vt coordinar.

coordination n coordinación f.

cop n (fam) poli m.

copier n copiadora f.

copious adj copioso/sa, abundante.

copper n cobre m.

copulate vi copularse.

copy n copia f.

copying machine n copiadora f.

coral n coral m.

cord n cuerda f; cable m.

cordial adj cordial.

corduroy n pana f.

core n cuesco m; interior m.

cork n alcornoque m; corcho m.

corkscrew n tirabuzón m.

corn n maíz m; grano m; callo m.

corncob n mazorca f.

cornea n córnea f.

corner n rincón m; esquina f.

cornet n corneta f.

cornflakes npl copos de maíz mpl.

cornice n cornisa f.

coronary n infarto m.

coronation n coronación f.

coroner n oficial que hace la inspección jurídica de los cadáveres m.

corporation n corporación f.

corps n cuerpo (de ejercito) m.

correct vt corregir; enmendar.

correctness n exactitud f.

correspond vi corresponder.

correspondence n correspondencia f.

corridor n pasillo m.

corrode vt corroer.

corrosive adj, n corrosivo m.

corrupt vt corromper; sobornar.

corruption n corrupción f; depravación f.

corset n corsé m.

cosily adv cómodamente.

cosmetic adj cosmético/ca.

cosmic adj cósmico/ca.

cosmonaut n cosmonauta m.

cosmopolitan adj cosmopolita.

cosset vt mimar.

cost n coste, precio m:—vi costar.

costume n traje m.

cosy adj cómodo/da.

cottage n casita, casucha f.

cotton n algodón m.

cotton wool n algodón hidrófilo m.

couch n sofá m.

couchette n litera f.

cough n tos f:—vi toser.

council n concilio, consejo m.

counsel n consejo, aviso m.

count vt contar, numerar; calcular.

counter n mostrador m; ficha f.

counterfeit vt contrahacer, imitar, falsear.

counterpart n parte correspondiente f.

countersign vt refrendar.

countess n condesa f.

countless adj innumerable.

countrified adj rústico/ca.

country n país m; campo m; región f; patria f.

county n condado m.

coup n golpe m.

couple n par m.

couplet n copla f; par m.

coupon n cupón m.

courage n coraje, valor f.

courageous adj corajudo/da, valeroso/sa:—**~ly** adv valerosamente.

courier n correo, mensajero/ra m/f, expreso m.

course n curso m; carrera f; camino m; ruta f.

court n corte f.

courteous adj cortés.

courtesy n cortesía f.

courthouse n palacio de justicia m.

courtyard n patio m.

cousin n primo m; prima f.

cove n (mar) ensenada, caleta f.

covenant n contrato m.

cover n cubierta f; abrigo m.

cover letter n carta de explicación f.

covert adj cubierto/ta; oculto/ta, secreto/ta.

cover-up n encubrimiento m.

covet vt codiciar.

cow n vaca f.

coward n cobarde m/f.

cowardice n cobardía, timidez f.

cowboy n vaquero m.

cower vi agacharse.

cowherd n vaquero m.

crab n cangrejo m.

crab apple n manzana silvestre f.

crack n crujido m; hendedura, quebraja f.

cracker n buscapiés m invar; galleta f.

crackle vi crujir, chillar.

cradle n cuna f.

craft n arte.

craftsman n artífice, artesano m.

craftsmanship n artesanía f.
crafty adj astuto/ta, artificioso/sa.
cramp n calambre m.
cranberry n arandilla f.
crane n grulla f; grua f.
crash vi estallar.
crash helmet n casco m.
crass adj craso/sa.
crater n cráter m; boca de volcán f.
cravat n pañuelo m.
crave vt rogar, suplicar.
craving adj insaciable.
crawl vi arrastrar.
crayfish n cangrejo de río m.
crayon n lápiz m.
craze n manía f.
craziness n locura f.
crazy adj loco/ca.
cream n crema f.
creamy adj cremoso.
crease n pliegue m.
create vt crear; causar.
creation n creación f; elección f.
creator n creador/a m/f.
creature n criatura f.
credence n creencia, fe f.
credibility n credibilidad f.
credible adj creíble.
credit n crédito m.
creditable adj estimable.
credit card n tarjeta de crédito f.
creed n credo m.
creek n arroyo, rio m.
creep vi arrastrar, serpear.
creeper n (bot) enredadera f.
cremate vt incinerar cadáveres.
cremation n cremación f.
crematorium n crematorio m.
crescent adj creciente.
cress n berro m.
crest n cresta f.
crevasse n grieta (de glaciar) f.

crevice n raja, hendedura f.
crew n banda, tropa f.
crib n cuna f; pesebre m.
cricket n grillo m; criquet m.
crime n crimen m.
criminal adj criminal.
crimson adj, n carmesí m.
cripple n, adj cojo/ja m/f.
crisis n crisis f.
crisp adj crujiente.
crispness n encrespadura f.
criss-cross adj entrelazado/da.
criterion n criterio m.
critic n crítico m; crítica f.
criticize vt criticar, censurar.
crochet n ganchillo m.
crockery n loza fl.
crocodile n cocodrilo m.
crook n (fam) ladrón m.
crooked adj torcido/da; perverso/sa.
cross n cruz f.
crossbar n travesaño m.
crossbreed n raza cruzada f.
cross-country n carrera a campo traviesa f.
crossing n cruce m; paso a nivel m.
cross-reference n contrarreferencia f.
crotch n entrepierna f.
crouch vi agacharse, bajarse.
crow n cuervo m.
crowd n publico m.
crown n corona f.
crown prince n príncipe real m.
crucial adj crucial.
crucible n crisol m.
crucifix n crucifijo m.
crucifixion n crucifixión f.
crude adj crudo/da, imperfecto/ta.
cruel adj cruel.
cruelty n crueldad f.
cruet n vinagrera f.
cruiser n crucero m.

crumb n miga f.

crumble vt desmigajar.

crumple vt arrugar.

crunchy adj crujiente.

crusade n cruzada f.

crush vt apretar, oprimir.

crust n costra f; corteza f.

crutch n muleta f.

crux n lo esencial.

cry vt, vi gritar; exclamar; llorar.

crypt n cripta (bóveda subterránea) f.

cryptic adj enigmático/ca.

crystal n cristal m.

cub n cachorro m.

cube n cubo m.

cuckoo n cuclillo, cuco m.

cucumber n pepino m.

cuddle vt abrazar.

cudgel n garrote, palo m.

cue n taco (de billar) m.

cuff n puñada f; vuelta f.

cull vt escoger, elegir.

culminate vi culminar.

culpable adj culpable.

cult n culto f.

cultivate vi cultivar.

cultivation n cultivación f.

cultural adj cultural.

culture n cultura f.

cumulative adj cumulativo/va.

cunning adj astuto/ta; intrigante.

cup n taza, jícara f; (bot) cáliz m.

cupboard n armario m.

curable adj curable.

curb n freno m; bordillo m.

curd n cuajada f.

cure n cura f; remedio m.

curiosity n curiosidad f; rareza f.

curious adj curioso/sa:—**~ly** adv curiosamente.

curl n rizo de pelo m.

curly adj rizado/da.

currant n pasa f.

currency n moneda f.

current adj corriente.

current affairs npl actualidades fpl.

currently adv corrientemente; actual-mente.

curry n curry m.

curse vt maldecir.

cursor n cursor m.

curt adj sucinto/ta.

curtail vt acortar.

curtain n cortina f; telón (en los teatros) m.

curvature n curvatura f.

curve vt encorvar:—n curva f.

cushion n cojín m; almohada f.

custard n natillas fpl.

custodian n custodio m.

custody n custodia f; prisión f.

custom n costumbre f, uso m.

customary adj usual, acostumbrado/da, ordinario/ria.

customer n cliente m/f.

customs npl aduana f.

customs duty n derechos de aduana mpl.

customs officer n aduanero/ra m/f.

cut vt cortar; separar.

cutback n reducción f.

cute adj lindo/da.

cutlery n cuchillería f.

cutlet n chuleta f.

cut-rate adj a precio reducido.

cut-throat n asesino m:—adj encar-nizado/da.

cutting n cortadura f:—adj cortante; mordaz.

cyanide n cianuro m.

cycle n ciclo m; bicicleta f:—vi ir en bicicleta.

cycling n ciclismo m.

cyclist n ciclista m/f.
cyclone n ciclón m.
cygnet n pollo del cisne m.
cylinder n cilindro m; rollo m.
cylindric(al) adj cilíndrico/ca.
cymbals n címbalo m.

cynic(al) adj cínico/ca; obsceno/na:— n cínico m (filósofo).
cynicism n cinismo m.
cypress n ciprés m.
cyst n quiste m.
czar n zar m.

D

dad(dy) n papa m.
daddy-long-legs n típula m.
daffodil n narciso m.
dagger n puñal m.
daily adj diario/ria.
dainty adj delicado/da.
dairy n lechería f.
dairy produce n productos lácteos mpl.
daisy n margarita f.
damage n daño m; perjuicio m.
damask n damasco m.
damn vt condenar.
damnation n perdición f.
damp adj húmedo/da.
dampen vt mojar.
dampness n humedad f.
dance n danza f; baile m.
dandelion n diente de león m.
dandruff n caspa f.
danger n peligro m.
dare vi atreverse.
daredevil n atrevido m.
dark adj oscuro/ra.
darling n, adj querido m.
darn vt zurcir.
dart n dardo m.
dartboard n diana f.
dash vi irse de prisa.
dashboard n tablero de instrumentos m.

data n datos mpl.
database n base de datos f.
date n fecha f; cita f.
daughter n hija f:—~ **in-law** nuera f.
dawn n alba f:—vi amanecer.
day n día m.
dazzle vt deslumbrar.
deacon n diácono m.
dead adj muerto/ta.
deadline n fecha tope f.
deadlock n punto muerto m.
deaf adj sordo/da.
deal n convenio m; transacción f.
dean n deán m.
dear adj querido/da. caro/ra.
dearness n carestía f.
death n muerte f.
debacle n desastre m.
debar vt excluir.
debase vt degradar.
debate n debate m; polémica f.
debilitate vt debilitar.
debt n deuda f.
decade n década f.
decadence n decadencia f.
decaffeinated adj descafeinado/da.
decay vi decaer; pudrirse.
deceit n engaño m.
deceive vt engañar.
December n diciembre m.
decent adj decente.

decide vt, vi decidir; resolver.
deciduous adj (bot) de hoja caduca.
decimal adj decimal.
decipher vt descifrar.
decision n decisión.
declare vt declarar.
decline vt (gr) declinar; evitar.
decompose vt descomponer.
decorate vt decorar, adornar.
decoration n decoración f.
decorum n decoro m.
decrease vt disminuir.
decree n decreto m.
dedicate vt dedicar; consagrar.
dedication n dedicación f.
deduce vt deducir.
deep adj profundo/da.
deep-freeze n congeladora f.
deer n ciervo m.
defamation n difamación f.
defeat n derrota f:—vt derrotar.
defect n defecto m.
defend vt defender.
defense n defensa f.
defensive adj defensivo/va.
defer vt aplazar.
deficient adj insuficiente.
deficit n déficit m.
define vt definir.
definition n definición f.
deflate vt desinflar.
deflect vt desviar.
deform vt desfigurar.
defraud vt estafar.
defuse vt desactivar.
degenerate vi degenerar.
degrade vt degradar.
degree n grado m; título m.
dehydrated adj deshidratado/da.
deity n deidad, divinidad f.
dejection n desaliento m.
delay vt demorar:—n retraso m.

delegate vt delegar:—n delegado m.
delete vt tachar; borrar.
delicacy n delicadeza f.
delicate adj delicado/da.
delicious adj delicioso/sa.
delight n delicia f.
delinquent n delincuente m.
delirium n delirio m.
deliver vt entregar.
delivery n entrega f; parto m.
delivery truck n camioneta f.
delude vt engañar.
deluge n diluvio m.
demagog(ue) n demagogo m.
demand n demanda f.
demean vi rebajarse.
demented adj demente.
demise n desaparición f.
democracy n democracia f.
democrat n demócrata m/f.
demolish vt demoler.
demon n demonio, diablo m.
demonstrate vt demostrar.
demoralize vt desmoralizar.
demote vt degradar.
demure adj modesto/ta.
den n guarida f.
denial n negación f.
denims npl vaqueros mpl.
denomination n valor m.
denote vt denotar.
denounce vt denunciar.
dense adj denso/sa.
density n densidad f.
dental adj dental.
dentist n dentista m/f.
denture npl dentadura postiza f.
denunciation n denuncia f.
deny vt negar.
deodorant n desodorante m.
depart vi partir(se).
department n departamento m.

department store n gran almacén m.

departure lounge n sala de embarque f.

depend vi depender.

depict vt pintar, retratar; describir.

deplore vt deplorar, lamentar.

deport vt deportar.

deposit vt depositar.

depositor n depositante m.

depot n depósito m.

deprave vt depravar.

depravity n depravación f.

deprecate vt lamentar.

depreciate vi depreciarse.

depreciation n depreciación f.

depress vt deprimir.

depressed adj deprimido/da.

depression n depresión f.

deprivation n privación f.

deprive vt privar.

depth n profundidad f.

deputation n diputación f.

deputize vi suplir a.

deputy n diputado m.

derelict adj abandonado/da.

deride vt burlar.

derision n mofa f.

derivative n derivado m.

derive vt, vi derivar(se).

derogatory adj despectivo/va.

descend vi descender.

descendant n descendiente m.

descent n descenso m.

describe vt describir.

description n descripción f.

descriptive adj descriptivo/va.

desecrate vt profanar.

desert n desierto m.

deserve vt merecer.

design vt diseñar.

designate vt nombrar.

designedly adv de propósito.

designer n diseñador m.

desirable adj deseable.

desire n deseo m.

desk n escritorio m.

desolate adj desierto/ta.

despair n desesperación f.

desperado n bandido m.

desperate adj desesperado/da.

despise vt despreciar.

despite prep a pesar de.

despoil vt despojar.

despondency n abatimiento m.

despot n déspota m/f.

dessert n postre m.

destination n destino m.

destine vt destinar.

destiny n destino m; suerte f.

destitute adj indigente.

destroy vt destruir.

destruction n destrucción.

detach vt separar.

detail n detalle m.

detain vt retener; detener.

detect vt detectar.

detection n descubrimiento m.

detective n detective m/f.

deter vt disuadir.

detergent n detergente m.

deteriorate vt deteriorar.

determination n resolución f.

determine vt determinar.

deterrent n fuerza de disuasión f.

detest vt detestar.

detonate vi detonar.

detonation n detonación f.

detour n desviación f.

detriment n perjuicio m.

devaluation n devaluación f.

devastate vt devastar.

develop vt desarrollar.

development n desarrollo m.

deviate vi desviarse.

deviation n desviación f.
device n mecanismo m.
devil n diablo, demonio m.
devious adj taimado/da.
devise vt inventar.
devote vt dedicar.
devour vt devorar.
devout adj devoto/ta.
dew n rocío m.
dexterity n destreza f.
diabetes n diabetes f.
diabetic n diabético m.
diadem n diadema f.
diagnosis n (med) diagnosis f.
diagonal adj, n diagonal (f).
diagram n diagrama m.
dial n cuadrante m.
dialect n dialecto m.
dialog(ue) n dialogo m.
diameter n diámetro m.
diamond n diamante m.
diaper n pañal m.
diaphragm n diafragma m.
diarrhea n diarrea f.
diary n diario m.
dice npl dados mpl.
dictate vt dictar.
dictation n dictado m.
dictatorship n dictadura f.
diction n dicción f
dictionary n diccionario m.
didactic adj didáctico/ca.
die[1] vi morir.
die[2] n dado m.
diesel n diesel m.
diet n dieta f; régimen m.
differ vi diferenciarse.
difference n diferencia f.
different adj diferente.
difficult adj difícil.
dig vt cavar.
digest vt digerir.

digestion n digestión f.
digger n excavadora f.
digit n dígito m.
digital adj digital.
dignity n dignidad f.
dike n dique m.
dilate vt, vi dilatar(se).
dilemma n dilema m.
dilute vt diluir.
dim adj turbio/bia.
dimension n dimensión, extensión f.
diminish vt, vi disminuir(se).
dimple n hoyuelo m.
din n alboroto m.
dine vi cenar.
diner n café m, restaurante (económico) m.
dinghy n lancha neumática f.
dingy adj sombrío/ria.
dinner n cena f.
dinosaur n dinosaurio m.
diocese n diócesis f.
dip vt mojar.
diphtheria n difteria f.
diploma n diploma m.
diplomacy n diplomacia f.
diplomat n diplomático/ca m/f.
dire adj calamitoso/sa.
direct adj directo/ta:—vt dirigir.
direction n dirección f.
directly adj directamente.
director n director/a m/f.
directory n guía f.
dirt n suciedad f.
disability n incapacidad f.
disabled adj minusválido/da.
disadvantage n desventaja f:—vt perjudicar.
disagree vi no estar de acuerdo.
disappear vi desaparecer.
disappoint vt decepcionar.
disapprove vt desaprobar.

disaster n desastre m.
disbelieve vt desconfiar.
discard vt descartar.
discern vt discernir, percibir.
discharge vt descargar; pagar (una deuda).
disciple n discípulo m.
discipline n disciplina f:—vt disciplinar.
disclose vi revelar.
disco n discoteca f.
discomfort n incomodidad f.
discontent n descontento m:—adj malcontento/ta.
discontinue vi interrumpir.
discord n discordia f.
discount n descuento m; rebaja f.
discover vt descubrir.
discreet adj discreto/ta.
discriminate vt distinguir.
discuss vt discutir.
discussion n discusión f.
disease n enfermedad f.
disembark vt, vi desembarcar.
disentangle vt desenredar.
disfigure vt desfigurar.
disgrace n ignominia f.
disgruntled adj descontento/ta.
disguise vt disfrazar.
disgust n aversión f:—vt repugnar.
dish n fuente f; plato m.
disheveled adj desarreglado/da.
dishonest adj deshonesto/ta.
dishonesty n falta de honradez f.
dishonor n deshonra, ignominia f.
dishtowel n trapo de fregar m.
dishwasher n lavaplatos m.
disillusion vt desilusionar.
disillusioned adj desilusionado/da.
disincentive n freno m.
disinclination n aversión f.
disinclined adj reacio/cia.

disinfect vt desinfectar.
disinfectant n desinfectante m.
disinherit vt desheredar.
disintegrate vi disgregarse.
disinterested adj desinteresado/da.
disjointed adj inconexo/xa.
disk n disco, disquete m.
diskette n disco, disquete m.
dislike n aversión f.
dislocate vt dislocar.
dislocation n dislocación f.
dislodge vt, vi desalojar.
disloyal adj desleal.
disloyalty n deslealtad f.
dismal adj triste.
dismantle vt desmontar.
dismay n consternación f.
dismember vt despedazar.
dismiss vt despedir.
dismissal n despedida f.
disobedience n desobediencia f.
disobedient adj desobediente.
disobey vt desobedecer.
disorderly adj desarreglado/da.
disorganized adj desorganizado/da.
disorientated adj desorientado/da.
disown vt desconocer.
disparage vt despreciar.
disparaging adj despreciativo/va.
disparity n disparidad f.
dispassionate adj desapasionado/da.
dispatch vt enviar.
dispel vt disipar.
dispensary n dispensario m.
dispense vt dispensar; distribuir.
disperse vt disipersar.
dispirited adj desalentado/da.
displace vt desplazar.
display vt exponer.
displeased adj disgustado/da.
displeasure n disgusto m.
disposable adj desechable.

disposal n disposición f.

dispose vt disponer; arreglar.

disposition n disposición f.

dispossess vt desposeer.

disproportionate adj despropor-cionado/da.

disprove vt refutar.

dispute n disputa, controversia f.

disqualify vt incapacitar.

disregard vt desatender:—n desdén m.

disreputable adj de mala fama.

disrespectful adj irreverente.

disrobe vt desnudar.

disrupt vt interrumpir.

disruption n interrupción f.

dissatisfaction n descontento/ta.

dissatisfied adj insatisfecho/cha.

dissect vt disecar.

dissection n disección.

dissent vi disentir.

dissertation n disertación f.

dissident n disidente m.

dissimilar adj distinto.

dissolution n disolución f.

dissolve vt disolver.

dissuade vt disuadir.

distance n distancia f.:—**at a ~** de lejos:—vt apartar.

distant adj distante.

distillery n destilería f.

distinct adj distinto/ta.

distinction n distinción f.

distinctive adj distintivo/va.

distinguish vt distinguir.

distort vt retorcer.

distorted adj distorsionado/da.

distortion n distorción f.

distract vt distraer.

distracted adj distraído/da.

distraction n distracción f; confusión f.

distraught adj enloquecido/da.

distress n angustia f.

distribute vt distribuir, repartir.

distribution n distribución f.

district n distrito m.

disturb vt molestar.

disturbance n disturbio m.

disturbing adj inquietante.

disused adj abandonado/da.

ditch n zanja f.

ditto adv ídem.

diuretic adj (med) diurético/ca.

diver n buzo m.

diverge vi divergir.

diverse adj diverso/sa, diferente.

diversion n diversión f.

diversity n diversidad f.

divert vt desviar; divertir.

divide vt dividir:—vi dividirse.

divine adj divino/na.

divinity n divinidad f.

divorce n divorcio m.

DJ n pinchadiscos m.

do vt hacer, obrar.

docile adj dócil, apacible.

dockyard n (mar) astillero m.

doctor n médico/ca m/f.

doctrine n doctrina f.

document n documento m.

documentary adj documental.

doe n gama f:—**~ rabbit** coneja f.

dog(ue) n perro m.

do-it-yourself n bricolaje m.

doll n muñeca f.

dollar n dólar m.

dolphin n delfín m.

dome n cúpula f.

domestic adj doméstico/ca.

domesticity n domesticidad f.

domicile n domicilio m.

dominant adj dominante.

dominate vi dominar.

domineer vi dominar.
dominion n dominio m.
dominoes npl domino m.
donate vt donar.
donation n donación f.
donkey n asno, borrico m.
donor n donante m.
door n puerta f.
doorbell n timbre m.
doorman n portero m.
doormat n felpudo m.
dormouse n lirón m.
dose n dosis f.
dossier n expediente m.
dot n punto m.
dote vi adorar.
double adj doble.
doubly adj doblemente.
doubt n duda, sospecha f.
doubtful adj dudoso/sa.
doubtless adv sin duda.
dough n masa f.
douse vt apagar.
dove n paloma f.
dovecot n palomar m.
dowdy adj mal vestido/da.
down n plumón m; flojel m:—prep abajo.
downfall n ruina f.
downhearted adj desanimado/da.
downpour n aguacero m.
downtown adv al centro (de la ciudad).
dowry n dote f.
doze vi dormitar.
dozen n docena f.
dozy adj soñoliento/ta.
drab adj gris.
draft n borrador m; quinta f; corriente de aire f.
dragon n dragón m.

dragonfly n libélula f.
drain vt desaguar.
drake n ánade macho m.
drama n drama m.
dramatic adj dramático/ca.
dramatize vt dramatizar.
dramatist n dramaturgo/ga m/f.
drape vt cubrir.
drapes npl cortinas fpl.
drastic adj drástico/ca.
draw vt tirar; dibujar.
drawback n desventaja f.
drawer n cajón m.
drawing n dibujo m.
drawing room n salón m.
dread n terror, espanto m:—vt temer.
dreadful adj espantoso/sa.
dream n sueno m:—vi sonar.
drench vt empapar.
dress vt vestir:—n vestido m.
dresser n aparador m.
dressing gown n bata f.
dressing table n tocador m.
dressmaker n modista f.
dried adj seco/ca.
drill n taladro m.
drink vt, vi beber.
drinkable adj potable.
drip vi gotear.
drive vt manejar.
driver n conductor m.
driveway n entrada f.
drizzle vi lloviznar.
droop vi decaer.
drop n gota f.
drought n seguía f.
drown vt anegar.
drowsiness n somnolencia f.
drowsy adj soñoliento/ta.
drudgery n trabajo monótono m.
drug n droga f:—vt drogar.

drug addict n drogadicto m.
drug store n farmacia f.
drum n tambor m:—vi tocar el tambor.
drummer n batería m.
drumstick n palillo de tambor m.
drunk adj borracho/cha.
drunkard n borracho m.
drunkenness n borrachera f.
dry adj seco/ca. * vt secar.
dry goods store n mercería, camisería f.
dry rot n podredumbre f.
dual adj doble.
dubbed adj doblado/da.
dubious adj dudoso/sa.
duck n pato m.
duckling n patito m.
dud adj estropeado/da.
due adj debido/da.
duel n duelo m.
duet n (mus) duo m.
dull adj lerdo/da. insípido/da.
duly adv debidamente; puntualmente.
dumb adj mudo/da.
dumbbell n pesa f.
dumbfounded adj pasmado/da.
dummy n maniquí m; imbécil m.
dumpling n bola de masa f.
dumpy adj gordito/ta.

dunce n zopenco m.
dune n duna f.
dung n estiércol m.
dungarees npl mono m.
dungeon n calabozo m.
dupe n bobo m.
duplicity n duplicidad f.
durability n durabilidad f.
durable adj duradero/ra.
duration n duración f.
during prep mientras, durante el tiempo que.
dusk n crepúsculo m.
dust n polvo m.
duster n plumero m.
dutch courage n valor fingido m.
duteous adj fiel, leal.
dutiful adj obediente.
duty n deber m; obligación f.
dwarf n enano m; enana f.
dwell vi habitar, morar.
dwelling n habitación f; domicilio m.
dwindle vi mermar, disminuirse.
dye vt teñir:—n tinte m.
dynamic adj dinámico/ca.
dynamite n dinamita f.
dynamo n dinamo f.
dynasty n dinastía f.
dysentery n disenteria f.
dyspepsia n (med) dispepsia f.

E

each pn cada uno, cada una.
eager adj entusiasmado/da.
eagle n águila f.
eaglet n aguilucho m.
ear n oreja f.
earache n dolor de oídos m.

eardrum n tímpano (del oído) m.
early adj temprano/na.
earn vt ganar; conseguir.
earnest adj serio/ria.
earth n tierra f.
earthenware n loza de barro f.

earthquake n terremoto m.
earthworm n lombriz f.
earthy adj sensual.
earwig n tijereta f.
ease n comodidad f; facilidad f.
easel n caballete m.
easily adv fácilmente.
east n este m; oriente m.
Easter n Pascua de Resurrección f.
easterly adj del este.
eastern adj del este, oriental.
easy adj fácil; cómodo/da.
easy chair n sillón m.
eat vt comer.
ebb n reflujo m.
ebony n ébano m.
eccentric adj excéntrico/ca.
echo n eco m.
eclectic adj ecléctico/ca.
eclipse n eclipse m.
ecology n ecología f.
economics npl economía f.
economy n economía f.
ecstasy n éxtasis m.
eczema n eczema m.
eddy n reflujo de agua m.
edge n filo m.
edict n edicto, mandato m.
edit vt dirigir; redactar.
edition n edición f.
editor n director m.
educate vt educar.
education n educación f.
eel n anguila f.
effect n efecto m.
effective adj eficaz..
effeminate adj afeminado/da.
effervescence n efervescencia f.
efficacy n eficacia f.
efficient adj eficaz.
effigy n efigie, imagen f.
effort n esfuerzo m.

egg n huevo m.
eggplant n berenjena f.
ego(t)ist n egoísta m/f.
eight num ocho.
eighteen num dieciocho.
eighth adj octavo.
eighty num ochenta.
either pn cualquiera.
eject vt expeler, desechar.
elastic adj elástico/ca.
elation n regocijo m.
elbow n codo m.
elder n saúco m (árbol):—adj mayor.
elect vt elegir.
election n elección f.
electrician n electricista m/f.
electricity n electricidad f.
elegance n elegancia f.
elegant adj elegante, delicado/da.
elegy n elegía f.
element n elemento m.
elephant n elefante m.
elevate vt elevar, alzar.
elevator n ascensor m.
eleven num once.
eleventh adj onceno, undécimo.
elf n duende m.
elicit vt sacar de.
eligible adj elegible.
eliminate vt eliminar, descartar.
elk n alce m.
elm n olmo m.
elocution n elocución f.
elongate vt alargar.
elope vi escapar, huir.
elopement n fuga f.
eloquence n elocuencia f.
else pn otro/ra.
elsewhere adv en otra parte.
elude vt eludir, evitar.
embargo n prohibición f.
embark vt embarcar.

embarrass vt avergonzar.
embarrassment n desconcierto m.
embassy n embajada f.
embed vt empotrar; clavar.
embellish vt hermosear.
embers npl rescoldo m.
embezzle vt desfalcar.
embitter vt amargar.
emblem n emblema m.
embrace vt abrazar.
embroider vt bordar.
embroil vt embrollar; confundir.
embryo n embrión m.
emerald n esmeralda f.
emerge vi salir, proceder.
emergency n emergencia f.
emery n esmeril m.
emigrant n emigrante m.
emigrate vi emigrar.
eminent adj eminente.
emission n emisión f.
emit vt emitir.
emotion n emoción f.
emperor n emperador m.
emphasis n énfasis m.
emphasize vt hablar con énfasis.
empire n imperio m.
employ vt emplear, ocupar.
employee n empleado m.
employer n patrón m; empresario m.
empress n emperatriz f.
empty adj vacío/cia.
emulate vt emular.
emulsion n emulsión f.
enable vt capacitar.
enact vt promulgar.
enamel n esmalte m.
enchant vt encantar.
enchanting adj encantador.
encircle vt cercar, circundar.
enclose vt cercar, circunvalar.
encore adv otra vez, de nuevo.

encounter n encuentro m.
encourage vt animar.
encouragement n estimulo, patrocinio m.
encroach vt usurpar.
encumber vt embarazar, cargar.
encyclopedia n enciclopedia f.
end n fin m.
endanger vt peligrar.
endear vt encarecer.
endeavor vi esforzarse; intentar.
endemic adj endémico/ca.
ending n conclusión.
endive n (bot) endibia f.
endless adj infinito/ta.
endorse vt endosar; aprobar.
endow vt dotar.
endure vt sufrir, soportar.
enemy n enemigo/ga.
energetic adj enérgico/ca.
energy n energía, fuerza f.
enforce vt hacer cumplir.
engine n motor m; locomotora f.
engineer n ingeniero m.
engrave vt grabar.
enhance vt aumentar.
enigma n enigma m.
enjoy vt gozar.
enjoyment n disfrute m; placer m.
enlarge vt engrandecer.
enlist vt alistar.
enliven vt animar.
enmity n enemistad f; odio m.
enormous adj enorme.
enough adv bastante; basta.
enrage vt enfurecer.
enrapture vt arrebatar.
enrich vt enriquecer.
enrol vt registrar.
enrolment n inscripción f.
ensign n (mil) bandera f.
enslave vt esclavizar.

ensue vi seguirse.
ensure vt asegurar.
entangle vt enmarañar.
enter vt entrar; admitir.
enterprise n empresa f.
entertain vt divertir; hospedar.
entertainer n artista m/f.
entertainment n entretenimiento, pasatiempo m.
enthralling adj cautivador.
enthusiasm n entusiasmo m.
entice vt tentar; seducir.
entire adj entero/ra, completo/ta.
entitle vt intitular; conferir algún derecho.
entity n entidad f.
entrance n entrada f.
entreat vt rogar, suplicar.
entrepreneur n empresario m.
entrust vt confiar.
entry n entrada f.
entwine vt entrelazar.
envelop n envolver.
envelope vt sobre m.
enviable adj envidiable.
environment n medio ambiente m.
environs npl vecindad f.
envisage vt prever; concebir.
envoy n enviado m.
envy n envidia.
ephemeral adj efímero/ra.
epic adj épico/ca.
epidemic adj epidémico/ca.
epilogue n epílogo m.
Epiphany n Epifanía f.
episcopacy n episcopado m.
episcopal adj episcopal.
episcopalian n anglicano m.
episode n episodio m.
epistle n epístola f.
epithet n epíteto m.
epoch n época f.

equal adj igual.
equalize vt igualar.
equality n igualdad, uniformidad f.
equally adv igualmente.
equate vt equiparar (con).
equation n ecuación f.
equator n ecuador m.
equatorial adj ecuatorial.
equestrian adj ecuestre.
equilibrium n equilibrio m.
equinox n equinoccio m.
equip vt equipar.
equipment n equipaje m.
equitable adj equitativo/va.
equity n equidadf.
equivalent adj, n equivalente m.
era n era f.
eradicate vt desarraigar.
eradication n extirpación f.
erase vt borrar.
eraser n goma de borrar f.
erect vt erigir; establecer.
ermine n armiño m.
erode vt erosionar.
erotic adj erótico/ca.
err vi vagar, errar.
errand n recado.
erratic adj errático/ca.
erroneous adj erróneo/nea.
error n error m.
erudite adj erudito/ta.
erupt vi entrar en erupción; hacer erupción.
eruption n erupción f.
escalate vi extenderse.
escalator n escalera móvil f.
escapade n travesura f.
escape vt evitar; escapar.
escapism n escapismo m.
escort n escolta f:—vt escoltar.
esoteric adj esotérico/ca.
especial adj especial.

essay n ensayo m.
essence n esencia f.
essential n esencia f:—adj esencial.
establish vt establecer.
establishment n establecimiento m.
estate n estado m.
esteem vt estimar, apreciar.
estimate vt estimar, apreciar.
estuary n estuario.
etch vt grabar al aguafuerte.
eternal adj eterno/na.
eternity n eternidad f.
ether n éter m.
ethical adj ético/ca.
ethics npl ética f.
ethnic adj étnico/ca.
ethos n genio m.
etiquette n etiqueta f.
etymology n etimología f.
Eucharist n Eucaristía f.
eulogy n elogio.
eunuch n eunuco m.
euphemism n eufemismo m.
evacuate vt evacuar.
evacuation n evacuación f.
evade vt evadir.
evaluate vt evaluar.
evangelical adj evangélico/ca.
evaporate vt evaporar.
evasion n evasión f.
evasive adj evasivo/va.
eve n víspera f.
even adj llano/na, igual; par, semejante:—adv aun; aun cuando;
supuesto que; no obstante.
evening n tarde f.
event n acontecimiento, evento m.
eventuality n eventualidad f.
ever adv siempre.
every adj cada uno o cada una.
evict vt desahuciar.
eviction n desahucio m.

evidence n evidencia f.
evil adj malo/la, depravado/da.
evocative adj sugestivo/va.
evoke vt evocar.
evolution n evolución f.
evolve vt, vi evolucionar.
ewe n oveja f.
exacerbate vt exacerbar.
exact adj exacto/ta.
exacting adj exigente.
exaggerate vt exagerar.
exaggeration n exageración f.
exalt vt exaltar.
exaltation n exaltación.
examination n examen m.
examine vt examinar.
examiner n inspector/a m/f.
example n ejemplar m; ejemplo m.
excavate vt excavar.
excavation n excavación f.
exceed vt exceder.
exceedingly adv extremamente, en
sumo grado.
excel vt sobresalir.
excellence n excelencia f.
excellent adj excelente.
except vt exceptuar, excluir:—~(ing)
prep excepto, a excepción de.)
exception n excepción, exclusión f.
exceptional adj excepcional.
excerpt n extracto m.
excess n exceso m.
excessive adj excesivo/va.
exchange vt cambiar; trocar.
exchange rate n tipo de cambio m.
excitability n excitabilidad f.
excitable adj excitable.
excite vt excitar; estimular.
excited adj emocionado/da.
excitement n estímulo m, excitación
f.
exclaim vi exclamar.

exclamation *n* exclamación f.

exclamation mark *n* punto de admiración m.

exclamatory *adj* exclamatorio/ria.

exclude *vt* excluir; exceptuar.

exclusion *n* exclusión, f.

exclusive *adj* exclusivo/va.

excommunicate *vt* excomulgar.

excommunication *n* excomunión f.

excrement *n* excremento m.

excruciating *adj* atroz.

excursion *n* excursión f.

excusable *adj* excusable.

excuse *vt* disculpar.

execute *vt* ejecutar.

execution *n* ejecución f.

executioner *n* ejecutor/a.

executive *adj* ejecutivo/va.

executor *n* testamentario/ria, albacea m/f.

exemplary *adj* ejemplar.

exemplify *vt* ejemplificar.

exempt *adj* exento/ta.

exemption *n* exención f.

exercise *n* ejercicio m.

exercise book *n* cuaderno m.

exertion *n* esfuerzo m.

exhale *vt* exhalar.

exhaust *n* escape m.

exhausted *adj* agotado/da.

exhaustion *n* agotamiento m.

exhaustive *adj* comprensivo/va.

exhibit *vt* exhibir; mostrar.

exhibition *n* exposición f.

exhilarating *adj* estimulante.

exhort *vt* exhortar, excitar.

exhume *vt* exhumar.

exile *n* destierro m.

exist *vi* existir.

existence *n* existencia f.

exit *n* salida f:—*vi* hacer mutis.

exit ramp *n* vía de acceso f.

exodus *n* éxodo m.

exonerate *vt* exonerar.

exhorbitant *adj* exorbitante.

exorcize *vt* exorcizar, conjurar.

exorcism *n* exorcismo m.

exotic *adj* exótico/ca.

expand *vt* extender, dilatar.

expatriate *vt* expatriar.

expect *vt* esperar.

expectant mother *n* mujer encinta f.

expediency *n* conveniencia f.

expedition *n* expedición f.

expel *vt* expeler, desterrar.

expend *vt* expender.

expendable *adj* prescindible.

expenditure *n* gasto, desembolso m.

expense *n* gasto m; coste m.

experience *n* experiencia f; practica f.

experienced *adj* experimentado/da.

experiment *n* experimento m.

expert *adj* experto/ta.

expertise *n* pericia f.

expiration *n* expiración f.

expire *vi* expirar.

explain *vt* explanar, explicar.

explanation *n* explanación, explicación f.

expletive *adj* expletivo/va.

explicit *adj* explícito/ta.

explode *vt, vi* estallar, explotar.

exploit *vt* explotar.

exploitation *n* explotación f.

exploration *n* exploración f.

exploratory *adj* exploratorio/ria.

explore *vt* explorar.

explorer *n* explorador m.

explosion *n* explosión f.

explosive *adj, n* explosivo m.

exponent *n* (*math*) exponente m.

export *vt* exportar.

expose *vt* exponer; mostrar.

exposed *adj* expuesto/ta.

exposition *n* exposición *f.*
expostulate *vi* debatir, contender.
exposure *n* exposición *f.*
expound *vt* exponer.
express *vt* exprimir; representar.
expression *n* expresión *f.*
expressionless *adj* sin expresión (cara).
expressway *n* autopista *f.*
expulsion *n* explosión *f.*
expurgate *vt* expurgar.
exquisite *adj* exquisito/ta.
extend *vt* extender.
extension *n* extensión *f.*
extensive *adj* extenso/sa.
extent *n* extensión *f.*
extenuate *vt* extenuar.
exterior *adj, n* exterior *m.*
exterminate *vt* exterminar.
extermination *n* exterminación *f.*
external *adj* externo/na.
extinct *adj* extinto/ta.
extinction *n* extinción *f.*
extinguish *vt* extinguir.
extinguisher *n* extintor *m.*
extol *vt* alabar, magnificar.
extort *vt* sacar por fuerza.
extortion *n* extorsión *f.*

extortionate *adj* excesivo/va.
extra *adv* extra.
extract *vt* extraer.
extracurricular *adj* extraescolar.
extradition *n* (law) extradición *f.*
extramarital *adj* extramatrimonial.
extraneous *adj* extraño/ña.
extraordinary *adj* extraordinario/ria.
extravagance *n* extravagancia *f.*
extravagant *adj* extravagante.
extreme *adj* extremo/ma.
extremist *adj, n* extremista *m/f.*
extremity *n* extremidad *f.*
extrovert *adj, n* extrovertido *m.*
exuberance *n* exuberancia *f.*
exuberant *adj* exuberante.
exult *vt* exultar.
exultation *n* exultación *f;* regocijo *m.*
eye *n* ojo *m:—vt* ojear, contemplar, observar.
eyeball *n* globo del ojo *m.*
eyebrow *n* ceja *f.*
eyelash *n* pestaña *f.*
eyelid *n* párpado *m.*
eyesight *n* vista *f.*
eyewitness *n* testigo ocular *m.*
eyrie *n* aguilera *f.*

F

fabric *n* tejido *m.*
fabricate *vt* fabricar.
fabulous *adj* fabuloso/sa.
facade *n* fachada *f.*
face *n* cara, faz *f;* superficie *f.*
facet *n* faceta *f.*
facetious *adj* chistoso/sa.
facile *adj* fácil.
facilitate *vt* facilitar.
facility *n* facilidad *f.*

facsimile *n* facsímile *m;* telefax *m.*
fact *n* hecho *m.*
faction *n* facción *f.*
factor *n* factor *m.*
factory *n* fabrica *f.*
faculty *n* facultad *f.*
fad *n* moda , manía *f.*
fade *vi* decaer.
fail *vt* suspender, reprobar; fallar a.
failure *n* falta *f;* culpa *f.*

faint vi desmayarse, debilitarse.
faint-hearted adj cobarde.
fair adj hermoso/sa, bello/la; blanco/ca; rubio/bia; claro/ra, sereno/na; favorable; recto/ta, justo/ta; franco/ca:—adv limpio:—n feria f.
fairly adv justamente.
fairy n hada f.
faith n fe f; dogma de fe m.
faithfulness n fidelidad f.
fake n falsificación f.
falcon n halcón m.
fall[1] n otoño m.
fall[2] vi caer(se).
fallacy n falacia.
fallible adj falible.
false adj falso/sa.
falsify vt falsificar.
fame n fama f.
famed adj celebrado/da, famoso/sa.
familiar adj familiar.
family n familia f.
famine n hambre f; carestía f.
famous adj famoso/sa.
fan n abanico m; aficionado m.
fanatic adj, n fanático m.
fanciful adj imaginativo/va.
fancy n fantasía, imaginación f.
fanfare n (mus) fanfarria f.
fang n colmillo m.
fantastic adj fantástico/ca.
fantasy n fantasía f.
far adv lejos.
faraway adj remoto/ta.
farce n farsa f.
fare n precio m; tarifa f.
farm n finca f, granja f.
farmer n estanciero m; granjero m.
fascinate vt fascinar, encantar.
fascism n fascismo.
fashion n moda f; forma f.

fashionable adj a la moda.
fashion show n desfile de modelos m.
fast vi ayunar; adv rápidamente.
fasten vt abrochar.
fastidious adj fastidioso/sa.
fat adj gordo/da.
fatal adj fatal.
fate n hado, destino m.
fateful adj fatídico/ca.
father n padre m.
father-in-law n suegro m.
fatherland n patria f.
fathom n braza (medida) f.
fatigue n fatiga f.
fatty adj graso/sa.
faucet n espita f.
fault n falta, culpa f.
fauna n fauna f.
faux pas n plancha f.
favor n favor.
favorite n favorito m.
fawn n cervato m.
fax n facsímil(e) m; telefax m.
fear vi temer:—n miedo m.
fearful adj medroso/sa, temeroso/sa.
feasible adj factible.
feast n banquete.
feat n hecho m.
feather n pluma f.
feature n característica f; rasgo m.
February n febrero m.
federal adj federal.
federalist n federalista m/f.
federation n federación f.
fed-up adj harto/ta.
fee n honorarios mpl.
feeble adj flaco/ca, débil.
feed vt nutrir; alimentar.
feedback n reacción f.
feel vt sentir; tocar.
feign vt inventar, fingir.

feline *adj* gatuno/na.
fellowship *n* compañerismo *m*.
felon *n* criminal *m/f*.
felony *n* crimen *m*.
felt *n* fieltro *m*.
female *n* hembra *f*:—*adj* femenino/-na.
feminine *adj* femenino/na.
feminist *n* feminista *m/f*.
fence *n* cerca *f*; defensa *f*.
fennel *n* (*bot*) hinojo *m*.
fern *n* (*bot*) helecho *m*.
ferocious *adj* feroz.
ferret *n* hurón *m*.
ferry *n* barca de pasaje *f*.
fertile *adj* fértil, fecundo/da.
fester *vi* enconarse.
festival *n* fiesta *f*; festival *m*.
fetch *vt* ir a buscar.
fete *n* fiesta *f*.
fetus *n* feto *m*.
feud *n* riña, contienda *f*.
feudal *adj* feudal.
fever *n* fiebre *f*.
feverish *adj* febril.
few *adj* poco/ca.
fewer *adj* menor.
fewest *adj* los menos.
fiancé *n* novio *m*.
fiancée *n* novia *f*.
fib *n* mentira *f*.
fibre *n* fibra, hebra *f*.
fickle *adj* voluble.
fiction *n* ficción *f*.
fiddle *n* violín *m*; trampa *f*.
fidelity *n* fidelidad *f*.
field *n* campo *m*.
fieldmouse *n* ratón de campo *m*.
fierce *adj* fiero/ra, feroz.
fierceness *n* fiereza, ferocidad *f*.
fiery *adj* ardiente; apasionado/da.
fifteen *adj, n* quince.

fifteenth *adj, n* decimoquinto/ta.
fifth *adj, n* quinto/ta.
fiftieth *adj, n* quincuagésimo/ma.
fifty *adj, n* cincuenta.
fig *n* higo *m*.
fight *vt, vi* reñir; batallar; combatir.
fig-leaf *n* hoja de higuera *f*.
figurative *adj* figurativo/va.
figure *n* figura.
filament *n* filamento *m*.
fill *vt* llenar; hartar.
fillet *n* filete *m*.
filling station *n* estación de servicio *f*.
fillip *n* (*fig*) estimulo *m*.
filly *n* potra *f*.
film *n* película *f*; film *m*.
filter *n* filtro *m*.
filth(iness) *n* inmundicia, porquería *f*.
fin *n* aleta *f*.
final *adj* final, último/ma.
finalize *vt* concluir.
finance *n* fondos *mpl*.
financier *n* financiero *m*.
find *vt* hallar, descubrir.
finesse *n* sutileza *f*.
finger *n* dedo *m*.
fingernail *n* uña *f*.
finish *vt* acabar, terminar, concluir.
finite *adj* finito/ta.
fir *n* abeto *m*.
fire *n* fuego *m*; incendio *m*.
firearm *n* arma de fuego *f*.
firefly *n* luciérnaga *f*.
firewood *n* leña *f*.
fireworks *npl* fuegos artificiales *mpl*.
firm *adj* firme, estable.
firmament *n* firmamento *m*.
firmness *n* firmeza *f*.
first *adj* primero/ra.
fiscal *adj* fiscal.
fish *n* pez *m*.
fishbone *n* espina *f*.

fisherman n pescador m.
fishy adj (fig) sospechoso/sa.
fist n puño m.
fitness n salud f.
five adj, n cinco.
fix vt fijar.
fixation n obsesión f.
fizzy adj gaseoso/sa.
flabbergasted adj pasmado/da.
flabby adj blando/da.
flaccid adj flojo/ja.
flag n bandera f.
flagpole n asta de bandera f.
flagrant adj flagrante; notorio/ria.
flagship n navío almirante m.
flair n aptitud especial f.
flake n copo m.
flamboyant adj vistoso/sa.
flame n llama f.
flamingo n flamenco m.
flammable adj inflamable.
flank n ijada f.
flannel n franela f.
flare vi lucir, brillar.
flash n flash m.
flashlight n antorcha f.
flask n frasco m.
flat adj llano/na, plano/na.
flatness n llanura f.
flatten vt allanar.
flatter vt adular.
flattery n adulación f.
flatulence n (med) flatulencia f.
flaunt vt ostentar.
flavor n sabor m.
flavorless adj soso/sa.
flaw n falta m.
flawless adj sin defecto.
flax n lino m.
flea n pulga f.
fleck n mota f.
flee vt huir de.

fleece n vellón m.
fleet n flota f.
flesh n carne f.
flex n cordón m.
flexibility n flexibilidad f.
flexible adj flexible.
flight n vuelo m.
flight attendant n tripulante auxiliar m.
flimsy adj débil; fútil.
flinch vi encogerse.
fling vt lanzar.
flint n pedernal m.
flip vt arrojar.
flippant adj petulante.
flipper n aleta f.
flirt vi coquetear:—n coqueta f.
flirtation n coquetería f.
flock n manada f.
flog vt azotar.
flogging n tunda, zurra f.
flood n diluvio m; inundación f.
flooding n inundación f.
floodlight n foco m.
floor n suelo, piso m.
floorboard n tabla f.
flop n fracaso m.
floppy adj flojo/ja.
flora n flora f.
floral adj floral.
florescence n florescencia f.
florid adj florido/da.
florist n florista m/f.
florist's (shop) n florería f.
flotilla n (mar) flotilla f.
flounder n platija (pez de mar) f.
flour n harina f.
flourish vi florecer.
flout vt burlarse de.
flow vi fluir.
flower n flor f.
flowerbed n cuadro (en un jardín) m.

flowerpot n tiesto de flores m.
flowery adj florido/da.
fluctuate vi fluctuar.
fluctuation n fluctuación f.
fluency n fluidez f.
fluent adj fluido/da.
fluff n pelusa f.
fluid adj, n fluido/da m.
fluidity n fluidez f.
fluke n (sl) chiripa f.
fluoride n fluoruro m.
flurry n ráfaga f; agitación f.
flute n flauta f.
flutter vi revolotear; estar en agitación.
flux n flujo m.
fly vt pilotar; transportar:—vi volar.
flying saucer n platillo volante m.
foal n potro m.
foam n espuma f.
foamy adj espumoso/sa.
focus n foco.
fodder n forraje m.
foe n adversario/ria m/f, enemigo m.
fog n niebla f.
foggy adj nebuloso/sa.
fold n redil m; pliegue m.
folder n carpeta f.
folding adj plegable.
foliage n follaje m.
folio n folio m.
folk n gente f.
folklore n folklore m.
folk song n canción folklórica f.
follow vt seguir; acompañar.
follower n seguidor/a m/f.
following adj siguiente.
folly n extravagancia f.
foment vt fomentar.
fond adj cariñoso/sa.
fondle vt acariciar.
fondness n gusto m; cariño m.

font n pila bautismal f.
food n comida f.
food mixer n batidora f.
food poisoning n botulismo m.
fool n loco/ca, tonto/ta m/f.
foolish adj bobo/ba, tonto/ta.
foolscap n papel tamaño folio m.
foot n pie m; pata f.
footage n imágenes fpl.
footnote n nota de pie f.
footpath n senda f.
footprint n huella f.
for prep por, a causa de; para.
forbid vt prohibir.
force n fuerza f; poder, vigor m.
forced adj forzado/da.
forceful adj enérgico/ca.
forceps n fórceps m.
ford n vado m.
fore n:—**to the ~** en evidencia.
forearm n antebrazo m.
foreboding n presentimiento m.
forecast vt pronosticar.
forecourt n patio m.
forefather n abuelo, antecesor m.
forefinger n índice m.
forefront n:—**in the ~ of** en la vanguardia de.
forego vt ceder.
foreground n delantera f.
forehead n frente f.
foreign adj extranjero/ra; extraño/ña.
foreigner n extranjero/ra, forastero/ra m/f.
foreign exchange n divisas fpl.
foreleg n pata delantera f.
foreman n capataz m.
foremost adj principal.
forensic adj forense.
forerunner n precursor/a m/f.
foresee vt prever.
foresight n previsión f.

forest n bosque m; selva f.
forester n guardabosque m.
forestry n silvicultura f.
foretaste n muestra f.
foretell vt predecir, profetizar.
forethought n providencia f.
forever adv para siempre.
foreword n prefacio m.
forfeit n confiscación f.
forge n fragua f; fabrica de metales f.
forger n falsificador/a m/f.
forgery n falsificación f.
forget vt olvidar.
forgetful adj olvidadizo/za.
forget-me-not n (bot) nomeolvides m.
forgive vt perdonar.
forgiveness n perdón m.
fork n tenedor m.
form n forma f; modelo m; modo m.
formal adj formal.
formality n formalidad f.
format n formato m.
formation n formación f.
formative adj formativo/va.
former adj precedente; anterior.
formidable adj formidable.
formula n fórmula f.
formulate vt formular.
forsake vt dejar.
fort n castillo m.
forthright adj franco/ca.
forthwith adj inmediatamente.
fortieth adj, n cuadragésimo m.
fortification n fortificación f.
fortify vt fortificar.
fortitude n fortaleza f.
fortnight n quince días mpl.
fortress n (mil) fortaleza f.
fortuitous adj impensado/da.
fortunate adj afortunado/da.
fortune n fortuna, suerte f.

fortune-teller n sortílego/ga.
forty adj, n cuarenta.
forum n foro m.
forward adj avanzado/da; delantero/ra.
forwardness n precocidad f; audacia f.
fossil adj, n fósil m.
foster vt criar.
foul adj sucio/cia, puerco/ca; impuro/ra.
found vt fundar, establecer.
foundation n fundación f.
founder n fundador/a m/f.
foundling n niño expósito m, niña expósita f.
foundry n fundería f.
fount, fountain n fuente f.
fountainhead n origen de fuente m.
four adj, n cuatro.
fourfold adj cuádruple.
fourteen adj, n catorce.
fourteenth adj, n decimocuarto/ta.
fourth adj, n cuarto/ta:—n cuarto m:— ~ly adv en cuarto lugar.
fowl n ave f.
fox n zorra f.
fracas n riña f.
fraction n fracción f.
fracture n fractura f.
fragile adj frágil; débil.
fragility n fragilidad f.
fragment n fragmento m.
fragrance n fragancia f.
fragrant adj fragante, oloroso/sa.
frail adj frágil, débil.
frailty n fragilidad f; debilidad f.
frame n armazón m; marco, cerco m.
franchise n sufragio m.
frank adj franco/ca, liberal.
frankly adv francamente.
frantic adj frenético/ca.

fraternize vi hermanarse.
fraternity n fraternidad f.
fraud n fraude m.
fraudulent adj fraudulento/ta.
fraught adj cargado/da, lleno/na.
freak n monstruo m; fenómeno m.
freckle n peca f.
freckled adj pecoso/sa.
free adj libre; liberal; suelto/ta.
freedom n libertad f.
freehold n propiedad vitalicia f.
free-for-all n riña general f.
freelance adj, adv por cuenta propia.
freemason n francmasón m.
freemasonry n francmasonería f.
freeway n autopista f.
freewheel vi ir en punto muerto.
freeze vi helar(se).
freezer n congeladora f.
freight n carga f; flete m.
freighter n fletador m.
frenzy n frenesí m; locura f.
frequency n frecuencia f.
fresco n fresco m.
fresh adj fresco/ca; nuevo/va.
freshly adv nuevamente.
freshman n novicio m.
freshwater adj de agua dulce.
fret vi agitarse.
friar n fraile m.
friction n fricción f.
Friday n viernes m:—**Good ~** Viernes Santo m.
friend n amigo m; amiga f.
friendship n amistad f.
frieze n friso m.
frigate n (mar) fragata f.
fright n espanto, terror m.
frighten vt espantar.
frigid adj frío/ría, frígido/da.
fringe n franja f.
frisk vt cachear.

frivolity n frivolidad f.
frock n vestido m.
frog n rana f.
frolic vi juguetear.
from prep de; después; desde.
front n parte delantera f; fachada f; paseo marítimo m; frente m.
frontal adj de frente.
frontier n frontera f.
frost n helada f; hielo m.
froth n espuma (de algún líquido) f.
frown vt mirar con ceño.
frozen adj helado/da.
fruit n fruta f; fruto m.
fruiterer n frutero m.
fruiterer's (shop) n frutería f.
fruit juice n jugo de fruta m.
fruitless adj estéril; inútil.
fruit salad n ensalada de frutas f.
fruit tree n frutal m.
frustrate vt frustrar; anular.
fry vt freír.
frying pan n sartén f.
fuchsia n (bot) fucsia f.
fuel n combustible m.
fuel tank n deposito m.
fugitive adj, n fugitivo m.
fulcrum n fulcro m.
fulfill vt cumplir; realizar.
fulfillment n cumplimiento m.
full adj lleno/na.
full moon n plenilunio m; luna llena f.
fulsome adj exagerado/da.
fumble vi manejar torpemente.
fume vi humear; encolerizarse.
fun n diversión f; alegría f.
function n función f.
functional adj funcional.
fund n fondo m.
fundamental adj fundamental.
funeral n funerales mpl.

fungus n hongo m; seta f.
funnel n embudo m.
funny adj divertido/da; curioso/sa.
fur n piel f.
furious adj furioso/sa.
furnace n horno m; hornaza f.
furnish vt amueblar.
furnishings npl muebles mpl.
furniture n muebles mpl.
furrow n surco m.
furry adj peludo/da.

furthermore adv además.
fury n furor m; furia f; ira f.
fuse vt, vi fundir; derretirse.
fuse box n caja de fusibles f.
fusion n fusión f.
fuss n lío m; alboroto m.
fussy adj jactancioso/sa.
futile adj fútil, frívolo/la.
futility n futilidad f.
future adj futuro/ra.
fuzzy adj borroso/sa; muy rizado/da.

G

gable n aguilón m.
gag n mordaza f; chiste m.
gage n calibre m.
gaiety n alegría f.
gain n ganancia f.
gala n fiesta f.
galaxy n galaxia f.
gale n vendaval m.
gallant adj galante.
gallery n galería f.
gallon n galón m (medida).
gallop n galope m.
gallows n horca f.
galore adv en abundancia.
gambit n estrategia f.
gamble vi jugar; especularf.
gambler n jugador m.
game n juego m; pasatiempo m.
gamekeeper n guardabosques m.
gaming n juego m.
gammon n jamón m.
gander n ganso m.
gang n pandilla, banda f.
gangrene n gangrena f.
gangster n gangster m.
gangway n pasarela f.
gap n hueco m; claro m; intervalo m.

garage n garaje m.
garbage n basura f.
garbage can n cubo de la basura m.
garden n jardín m.
gargoyle n gárgola f.
garish adj ostentoso/sa.
garland n guirnalda f.
garlic n ajo m.
garment n prenda f.
garnish vt guarnecer m.
garter n liga f.
gas n gas m.
gasoline, gas n gasolina f.
gash n cuchillada f.
gasp vi jadear.
gastric adj gástrico/ca.
gastronomic adj gastronómico/ca.
gate n puerta f.
gateway n puerta f.
gather vt recoger.
gathering n reunión f.
gaudy adj chillón/ona.
gauze n gasa f.
gay adj alegre; vivo/va; gay.
gazelle n gacela f.
gazette n gaceta f.
gazetteer n gacetero m.

gear n atavío m; vestido m.
gearbox n caja de cambios f.
gel n gel m.
gelatin(e) n jaletina, jalea f.
gelignite n gelignita f.
gem n joya f.
Gemini n Géminis m (signo del zodiaco).
gender n género m.
gene n gen m.
genealogy n genealogía f.
general adj general, común.
generalize vt generalizar.
generation n generación f.
generic adj genérico/ca.
generosity n generosidad.
generous adj generoso/sa.
genetics npl genética f.
genial adj genial.
genitals npl genitales mpl.
genius n genio m.
genteel adj refinado, elegante.
gentile n gentil.
gentle adj suave.
gentleman n caballero m.
gentry n alta burguesía f.
gents n aseos mpl.
genuine adj genuino/na.
genus n genero m.
geographer n geógrafo/fa m/f.
geography n geografía f.
geology n geología f.
geometry n geometría f.
geranium n (bot) geranio m.
germ n (bot) germen m.
germinate vi brotar.
gesticulate vi gesticular.
gesture n gestom.
get vt ganar; conseguir, obtener.
geyser n géiser m m.
ghastly adj espantoso/sa.
gherkin n pepinillo m.

ghost n fantasma m.
ghostly adj fantasmal.
giant n gigante m.
giddy adj vertiginoso/sa.
gift n regalom.
giggle vi reírse tontamente.
gin n ginebra f.
ginger n jengibre m.
ginger-haired adj pelirrojo/ja.
giraffe n jirafa f.
girl n muchacha, chica f.
girlfriend n amiga f; novia f.
giro n giro postal m.
girth n cincha f; circunferencia f.
give vt, vi dar.
glacier n glaciar m.
glad adj alegre, contento/ta.
gladiator n gladiator m.
glamor n encantom.
gland n glándula f.
glare n deslumbramiento m.
glass n vidrio.
glean vt espigar; recoger.
glee n alegría f; gozo m.
glib adj con poca sinceridad, elocuente pero falso.
glide vi resbalar.
glimmer n vislumbre f.
glimpse n vislumbre f.
glint vi centellear.
glisten, glitter vi relucir, brillar.
gloat vi ojear con admiración.
global adj mundial.
globe n globo m; esfera f.
gloom, gloominess n oscuridad f; melancolía.
glorify vt glorificar, celebrar.
glory n gloria, fama, celebridad f.
gloss n glosa f; lustre m.
glossary n glosario m.
glove n guante m.
glow vi arder; inflamarse; relucir.

glower vi mirar con ceño.

glue n cola f.

glum adj abatido/da, triste.

glut n hartura, abundancia f.

gluttony n glotonería f.

glycerine n glicerina f.

gnarled adj nudoso/sa.

gnash vt, vi rechinar; crujir los dientes.

gnat n mosquito m.

gnaw vt roer.

gnome n gnomo m.

go vi ir, irse.

goal n meta f; fin m.

goaltender n portero m.

gobble vt engullir, tragar.

go-between n mediador/a m/f.

goblet n copa f.

goblin n espíritu ambulante, duende m.

God n Dios m.

godchild n ahijado, hijo de pila m.

goddaughter n ahijada, hija de pila f.

goddess n diosa f.

godfather n padrino m.

godmother n madrina f.

godsend n don del cielo m.

godson n ahijado m.

goggle-eyed adj bizco/ca.

goggles npl anteojos mpl.

gold n oro m.

goldfish n pez de colores m.

gold-plated adj chapado/da en oro.

golf n golf m.

golf course n campo de golf m.

golfer n golfista m/f.

gondolier n gondolero/ra m/f.

gone adj ido/da; perdido/da; pasado/da; gastado/da; muerto/ta.

gong n atabal chino m.

good adj bueno/na.

goodbye ! excl ¿adiós!

Good Friday n Viernes Santo m.

good-looking adj guapo/pa.

goodness n bondad f.

goodwill n benevolencia, bondad f.

goose n ganso m; oca f.

gooseberry n grosella espinosa f.

gorge n barranco m.

gorgeous adj maravilloso/sa.

gorilla n gorila m.

gorse n aulaga f.

gory adj sangriento/ta.

goshawk n azor m.

gospel n evangelio m.

gossamer n vello m.

gossip n charla f.

gothic adj gótico/ca.

gout n gota f (enfermedad).

govern vt gobernar, dirigir.

governess n gobernadora f.

government n gobierno m.

governor n gobernador m.

gown n toga f.

grab vt agarrar.

grace n gracia.

graceful adj gracioso/sa.

gracious adj gracioso/sa.

gradation n gradación f.

grade n grado m.

grade crossing n paso a nivel m.

gradient n (rail) pendiente.

gradual adj gradual.

graduate vi graduarse.

graduation n graduación f.

graffiti n pintadas fpl.

graft n injerto m.

grain n grano m.

gram n gramo m (peso).

grammar n gramática f.

granary n granero m.

grand adj grande, ilustre.

grandchild n nieto m; nieta f.

grandad n abuelo m.

granddaughter n nieta f.
grandeur n grandeza f.
grandfather n abuelo m.
grandiose adj grandioso/sa.
grandma n abuelita f.
grandmother n abuela f.
grandparents npl abuelos mpl.
grand piano n piano de cola m.
grandson n nieto m.
grandstand n tribuna f.
granite n granito m.
granny n abuelita f.
grant vt conceder.
granule n gránulo m.
grape n uva f:—**bunch of ~s** racimo de uvas m.
grapefruit n toronja f.
graph n gráfica f.
graphics n artes gráficas fpl; gráficos mpl.
grasp vt empuñar.
grass n hierba f.
grasshopper n saltamontes m.
grassland n pampa , pradera f.
grass snake n culebra f.
gratify vt contentar; gratificar.
gratifying adj grato/ta.
grating n rejado m.
gratis adv gratis.
gratitude n gratitud f.
grave n sepultura f.
gravel n cascajo m.
gravestone n piedra sepulcra f.
graveyard n cementerio m.
gravity n gravedad f.
gravy n jugo de la carne f; salsa f.
gray adj gris.
graze vt pastorear.
grease n grasa f:—vt untar.
greasy adj grasiento/ta.
great adj gran, grande.
greatcoat n sobretodo m.

greatness n grandeza f.
greedily adv vorazmente.
greediness, greed n gula f; codicia f.
Greek n griego (idioma) m.
green adj verde.
greengrocer n verdulero m.
greenhouse n invernadero m.
greet vt saludar, congratular.
greeting n saludo m.
greeting(s) card n tarjeta de felicitaciones f.
grenade n (mil) granada f.
grenadier n granadero m.
greyhound n galgo m.
greyish adj pardusco/ca.
grid n reja f; red f.
grief n dolor m.
grieve vt agraviar.
grievous adj doloroso/sa.
griffin n grifo m.
grill n parrilla f.
grim adj feo, fea.
grimace n visaje m.
grime n porquería f.
grin n mueca f.
grind vt moler.
grinder n molinero m.
grip n asimiento m.
grisly adj horroroso/sa.
gristle n tendón, nervio m.
grit n gravilla f; valor m.
groan vi gemir, suspirar.
grocer n tendero/ra, abarrotero/ra m/f.
groceries npl comestibles mpl.
groin n ingle f.
groom n establero m.
groove n ranura f.
gross adj grueso/sa.
grotesque adj grotesco/ca.
grotto n gruta f.
ground n tierra f.

ground floor n planta baja f.
group n grupo m..
grouse n urogallo m:—vi quejarse.
grove n arboleda f.
grovel vi arrastrarse.
grow vt cultivar:—vi crecer, aumen-
tarse.
growl vi regañar, gruñir.
grown-up n adulto m.
grub n gusano m.
grubby adj sucio/cia.
grudge n rencor, odio m; envidia f:—
vt, vienvidiar.
gruesome adj horrible.
gruff adj brusco/ca.
grumble vi gruñir; murmurar.
grunt vi gruñir.
G-string n taparrabo m.
guarantee n garantía f.
guard n guardia f.
guardianship n tutela f.
guerrilla n guerrillero m.
guess vt, vi conjeturar; adivinar;
suponer.
guest n huésped/a.
guffaw n carcajada f.
guide vt guiar, dirigir:—n guía m.
guidebook n guía f.
guild n gremio m.
guile n astucia f.

guilt n culpabilidad f.
guilty adj reo, rea, culpable.
guinea pig n cobayo m.
guise n manera f.
guitar n guitarra f.
gulf n golfo m.
gull n gaviota f.
gullet n esófago m.
gullible adj crédulo/la.
gully n barranco m.
gulp n trago m.
gum n goma f.
gum tree n árbol gomero m.
gun n pistola f; escopeta f.
gunboat n cañonera f.
gunpowder n pólvora f.
gunshot n escopetazo m.
gurgle vi gorgotear.
guru n gurú m.
gush vi brotar.
gusset n escudete m.
gut n intestino m.
gutter n canalón m; arroyo m.
guy n tío m; tipo m.
gym(nasium) n gimnasio m.
gymnast n gimnasta m/f.
gynecologist n ginecólogo/ga m/f.
Gypsy n gitano/na m/f.
gyrate vi girar.

H

haberdasher n camisero/ra, mercero/
ra m/f.
habit n costumbre f.
habitable adj habitable.
habitat n hábitat m.
habitual adj habitual.
haddock n merlango m.
hag n bruja f.

hail n granizo m.
hair n pelo; cabello m.
hairbrush n cepillo m.
haircut n corte de pelo m.
hairdresser n peluquero m.
hairdryer n secador de pelo m.
hairspray n laca f.
hairstyle n peinado m.

half n mitad f.
half-caste adj mestizo/za.
hall n vestíbulo m.
hallow vt consagrar, santificar.
hallucination n alucinación f.
halo n halo m.
halt vi parar.
halve vt partir por mitad.
ham n jamón m.
hamburger n hamburguesa f.
hamlet n aldea f.
hammer n martillo m.
hammock n hamaca f.
hamper n cesto f.
hamstring vt desjarretar.
hand n mano f.
handbag n cartera f.
handful n puñado m.
handicap n desventaja f.
handicraft n artesanía f.
handkerchief n pañuelo m.
handle n mango, puño m; asa; manija f.
handshake n apretón de manos m.
handsome adj guapo/pa.
handwriting n letra f.
handy adj practico/ca.
hang vt colgar.
hanger n percha f.
hangover n resaca f.
happen vi pasar; acontecer.
happiness n felicidad f.
happy adj feliz.
harass vt cansar, fatigar.
harbinger n precursor m.
harbor n puerto m.
hard adj duro/ra, firme.
harden vt, vi endurecer(se).
hardiness n robustez f.
hardly adv apenas.
hardship n penas fpl.
hard-up adj sin plata.

hardware store n ferretería f.
hardy adj fuerte.
hare n liebre f.
hare-lipped adj labihendido/da.
haricot n alubia f.
harlequin n arlequín m.
harm n mal, daño m.
harmful adj perjudicial.
harmless adj inocuo/cua.
harmonic adj armónico/ca.
harmonious adj armonioso/sa.
harmonize vt armonizar.
harmony n armonía f.
harp n arpa f.
harpoon n arpón m.
harsh adj duro/ra; austero/ra.
harvest n cosecha f.
harvester n cosechadora f.
hash n hachís m.
hassock n cojín de paja m.
haste n apuro m.
hasten vt acelerar.
hasty adj apresurado/da.
hat n sombrero m.
hatch vt incubar; tramarf.
hatchet n hacha f.
hatchway n (mar) escotilla f.
hate n odio.
hateful adj odioso/sa.
hatred n odio, aborrecimiento m.
haughty adj altanero/ra, orgulloso/sa.
haul vt tirar:—n botín m.
hauler n transportista m/f.
haunch n anca f.
haunt vt frecuentar, rondar.
have vt haber; tener, poseer.
haven n asilo m.
havoc n estrago m.
hawk n halcón m.
hawthorn n espino blanco m.
hay n heno m.
hazard n riesgo m.

haze n niebla f.
hazel n avellano m.
hazelnut n avellana f.
hazy adj oscuro/ra.
he pn el. **head** n cabeza f.
head n cakeza f.
headache n dolor de cabeza m.
headlamp n faro m.
headline n titular m.
headmaster n director m.
headphones npl auriculares mpl.
heal vt, vi curar.
health n salud f
healthy adj sano/na.
heap n montón m.
hear vt oír; escuchar.
hearing n oído m.
hearing aid n audífono m.
hearse n coche fúnebre m.
heart n corazón m.
heart attack n infarto m.
heartburn n acedia f.
hearth n hogar m.
heartily adv sinceramente.
heartless adj cruel.
hearty adj cordial.
heat n calor m.
heater n calentador m.
heathen n pagano m.
heating n calefacción f.
heatwave n ola de calor f.
heaven n cielo m.
heavily adv pesadamente.
heavy adj pesado/da.
Hebrew n hebreo m.
heckle vt interrumpir.
hectic adj agitado/da.
hedge n seto m.
hedgehog n erizo m.
heed vt hacer caso de.
heedless adj descuidado/da.
heel n talón m.

hefty adj grande.
heifer n ternera f.
height n altura f; altitud f.
heinous adj atroz.
heir n heredero/ra m/f.
heirloom n reliquia de familia f.
helicopter n helicóptero m.
hell n infierno m.
helm n (mar) timón m.
helmet n casco m.
help vt, vi ayudar, socorrer.
helper n ayudante m.
helpful adj útil.
helping n ración f.
helpless adj indefenso/sa.
hem n ribete m.
he-man n macho m.
hemisphere n hemisferio m.
hemorrhage n hemorragia f.
hemorrhoids npl hemorroides mpl.
hemp n cáñamo m.
hen n gallina f.
henchman n secuaz m.
henceforth, henceforward adv de aquí en adelante. **hepatitis** n hepatitis f.
her pn su; ella; de ella; a ella.
herald n heraldo m.
heraldry n heráldica f.
herb n hierba fl.
herbaceous adj herbáceo/cea.
herbalist n herbolario m.
herbivorous adj herbívoro/ra.
herd n rebaño m.
here adv aquí, acá.
hereabout(s) adv aquí alrededor.
hereafter adv en el futuro.
hereby adv por esto.
hereditary adj hereditario/ria.
heresy n herejía f.
heretic n hereje m/f.
heritage n patrimonio m.

hermetic *adj* hermético/ca.
hermit *n* ermitaño/ña *m/f.*
hermitage *n* ermita *f.*
hernia *n* hernia *f.*
hero *n* héroe *m.*
heroic *adj* heroico/ca.
heroine *n* heroína *f.*
heroism *n* heroísmo *m.*
heron *n* garza *f.*
herring *n* arenque *m.*
herself *pn* ella misma.
hesitant *adj* vacilante.
hesitate *vt* dudar; tardar.
heterosexual *adj, n* heterosexual *m.*
hew *vt* tajar; cortar.
heyday *n* apogeo *m.*
hi *excl* ¿hola!
hiatus *n* (gr) hiato *m.*
hibernate *vi* invernar.
hiccup *n* hipo *m.*
hickory *n* noguera americana *f.*
hide *vt* esconder*f.*
hideaway *n* escondite *m.*
hideous *adj* horrible.
hierarchy *n* jerarquía *f.*
hieroglyphic *adj* jeroglífico/ca.
hi-fi *n* estéreo, hi-fi *m.*
high *adj* alto/ta; elevado/da.
highlight *n* punto culminante *m.*
highway *n* carretera *f.*
hike *vi* ir de excursión.
hijack *vt* secuestrar.
hilarious *adj* alegre.
hill, hillock *n* colina *f.*
him *pn* le, lo, el.
himself *pn* el mismo, se, si mismo.
hinder *vt* impedir.
hindrance *n* impedimento, obstáculo *m.*
hinge *n* bisagra *f.*
hip *n* cadera *f.*
hippopotamus *n* hipopótamo *m.*

hire *vt* alquilar.
his *pn* su, suyo, de el.
Hispanic *adj* hispano/na; hispánico/ca.
hiss *vt, vi* silbar.
historian *n* historiador *m.*
history *n* historia *f.*
hit *vt* golpear.
hitch *vt* atar.
hitch-hike *vi* hacer autostop.
hive *n* colmena *f.*
hoax *n* trampa *f.*
hobble *vi* cojear.
hobby *n* pasatiempo *m.*
hockey *n* hockey *m.*
hodge-podge *n* mezcolanza *f.*
hoe *n* azadón *m.*
hog *n* cerdo, puerco *m.*
hoist *vt* alzar.
hold *vt* tener; detener; contener.
hole *n* agujero *m.*
holiday *n* día de fiesta *m:*—~s *pl* vacaciones *fpl.*
hollow *adj* hueco/ca.
holly *n* (bot) acebo *m.*
hollyhock *n* malva hortense *f.*
holocaust *n* holocausto *m.*
holster *n* pistolera *f.*
holy *adj* santo/ta.
holy week *n* semana santa *f.*
homage *n* homenaje *m.*
home *n* casa *f.*
home address *n* domicilio *m.*
homely *adj* casero/ra.
homeopathist *n* homeopatista *m/f.*
homeopathy *n* homeopatía *f.*
homesick *adj* nostálgico/ca.
homework *n* deberes *mpl.*
homicide *n* homicidio *m*; homicida *m.*
homosexual *adj, n* homosexual *m.*
honest *adj* honrado/da.
honesty *n* honradez *f.*

honey n miel f.
honeycomb n panal m.
honeymoon n luna de miel f.
honeysuckle n (bot) madreselva f.
honor n honra f; honor m:—vt honrar.
honorary adj honorario/ria.
hood n capo m; capucha f.
hoof n pezuña f.
hook n gancho m.
hooligan n gamberro m.
hoop n aro m.
hooter n sirena f.
hop n (bot) lúpulo.
hope n esperanza f.
horde n horda f.
horizon n horizonte m.
horizontal adj horizontal.
hormone n hormona f.
horn n cuerno m.
hornet n avispón m.
horny adj calloso/sa.
horoscope n horóscopo m.
horrendous adj horrendo/da.
horrible adj horrible.
horrid adj horrible.
horrific adj horroroso/sa.
horrify vt horrorizar.
horror n horror, terror m.
hors d'oeuvre n entremeses mpl.
horse n caballo m
horse chestnut n castaño de Indias m.
horsefly n moscarda f.
horseradish n rábano silvestre m.
horticulture n horticultura, jardinería f.
horticulturist n jardinero/ra m/f.
hosepipe n manga f.
hosiery n calcetería f.
hospital n hospital m.
hospitality n hospitalidad f.
host n anfitrión m; hostia f.

hostage n rehén m.
hostess n anfitriona f.
hostile adj hostil.
hot adj caliente; cálido/da.
hotbed n semillero m.
hotel n hotel m.
hotelier n hotelero/ra m/f.
hour n hora f.
hour-glass n reloj de arena m.
house n casa f.
household n familia f.
houseless adv sin casa.
housewife n ama de casa f.
hovel n choza, cabaña f.
hover vi flotar.
how adv cómo.
howl vi aullar.
hub n centro m.
hue n color m.
hug vt abrazar:—n abrazo m.
huge adj vasto/ta, enorme.
hum vi canturrear.
human adv humano/na.
humane adv humano/na.
humanist n humanista m/f.
humanitarian adj humanitario/ria.
humanity n humanidad f.
humble adj humilde.
humid adj húmedo/da.
humidity n humedad f.
humiliate vt humillar.
humming-bird n colibrí m.
humor n sentido del humor m.
humorist n humorista m./f
humorous adj gracioso/sa.
hundred adj ciento.
hundredth adj centésimo.
hundredweight n quintal m.
hunger n hambre f.
hunt vt cazar; perseguir.
hunter n cazador/a m/f.
hurdle n valla f.

hurricane n huracán m.
hurt vt hacer daño; ofender.
hurtful adj dañoso/sa:—~ly adv dañosamente.
husband n marido m.
hush! excl ¡chitón!, ¡silencio!.
husk n cáscara f.
hut n cabaña f.
hutch n conejera f.
hyacinth n jacinto m.
hydraulic adj hidráulico/ca.

hydrofoil n aerodeslizador m.
hydrogen n hidroala f.
hyena n hiena f.
hygiene n higiene f.
hymn n himno m.
hypermarket n hipermercado m.
hyphen n (gr) guión m.
hypocrisy n hipocresía f.
hypocrite n hipócrita m/f.
hysterical adj histérico/ca.
hysterics npl histeria f.

I

I pn yo.
ice n hielo m:—vt helar.
ice cream n helado m.
ice rink n pista de hielo f.
icicle n carámbano m.
idea n idea f.
ideal adj ideal.
identical adj idéntico/ca.
identification n identificación f.
identify vt identificar.
identity n identidad f.
ideology n ideología f.
idiom n idioma m.
idiosyncrasy n idiosincrasia f.
idiot n idiota, necio m.
idiotic adj tonto/ta, bobo/ba.
idle adj desocupado/da.
idol n ídolo m.
idolatry n idolatría f.
idyllic adj idílico/ca.
i.e. adv esto es.
if conj si, aunque.
ignite vt encender.
ignoble adj innoble.
ignorance n ignorancia f.
ignorant adj ignorante.
ignore vt no hacer caso de.

ill adj malo/la, enfermo/ma.
ill-advised adj imprudente.
illegal adj ~ly adv ilegal(mente).
illegible adj ilegible.
illegitimate adj ilegítimo/ma.
ill feeling n rencor m.
illiterate adj analfabeto/ta.
illness n enfermedad f.
illogical adj ilógico/ca.
illuminate vt iluminar.
illusion n ilusión f.
illustrate vt ilustrar.
illustration n ilustración f.
image n imagen f.
imagination n imaginación f.
imagine vt imaginarse.
imbalance n desequilibrio m.
imbecile adj imbécil.
imitate vt imitar, copiar.
imitation n imitación, copia f.
immaculate adj inmaculado/da.
immature adj inmaduro/ra.
immediate adj inmediato/ta.
immense adj inmenso/sa.
immigrant n inmigrante m.
immigration n inmigración f.
imminent adj inminente.

immodest adj inmodesto/ta.
immoral adj inmoral.
immortal adj inmortal.
immune adj inmune.
imp n diablillo, duende m.
impact n impacto m.
impair vt disminuir.
impartial adj **~ly** adv imparcial (mente).
impatience n impaciencia f.
impede vt estorbar.
impel vt impeler.
impending adj inminente.
imperative adj imperativo/va.
imperfect adj imperfecto/ta
imperial adj imperial.
impersonal adj, **~ly** adv impersonal-(mente).
impetus n ímpetu m.
impiety n irmpiedad f.
implant vt implantar.
implement n herramienta.
implore vt suplicar.
imply vt suponer.
impolite adj maleducado/da.
import vt importar.
importance n importancia f.
important adj importante.
impose vt imponer.
impostor n impostor m.
impotence n impotencia f.
impotent adj impotente.
impound vt embargar.
impoverish vt empobrecer.
impractical adj poco práctico/ca.
imprecise adj impreciso/sa.
impress vt impresionar.
impression n impresión f; edición f.
impressive adj impresionante.
imprint n sello m:—vt imprimir; estampar.
improbable adj improbable.

improper adj impropio/pia.
improve vt, vi mejorar.
improvise vt improvisar.
impulse n impulso m.
impure adj impuro/ra.
impurity n impureza f.
in prep en.
inability n incapacidad f.
inaccessible adj inaccesible.
inaccurate adj inexacto/ta.
inadequate adj inadecuado/da, defec-tuoso/sa.
inadmissible adj inadmisible.
inadvertently adv sin querer.
inappropriate adj impropio/pia.
inaudible adj inaudible.
inaugurate vt inaugurar.
in-between adj intermedio/dia.
inborn, inbred adj innato/ta.
incapable adj incapaz.
incarcerate vt encarcelar.
incarnation n encarnación f.
incendiary n bomba incendiaria f.
incense n incienso m.
incentive n incentivo m.
incessant adj incesante.
incest n incesto m.
inch n pulgada f.
incident n incidente m.
incinerator n incinerador m.
inclination n inclinación.
incline vt, vi inclinar(se).
include vt incluir.
inclusive adj inclusivo/va.
incognito adv de incógnito.
incoherent adj incoherente.
income n renta f
incompatible adj incompatible.
incompetence n incompetencia f.
incomplete adj incompleto/ta.
incomprehensible adj incomprensi-ble.

inconceivable *adj* inconcebible.
incontinence *n* incontinencia *f.*
inconvenience *n* incomodidad *f.*
incorrect *adj* incorrecto/ta.
increase *vt* acrecentar, aumentar
incredible *adj* increíble.
incubate *vi* incubar.
incubator *n* incubadora *f.*
incurable *adj* incurable.
indecency *n* indecencia *f.*
indecent *adj* indecente:—~ly *adv* indecentemente.
indecisive *adj* indeciso/sa.
indeed *adv* verdaderamente, de veras.
independence *n* independencia *f.*
independent *adj* independiente.
indescribable *adj* indescriptible.
index *n* índice *m.*
indicate *vt* indicar.
indifference *n* indiferencia *f.*
indigenous *adj* indígena.
indigestion *n* indigestión *f.*
indignation *n* indignación *f.*
indigo *n* añil *m.*
indirect *adj* indirecto/ta.
indiscreet *adj* indiscreto/ta.
indispensable *adj* indispensable.
indistinguishable *adj* indistinguible.
individual *adj* individual *m.*
indoors *adv* dentro.
indulge *vt, vi* conceder; ser indulgente.
industrialist *n* industrial *m.*
industry *n* industria *f.*
inedible *adj* no comestible.
ineffective, ineffectual *adj* ineficaz.
inefficiency *n* ineficacia *f.*
ineligible *adj* ineligible.
inept *adj* incompetente.
inequality *n* desigualdad *f.*
inevitable *adj* inevitable.

inexpensive *adj* económico/ca.
inexperience *n* inexperiencia *f.*
inexpert *adj* inexperto/ta.
inexplicable *adj* inexplicable.
infallible *adj* infalible.
infamy *n* infamia *f.*
infancy *n* infancia *f.*
infant *n* niño/ña *m/f.*
infantile *adj* infantil.
infantry *n* infantería *f.*
infatuation *n* infatuación *f.*
infect *vt* infectar.
infection *n* infección *f.*
inferior *adj* inferior.
infernal *adj* infernal.
inferno *n* infierno *m.*
infest *vt* infestar.
infidelity *n* infidelidad *f.*
infinite *adj* infinito/ta.
infinitive *n* infinitivo *m.*
infinity *n* infinito *m;* infinidad *f.*
infirm *adj* enfermo/ma.
infirmary *n* enfermería *f.*
infirmity *n* fragilidad, enfermedad *f.*
inflammation *n* inflamación *f.*
inflatable *adj* inflable.
inflate *vt* inflar, hinchar.
inflation *n* inflación *f.*
inflict *vt* imponer.
influence *n* influencia *f.*
influenza *n* gripe *f.*
inform *vt* informar.
informal *adj* informal.
information *n* información *f.*
infrastructure *n* infraestructura *f.*
infuriate *vt* enfurecer.
infusion *n* infusión *f.*
ingenious *adj* ingenioso/sa.
ingenuity *n* ingeniosidad *f.*
ingot *n* barra de metal *f.*
ingrained *adj* inveterado/da.
ingratitude *n* ingratitud *f.*

ingredient n ingrediente m.
inhabit vt, vi habitar.
inhabitant n habitante m.
inhale vt inhalar.
inherent adj inherente.
inherit vt heredar.
inheritance n herencia f.
inhibit vt inhibir.
inhospitable adj inhospitalario/ria.
inhuman adj inhumano/na.
inhumanity n inhumanidad, crueldad f.
initial adj inicial.
initiate vt iniciar.
initiative n iniciativa f.
inject vt inyectar.
injection n inyección f.
injure vt herir.
injury n daño m.
injustice n injusticia f.
ink n tinta f.
inkling n sospecha f.
inlaid adj taraceado/da.
in-laws npl suegros mpl.
inlay vt taracear.
inlet n entsenada f.
inmate n preso m.
inn n posada f; mesón m.
innkeeper n posadero/ra, mesonero/ra m/f.
innocence n inocencia f.
innocent adj inocente.
innovate vt innovar.
innovation n innovación f.
innuendo n indirecta, insinuación f.
inoffensive adj inofensivo/va.
inorganic adj inorgánico/ca.
inpatient n paciente interno m.
input n entrada f.
inquest n encuesta judicial i.
inquire vt, vi preguntar.
inquiry n pesquisa f.

inquisition n inquisición f.
inquisitive adj curioso/sa.
insane adj loco/ca, demente.
insanity n locura f.
inscription n inscripción f.
inscrutable adj inescrutable.
insect n insecto m.
insecticide n insecticida m.
insecure adj inseguro/ra.
insensitive adj insensible.
inseparable adj inseparable.
insert vt introducir.
insertion n inserción f.
inside n interior m:—adv dentro.
inside out adv al revés; a fondo.
insignia npl insignias fpl.
insignificant adj insignificante.
insincere adj poco sincero/ra.
insipid adj insípido/da.
insist vi insistir.
insole n plantilla f.
insolence n insolencia f.
insoluble adj insoluble.
insomnia n insomnio m.
insomuch conj puesto que.
inspect vt examinar, inspeccionar.
inspection n inspección f.
inspire vt inspirar.
instability n inestabilidad f.
instance n ejemplo m.
instant adj inmediato/ta.
instead (of) pr por, en lugar de, en vez de.
instill vt inculcar.
instinct n instinto m.
instinctive adj instintivo/va.
institute vt establecer:—n instituto m.
institution n institución f.
instruct vt instruir, enseñar.
instruction n instrucción f.
instrument n instrumento m.
instrumental adj instrumental.

insufferable *adj* insoportable.
insufficient *adj* insuficiente.
insulate *vt* aislar.
insulin *n* insulina *f.*
insult *vt* insultar:—*n* insulto *m.*
insurance *n* (com) seguro *m.*
insure *vt* asegurar.
intact *adj* intacto/ta.
integral *adj* íntegro/gra.
integrate *vt* integrar.
integrity *n* integridad *f.*
intellect *n* intelecto *m.*
intelligence *n* inteligencia *f.*
intend *vi* tener intención.
intense *adj* intenso/sa.
intensity *n* intensidad *f.*
intention *n* intención *f.*
inter *vt* enterrar.
interaction *n* interacción *f.*
intercourse *n* relaciones sexuales *fpl.*
interest *vt* interesar.
interesting *adj* interesante.
interest rate *n* tipo de interés *m.*
interfere *vi* entrometerse.
interference *n* interferencia *f.*
interior *adj* interior.
interlude *n* intermedio *m.*
intermediate *adj* intermedio/dia.
interment *n* entierro *m;* sepultura *f.*
intermission *n* descanso *m.*
intermittent *adj* intermitente.
internal *adj* interno/na.
international *adj* internacional.
interpret *vt* interpretar.
interpretation *n* interpretación *f.*
interpreter *n* intérprete *m/f.*
interregnum *n* interregno *m.*
interrelated *adj* interrelacionado/da.
interrogate *vt* interrogar.
interrogation *n* interrogatorio *m.*
interrogative *adj* interrogativo/va.
interrupt *vt* interrumpir.

interruption *n* interrupción *f.*
intersect *vi* cruzarse.
intersection *n* cruce *m.*
intersperse *vt* esparcir.
intertwine *vt* entretejer.
interval *n* intervalo *m.*
intervene *vi* intervenir.
intervention *n* intervención *f.*
interview *n* entrevista *f.*
interviewer *n* entrevistador/a *m/f.*
intestine *n* intestino *m.*
intimacy *n* intimidad *f.*
intimate *n* amigo/ga íntimo/ma.
intimidate *vt* intimidar.
into *prep* en, dentro, adentro.
intolerable *adj* intolerable.
intolerance *n* intolerancia *f.*
intoxicate *vt* embriagar.
intravenous *adj* intravenoso/sa.
intrepid *adj* intrépido/da.
intricate *adj* intricado/da.
intrigue *n* intriga *f:*—*vi* intrigar.
intriguing *adj* fascinante.
intrinsic *adj* intrínseco/ca.
introduce *vt* introducir.
introduction *n* introducción *f.*
introvert *n* introvertido *m.*
intrude *vi* entrometerse.
intruder *n* intruso/sa *m/f.*
intuition *n* intuición *f.*
intuitive *adj* intuitivo/va.
inundate *vt* inundar.
inundation *n* inundación *f.*
invade *vt* invadir.
invalid *adj* inválido/da.
invalidate *vt* invalidar, anular.
invaluable *adj* inapreciable.
invariable *adj* invariable.
invariably *adv* invariablemente.
invasion *n* invasión *f.*
invent *vt* inventar.
invention *n* invento *m.*

inventor n inventor m.
inventory n inventario m.
inversion n inversión f.
invert vt invertir.
invest vt invertir.
investigate vt investigar.
investment n inversión f.
invigilate vt vigilar.
invigorating adj vigorizante.
invincible adj invencible.
invisible adj invisible.
invitation n invitación f.
invite vt invitar.
invoice n (com) factura f.
involuntarily adv involuntariamente.
involve vt implicar.
involvement n compromiso m.
iodine n (chem) yodo m.
IOU (I owe you) n vale m.
irate, ireful adj enojado/da.
iris n iris m.
irksome adj fastidioso/sa.
iron n hierro m:—adj férreo/rea:—vt planchar.
ironic adj irónico/ca:—~ly adv con ironía.
ironwork n herraje m:——~s pl herrería f.

irony n ironía f.
irradiate vt irradiar.
irrational adj irracional.
irreconcilable adj irreconciliable.
irregular adj ~ly adv irregular (mente).
irrelevant adj impertinente.
irreparable adj irreparable.
irresistible adj irresistible.
irresponsible adj irresponsable.
irrigate vt regar.
irrigation n riego m.
irritable adj irritable.
irritant n (med) irritante m.
irritate vt irritar.
island n isla f.
isle n isla f.
isolate vt aislar.
issue n asunto m.
it pn el, ella, ello, lo, la, le.
italic n cursiva f.
itch n picazón f:—vi picar.
item n artículo m.
itemize vt detallar.
itinerary n itinerario m.
its pn su, suyo.
itself pn el mismo, la misma, lo mismo.
ivory n marfil m.
ivy n hiedra f.

J

jab vt clavar.
jabber vi farfullar.
jack n gato m; sota f.
jackal n chacal m.
jackboots npl botas militares fpl.
jackdaw n grajo m.
jacket n chaqueta f.
jack-knife vi colear.
jackpot n premio gordo m.
jade n jade m.

jagged adj dentado/da.
jaguar n jaguar m.
jail n cárcel f.
jailer n carcelero/ra m/f.
jam n conserva f; mermelada de frutas f.
jangle vi sonar.
January n enero m.
jargon n jerigonza f.
jasmine n jazmín m.

jaundice n ictericia f.
jaunt n excursión f.
jaunty adj alegre.
javelin n jabalina f.
jaw n mandíbula f.
jay n arrendajo m.
jazz n jazz m.
jealous adj celoso/sa.
jealousy n celos mpl; envidia f.
jeans npl vaqueros mpl.
jeep n jeep m.
jeer vi befar.
jelly n jalea, gelatina f.
jellyfish n aguamar m; medusa f.
jeopardize vt arriesgar.
jersey n jersey m.
jest n broma f.
jester n bufón/ona m/f.
Jesuit n jesuita m.
Jesus n Jesús m.
jet n avión a reacción m
jettison vt desechar.
jetty n muelle m.
Jew n judío/día m/f.
jewel n joya f.
jewelry n joyería f.
Jewish adj judío/día.
jib n (mar) foque m.
jibe n mofa f.
jig n giga f.
jigsaw n rompecabezas m.
jilt vt dejar.
job n trabajo m.
jockey n jinete m/f.
jocular adj jocoso/sa, alegre.
jog vi hacer footing.
jogging n footing m.
join vt juntar, unir.
joiner n carpintero/ra m/f.
joinery n carpintería f.
joint n articulación f.
jointly adv conjuntamente.

joke n broma f:—vi bromear.
joker n comodín m.
jollity n alegría f.
jolly adj alegre.
jolt vt sacudir:—n sacudida f.
jostle vt codear.
journal n revista f.
journalism n periodismo m.
journalist n periodista m/f.
journey n viaje m:—vt viajar.
jovial adj jovial.
joy n alegría f; jubilo m.
jubilant adj jubiloso/sa.
jubilation n jubilo/la, regocijo m.
jubilee n jubileo m.
Judaism n judaísmo m.
judge n juez/a m/f:—vt juzgar.
judgment n juicio m.
judicial adj ~ly adv judicial(mente).
judiciary n judicatura m.
judicious adj prudente.
judo n judo m.
juggle vi hacer juegos malabares.
juggler n malabarista m/f.
juice n jugo m; suco m.
juicy adj jugoso/sa.
jukebox n gramola f.
July n julio m.
jumble vt mezclar
jump vi saltar
jumper n suéter m.
jumpy adj nervioso/sa.
juncture n coyuntura f.
June n junio m.
jungle n selva f.
junior adj más joven.
juniper n (bot) enebro m.
junk n basura f; baratijas fpl.
junta n junta f.
jurisdiction n jurisdicción f.
jurisprudence n jurisprudencia f.
jurist n jurista m/f.

jury n jurado m.
just adj justo/ta.
justice n justicia f.
justification n justificación f.
justify vt justificar.
justly adv justamente.

justness n justicia f.
jut vi:—**to ~ out** sobresalir.
jute n yute m.
juvenile adj juvenil.
juxtaposition n yuxtaposición f.

K

kaleidoscope n calidoscopio m.
kangaroo n canguro m.
karate n karate m.
kebab n pincho m.
keel n (mar) quilla f.
keen adj agudo/da; vivo/va.
keep vt mantener; guardar; conservar.
keeper n guardián/ana m/f.
keepsake n recuerdo m.
keg n barril m.
kennel n perrera f.
kernel n fruta f; meollo m.
kerosene n kerosene m.
ketchup n catsup m.
kettle n hervidor m.
key n llave f; (mus) clave f; tecla f.
keyboard n teclado m.
keyhole n ojo de la cerradura m.
key ring n llavero m.
khaki n caqui m.
kick vt, vi patear.
kid n chico m.
kidnap vt secuestrar.
kidnapper n secuestrador/a m/f.
kidney n riñón m.
killer n asesino/na m/f.
killing n asesinato m.
kiln n horno m.
kilo n kilo m.
kilobyte n kiloocteto m.
kilogram n kilo m.

kilometer n kilómetro m.
kilt n falda escocesa f.
kin n parientes mpl.
kind adj cariñoso/sa:—n genero m.
kind-hearted adj bondadoso/sa.
kindle vt, vi encender.
kindly adj bondadoso/sa.
kindness n bondad f.
kindred adj emparentado/da.
kinetic adj cinético/ca.
king n rey m.
kingdom n reino m.
kingfisher n martín pescador m.
kiosk n quiosco m.
kiss n beso m:—vt besar.
kit n equipo m.
kitchen n cocina f.
kite n cometa f.
kitten n gatillo m.
knack n don m.
knapsack n mochila f.
knave n bribón m.
knead vt amasar.
knee n rodilla f.
kneel vi arrodillarse.
knell n toque de difuntos m.
knife n cuchillo m.
knight n caballero m.
knit vt, vi tejer.
knitting needle n aguja de tejer f.
knitwear n prendas de punto fpl.
knob n bulto m.

knock *vt, vi* golpear.
knocker *n* aldaba *f.*
knock-kneed *adj* patizambo/ba.
knock-out *n* K.O. *m.*
knoll *n* cima de una colina *f.*
knot *n* nudo *m*; lazo *m*:—*vt* anudar.
knotty *adj* escabroso/sa.
know *vt, vi* conocer; saber.

know-all *n* sabelotodo *m/f.*
know-how *n* conocimientos *mpl.*
knowing *adj* entendido/da:—**~ly** *adv*
   a sabiendas.
knowledge *n* conocimiento *m.*
knowledgeable *adj* bien informado/
   da.
knuckle *n* nudillo *m.*

L

label *n* etiqueta *f.*
laboratory *n* laboratorio *m.*
laborious *adj* laborioso/sa.
labor *n* trabajo *m.*
laborer *n* peón *m.*
labyrinth *n* laberinto *m.*
lace *n* cordón.
lacerate *vt* lacerar.
lack *vt, vi* faltar.
lacquer *n* laca *f.*
lad *n* muchacho *m.*
ladder *n* escalera *f.*
ladle *n* cucharón *m.*
lady *n* señora *f.*
lag *vi* quedarse atrás.
lager *n* cerveza (rubia) *f.*
lagoon *n* laguna *f.*
lake *n* lago *m.*
lamb *n* cordero *m*:—*vi* parir.
lame *adj* cojo/ja.
lament *vt, vi* lamentar(se).
lamp *n* lámpara *f.*
lampoon *n* sátira *f.*
lampshade *n* pantalla *f.*
lance *n* lanza *f.*
lancet *n* lanceta *f.*
land *n* país *m*; tierra *f.*
landing *n* desembarco *m.*
landmark *n* lugar conocido *m.*
landscape *n* paisaje *m.*

lane *n* callejuela *f.*
language *n* lengua *f*; lenguaje *m.*
lank *adj* lacio/cia.
lanky *adj* larguirucho.
lantern *n* linterna *f*; farol *m.*
lap *n* regazo *m.*
lapel *n* solapa *f.*
lapse *n* lapso *m.*
larceny *n* latrocinio *m.*
larch *n* alerce *m.*
lard *n* manteca de cerdo *f.*
larder *n* despensa *f.*
large *adj* grande.
lark *n* alondra *f.*
larva *n* larva, oruga *f.*
laryngitis *n* laringitis *f.*
larynx *n* laringe *f.*
lascivious *adj* lascivo/va.
laser *n* láser *m.*
lash *n* latigazo *m.*
lasso *n* lazo *m.*
last *adj* último/ma.
lasting *adj* duradero/ra, permanente.
latch *n* picaporte *m.*
late *adj* tarde; difunto/ta.
latent *adj* latente.
lathe *n* torno *m.*
lather *n* espuma *f.*
latitude *n* latitud *f.*
latter *adj* último/ma.

lattice n celosía f.
laugh vi reir.
laughter n risa f.
launch vt, vi lanzar(se):—n (mar) lancha f.
launching n lanzamiento m.
launder vt lavar.
laundry n lavandería f.
laurel n laurel m.
lava n lava f.
lavatory n water m.
lavender n (bot) espliego m, lavándula f.
lavish adj pródigo/ga:—~ly adv pródigamente:—vt disipar.
law n ley f; derecho m.
law court n tribunal m.
lawn n pasto m.
lawnmower n cortacésped m.
law suit n proceso m.
lawyer n abogado/da m/f.
laxative n laxante m.
lay vt poner.
layabout n vago/ga m/f.
layer n capa f.
layout n composición f.
laze vi holgazanear.
laziness n pereza f.
lazy adj perezoso/sa.
lead n plomo m.
leader n jefe/fa m/f.
leaf n hoja f.
leaflet n folleto m.
league n liga, alianza f.
leak n escape m.
lean vt, vi apoyar(se).
leap vi saltar.
leap year n año bisiesto m.
learn vt, vi aprender.
lease n arriendo m:—vt arrendar.
leash n correa f.
least adj mínimo/ma.

leather n cuero m.
leave n licencia f; permiso m.
lecherous adj lascivo/va.
lecture n conferencia f.
ledge n reborde m.
ledger n (com) libro mayor m.
leech n sanguijuela f.
leek n (bot) puerro m.
left adj izquierdo/da.
left-handed adj zurdo/da.
leftovers npl sobras fpl.
leg n pierna f
legacy n herencia f.
legal adj legal.
legalize vt legalizar.
legend n leyenda f.
legendary adj legendario/ria.
legible adj legible.
legion n legión f.
legislate vt legislar.
legislation n legislación f.
leisure n ocio m:—~ly adj sin prisa:—at ~ desocupado/da.
lemon n limón m.
lemonade n limonada f.
lend vt prestar.
length n largo m; duración f.
lenient adj indulgente.
lens n lente f.
Lent n Cuaresma f.
lentil n lenteja f.
leopard n leopardo m.
leotard n leotardo m.
leper n leproso/sa m/f.
leprosy n lepra f.
lesbian n lesbiana f.
less adj menor.
lesson n lección f.
let vt dejar, permitir.
lethal adj mortal.
lethargy n letargo m.
letter n letra f; carta f.

lettuce n lechuga f.
leukemia n leucemia f.
level adj llano/na, igual.
lever n palanca f.
leverage n influencia f.
levy n leva (de tropas) f.
lexicon n léxico m.
liability n responsabilidad f.
liable adj sujeto/ta; responsable.
liaise vi enlazar.
liaison n enlace m.
liar n embustero m.
libel n difamación f:—vt difamar.
liberal adj liberal.
liberate vt libertar.
liberation n liberación f.
liberty n libertad f.
Libra n Libra f.
librarian n bibliotecario m.
library n biblioteca f.
license n licencia f.
lick vt lamer.
lid n tapa f.
lie n mentira f.
life n vida f.
lifelike adj natural.
life preserver n chaleco salvavidas m.
lift vt levantar.
ligament n ligamento m.
light n luz f.
light bulb n foco m; bombilla f.
lighter n encendedor m.
lighthouse n (mar) faro m.
lightning n relámpago m.
like adj semejante; igual.
likeness n semejanza f.
lilac n lila f.
lily n lirio m.
lima beans npl haba gruesa f.
limb n miembro m.
lime n cal f; lima f.
limestone n piedra caliza f.

limit n limitem.
line n línea f.
linen n lino m.
liner n transatlántico m.
linger vi persistir.
lingerie n ropa interior f.
linguist n lingüista m.
lining n forro m.
link n eslabón m.
linoleum n linóleo m.
lintel n dintel m.
lion n león m.
lip n labio m.
liqueur n licor m.
liquid adj líquido/da
liquor n licor m.
liquorice n orozuz m; regalicia f.
lisp vi cecear.
list n lista f.
listen vi escuchar.
literature n literatura f.
lithe adj ágil.
lithograph n litografía f.
litigation n litigio m.
liter n litro m.
litter n litera f.
little adj pequeño/ña, poco/ca
live vi vivir; habitar.
liver n hígado m.
livestock n ganado m.
living n vida f:—adj vivo/va.
living room n sala de estar f.
lizard n lagarto m.
load vt cargar
loaf n pan m.
loam n marga f.
loan n préstamo m.
loathe vt aborrecer.
loathing n aversión f.
lobby n vestíbulo m.
lobe n lóbulo m.
lobster n langosta f.

local *adj* local.
locality *n* localidad *f.*
locate *vt* localizar.
location *n* situación *f.*
loch *n* lago *m.*
lock *n* cerradura *f.*
locker *n* vestuario *m.*
locket *n* medallón *m.*
locomotive *n* locomotora *f.*
locust *n* langosta *f.*
loft *n* desván *m.*
lofty *adj* alto/ta.
log *n* leño *m.*
logic *n* lógica *f.*
logo *n* logotipo *m.*
loiter *vi* merodear.
lollipop *n* pirulí *m.*
loneliness *n* soledad *f.*
long *adj* largo/ga.
longitude *n* longitud *f.*
look *vi* mirar *f.*
looking glass *n* espejo *m.*
loop *n* lazo *m.*
loose *adj* suelto/ta.
loot *vt* saquear:—*n* botín *m.*
lop *vt* desmochar.
lord *n* señor *m.*
lose *vt* perder.
loss *n* perdida *f.*
lotion *n* loción *f.*
lottery *n* lotería *f.*
loud *adj* fuerte:—~**ly** *adv* fuerte.
loudspeaker *n* altavoz *m.*
lounge *n* salón *m.*
louse *n* piojo (*pl* **lice**) *m.*

lout *n* gamberro *m.*
love *n* amor, cariño *m.*
lovely *adj* hermoso/sa.
lover *n* amante *m.*
low *adj* bajo/ja.
loyal *adj* leal; fiel.
lozenge *n* pastilla *f.*
lubricant *n* lubricante *m.*
lubricate *vt* lubricar.
luck *n* suerte *f;* fortuna *f.*
lucrative *adj* lucrativo/va.
ludricrous *adj* absurdo/da.
lug *vt* arrastrar.
luggage *n* equipaje *m.*
lull *vt* acunar:—*n* tregua *f.*
lullaby *n* nana *f.*
lumbago *n* lumbago *m.*
lumber *n* madera de construccion *f*
luminous *adj* luminoso/sa.
lump *n* terrón *m.*
lunacy *n* locura *f.*
lunar *adj* lunar.
lunatic *adj* loco/ca.
lunch, luncheon *n* merienda *f.*
lungs *npl* pulmones *mpl.*
luscious *adj* delicioso/sa.
lush *adj* exuberante.
lust *n* lujuria, sensualidad *f.*
luster *n* lustre *m.*
luxurious *adj* lujoso/sa.
luxury *n* lujo *m.*
lymph *n* linfa *f.*
lynx *n* lince *m.*
lyrical *adj* lírico/ca.
lyrics *npl* letra *f.*

M

macaroni *n* macarrones *mpl.*
macaroon *n* almendrado *m.*
mace *n* maza *f;* macis *f.*

machine *n* maquina *f.*
machinery *n* maquinaria, mecanica *f.*
mackerel *n* escombro *m.*

mad adj loco, furioso, rabioso.
madam n madama, senora f.
madhouse n casa de locos f.
madness n locura f.
magazine n revista f.
maggot n gusano m.
magic n magia f.
magician n mago m
magistrate n magistrado m.
magnet n iman m.
magnetic adj magnetico.
magnificent adj magnifico.
magnify vt aumentar.
magnifying glass n lupa f.
magnitude n magnitud f.
magpie n urraca f.
mahogany n caoba f.
mail n correo m.
mailman n cartero m.
maim vt mutilar.
main adj principal.
maintain vt mantener.
maintenance n mantenimiento m.
maize n maiz m.
majesty n majestad f.
major adj principal
make vt hacer, crear.
make-up n maquillaje m.
malaria n malaria f.
male adj masculino:—n macho m.
malice n malicia f.
malicious adj malicioso.
mall n centro comercial m.
malleable adj maleable.
mallet n mazo m.
mallows n (bot) malva f.
malnutrition n desnutricion f.
malpractice n negligencia f.
malt n malta f.
maltreat vt maltratar.
mammal n mamifero m.
mammoth adj gigantesco.

man n hombre m.
manage vt, vi manejar, dirigir.
management n direccion f.
manager n director m.
mandate n mandato m.
mane n crines del caballo fpl.
maneuvre n maniobra f.
mangle n rodillo m.
mangy adj sarnoso.
manhood n edad viril f.
mania n mania f.
maniac n maniaco m.
manipulate vt manejar.
mankind n genero humano m.
man-made n artificial.
manner n manera f; modo m
mansion n palacio m.
mantelpiece n repisa de chimenea f.
manual adj, n manual m.
manufacture n fabricacion f.
manufacturer n fabricante m.
manuscript n manuscrito m.
many adj muchos, muchas.
map n mapa m.
maple n arce m.
mar vt estropear.
marathon n maraton m.
marble n marmol m.
March n marzo m.
mare n yegua f.
margarine n margarina f.
margin n margen m; borde m.
marigold n (bot) calendula f.
marijuana n marijuana f.
marine adj marinom.
marital adj marital.
mark n marca f.
market n mercado m.
marmalade n mermelada de naranja f.
maroon adj marron.
marquee n entoldado m.

marriage n matrimonio m
marrow n medula f.
marry vi casar(se).
marsh n pantano m.
marshy adj pantanoso.
martyr n martir m.
marvel n maravilla f.
marvelous adj maravilloso.
marzipan n mazapan m.
mascara n rimel m.
masculine adj masculino.
mask n mascara f.
masochist n masoquista m.
mason n albanil m.
mass n masa f; misa f;
massacre n carniceria, matanza f.
massage n masaje m.
massive adj enorme.
mast n mastil m.
masterpiece n obra maestra f.
masticate vt masticar.
mat n estera f.
match n fosforo m, cerilla f.
mate n companero m:—vt acoplar.
mathematics npl matematicas fpl.
matinee n funcion de la tarde f.
mating n aparejamiento m.
matriculate vt matricular.
matriculation n matriculacion f.
matt adj mate.
matter n materia, substancia f.
mattress n colchon m.
mature adj maduro.
mauve adj de color malva.
maximum n maximo m.
May n mayo m.
mayonnaise n mayonesa f.
mayor n alcalde m.
maze n laberinto m.
me pn me; mi.
meal n comida f; harina f.
mean adj tacano.

meander vi serpentear.
meaning n sentido, significado m.
meantime, meanwhile adv mientras tanto.
measles npl sarampion m.
measurement n medida f.
meat n carne f.
mechanic n mecanico m.
mechanism n mecanismo m.
medal n medalla f.
media npl medios de comunicacion mpl.
medical adj medico.
medicate vt medicinar.
medicine n medicina f.
medieval adj medieval.
mediocre adj mediocre.
meditate vi meditar.
meditation n meditacion f.
Mediterranean adj mediterraneo.
medium n medio m.
meet vt encontrar.
meeting n reunion f.
megaphone n megafono m.
melancholy n melancolia f.
mellow adj maduro.
mellowness n madurez f.
melody n melodia f.
melon n melon m.
melt vt derretir.
member n miembro m.
membrane n membrana f.
memento n memento m.
memoir n memoria f.
memorandum n memorandum m.
memorial n monumento conmemorativo m.
memory n memoria f; recuerdo m.
menace n amenaza f.
menagerie n casa de fieras f.
mend vt reparar.
menial adj domestico.

meningitis n meningitis f.
menopause n menopausia f.
menstruation n menstruacion f.
mental adj mental.
mention n mencion f.
mentor n mentor m.
menu n menu m; carta f.
merchandise n mercancia f.
merchant n comerciante m.
mercury n mercurio m.
mercy n compasion f.
mere adj mero.
meridian n meridiano m.
merit n merito m.
mermaid n sirena f.
merry adj alegre.
merry-go-round n tiovivo m.
mesh n malla f.
mesmerize vt hipnotizar.
mess n lio m.
message n mensaje m.
metabolism n metabolismo n.
metal n metal m.
metallic adj metalico.
metamorphosis n metamorfosis f.
metaphor n metafora f.
meteor n meteoro m.
meteorological adj meteorológico.
meteorology n meteorologia f.
meter[1] n medidor m.
meter[2] n metro m.
method n metodo m.
methodical adj metodico.
Methodist n metodista m.
metric adj metrico.
metropolis n metropoli f.
metropolitan adj metropolitano.
mettle n valor m.
mew vi maullar.
mezzanine n entresuelo m.
microbe n microbio m.
microphone n microfono m.

microchip n microplaqueta f.
microscope n microscopio m.
microwave n horno microondas m.
mid adj medio.
midday n mediodia m.
middle adj mediom.
midge n mosca f.
midget n enano m.
midnight n medianoche f.
midst n medio, centro m.
midsummer n pleno verano m.
midwife n partera f.
might n poder m; fuerza f.
mighty adj fuerte.
migraine n jaqueca f.
migrate vi emigrar.
migration n emigracion f.
mike n microfono m.
mild adj apacible; suave.
mildew n moho m.
mileage n kilometraje m.
milieu n ambiente m.
militant adj militante.
military adj militar.
milk n leche f.
milkshake n batido m
milky adj lechoso:—**M~ Way** n Via
   Lactea f.
mill n molino m.
millennium n milenio m.
miller n molinero m.
milligram n miligramo m.
milliliter n mililitro m.
millimeter n milimetro m.
milliner n sombrerero.
million n millon m.
millionaire n millonario m.
millionth adj n millonésimo.
mime n mimo m.
mimic vt imitar.
mince vt picar.
mind n mente f.

mine *pn* mio, mia, mi:—*n* mina:—*vi* minar.

miner *n* minero *m*.

mineral *adj, n* mineral *m*.

mineral water *n* agua mineral *f*.

mingle *vt* mezclar.

miniature *n* miniatura *f*.

minimal *adj* minimo.

minimum *n* minimum *m*.

mining *n* explotacion minera *f*.

minister *n* ministro *m*.

mink *n* vison *m*.

minnow *n* pecicillo *m* (pez).

minor *adj* menor.

mint *n* (*bot*) menta *f*.

minus *adv* menos.

minute *adj* diminuto.

minute *n* minuto *m*.

miracle *n* milagro *m*.

mirage *n* espejismo *m*.

mire *n* fango *m*.

mirror *n* espejo *m*.

mirth *n* alegria *f*.

misbehave *vi* portarse mal.

miscarry *vi* abortar.

miscellaneous *adj* varios, varias.

miser *n* avaro *m*.

miserable *adj* miserable.

miserly *adj* mezquino, tacano.

misery *n* miseria *f*.

mislay *vt* extraviar.

mislead *vt* enganar.

misogynist *n* misogino *m*.

Miss *n* senorita *f*.

miss *vt* perder; echar de menos.

missile *n* misil *m*.

mission *n* mision *f*.

missionary *n* misionero *m*.

mist *n* niebla *f*.

mistake *vt* entender mal

Mister *n* Senor *m*.

mistletoe *n* (*bot*) muerdago *m*.

mistress *n* amante *f*.

mistrust *vt* desconfiar.

mitigate *vt* mitigar.

mitigation *n* mitigacion *f*.

miter *n* mitra *f*.

mittens *npl* manoplas *fpl*.

mix *vt* mezclar.

mixer *n* licuadora *f*.

mixture *n* mezcla *f*.

moan *n* gemido *m*.

moat *n* foso *m*.

mob *n* multitud *f*.

mobile *adj* movil.

mode *n* modo *m*.

model *n* modelo *m*.

moderate *adj* moderado.

moderation *n* moderacion *f*.

modern *adj* moderno.

modernize *vt* modernizar.

modest *adj* modesto.

modesty *n* modestia *f*.

modify *vt* modificar.

module *n* modulo *m*.

mogul *n* magnate *m*.

mohair *n* mohair *m*.

moist *adj* humedo.

moisture *n* humedad *f*.

mold *n* molde *m*.

mole *n* topo *m*.

molecule *n* molecula *f*.

molest *vt* importunar.

mom *n* mama *f*.

moment *n* momento *m*.

momentum *n* impetu *m*.

mommy *n* mama *f*.

monarch *n* monarca *m*.

monarchy *n* monarquia *f*.

monastery *n* monasterio *m*.

Monday *n* lunes *m*.

monetary *adj* monetario.

money *n* moneda *f*; dinero *m*.

mongol *n* mongolico *m*.

mongrel *adj, n* mestizo *m.*

monk *n* monje *m.*

monkey *n* mono *m.*

monopoly *n* monopolio *m.*

monotonous *adj* monotono.

monsoon *n* (*mar*) monzon *m.*

monster *n* monstruo *m.*

month *n* mes *m.*

monthly *adj, adv* mensual (mente).

monument *n* monumento *m.*

mood *n* humor *m.*

moody *adj* malhumorado.

moon *n* luna *f.*

moor *n* paramo.

moorland *n* paramo *m.*

moose *n* alce *m.*

mop *n* fregona *f.*

mope *vi* estar triste.

moped *n* ciclomotor *m.*

morality *n* etica, moralidad *f.*

morbid *adj* morboso.

more *adj, adv* mas.

moreover *adv* ademas.

morgue *n* deposito de cadaveres *m.*

morning *n* manana *f.:*—**good ~** buenos dias *mpl.*

moron *n* imbecil *m.*

morphine *n* morfina *f.*

morse *n* morse *m.*

morsel *n* bocado *m.*

mortal *adj* mortal

mortality *n* mortalidad *f.*

mortar *n* mortero *m.*

mortgage *n* hipoteca *f.*

mortify *vt* mortificar.

mortuary *n* deposito de cadaveres *m.*

mosaic *n* mosaico *m.*

mosque *n* mezquita *f.*

mosquito *n* mosquito *m.*

moss *n* (*bot*) musgo *m.*

most *adj* la mayoria de.

motel *n* motel *m.*

moth *n* polilla *f.*

mother *n* madre *f.*

mother-in-law *n* suegra *f.*

mother-of-pearl *n* nacar *m.*

motif *n* tema *m.*

motion *n* movimiento *m.*

motive *n* motivo *m.*

motor *n* motor *m.*

motorbike *n* moto *f.*

motorcycle *n* motocicleta *f.*

motor vehicle *n* automovil *m.*

motto *n* lema *m.*

mount *n* monte *m.*

mountain *n* montana *f.*

mountaineering *n* montañismo *m.*

mourn *vt* lamentar.

mourner *n* doliente *m.*

mourning *n* luto *m.*

mouse *n* (*pl* mice) raton *m.*

mousse *n* mousse *f.*

mouth *n* boca *f*;

mouthful *n* bocado *m.*

mouthwash *n* enjuague *m.*

mouthwatering *adj* apetitoso.

move *vt* mover.

movement *n* movimiento *m.*

movies *n* pelicula *f*; el cine

moving *adj* conmovedor.

mow *vt* segar.

mower *n* cortacesped *m*; mocion *f.*

Mrs *n* senora *f.*

much *adj, adv* mucho.

muck *n* suciedad *f.*

mucous *adj* mocoso.

mud *n* barro *m.*

muddle *vt* confundir *m*; confusion *f.*

muffle *vt* embozar.

mug *n* jarra *f.*

mulberry *n* mora *f.*

mule *n* mulo *m*, mula *f.*

multiple *adj* multiplo *m.*

multiplication *n* multiplicacion *f.*

multiply *vt* multiplicar.
multitude *n* multitud *f.*
mumble *vt, vi* refunfunar.
mummy *n* momia *f.*
mumps *npl* paperas *fpl.*
munch *vt* mascar.
mundane *adj* trivial.
municipal *adj* municipal.
municipality *n* municipalidad *f.*
mural *n* mural *m.*
murder *n* asesinato *m;* homicidio *m.*
murky *adj* sombrio.
murmur *n* murmullo.
muscle *n* musculo *m.*
muse *vi* meditar.
museum *n* museo *m.*
mushroom *n* (*bot*) seta *f;* champinon *m.*
music *n* musica *f.*
musician *n* musico *m.*
musk *n* musco *m.*
muslin *n* muselina *f.*

mussel *n* marisco *m.*
must *v aux* estar obligado.
mustache *n* bigote *m.*
mustard *n* mostaza *f.*
mute *adj* mudo, silencioso.
mutilate *vt* mutilar.
mutter *vt, vi* murmurar.
mutton *n* carnero *m.*
mutual *adj* mutuo, mutual.
muzzle *n* bozal *m.*
my *pn* mi, mis; mio, mia; mios, mias.
myriad *n* miriada *f.*
myrrh *n* mirra *f.*
myrtle *n* mirto, arrayan *m.*
myself *pn* yo mismo.
mysterious *adj* misterioso.
mystery *n* misterio *m.*
mystic(al) *adj* mistico.
mystify *vt* dejar perplejo.
mystique *n* misterio *m.*
myth *n* mito *m.*
mythology *n* mitologia *f.*

N

nag *n* jaca *f:*—*vt* reganar.
nagging *adj* persistente.
nail *n* una *f;* garra *f;* clavo *m.*
naive *adj* ingenuo.
naked *adj* desnudo.
name *n* nombre *m.*
nameless *adj* anonimo.
namely *adv* a saber.
namesake *n* tocayo *m.*
nanny *n* ninera *f.*
nap *n* sueno ligero *m.*
nape *n* nuca *f.*
napkin *n* servilleta *f.*
narcissus *n* (*bot*) narciso *m.*
narcotic *adj, n* narcotico *m.*

narrate *vt* narrar.
narrative *adj* narrativo.
narrow *adj* angosto, estrecho.
nasal *adj* nasal.
nasty *adj* sucio, puerco.
natal *adj* nativo; natal.
nation *n* nacion *f.*
nationalize *vt* nacionalizar.
nationalism *n* nacionalismo *m.*
nationalist *adj, n* nacionalista *m.*
nationality *n* nacionalidad *f.*
native *adj* nativo *m.*
native language *n* lengua materna *f.*
Nativity *n* Navidad *f.*
natural *adj* natural.

naturalize vt naturalizar.
naturalist n naturalista m.
nature n naturaleza f.
naught n cero m.
naughty adj malo.
nausea n nausea.
nauseous adj fastidioso.
nautic(al), naval adj nautico, naval.
nave n nave (de la iglesia) f.
navel n ombligo m.
navigate vi navegar.
navigation n navegacion f.
navy n marina f.
Nazi n nazi m.
near prep cerca de.
nearby adj cercano.
nearly adv casi.
near-sighted adj miope.
nebulous adj nebuloso.
necessarily adv necesariamente.
necessary adj necesario.
necessity n necesidad f.
neck n cuello m.
necklace n collar m.
necktie n corbata f.
nectar n nectar m.
need n necesidad f.
needle n aguja f.
needless adj superfluo.
needlework n costura f
needy adj necesitado, pobre.
negation n negacion f.
negative adj negativo.
neglect vt descuidar.
negligee n salto de cama m.
negligence n negligencia f
negligible adj insignificante.
negotiate vt, vi negociar (con).
negotiation n negociacion f; negocio m.
Negress n negra f.
Negro adj, n negro m.

neighbor n vecino m.
neighborhood n vecindad f; vecindariom.
neither conj ni:—pn ninguno.
neon n neon m.
neon light n luz de neon f.
nephew n sobrino m.
nepotism n nepotismo m.
nerve n nervio m; valor m.
nerve-racking adj espantoso.
nervous adj nervioso; nervudo.
nervous breakdown n crisis nerviosa f.
nest n nido m.
nest egg n (fig) ahorros mpl.
nestle vt anidarse.
net n red f.
netball n basquet m.
nettle n ortiga f.
network n red f.
neurosis n neurosis f invar.
neurotic adj, n neurotico m.
neuter adj (gr) neutro.
neutral adj neutral.
neutrality n neutralidad f.
neutron n neutron m.
never adv nunca, jamas.
nevertheless adv no obstante.
new adj nuevo.
news npl novedad, noticias fpl.
newscaster n presentador m.
newspaper n periodico m.
next adj proximo.
nib n pico m.
nibble vt picar.
nice adj simpatico.
niche n nicho m.
nickel n niquel m
nickname n mote.
nicotine n nicotina f.
niece n sobrina f.
niggling adj insignificante.
night n noche f.

nightclub n cabaret m.
nightfall n anochecer m.
nightingale n ruisenor m.
nightmare n pesadilla f.
nihilist n nihilista m.
nimble adj ligero, activo, listo, agil.
nine adj, n nueve.
nineteen adj, n diecinueve.
nineteenth adj, n decimonono.
ninetieth adj, n nonagesimo.
ninety adj, n noventa.
ninth adj, n nono, noveno.
nip vt pellizcar; morder.
nipple n pezon m; tetilla f.
nit n liendre f.
nitrogen n nitrogeno m.
no adv no.
nobility n nobleza f.
noble adj noble.
nobleman n noble m.
nobody n nadie, ninguna persona f.
nocturnal adj nocturnal.
noise n ruido m.
noisy adj ruidoso, turbulento.
nominate vt nombrar.
nomination n nominacion f.
nominee n candidato m.
non-alcoholic adj no alcoholico.
nonchalant adj indiferente.
nondescript adj no descrito.
none adj nadie, ninguno.
nonentity n nulidad f.
nonetheless adv sin embargo.
nonsense n disparate m.
noodles npl fideos mpl.
noon n mediodia m.
noose n lazo corredizo m.
nor conj ni.
normal adj normal.
north n norte m.
North America n America del Norte f.

northeast n nor(d)este m.
northerly, northern adj norteno.
North Pole n polo artico m.
northwest n nor(d)oeste m.
nose n nariz f
nosebleed n hemorragia nasal f.
nostalgia n nostalgia f.
nostril n ventana de la nariz f.
not adv no.
notable adj notable.
notably adv especialmente.
notary n notario m.
notch n muesca f.
note n nota, marca f.
notebook n librito de apuntes m.
noted adj afamado, celebre.
nothing n nada f.
notice n noticia f; aviso m.
notification n notificacion f.
notify vt notificar.
notion n nocion f.
notoriety n notoriedad f.
notwithstanding conj no obstante, aunque.
nougat n turron m.
nought n cero m.
noun n (gr) sustantivo m.
nourish vt nutrir, alimentar.
novel n novela f.
novelist n novelista m.
novelty n novedad f.
November n noviembre m.
novice n novicio m.
now adv ahora.
nowadays adv hoy (en) dia.
nowhere adv en ninguna parte.
noxious adj nocivo, danoso.
nozzle n boquilla f.
nuance n matiz m.
nuclear adj nuclear.
nucleus n nucleo m.
nude adj desnudo.

nudge vt dar un codazo a.
nudist n nudista m.
nudity n desnudez f.
null adj nulo.
nullify vt anular.
numb adj entorpecido.
number n numero m.
numerous adj numeroso.
nun n monja f.
nunnery n convento de monjas m.
nuptial adj nupcial fpl.
nurse n enfermera f.

nursery n guarderia infantil f
nursery rhyme n cancion infantil f.
nursery school n parvulario m.
nursing home n clinica de reposo f.
nurture vt criar.
nut n nuez f.
nutcrackers npl cascanueces m.
nutmeg n nuez moscada f.
nutritious adj nutritivo.
nut shell n cascara de nuez f.
nylon n nilon m.

O

oak n roble m.
oar n remo m.
oasis n oasis f.
oat n avena f.
oath n juramento m.
obedience n obediencia f.
obese adj obeso, gordo.
obey vt obedecer.
obituary n necrologia f.
object n objeto m:—vt objetar.
objective adj, n objetivo m.
oblige vt obligar.
obliterate vt borrar.
oblivion n olvido m.
oblong adj oblongo.
obnoxious adj odioso.
oboe n oboe m.
obscene adj obsceno.
obscenity n obscenidad f.
obscure adj oscuro.
observatory n observatorio m.
observe vt observar, mirar.
obsess vt obsesionar.
obsolete adj en desuso.
obstacle n obstaculo m.

obstinate adj obstinado.
obstruct vt obstruir; impedir.
obtain vt obtener, adquirir.
obvious adj obvio, evidente.
occasion n ocasion f.
occupant, occupier n ocupador m
occupation n ocupacion f; empleo m.
occupy vt ocupar.
occur vi pasar.
ocean n oceano m; alta mar f.
ocher n ocre m.
octave n octava f.
October n octubre m.
octopus n pulpo m.
odd adj impar.
oddity n singularidad.
odious adj odioso.
odor n olor m.
of prep de.
off adv desconectado; apagado.
offence n ofensa f.
offend vt ofender.
offensive adj ofensivo.
offer vt ofrecer.

offering n sacrificio m.
office n oficina f.
officer n oficial, empleado m.
official adj oficial.
offspring n prole f.
ogle vt comerse con los ojos.
oil n aceite m.
oil painting n pintura al oleo f.
oil rig n torre de perforacion f.
oil tanker n petrolero m.
ointment n unguento m.
OK, okay excl vale.
old adj viejo; antiguo.
old age n vejez f.
olive n olivo m.
omelet n tortilla de huevos f.
omen n agüero.
ominous adj ominoso.
omission n omisión f.
omit vt omitir.
omnipotence n omnipotencia f.
on prep sobre, encima, en; de; a.
one adj un, uno.
oneself pn si mismo; si misma.
ongoing adj continuo.
onion n cebolla f.
onlooker n espectador m.
only adj unico, solo.
onus n responsabilidad f.
onwards adv adelante.
opaque adj opaco.
open adj abierto; vi abrirse.
open-minded adj imparcial.
opera n opera f.
operate vi obrar.
operation n operacion f.
operational adj operacional.
operative adj operativo.
operator n operario m; operador m.
ophthalmic adj oftálmico.
opinion n opinion f.

opinion poll n sondeo m.
opponent n antagonista m.
opportune adj oportuno.
opportunity n oportunidad f.
oppose vt oponerse.
opposite adj opuesto; contrario.
opposition n oposicion f.
oppress vt oprimir.
oppression n opresion f.
optic(al) adj optico f.
optician n optico m.
optimist n optimista m.
optimum adj optimum.
option n opcion f; deseo m.
opulent adj opulento.
or conj o; u.
oracle n oraculo m.
oral adj oral.
orange n naranja f.
orbit n orbita f.
orchard n huerto m.
orchestra n orquesta f.
orchid n orquidea f.
order n orden mf; regla f; mandar.
ordinary adj ordinario.
ore n mineral m.
organ n organo m.
organic adj organico.
organization n organizacion f.
organize vt organizar.
organism n organismo m.
organist n organista m.
orgasm n orgasmo m.
orgy n orgia f.
oriental adj oriental.
orifice n orificio m.
origin n origen m.
original adj original.
originate vi originar.
ornament n ornamento m.
ornate adj adornado.

orphan *adj, n* huerfano *m.*
orphanage *n* orfanato *m.*
orthodox *adj* ortodoxo.
orthopedic *adj* ortopedico.
oscillate *vi* oscilar.
osprey *n* aguila marina *f.*
ostensibly *adv* aparentemente.
ostentatious *adj* ostentoso.
osteopath *n* osteopata *m.*
ostrich *n* avestruz *m.*
other *pn* otro.
otter *n* nutria *f.*
ouch *excl* ¡ay!
ought *v aux* deber, ser menester.
ounce *n* onza *f.*
our, ours *pn* nuestro, nuestra, nuestros, nuestras.
ourselves *pn pl* nosotros mismos.
out *adv* fuera.
outbreak *n* erupcion *f.*
outcast *n* paria *m.*
outcome *n* resultado *m.*
outcry *n* clamor *m.*
outdo *vt* exceder a otro, sobrepujar.
outer *adj* exterior.
outermost *adj* extremo; lo mas exterior.
outfit *n* vestidos *mpl;* ropa *f.*
outlet *n* enchufe *m.*
outline *n* contorno *m*
outlook *n* perspectiva *f.*
out-of-date *adj* caducado; pasado de moda.
outpatient *n* paciente externo *m.*
output *n* rendimiento *m.*
outrage *n* ultraje *m.*
outrageous *adj* ultrajoso.
outside *n* superficie *f;* exterior *m.*
outsider *n* forastero *m.*
outskirts *npl* alrededores *mpl.*

outstanding *adj* excepcional.
outwit *vt* enganar a uno a fuerza de tretas.
oval *n* ovalo *m:—adj* oval.
ovary *n* ovario *m.*
oven *n* horno *m.*
ovenproof *adj* resistente al horno.
over *prep* sobre, encima.
overbearing *adj* despotico.
overcharge *vt* sobrecargar.
overcoat *n* abrigo *m.*
overdose *n* sobredosis *f.*
overdue *adj* retrasado.
overeat *vi* atracarse.
overflow *vt, vi* inundar.
overhaul *vt* revisar.
overkill *n* exceso de medios *m.*
overlap *vi* traslaparse.
overleaf *adv* al dorso.
overload *vt* sobrecargar.
overpower *vt* predominar, oprimir.
overseas *adv* en ultramar:—*adj* extranjero.
oversee *vt* inspeccionar.
overshadow *vt* eclipsar.
overstate *vi* exagerar.
overstep *vt* exceder, pasar de.
overtake *vt* sobrepasar.
overtime *n* horas extra *fpl.*
overtone *n* tono *m.*
owe *vt* deber.
owl *n* buho *m.*
own *adj* propio.
owner *n* dueno, propietario *m.*
ownership *n* posesion *f.*
ox *n* buey *m.*
oxidize *vt* oxidar.
oxygen *n* oxigeno *m.*
oyster *n* ostra *f.*
ozone *n* ozono *m.*

P

pa n papa m.

pace n paso m.

pacemaker n marcapasos m.

pacific(al) adj pacifico.

pacify vt pacificar.

package n paquete m.

packet n paquete m.

packing n embalaje m.

pact n pacto m.

pad n bloc m.

paddle vi remar

paddock n corral m.

paddy n arrozal m.

pagan adj, n pagano m.

page n pagina f.

pain n pena f; castigo m; dolor m.

painkiller n analgesico m.

paint vt pintar.

paintbrush n pincel m.

painter n pintor m.

painting n pintura f.

pair n par m.

pajamas npl pijama m.

palatial adj palatino.

pale adj palido; claro.

pallet n pallet m.

palliative adj, n paliativo m.

pallid adj palido.

pallor n palidez f.

palm n (bot) palma f.

Palm Sunday n Domingo de Ramos m.

palpable adj palpable.

paltry adj irrisorio; mezquino.

pamphlet n folleto m.

pan n cazuela f.

pancake n bunuelo m.

pandemonium n jaleo m.

pane n cristal m.

panel n panel m pang n angustia f.

panic adj, n panico m.

pansy n (bot) pensamiento m.

pant vi jadear.

panther n pantera f.

pantry n despensa f.

pants npl pantalones mpl.

papacy n papado m.

papal adj papal.

paper n papel m.

paperback n libro de bolsillo m.

paper clip n clip m.

paperweight n sujetapapeles m.

paprika n pimienta hungara f.

parachute n paracaidas m.

paradise n paraiso m.

paradox n paradoja f.

paragon n modelo perfecto m.

paragraph n parrafo m.

parallel adj paralelo.

paralysis n paralisis f.

paralytic(al) adj paralitico.

paralyze vt paralizar.

paramedic n ambulanciero m.

paramount adj supremo.

paranoid adj paranoico.

parasite n parásito m.

parasol n parasol m.

parcel n paquete m.

parch vt resecar.

pardon n perdon m.

parent n padre m; madre f.

parentage n parentela f.

parental adj paternal.

parenthesis n parentesis m.

parish n parroquia f.

parity n paridad f.

park n parque m.

parliament n parlamento m.

parlor n sala de recibimiento f.

parody n parodia f.

parrot n papagayo m.
parsley n (bot) perejil m.
parsnip n (bot) chirivia f.
part n parte f.
participate vi participar (en).
particle n particula f.
particular adj particular.
parting n separacion f.
partition n particion.
partner n socio, companero m.
partridge n perdiz f.
party n partido m; fiesta f.
pass vt pasar.
passage n pasaje m
passbook n libreta de depositos f.
passenger n pasajero m.
passion n pasion f
passionate adj apasionado.
passive adj pasivo.
Passover n Pascua f.
passport n pasaporte m.
password n contrasena f.
past adj pasado.
pasta n pasta f.
paste n pasta f.
pastime n pasatiempo m f.
pastor n pastor m.
pastry n pasteleria f.
pasture n pasto m.
patch n remiendo m; parche m.
patent adj patente.
pathetic adj patetico.
patience n paciencia f.
patient adj paciente.
patio n patio m.
patriot n patriota m.
patriotism n patriotismo m.
patrol n patrulla f.
patron n patron m.
patronize vt patrocinar.
pattern n patron m; dibujo m.
pauper n pobre m.

pause n pausa f.
pave vt empedrar.
pavilion n pabellon m.
paw n pata f.
pay vt pagar.
pea n guisante m.
peace n paz f.
peach n melocoton m.
peacock n pavon, pavo real m.
peak n cima f.
peanut n cacahuete m.
pear n pera f.
pearl n perla f.
peasant n campesino m.
pebble n guija f.
peculiar adj peculiar.
pedal n pedal m.
pedestal n pedestal m.
pedestrian n peaton m.
pedigree n genealogia f.
peel vt pelar.
peg n clavija f.
pelican n pelicano m.
pen n boligrafo m; pluma f
penal adj penal.
pence n d pl of penny.
pencil n lapiz m.
pendulum n pendulo m.
penetrate vt penetrar.
penguin n pinguino m.
penicillin n penicilina f.
peninsula n peninsula f.
penis n pene m.
penitence n penitencia f.
penitentiary n encierro m.
penknife n navaja f.
penny n penique m.
pension n pension f.
pensive adj pensativo.
Pentecost n Pentecostes m.
penthouse n atico m.
people n pueblo m; nacion f; gente f.

pepper n pimienta f.
peppermint n menta f.
perceive vt percibir.
percentage n porcentaje m.
perception n percepcion f.
percolator n cafetera de filtro f.
percussion n percusion f; golpe m.
perennial adj perenne; perpetuo.
perfect adj perfecto.
perform vt ejecutar.
performance n ejecucion f.
perfume n perfume m; fragancia f:— vt perfumar.
perhaps adv quiza, quizas.
peril n peligro m.
period n periodo m.
periodical adj jornal, periodico m.
perk n extra m.
perm n permanente f.
permanent adj, ~ly adv permanente (mente).
permissible adj licito.
permission n permiso m.
permit vt permitir.
perplex vt confundir.
persecute vt perseguir.
persevere vi perseverar.
persist vi persistir.
person n persona f.
personality n personalidad f.
personnel n personal m.
perspective n perspectiva f.
perspiration n transpiracion f.
perspire vi transpirar.
persuade vt persuadir.
perturb vt perturbar.
peruse vt leer.
perverse adj perverso.
pessimist n pesimista m.
pester vt molestar.
pet n animal domestico m.
petal n (bot) petalo m.

petition n presentacion, peticion f.
petroleum n petroleo m.
petticoat n enaguas fpl.
petty adj mezquino.
pewter n peltre m.
phantom n fantasma m.
pharmacist n farmacéutico m.
pharmacy n farmacia f.
phase n fase f.
pheasant n faisan m.
phenomenon n fenomeno m.
phial n redomilla f.
philosopher n filosofo m.
philosophy n filosofia f.
phlegm n flema f.
phobia n fobia f.
phone n telefono m.
photocopier n fotocopiadora f.
photocopy n fotocopia f.
photograph n fotografia f:—vt fotografiar.
photographic adj fotografico.
photography n fotografia f.
phrase n frase f.
physical adj fisico.
physician n medico m.
physicist n fisico m.
physiotherapy n fisioterapia f.
physique n fisico m.
pianist n pianista m, f.
piano n piano m.
piccolo n flautin m.
pick vt escoger, elegir.
pickle n escabeche m.
picnic n comida, merienda f.
picture n pintura f.
picturesque adj pintoresco.
pie n pastel m; tarta f.
piece n pedazo m; pieza f.
pierce vt penetrar, agujerear.
pig n cerdo m.
pigeon n paloma f.

pigtail n trenza f.
pike n lucio m; pica f.
pile n estaca f; pila f; monton m.
pilgrim n peregrino m.
pill n pildora f.
pillar n pilar m.
pillow n almohada f.
pilot n piloto m.
pimple n grano m.
pin n alfiler m.
pinball n fliper m.
pincers n pinzas fpl.
pinch vt pellizcar.
pine n (bot) pino m.
pineapple n pina f, ananas m.
pink n rosa f.
pinnacle n cumbre f.
pint n pinta f.
pioneer n pionero m.
pious adj pio.
pip n pepita f.
pipe n tubo.
pirate n pirata m.
pirouette n pirueta.
Pisces n Piscis m (signo del zodiaco).
piss n (sl) meados mpl.
pistol n pistola f.
piston n embolo m.
pit n hoyo m; mina f.
pitcher n cantaro, jarro m.
pitchfork n horca f.
pity n piedad, compasion f.
pivot n eje m.
pizza n pizza f.
placard n pancarta f.
placate vt apaciguar.
place n lugar, sitio m.
placid adj placido.
plagiarism n plagio m.
plague n peste, plaga f.
plaice n platija f (pez).
plaid n tartan m.

plain adj liso, llano
plaintiff n (law) demandador m.
plan n plano m.
plane n avion m; plano m.
planet n planeta m.
plank n tabla f.
plant n planta f.
plantation n plantacion f.
plaque n placa f.
plaster n yeso m.
plastic adj plastico.
plate n plato m.
plateau n meseta f.
platform n plataforma f.
platinum n platino m.
platoon n (mil) peloton m.
play n juego m.
playboy n playboy m.
player n jugador m
plea n defensa f.
pleasant adj agradable.
please vt agradar.
pleasure n gusto, placer m.
pleat n pliegue m.
plentiful adj copioso.
plethora n pletora, replecion f.
pleurisy n pleuresia f.
pliers npl alicates mpl.
plinth n plinto m.
plough n arado m.
ploy n truco m.
plug n tapon m.
plum n ciruela f.
plumage n plumaje m.
plumb n plomada f.
plumber n plomero m.
plume n pluma f.
plump adj gordo.
plunder vt saquear.
plunge vi sumergir(se), precipitarse.
pluperfect n (gr) pluscuamperfecto m.
plural adj, n plural m.

plus n signo de mas m.
plush adj de felpa.
plutonium n plutonio m.
plywood n madera contrachapada f.
pneumatic adj neumatico.
pneumonia n pulmonia f.
poach vt escalfar.
pocket n bolsillo m.
pod n vaina f.
poem n poema m.
poet n poeta m.
poetry n poesia f.
poignant adj punzante.
point n punta f; punto m.
point-blank adv directamente.
poise n peso m; equilibrio m.
poison n veneno m.
poker n atizador m; poker m.
polar adj polar.
pole n polo m.
police n policia f.
policy n politica f.
polio n polio f.
polish vt pulir, alisar.
polite adj pulido, cortes.
politician n politico m.
politics npl politica f.
polka n polca f.
pollen n (bot) polen m.
pollute vt ensuciar.
pollution n polucion, contaminacion f.
polo n polo m.
polyester n poliester m.
polytechnic n politecnico m.
pomegranate n granada f.
pomp n pompa f; esplendor m.
pompom n borla f.
pompous adj pomposo.
pond n estanque m.
ponder vt ponderar, considerar.
ponderous adj ponderoso, pesado.

pontoon n ponton m.
pony n jaca f.
pool n charca f; piscina.
poor adj pobre.
pop n papá m.
popcorn n palomitas fpl.
Pope n papa m.
poplar n alamo m.
poppy n (bot) amapola f.
popular adj, **~ly** adv popular(mente).
populate vi poblar.
population n poblacion f.
porcelain n porcelana f.
porch n portico m.
porcupine n puerco espin m.
pore n poro m.
pork n carne de puerco f.
pornography n pornografia f.
porous adj poroso.
porpoise n marsopa f.
porridge n gachas de avena fpl.
port n puerto m m.
portable adj portatil.
portal n portal m f.
porter n portero m.
portfolio n cartera f.
porthole n portilla f.
portico n portico m.
portion n porcionf.
portly adj rollizo.
portrait n retrato m.
portray vt retratar.
pose n postura f; pose f.
posh adj elegante.
position n posicion f.
positive adj positivo.
posse n peloton m.
possess vt poseer.
possession n posesion f.
possibility n posibilidad f.
possible adj posible.
post n correo m; puesto m.

postage stamp *n* sello *m*.
postcard *n* tarjeta postal *f*.
poster *n* cartel *m*.
posterior *n* trasero *m*.
posterity *n* posteridad *f*.
postgraduate *n* posgraduado *m*.
posthumous *adj* postumo.
post office *n* correos *m*.
postpone *vt* diferir.
posture *n* postura *f*.
posy *n* ramillete de flores *m*.
pot *n* marmita *f*.
potato *n* patata *f*; papa *f*.
potent *adj* potente.
potential *adj* potencial.
pothole *n* bache *m*.
potion *n* pocion *f*.
potter *n* alfarero *m*.
pottery *n* cerámica *f*.
pouch *n* bolsa *f*.
poultice *n* cataplasma *f*.
poultry *n* aves caseras *fpl*.
pound *n* libra *f*; libra esterlina *f*.
pour *vt* echar; servir.
pout *vi* ponerse cenudo.
poverty *n* pobreza *f*.
powder *n* polvo *m*.
power *n* poder *m*.
practicable *adj* practicable; hacedero.
practical *adj* práctico:—~ly *adv* prácticamente.
practicality *n* factibilidad *f*.
practice *n* practica *f*.
pragmatic *adj* pragmático.
prairie *n* pampa *f*.
praise *n* renombre *m*.
prattle *vi* charlar:—*n* charla *f*.
prawn *n* gamba *f*.
pray *vi* rezar.
prayer *n* oracion *f*.
preach *vi* predicar.

preacher *n* pastor *m*.
precaution *n* precaucion *f*.
precede *vt* anteceder.
precious *adj* precioso.
precise *n* preciso.
precision *n* precision *f*.
preconception *n* preocupacion *f*.
predator *n* animal de rapina *m*.
predict *vt* predecir.
prediction *n* prediccion *f*.
predominant *adj* predominante.
predominate *vt* predominar.
preface *n* prefacio *m*.
prefer *vt* preferir.
preference *n* preferencia *f*.
prefix *vt* prefijar.
pregnancy *n* embarazo *m*.
pregnant *adj* embarazada.
prehistoric *adj* prehistorico.
prejudice *n* perjuicio *m*.
preliminary *adj* preliminar.
prelude *n* preludio *m*.
premature *adj* prematuro.
premier *n* primer ministro *m*.
premises *npl* establecimiento *m*.
premium *n* premio *m*.
premonition *n* presentimiento *m*.
prepare *vt* preparar(se).
preposition *n* preposicion *f*.
preposterous *adj* prepostero; absurdo.
prerequisite *n* requisito *m*.
prerogative *n* prerrogativa *f*.
prescribe *vi* prescribir; recetar.
prescription *n* prescripcion *f*.
present *n* regalo *m*.
presentation *n* presentacion *f*.
preservation *n* preservacion *f*.
preservative *n* preservativo *m*.
preserve *vt* preservar.
preside *vi* presidir.
presidency *n* presidencia *f*.

president n presidente m.

press vt empujar n prensa.

pressure n presion f.

prestige n prestigio m.

presume vt presumir, suponer.

pretence n pretexto m; pretension f.

pretend vi pretender.

preterite n preterito m.

pretext n pretexto m.

pretty adj lindo.

prevent vt prevenir.

preview n preestreno m.

previous adj previo.

prey n presa f.

price n precio m; premio m.

prick vt punzar, picar.

pride n orgullo m.

priest n sacerdote m.

priggish adj afectado.

prim adj peripuesto.

primary adj primario.

primate n primado m.

primeval adj primitivo.

primitive adj primitivo.

primrose n (bot) primula f.

prince n principe m.

princess n princesa f.

principle n principio m.

printer n impresor m.

prior adj anterior.

priority n prioridad f.

priory n priorato m.

prism n prisma m.

prison n prision, carcel f.

prisoner n prisionero m.

pristine adj pristino.

privacy n soledad f.

private adj secreto, privado; particular.

private eye n detective privado m.

privet n alhena f.

privilege n privilegio m.

prize n premio m.

probability n probabilidad f.

probable adj probable.

probation n prueba f.

problem n problema m.

procedure n procedimiento

proceed vi proceder.

process n proceso m.

procession n procesion f.

proclaim vt proclamar.

proclamation n proclamacion f.

procure vt procurar.

prod vt empujar.

prodigal adj prodigo.

prodigious adj prodigioso.

prodigy n prodigio m.

produce vt producir

product n producto m; obra f; efecto m.

production n produccion f.

profane adj profano.

profess vt profesar.

profession n profesion f.

professor n profesor, catedrático m.

proficient adj proficiente.

profile n perfil m.

profit n ganancia f.

profound adj profundo.

profuse adj profuso.

program n programa m.

progress n progreso m.

prohibit vt prohibir.

project vt proyectar

prominent adj prominente, saledizo.

promiscuous adj promiscuo.

promise n promesa f.

promontory n promontorio m.

promote vt promover.

promotion n promocion f.

prone adj inclinado.

prong n diente m.
pronoun n pronombre m.
pronounce vt pronunciar.
proof n prueba f.
propaganda n propaganda f.
propel vt impeler.
propeller n helice f.
propensity n propension f.
proper adj propio.
property n propiedad f.
prophecy n profecia f.
prophesy vt profetizar.
prophet n profeta m.
prophetic adj profetico.
proportion n proporcion f.
proportional adj proporcional.
proposal n propuesta f.
propose vt proponer.
proposition n proposicion f.
proprietor n propietario m.
propriety n propiedad f.
pro rata adv a prorrateo.
prosaic adj prosaico.
prose n prosa f.
prosecute vt proseguir.
prosecution n prosecucion f.
prosecutor n acusador m.
prospect n perspectiva f.
prospectus n prospecto m.
prosper vi prosperar.
prosperity n prosperidad f.
prostitute n prostituta f.
prostitution n prostitucion f.
prostrate adj postrado.
protagonist n protagonista m.
protect vt proteger.
protection n proteccion f.
protective adj protectorio.
protector n protector, patrono m.
protege n protegido m.
protein n proteina f.

protest vi protestar.
Protestant n protestante m.
protester n manifestante m.
protocol n protocolo m.
prototype n prototipo m.
protracted adj prolongado.
protrude vi sobresalir.
proud adj soberbio, orgulloso.
prove vt probar.
proverb n proverbio m.
provide vt proveer.
provided conj:—~ that con tal que.
providence n providencia f.
province n provincia f
provincial adj, n provincial m.
provision n provision f.
proviso n estipulacion f.
provocation n provocacion f.
provocative adj provocativo.
provoke vt provocar.
prowess n proeza f.
prowl vi rondar.
proximity n proximidad f.
proxy n poder m; apoderado m.
prudence n prudencia f.
prudent adj prudente.
prudish adj gazmono.
prussic acid n acido prúsico m.
pry vi espiar, acechar.
psalm n salmo m.
pseudonym n seudonimo m.
psyche n psique f.
psychiatrist n psiquiatra m.
psychiatry n psiquiatria f.
psychic adj psiquico.
psychoanalysis n psicoanalisis m.
psychoanalyst n psicoanalista m.
psychological adj psicologico.
psychologist n psicologo m.
psychology n psicologia f.
puberty n pubertad f.

public *adj* publico
publicize *vt* publicitar.
publicity *n* publicidad *f.*
publish *vt* publicar.
publisher *n* publicador *m.*
pucker *vt* arrugar, hacer pliegues.
puddle *n* charco *m.*
puff *n* soplo *m.*
pull *vt* tirar.
pulley *n* polea *f.*
pullover *n* jersey *m.*
pulp *n* pulpa *f.*
pulpit *n* pulpito *m.*
pulsate *vi* pulsar.
pulse *n* pulso *m*; legumbres *fpl.*
pumice *n* piedra pomez *f.*
pummel *vt* aporrear.
pump *n* bomba *f.*
pumpkin *n* calabaza *f.*
pun *n* equivoco, chiste *m.*
punch *n* punetazo *m.*
punctual *adj* puntual.
punctuate *vi* puntuar.
punctuation *n* puntuacion *f.*
pungent *adj* picante.
punish *vt* castigar.
punishment *n* castigo *m.*
punk *n* punki *m.*
punt *n* barco llano *m.*

pup *n* cachorro *m.*
pupil *n* alumno *m.*
puppet *n* titere *m.*
puppy *n* perrito *m.*
purchase *vt* comprar.
pure *adj* puro.
puree *n* pure *m.*
purification *n* purificacion *f.*
purify *vt* purificar.
puritan *n* puritano *m.*
purity *n* pureza *f.*
purple *adj* purpureo.
purpose *n* intencion *f.*
purr *vi* ronronear.
purse *n* bolsa *f*; cartera *f.*
pursue *vi* perseguir.
pursuit *n* perseguimiento *m.*
purveyor *n* abastecedor *m.*
push *vt* empujar
pusher *n* traficante de drogas *m.*
push-up *n* plancha *f.*
put *vt* poner, colocar.
putrid *adj* podrido.
putty *n* masilla *f.*
puzzle *n* acertijo *m.*
puzzling *adj* extrano.
pylon *n* torre de conduccion electrica *f.*
pyramid *n* piramide *f.*
python *n* piton atigrado *m.*

Q

quack *vi* graznar.
quadrangle *n* cuadrangulo *m.*
quadrant *n* cuadrante *m.*
quadrilateral *adj* cuadrilatero.
quadruped *n* cuadrupedo *m.*
quadruple *adj* cuadruplo.
quadruplet *n* cuatrillizo *m.*
quagmire *n* tremedal *m.*
quail *n* codorniz *f.*

quaint *adj* pulido; exquisito.
quake *vi* temblar; tiritar.
qualification *n* calificacion *f.*
qualify *vt* calificar.
quality *n* calidad *f.*
qualm *n* escrupulo *m.*
quandary *n* incertidumbre *f.*
quantitative *adj* cuantitativo.
quantity *n* cantidad *f.*

quarantine n cuarentena f.
quarrel n rina, contienda f.
quarrelsome adj pendenciero.
quarry n cantera f.
quarter n cuarto mr.
quarterly adj trimestral.
quartermaster n (mil) comisario m.
quartet n (mus) cuarteto m.
quartz n (min) cuarzo m.
quash vt fracasar; anular.
quay n muelle m.
queasy adj nauseabundo.
queen n reina f.
queer adj extrano.
quell vt calmar.
quench vt apagar.
query n cuestion.
quest n pesquisa f.
question n pregunta f; cuestion f.
questionable adj cuestionable.
question mark n punto de interrogación m.
questionnaire n cuestionario m.
quibble vi buscar evasivas.

quick adj rapido.
quicken vt apresurar.
quicksand n arena movediza f.
quicksilver n azogue, mercurio m.
quick-witted adj agudo, perspicaz.
quiet adj callado.
quinine n quinina f.
quintet n (mus) quinteto m.
quintuple adj quintuplo.
quintuplet n quintillizo m.
quip n indirecta f:—vt echar pullas.
quirk n peculiaridad f.
quit vt dejar.
quite adv bastante.
quits adv ien paz!.
quiver vi temblar.
quixotic adj quijotesco.
quiz n concurso m.
quizzical adj burlon.
quota n cuota f.
quotation n citacion, cita f.
quotation marks npl comillas fpl.
quote vt citar.
quotient n cociente m.

R

rabbi n rabi m.
rabbit n conejo m.
rabble n gentuza f.
rabid adj rabioso.
rabies n rabia f.
race n raza.
rack n rejilla f.
racket n ruido m; raqueta f.
racy adj picante.
radiance n brillantez f.
radiant adj radiante.
radiate vt, vi radiar.
radiation n radiacion f.
radiator n radiador m.

radical adj, ~ly adv radical(mente).
radio n radio f.
radioactive adj radioactivo.
radish n rabano m.
radius n radio f.
raffle n rifa f.
raft n balsa f.
rafter n par m; viga f.
rag n trapo m.
rage n rabia f.
raid n incursion f.
rail n baranda, barandilla f.
railroad, railway n ferrocarril m.
rain n lluvia f.

rainbow n arco iris m.
raise vt levantar, alzar.
raisin n pasa f.
rake n rastro m.
ram n carnero m.
ramble vi divagar.
ramification n ramificacion f.
ramp n rampa f.
rampant adj exuberante.
ramshackle adj en ruina.
ranch n hacienda f.
rancid adj rancio.
rancor n rencor m.
random adj fortuito, sin orden.
range vt colocar, ordenar.
ransack vt saquear.
ransom n rescate m.
rape n violacion f.
rapid adj rapido.
rapist n violador m.
rapture n rapto m.
rare adj raro.
rascal n picaro m.
rash adj precipitado m; erupción (cutánea) f.
raspberry n frambuesa f.
rat n rata f.
rate n tasa f, precio, valor m.
rather adv mas bien; antes.
ratification n ratificacion f.
ratify vt ratificar.
ratio n razon f.
ration n racion f.
rational adj racional.
ravage vt saquear.
rave vi delirar.
raven n cuervo m.
ravine n barranco m.
ravish vt encantar.
ravishing adj encantador.
raw adj crudo.
ray n rayo de luz m; raya f (pez).

raze vt arrasar.
razor n navaja.
reach vt alcanzar.
react vi reaccionar.
reaction n reaccion f.
read vt leer.
readable adj legible.
reader n lector m.
readjust vt reajustar.
ready adj listo, pronto.
real adj real.
realization n realizacion f.
realize adv darse cuenta de; realizar.
reality n realidad f.
realm n reino m.
ream n resma f.
reap vt segar.
reappear vi reaparecer.
rear n parte trasera fr.
rearmament n rearme m.
reason n razon f; causa f:—vt, vi razonar.
reassure vt tranquilizar, alentar; (com) asegurar.
rebel n rebelde m/f.
rebellion n rebelion f.
rebound vi rebotar.
rebuke vt reprender.
rebut vi repercutir.
recede vi retroceder.
receipt n recibo m.
receive vt recibir.
recent adj reciente.
reception n recepcion f.
recess n descanso m.
recession n retirada f; (com) recesion f.
recipe n receta f.
recipient n recipiente m.
recital n recital m.
recite vt recitar.
reckless adj temerario.

reckon vt contar.

recline vt, vi reclinar(se).

recluse n recluso/a m/f.

recognize vt reconocer.

recommend vt recomendar.

recommendation n recomendacion f.

recompense n recompensa f.

reconcile vt reconciliar.

reconsider vt considerar de nuevo.

record vt registrar; grabar.

recourse n recurso m.

recover vt recobrar; recuperar.

recovery n convalecencia f; recobro m.

recreation n recreacion f; recreo m.

recruit vt reclutar.

rectangle n rectangulo m.

rectify vt rectificar.

rectilinear adj rectilineo.

rector n rector m.

recur vi repetirse.

red adj rojo; tinto:—n rojo m.

redeem vt redimir.

redemption n redencion f.

redhot adj candente, ardiente.

redress vt corregir.

reduce vt reducir.

reduction n reduccion f.

reed n cana f.

reek n mal olor.

refectory n refectorio m.

refer vt, vi referir.

referee n arbitro m.

reference n referencia.

refine vt refinar.

refit vt reparar.

reflect vt, vi reflejar.

reflection n reflexion f.

reflex adj reflejo.

reform vt, vi reformar(se).

refresh vt refrescar.

refreshment n refresco.

refrigerator n nevera f.

refuge n refugio, asilo m.

refugee n refugiado m/f.

refund vt devolver.

refurbish vt restaurar.

refusal n negativa f.

refuse vt rehusar.

refute vt refutar.

regal adj real.

regard vt estimar.

regardless adv a pesar de todo.

regatta n regata f.

regime n regimen m.

region n region f.

register n registro m.

registrar n registrador m.

registration n registro m.

registry n registro m.

regular adj regular.

regulation n regulacion f.

reign n reinado, reino m.

reinforce vt reforzar.

reinstate vt reintegrar.

reject vt rechazar.

rejection n rechazo m.

rejoice vt, vi regocijar(se).

relapse vi recaer.

relate vt, vi relatar.

relation n relacion f.

relationship n parentesco m; relacion f.

relative adj relativo.

relax vt, vi relajar.

release vt soltar, libertar.

relic n reliquia f.

relief n relieve m.

relieve vt aliviar.

religion n religion f.

rely vi confiar en; contar con.

remain vi quedar.

remains npl restos mpl.

remark n observacion, nota f.

remedial adv curativo.
remedy n remedio m.
remember vt acordarse de; recordar.
remind vt recordar.
remit vt, vi remitir.
remorse n remordimiento m.
remote adj remoto.
remove vt quitar.
renew vt renovar.
renovate vt renovar.
rent n renta f.
rental n alquiler m.
repair vt reparar.
repeat vt repetir.
repel vt repeler.
repetition n repeticion f.
replace vt reemplazar.
reply n respuesta f.
repose vt, vi reposar.
represent vt representar.
reproduce vt reproducir.
reproduction n reproduccion f.
reptile n reptil m.
republic n republica f.
repugnance n repugnancia f.
repulse vt repulsar.
request n peticion.
require vt requerir.
rescue vt librar.
research vt investigar.
resemble vt asemejarse.
resent vt resentirse.
reserve vt reservar.
residence n residencia f.
resign vt, vi resignar.
resin n resina f.
resist vt resistir, oponerse.
resolve vt, vr resolver(se).
resort vi recurrir.
resource n recurso m.
respect n respecto m.
respite n suspension f.

respond vt responder.
rest n reposo m.
restless adj insomne.
restore vt restaurar.
restrict vt restringir.
result vi resultar.
resume vt resumir.
résumé n currículum m.
resurrection n resurreccion f.
resuscitate vt resucitar.
retail vt revender f.
retain vt retener.
reticence n reticencia f.
retina n retina f.
retire vt, vi retirar(se).
retreat n retirada f.
return vt retribuir; restituir; devolver.
reveal vt revelar.
revenge vt vengar:—n venganza f.
revenue n renta f .
revere vt reverenciar.
reverse vt trastrocar.
review vt rever.
revise vt rever; repasar.
revival n restauracion f.
revolt vi rebelarse.
revolution n revolucion f.
revolve vt revolver.
revue n revista f.
reward n recompensa f.
rheumatism n reumatismo m.
rhinoceros n rinoceronte m.
rhombus n rombo m.
rhubarb n ruibarbo m.
rhyme n rima f.
rhythm n ritmo m.
rib n costilla f.
ribbon n liston m.
rice n arroz m.
rich adj rico.
riches npl riqueza f.
rickets n raquitis f.

rid vt librar.

riddle n enigma m.

ride vi cabalgar.

ridge n espinazo.

ridiculous adj ridiculoso.

rifle n rifle m.

right adj derecho, recto; justo.—n derecho m; título m; privilegio m.

rigid adj rigido.

rigor n rigor m.

rind n corteza f.

rinse vt lavar, limpiar.

rise vi levantarse.

risk n riesgo, peligro m.

rite n rito m.

ritual adj, n ritual m.

rival adj emulo.

river n rio m.

road n camino m.

roadsign n senal de trafico f.

roar vi rugir.

roast vt asar.

rob vt robar.

robber n robador, ladron m.

robbery n robo m.

robust adj robusto.

rock n roca f.

rocket n cohete m.

rodent n roedor m.

rogue n bribon m.

roll vt rodar.

Roman Catholic adj, n catolico/a m/f (romano/a).

romance n romance m.

roof n tejado m.

room n habitacion, sala f.

roomy adj espacioso.

root n raiz f.

rope n cuerda f.

rosary n rosario m.

rose n rosa f.

rosebed n campo de rosales m.

rosebud n capullo de rosa m.

rosemary n (bot) romero m.

rosette n roseta f.

rot vi pudrirse.

rotten adj podrido.

rouble n rublo m.

rouge n arrebol m.

rough adj aspero.

roulette n ruleta f.

round adj redondo.

rouse vt despertar.

route n ruta f.

routine adj rutinario.

row n camorra f.

row n (line) hilera, fila f:—vt (mar) remar, bogar.

royal adj real.

royalty n realeza, dignidad real f.

rub vt estregar, fregar, frotar.

rubber n caucho m, goma f.

rubber-band n goma, gomita f.

rubric n rubrica f.

ruby n rubi m.

rudder n timon m.

rude adj rudo, brutal.

rudiment n rudimentos mpl.

rue vi compadecerse.

rug n alfombra f.

rugby n rugby m.

ruin n ruina f.

ruinous adj ruinoso.

rule n mando m; regla f.

ruler n gobernador m; regla f.

rum n ron m.

rumor n rumor m.

run vt dirigir; organizar, vi correr.

runaway n fugitivo.

rung n escalon.

runway n pista de aterrizaje f.

rupture n rotura f.

rural adj rural.

ruse n astucia f.

rush n junco m; rafaga f.
rusk n galleta f.
russet adj bermejo.
rust n herrumbre f.
rustic adj rustico.

rustle vi crujir.
rut n celo m.
ruthless adj cruel.
rye n (bot) centeno m.

S

Sabbath n sabado m.
sabotage n sabotaje m.
saccharin n sacarina f.
sachet n sobrecito m.
sack n saco m:—vt despedir.
sacrament n sacramento m.
sacred adj sagrado.
sacredness n santidad f.
sacrifice n sacrificio m.
sacrilege n sacrilegio m.
sad adj triste.
saddle n silla f.
sadness n tristeza f.
safari n safari m.
safe adj seguro; n caja fuerte f.
safety n seguridad f
saffron n azafran m.
sage n (bot) salvia f.
Sagittarius n Sagitario m (signo del zodiaco).
sago n (bot) zagu m.
sail n vela f.
sailor n marinero m.
saint n santo m; santa f.
sake n causa, razon f.
salad n ensalada f.
salamander n salamandra f.
salary n sueldo m.
sale n venta f.
sales clerk n dependiente m.
salient adj saliente.
saline adj salino.
saliva n saliva f.

salmon n salmon m.
salmon trout n trucha salmonada f.
saloon n bar m.
salt n sal f.
salubrious adj salubre.
salutation n salutacion f.
salute vt saludar.
same adj mismo, idéntico/a
sample n muestra f; ejemplo m.
sanctify vt santificar.
sanctuary n santuario m.
sand n arena f.
sandal n sandalia f.
sandstone n piedra arenisca f.
sandwich n bocadillo m.
sane adj sapo.
sanitarium n sanatorio m.
sanity n juicio sano m.
sap n savia f.
sapling n arbolito m.
sapphire n zafir m.
sarcasm n sarcasmo m.
sarcophagus n sarcofago.
sardine n sardina f.
Satan n Satanas m.
satchel n mochila f.
satellite n satelite m.
satin n raso m.
satire n satira f.
satisfaction n satisfaccion f.
satisfy vt satisfacer.
Saturday n sabado m.
satyr n satiro m.

sauce *n* salsa *f.*

saucepan *n* cazo *m.*

saucer *n* platillo *m.*

sausage *n* salchicha *f.*

savage *adj* salvaje

savagery *n* crueldad *f.*

savannah *n* sabana *f.*

save *vt* salvar.

saveloy *n* chorizo *m.*

Savior *n* Salvador *m.*

savory *adj* sabroso.

saw *n* sierra *f.*

saxophone *n* saxofono *m.*

say *vt* decir.

saying *n* dicho *m.*

scab *n* rona *f.*

scald *vt* escaldar.

scale *n* balanza *f.*

scalp *n* cabellera *f.*

scamp *n* bribon.

scampi *npl* gambas *fpl.*

scan *vt* escudrinar.

scandal *n* escandalo *m.*

scandalize *vt* escandalizar.

scar *n* cicatriz *f.*

scarce *adj* raro.

scare *vt* espantar.

scarf *n* bufanda *f.*

scarlet *n* escarlata *f.*

scarp *n* escarpa *f.*

scene *n* escena *f.*

scenery *n* vista *f.*

schedule *n* horario *m.*

scheme *n* proyecto, plan *m.*

schism *n* cisma *m.*

scholar *n* estudiante *m*

school *n* escuela *f.*

schoolteacher *n* maestro, tra *m/f;* profesor, ra *m/f.*

science *n* ciencia *f.*

scientist *n* cientifico, ca *m/f.*

scissors *npl* tijeras *fpl.*

scooter *n* moto *f.*

scorch *vt* quemar.

scorn *vt, vi* despreciar.

Scorpio *n* Escorpion *m* (signo del zodiaco).

scorpion *n* escorpion *m.*

Scotch *n* whisky escoces *m.*

scoundrel *n* picaro *m.*

scramble *vi* arrapar.

scrap *n* migaja *f;* sobras *fpl.*

scrape *vt, vi* raer, raspar.

scraper *n* rascador *m.*

scratch *vt* rascar.

scrawl *vt, vi* garrapatear.

scream, screech *vi* chillar.

screen *n* pantalla *f.*

screenplay *n* guion *m.*

screw *n* tornillo *m.*

screwdriver *n* destornillador *m.*

scribble *vt* escarabajear.

scribe *n* escritor *m.*

script *n* guion *m;* letra *f.*

Scripture *n* Escritura sagrada *f.*

scruffy *adj* desalinado.

scruple *n* escrupulo *m.*

scullery *n* fregadero *m.*

sculptor *n* escultor, ra *m/f.*

sculpture *n* escultura *f.*

scum *n* espuma *f;* escoria *f.*

scurvy *n* escorbuto *m.*

scythe *n* guadana *f.*

sea *n* mar *m/f:—adj* de mar.

sea breeze *n* viento de mar *m.*

seafood *n* mariscos *mpl.*

sea front *n* paseo maritimo *m.*

seagull *n* gaviota *f.*

sea horse *n* hipocampo *m.*

seal *n* sello *m;* foca *f.*

seam *n* costura *f.*

seaman *n* marinero *m.*

sea plane *n* hidroavion *m.*

sear *vt* cauterizar.

search *vt* examinar, buscar.
seashore *n* ribera *f*, litoral *m*.
seasick *adj* mareado.
season *n* estacion *f*.
seasoning *n* condimento *m*.
seat *n* asiento *m*; silla *f*.
seat belt *n* cinturon de seguridad *m*.
seaweed *n* alga marina *f*.
seclude *vt* apartar.
seclusion *n* separacion *f*.
second *adj* segundo.
secondary *adj* secundario.
secondhand *n* segunda mano *f*.
secret *adj, n* secreto *m*.
secretary *n* secretario, ria *m/f*.
sect *n* secta *f*.
section *n* seccion *f*.
sector *n* sector *m*.
secular *adj* secular.
secure *adj* seguro.
security *n* seguridad *f*.
sedate *adj* sosegado.
sedative *n* sedativo *m*.
sedge *n* (bot) junco *m*.
sediment *n* sedimento *m*
sedition *n* sedicion *f*.
seduce *vt* seducir.
seducer *n* seductor *m*.
seduction *n* seduccion *f*.
seductive *adj* seductivo.
see *vt, vi* ver.
seed *n* semilla.
seedy *adj* desaseado.
seek *vt, vi* buscar.
seem *vi* parecer.
seemliness *n* decensia *f*.
seesaw *n* vaiven *m*.
seethe *vi* hervir.
segment *n* segmento *m*.
seize *vt* asir.
seizure *n* captura *f*.
seldom *adv* raramente.

select *vt* elegir.
selection *n* seleccion *f*.
self *n* uno mismo.
selfish *adj* egoista.
self-portrait *n* autorretrato *m*.
selfsame *adj* identico.
sell *vt, vi* vender.
semen *n* semen *m*.
semester *n* semestre *m*.
semicircle *n* semicirculo *m*.
semicircular *adj* semicircular.
semicolon *n* punto y coma *m*.
seminary *n* seminario *m*.
senate *n* senado *m*.
senator *n* senador, ra *m/f*.
send *vt* enviar.
sender *n* remitente *m*.
senile *adj* senil.
senior *n* mayor *m*.
senna *n* (bot) sena *f*.
sensation *n* sensacion *f*.
sense *n* sentido *m*.
sensibility *n* sensibilidad *f*.
sensible *adj* sensato/a, juicioso/a..
sensitive *adj* sensitivo.
sensual, sensuous *adj* sensual.
sensuality *n* sensualidad *f*.
sentence *n* oracion *f*; sentencia *f*.
sentiment *n* sentimiento *m*.
sentinel, sentry *n* centinela *m*.
separate *vt* (vi) separar(se).
separation *n* separacion *f*.
September *n* se(p)tiembre *m*.
sepulcher *n* sepulcro *m*.
sequel *n* continuacion *f*.
sequence *n* serie *f*.
seraph *n* serafin *m*.
serenade *n* serenata *f*.
serene *adj* seneno.
serenity *n* serenidad *f*.
serf *n* siervo *m*.
sergeant *n* sargento *m*.

serial adj consecutivo.

series n serie f.

serious adj serio, grave.

sermon n sermon f.

serious adj seroso.

serpent n serpiente f.

serpentine adj serpentino.

serrated adj serrado.

serum n suero m.

servant n criado m; criada f.

serve vt, vi servir.

service n servicio m.

servile adj servil.

session n junta f; sesion f.

set vt poner, colocar, fijar.

setter n perro de muestra m.

seven adj, n siete.

seventeen adj, n diez y siete, diecisiete.

seventeenth adj, n decimoseptimo.

seventh adj, n septimo.

seventieth adj, n septuagesimo.

seventy adj, n setenta.

sever vt, vi separar.

several adj, pn varios.

severance n separacion f.

severe adj severo.

severity n severidad f.

sew vt, vi coser.

sewer n albanal m.

sex n sexo m.

sexist adj n sexista m/f.

sexual adj sexual.

sexy adj sexy.

shade n sombra.

shadow n sombra f.

shaft n flecha, saeta f.

shake vt sacudir; agitar.

shallow adj somero.

sham vt enganar.

shame n verguenza f.

shamefaced adj vergonzoso.

shampoo champu m.

shamrock n trebol m.

shank n pierna f.

shanty n chabola f.

shantytown n barrio de chabolas m.

shape vt, vi formar; n forma m.

shapeless adj informe.

shapely adj bien hecho.

share n parte, porcion f; compartir.

shark n tiburon m.

sharp adj agudo.

shatter vt destrozar.

shave vt afeitar.

shaver n maquina de afeitar f.

shawl n chal m.

she pn ella.

sheaf n gavilla f

shear vt atusar.

sheath n vaina f.

shed vt verter; cabana f.

sheen n resplandor m.

sheep n oveja f.

sheer adj puro, claro.

sheet n sabana f.

sheet lightning n relampagueamiento m.

shelf n anaquel m.

shell n cascara f; concha f.

shelter n guardia f; amparo m.

shepherd n pastor m.

sherbet n sorbete m.

sheriff n sherif m.

sherry n jerez m.

shield n escudo m.

shift vi cambiarse.

shinbone n espinilla f.

shine vi lucir, brillar.

shiny adj brillante.

ship n nave f; barco m.

shipwreck n naufragio m.

shirt n camisa f.

shit excl (sl) imierda!

shiver *vi* tiritar de frio.
shoal *n* banco *m.*
shock *n* choque *m.*
shock absorber *n* amortiguador *m.*
shoddy *adj* de pacotilla.
shoe *n* zapato *m.*
shoelace *n* correa de zapato *f.*
shoemaker *n* zapatero *m.*
shoot *vt* tirar.
shopper *n* comprador, ra *m/f.*
shopping *n* compras *fpl.*
shopping mall *n* centro comercial *m.*
shore *n* costa, ribera *f.*
short *adj* corto breve.
short-sighted *adj* corto de vista.
shot *n* tiro *m.*
shotgun *n* escopeta *f.*
shoulder *n* hombro *m.*
shout *vi* gritar, aclamar.
shove *vt, vi* empujar.
shovel *n* pala *f.*
show *vt* mostrar.
shower *n* nubada *f;* llovizna *f;* ducha *f.*
showy *adj* ostentoso.
shred *n* cacho, pedazo.
shrewd *adj* astuto.
shriek *vt, vi* chillar
shrimp *n* camaron *m.*
shrine *n* relicario *m.*
shrink *vi* encogerse.
shroud *n* cubierta *f.*
Shrove Tuesday *n* martes de carnaval *m.*
shrub *n* arbusto *m.*
shrug *vt* encogerse de hombros.
shun *vt* huir, evitar.
shut *vt* cerrar.
shutter *n* contraventana *f.*
shuttle *n* lanzadera *f.*
shuttlecock *n* volante *m.*
shy *adj* timido.

shyness *n* timidez *f.*
sick *adj* malo, enfermo.
sickle *n* hoz *f.*
sickness *n* enfermedad *f.*
side *n* lado *m.*
sideboard *n* aparador *m;* alacena *f.*
sidewalk *n* calzada *f.*
siege *n* (*mil*) sitio *m.*
sieve *n* tamiz *m.*
sift *vt* cerner.
sigh *vi* suspirar.
sight *n* vista *f.*
sightseeing *n* excursionismo, turismo *m.*
sign *n* senal *f.*
signal *n* senal *f.*
signature *n* firma *f.*
significance *n* importancia *f.*
signify *vt* significar.
signpost *n* indicador *m.*
silence *n* silencio *m.*
silk *n* seda *f.*
silky *adj* hecho de seda; sedeno.
sill *n* repisa *f.*
silly *adj* tonto.
silver *n* plata *f.*
similar *adj* similar; semejante.
similarity *n* semejanza *f.*
simile *n* simil *m.*
simmer *vi* hervir a fuego lento.
simple *adj* simple.
simplicity *n* sencillez *ff.*
simulate *vt* simular.
simulation *n* simulacion *f.*
sin *n* pecado *m.*
since *adv* desde.
sincerity *n* sinceridad *f.*
sinew *n* tendon *m;* nervio *m.*
sing *vi, vt* cantar.
singe *vt* chamuscar.
singer *n* cantor *m;* cantora *f.*

single *adj* solo; soltero, soltera.

singly *adv* separadamente.

singular *adj* singular.

sinister *adj* siniestro.

sink *vi* hundirse.

sinner *n* pecador *m*; pecadora *f.*

sinus *n* seno *m.*

sip *vt* sorber:—*n* sorbo *m.*

siphon *n* sifon *m.*

sir *n* senor *m.*

siren *n* sirena *f.*

sister *n* hermana *f.*

sister-in-law *n* cunada *f.*

sisterly *adj* con hermandad.

sit *vi* sentarse.

site *n* sitio *m*; situacion *f.*

sit-in *n* ocupacion *f.*

sitting room *n* sala de estar *f.*

situation *n* situacion *f.*

six *adj*, *n* seis.

sixteen *adj*, *n* diez y seis, dieciseis.

sixteenth *adj*, *n* decimosexto.

sixth *adj*, *n* sexto.

sixtieth *adj*, *n* sexagesimo.

sixty *adj*, *n* sesenta.

size *n* tamano *m.*

skate *n* patin *m*:—*vi* patinar.

skeleton *n* esqueleto *m.*

skeptic *n* esceptico.

skepticism *n* escepticismo *m.*

sketch *n* esbozo *m.*

ski *n* esqui *m*:—*vi* esquiar.

skid *n* patinazo *m.*

skill *n* destreza *f.*

skim *vt* espumar.

skin *n* piel *f*; cutis *m/f.*

skip *vi* saltar, brincar.

skirt *n* falda.

skittle *n* bolo *m.*

skulk *vi* escuchar, acechar.

skull *n* craneo *m.*

sky *n* cielo *m.*

skyscraper *n* rascacielos *m invar.*

slab *n* losa *f.*

slack *adj* flojo.

slag *n* escoria *f.*

slander *vt* calumniar *f.*

slang *n* argot *m f.*

slap *n* manotada *f.*

slate *n* pizarra *f.*

slave *n* esclavo *m.*

slaver *n* baba *f*:—*vi* babosear.

slay *vt* matar.

sled, sleigh *n* trineo *m.*

sleek *adj* liso.

sleep *vi* dormir.

sleeping bag *n* saco de dormir *m.*

sleeping pill *n* somnifero *m.*

sleepwalking *n* sonambulismo *m.*

sleet *n* aguanieve *f.*

sleeve *n* manga *f.*

slender *adj* delgado.

slice *n* rebanada *f.*

slide *vi* resbalar, deslizarse.

slight *adj* ligero.

slim *adj* delgado.

slime *n* lodo *m/f.*

slimy *adj* viscoso, pegajoso.

sling *n* honda *f*; cabestrillo *m.*

slingshot *n* catapulta *f.*

slip *vi* resbalar; escapar.

slipper *n* zapatilla *f.*

slogan *n* eslogan, lema *m.*

slope *n* cuesta *f.*

slow *adj* tardio, lento, torpe.

slum *n* tugurio *m.*

slump *n* depresion *f.*

slur *vt* ensuciar; calumniar.

slut *n* marrana *f.*

sly *adj* astuto.

smack *n* sabor, gusto *m*; chasquido de latigo *m.*

small adj pequeno.

smallpox n viruelas fpl.

smalltalk n charla, prosa f.

smart adj elegante; listo.

smash vt romper, quebrantar

smell vt, vi oler.

smile vi sonreirse:—n sonrisa f.

smoke n humo m; fumar.

smoker n fumador, ra m/f.

smooth adj liso.

smug adj presumido.

smut n tiznon m.

snack n bocadom.

snag n problema m.

snail n caracol m.

snake n culebra f.

snap vt, vi romper.

snapdragon n (bot) antirrino m.

snatch vt arrebatar.

sneeze vi estornudar.

sniff vt oler:—vi resollar con fuerza.

snob n (e)snob m/f.

snore vi roncar.

snow n nieve f.

snowdrop n (bot) campanilla blanca f.

snowman n figura de nieve f.

snub vt reprender.

snuff n rape m.

so adv asi; de este modo; tan.

soap n jabon m.

soap opera n telenovela f.

soar vi remontarse.

sob n sollozo m:—vi sollozar.

soccer n balón m; fútbol m.

soccer player n futbolista m/f.

sociable adj sociable.

social adj social.

socialism n socialismo m.

society n sociedad f.

sociologist n sociologo, ga m/f.

sociology n sociologia f.

sock n calcetin m.

sod n cesped m.

soda n sosa f.

sofa n sofa m.

soft adj blando.

soil vt ensuciar, tierra f.

solar adj solar.

soldier n soldado m.

sole n planta del pie f.

solemn adj, ~ly adv solemne (mente).

solicitor n representante, agente m/f.

solid adj solido.

solitaire n solitario m; grueso diamante m.

solitude n soledad f.

solo n (mus) solo m.

solstice n solsticio m.

soluble adj soluble.

solution n solucion f.

solve vt resolver.

some adj algo de, un poco, algun, alguno, alguna, unos, pocos, ciertos.

somebody n alguien m.

something n alguna cosa, algo.

sometimes adv a veces.

somnambulism n somnambulismo m.

somnambulist n somnambulo m.

somnolence n somnolencia f.

son n hijo m.

sonata n (mus) sonata f.

song n cancion f.

son-in-law n yerno m.

sonnet n soneto m.

soon adv pronto.

soot n hollin m.

soothe vt adular; calmar.

sop n sopa f.

sophisticate vt sofisticar.

sophisticated adj sofisticado.

sorcerer n hechicero m.
sorcery n hechizo m.
sordid adj sordido.
sore n llaga, ulcera f.
sorrow n pesar m; tristeza f.
sorry adj triste.
soul n alma f.
sound adj sano; sonido, vi sonar.
soup n sopa f.
sour adj agrio.
souvenir n recuerdo m.
south n sur m.
sovereign adj, n soberano, na (m/f).
sovereignty n soberania f.
sow n puerca f.
sow vt sembrar.
space n espacio m.
spacious adj espacioso.
spade n laya.
spaghetti n espaguetis mpl.
span n palmo m.
spangle n lentejuela f.
spaniel n perro de aguas m.
Spanish adj espanol(a)
spar n palo m.
spark n chispa f.
sparkle n centella.
sparrow n gorrion m.
sparse adj delgado.
spasm n espasmo m.
spatula n espatula f.
spawn n freza f.
speak vt, vi hablar.
spear n lanza f.
special adj especial.
species n especie f.
specific adj especifico m.
specimen n muestra f.
spectacle n espectaculo m.
spectator n espectador, ra m/f.
specter n espectro m.
speculate vi especular.

speculation n especulacion f.
speed n prisa f; velocidad f.
spell n hechizo m.
spelling n ortografia f.
spend vt gastar.
sperm n esperma f.
spew vi (sl) vomitar.
sphere n esfera f.
spherical adj esferico.
spice n especia f.
spicy adj aromatico.
spider n arana f.
spike n espigon m.
spill vt derramar.
spin vt hilar.
spinach n espinaca f.
spinal adj espinal.
spine n espinazo m.
spinster n soltera f.
spiral adj espiral.
spire n espira f.
spirit n aliento m; espiritu m.
spiritual adj, ~ly adv espiritual (mente).
spiritualist n espiritualista m.
spit n asador m; saliva f.
spite n rencor m.
splash vt salpicar.
spleen n bazo m.
splendid adj esplendido.
splendor n esplendor m.
splint n tablilla f.
splinter n cacho m.
split n hendedura f.
spoil vt despojar.
spoke n rayo de la rueda m.
spokesman n portavoz m.
sponge n esponja f.
sponsor n fiador m.
spontaneity n espontaneidad f.
spool n carrete m.
spoon n cuchara f.

spoonful *n* cucharada *f.*

sport *n* deporte *m*

spot *n* mancha *f.*

spouse *n* esposo *m*; esposa *f.*

sprain *adj* descoyuntar.

sprat *n* meleta, nuesa *f* (pez).

sprawl *vi* revolcarse.

spray *n* rociada *f*; espray *m.*

spread *vt* extender

spree *n* fiesta *f*; juerga *f.*

sprig *n* ramito *m.*

sprinkle *vt* rociar.

spur *n* espuela *f.*

spurn *vt* despreciar.

spy *n* espia *m.*

squad *n* escuadra *f.*

squadron *n* (mil) escuadron *m.*

squalid *adj* sucio.

squall *n* rafaga *f.*

squalor *n* porqueria *f.*

squander *vt* malgastar.

square *adj* cuadrado *m*; plaza *f.*

squash *vt* aplastar.

squaw *n* hembra de un indiano *f*

squeak *vi* planir.

squeamish *adj* fastidioso.

squeeze *vt* apretar.

squid *n* calamar *m.*

squint *adj* bizco.

squirrel *n* ardilla *f.*

stable *n* establo *m.*

stack *n* pila *f.*

staff *n* personal *m.*

stag *n* ciervo *m.*

stage *n* etapa *f*; escena *f.*

stagnate *vi* estancarse.

stain *vt* manchar.

stair *n* escalon *m.*

staircase *n* escalera *f.*

stale *adj* anejo.

stalk, tronco. *m.*

stall *n* pesebre *m*; tienda portatil *f.*

stallion *n* semental *m.*

stamina *n* resistencia *f.*

stammer *vi* tartamudear.

stamp estampar, imprimir; sello *m.*

stampede *n* estampida *f.*

stand *vi* estar de pie o derecho; stand *m.*

standard *n* estandarte *m.*

staple *n* grapa *f.*

star *n* estrella *f.*

starch *n* almidon *m.*

stark *adj* fuerte, aspero.

starling *n* estornino *m.*

start *vi* empezar.

startle *vt* sobresaltar.

starvation *n* hambre *f.*

state *n* estado *m*; condicion *f.*

statement *n* afirmacion *f.*

static *adj* estatico.

station *n* estacion *f.*

stationary *adj* estacionario, fijo.

stationery *n* papeleria *f.*

statistics *npl* estadistica *f.*

statuary *n* estatuario *m.*

statue *n* estatua *f.*

stature *n* estatura *f.*

statute *n* estatuto *m.*

stay *n* estancia *f.*

steak *n* filete *m*; bistec *m.*

steal *vt, vi* robar.

stealth *n* hurto *m.*

steam *n* vapor *m.*

steel *n* acero *m.*

steep *adj* escarpado.

steeple *n* torre *f*; campanario *m.*

steer *n* novillo *m:*—*vt* manejar, conducir.

steering wheel *n* volante *m.*

stem *n* vastago.

stench *n* hedor *m.*

stencil *n* cliche *m.*

stenographer *n* taquigrafo, fa *m/f.*

stenography n taquigrafia f.

step n paso, escalon m.

stepbrother n hermanastro m.

stepdaughter n hijastra f.

stepfather n padrastro m.

stepmother n madrastra f.

stepsister n hermanastra f.

stepson n hijastro m.

stereo n estereo m.

stereotype n estereotipo m.

sterile adj esteril.

sterling n libras esterlinas fpl.

stethoscope n (med) estetoscopio m.

stew vt estofar f.

steward n mayordomo m

stick n palo, pegarse.

stiff adj tieso.

stifle vt sufocar.

stigma n estigma m.

stigmatize vt infamar.

stiletto n estilete m

still tranquilo; adv todavia.

stillborn adj nacido muerto.

stilts npl zancos mpl.

stimulant n estimulante m.

stimulate vt estimular.

stimulus n estimulo m.

sting vt picar o morder (un insecto).

stingy adj mezquino.

stink vi heder.

stint n tarea f.

stipulate vt estipular.

stipulation n estipulacion f.

stir vt agitar.

stirrup n estribo m.

stitch vt coser.

stoat n comadreja f.

stock n ganado m; caldo m.

stockbroker n agente de bolsa m/f.

stock exchange n bolsa f.

stocking n media f.

stock market n bolsa f.

stoic n estoico m.

stoical adj estoico.

stole n estola f.

stomach n estomago m.

stone n piedra f.

stop vt detener, parar.

stopwatch n cronometro m.

store n provision f; almacen m.

stork n ciguena f.

storm n tempestad.

story n historia f.

stout adj robusto.

stove n estufa f.

straight adj derecho.

strain vt colar, filtrar; n tension f.

strainer n colador m.

strange adj raro/a, extranjero.

stranger n desconocido m; extranjero, ra m/f.

strangle vt ahogar.

strap n correa.

strapping adj abultado.

stratagem n estratagema f; astucia f.

strategic adj estrategico m.

strategy n estrategia f.

stratum n estrato m.

straw n paja m; pajita f.

strawberry n fresa f.

stray vi extraviarse.

streak n raya.

street n calle f.

streetcar n tranvia f.

strength n fuerza f.

strenuous adj arduo.

stress n presion f; estres m.

stretch vt, vi extender.

stretcher n camilla f.

strew vt esparcir.

strict adj estricto.

stride n tranco m.

string n cordon m.

stringent adj astringente.

strip vt desnudar.

stripe n raya.

strive vi esforzarse.

stroll n paseo.

strong adj fuerte.

strongbox n cofre fuerte m.

structure n estructura f.

struggle vi esforzarse.

strum vt (mus) rasguear.

strut vi pavonearse.

stubborn adj obstinado.

stucco n estuco m.

stud n corchete m.

student n estudiante m/f.

studio n estudio de un artista m.

studious adj estudioso.

study n estudio m.

stuff n materia f.

stuffing n relleno m.

stumble vi tropezar

stump n tronco m.

stun vt aturdir.

stunt n vuelo acrobático m; truco publicitario m.

stuntman n especialista m.

stupid adj estupido.

sturdy adj fuerte.

sturgeon n esturion m.

stutter vi tartamudear.

sty n zahurda f.

stye n orzuelo m.

style n estilo m.

stylish adj elegante.

suave adj afable.

subdivide vt subdividir.

subdue vt sojuzgar, sujetar.

subject adj sujeto.

subjunctive n subjuntivo m.

sublime adj sublime

submarine adj submarino.

submerge vt sumergir.

submit vt, (vi) someter(se).

subordinate adj subordinado, inferior:—vt subordinar.

subscribe vt, vi suscribir.

subsequent adj, ~ly adv subsiguiente (mente).

subservient adj subordinado.

subside vi sumergirse.

subsidence n derrumbamiento m.

subsidiary adj subsidiario.

subsidize vt subvencionar.

subsidy n subvencion f.

substance n substancia f.

substitute vt sustituir.

substratum n lecho m.

subterranean adj subterraneo.

subtitle n subtitulo m.

subtle adj sutil.

suburb n suburbio m.

subversion n subversion f.

subway n metro m.

succeed vt, vi seguir; conseguir, lograr, tener exito.

success n exito m.

succumb vi sucumbir.

such adj tal.

suck vt, vi chupar.

sudden adj repentino, no previsto.

sue vt poner por justicia; suplicar.

suede n ante m.

suffer vt, vi sufrir, padecer.

sufficient adj suficiente.

suffocate vt sufocar.

suffrage n sufragio.

sugar n azucar m.

sugar cane n cana de azucar f.

suggest vt sugerir.

suggestion n sugestion f.

suicide n suicidio m.

suit n conjunto m; traje m.

suitcase n maleta f.

suitor n suplicante m.

sultan n sultan m.

sultana n sultana f.

sum n suma f.

summary adj, n sumario (m).

summer n verano m.

summit n apice m.

summon vt citar.

summons n citacion f.

sumptuous adj suntuoso.

sun n sol m.

sunbathe vi tomar el sol.

Sunday n domingo m.

sundial n reloj de sol m.

sundry adj varios.

sunflower n girasol m.

sunglasses npl gafas o antojos de sol mpl.

sunlight n luz del sol f.

sunrise n salida del sol f.

sunset n puesta del sol f.

sunshade n quitasol m.

sunstroke n insolacion f.

suntan n bronceado m.

suntan oil n aceite bronceador m.

superb adj magnifico.

superficial adj superficial.

superfluity n superfluidad f.

superior adj, n superior (m).

supermarket n supermercado m.

supernatural n sobrenatural.

superpower n superpotencia f.

superstition n supersticion f.

supertanker n superpetrolero m.

supervise vt inspeccionar.

supper n cena f.

supple adj flexible.

supplement n suplemento m.

supplementary adj adicional.

suppleness n flexibilidad f.

suppli(c)ant n suplicante m.

supplicate vt suplicar.

supplication n suplica, suplicacion f.

supplier n distribuidor, ra m/f.

supply vt suministrar; suplir, completar; surtir:—n provision f; suministro m.

support vt sostener; soportar, asistir:—n apoyo m.

supportable adj soportable.

supporter n partidario, ria; aficionado, dam/f.

suppose vt, vi suponer.

supposition n suposicion f.

suppress vt suprimir.

suppression n supresion f.

supremacy n supremacia f.

supreme adj supremo:—~ly adv supremamente.

surcharge vt sobrecargar:—n sobretasa f.

sure adj seguro, cierto; firme; estable:—**to be ~** sin duda; ya se ve:—~ly adv ciertamente, seguramente, sin duda.

sureness n certeza, seguridad f.

surety n seguridad f; fiador m.

surf n (mar) resaca f.

surface n superficie f:—vt revestir:—vi salir a la superficie.

surfboard n plancha (de surf) f.

surfeit n exceso m.

surge n ola, onda f:—vi avanzar en tropel.

surgeon n cirujano, na m/f.

surgery n cirujia m.

surgical adj quirurgico.

surliness n mal humor m.

surly adj aspero de genio.

surmise vt sospechar:—n sospecha f.

surmount vt sobrepujar.

surmountable adj superable.

surname n apellido, sobrenombre m.

surpass vt sobresalir, sobrepujar, exceder, aventajar.

surpassing adj sobresaliente.

surplice n sobrepelliz f.

surplus n excedente m; sobrante m:—adj sobrante.

surprise vt sorprender:—n sorpresa f.

surprising adj sorprendente.

surrender vt, vi rendir; ceder; rendirse:—n rendicion f.

surreptitious adj subrepticio:—~ly adv subrepticiamente.

surrogate vt subrogar:—n subrogado m.

surrogate mother n madre portadora f.

surround vt circundar, cercar, rodear.

survey vt inspeccionar, examinar; apear:—n inspeccion f; apeo (de tierras) m.

survive vi sobrevivir:—vt sobrevivir a.

survivor n sobreviviente m/f.

susceptibility n susceptibilidad f.

susceptible adj susceptible.

suspect vt, vi sospechar:—n sospechoso, sa m/f.

suspend vt suspender.

suspense n suspense m; detencion f; incertidumbre f.

suspension n suspension f.

suspension bridge n puente colgante o colgado m.

suspicion n sospecha f.

suspicious adj suspicaz:—~ly adv sospechosamente.

suspiciousness n suspicacia f.

sustain vt sostener, sustentar, mantener; apoyar; sufrir.

sustenance n sostenimiento, sustento m.

suture n sutura, costura f.

swab n algodon m; frotis m invar.

swaddle vt fajar.

swaddling-clothes npl panales mpl.

swagger vi baladronear.

swallow n golondrina f:—vt tragar, engullir.

swamp n pantano m.

swampy adj pantanoso.

swan n cisne m.

swap vt canjear:—n intercambio m.

swarm n enjambre m; gentio m; hormiguero m:—vi enjam brar; hormiguear de gente; abundar.

swarthy adj atezado.

swarthiness n tez morena f.

swashbuckling adj fanfarron.

swath n tranco m.

swathe vt fajar:—n faja f.

sway vt mover:—vi ladearse, inclinarse:—n balanceo m; poder, imperio, influjo m.

swear vt, vi jurar; hacer jurar; juramentar.

sweat n sudor m:—vi sudar; trabajar con fatiga.

sweater, sweatshirt n sueter m.

sweep vt, vi barrer; arrebatar; deshollinar; pasar o tocar liger amente; oscilar:—n barredura f; vuelta f; giro m.

sweeping adj rapido:—~s pl barreduras fpl.

sweepstake n loteria f.

sweet adj dulce, grato, gustoso; suave; oloroso; melodioso; hermoso; amable:—adv dulcemente, suavemente.

sweetbread n mellejas de ternera fpl.

sweeten vt endulzar; suavizar; aplacar; perfumar.

sweetener n edulcorante m.

sweetheart n novio, via m/f; querida f.

sweetmeats npl dulces secos mpl.

sweetness n dulzura, suavidad f.

swell *vi* hincharse; ensoberbecerse; embravecerse:—*vt* hin char, inflar, agravar:—*n* marejada *f:*—*adj* (*fam*) estupendo, fenomenal.

swelling *n* hinchazon *f;* tumor *m.*

swelter *vi* ahogarse de calor.

swerve *vi* vagar; desviarse.

swift *adj* veloz, ligero, rapido:—*n* vencejo, *m.*

swiftly *adv* velozmente.

swiftness *n* velocidad, rapidez *f.*

swill *vt* beber con exceso:—*n* bazofia *f.*

swim *vi* nadar; abundar en:—*vt* pasar a nado:—*n* nadada *f.*

swimming *n* natacion *f;* vertigo *m.*

swimming pool *n* piscina *f.*

swimsuit *n* traje de bano *m.*

swindle *vt* estafar.

swindler *n* trampista *m.*

swine *n* puerco, cochino *m.*

swing *vi* balancear, columpiarse; vibrar; agitarse:—*vt* colum piar; balancear; girar:—*n* vibracion *f;* balanceo *m.*

swinging *adj* (*fam*) alegre.

swinging door *n* puerta giratoria *f.*

swirl *n* hacer remolinos (en el agua).

switch *n* varilla *f;* interruptor *m;* (*rail*) aguja *f:*—*vt* cambiar de:—**to ~ off** apagar; parar:—**to ~ on** encender, prender.

switchboard *n* centralita (de teléfonos) *f.*

swivel *vt* girar.

swoon *vi* desmayarse:—*n* desmayo, deliquio, pasmo *m.*

swoop *vi* calarse:—*n* calada; redada *f:*—**in one ~** de un golpe.

sword *n* espada *f.*

swordfish *n* pez espada *f.*

swordsman *n* guerrero *m.*

sycamore *n* sicomoro *m* (arbol).

sycophant *n* sicofante *m.*

syllabic *adj* silabico.

syllable *n* silaba *f.*

syllabus *n* programa de estudios *m.*

syllogism *n* silogismo *m.*

sylph *n* silfio *m;* silfida *f.*

symbol *n* simbolo *m.*

symbolic(al) *adj* simbolico.

symbolize *vt* simbolizar.

symmetrical *adj* simetrico:—**~ly** *adv* con simetria.

symmetry *n* simetria *f.*

sympathetic *adj* simpatico:—**~ally** *adv* simpaticamente.

sympathize *vi* compadecerse.

sympathy *n* simpatia *f.*

symphony *n* sinfonia *f.*

symposium *n* simposio *m.*

symptom *n* sintoma *m.*

synagogue *n* sinagoga *f.*

synchronism *n* sincronismo *m.*

syndicate *n* sindicato *m.*

syndrome *n* sindrome *m.*

synod *n* sinodo *m.*

synonym *n* sinonimo *m.*

synonymous *adj* sinonimo:—**~ly** *adv* con sinonimia.

synopsis *n* sinopsis *f;* sumario *m.*

synoptical *adj* sinoptico.

syntax *n* sintaxis *f.*

synthesis *n* sintesis *f.*

syringe *n* jeringa, lavativa *f:*—*vt* jeringar.

system *n* sistema *m.*

systematic *adj* sistematico:—**~ally** *adv* sistematicamente.

systems analyst *n* analista de sistemas *m/f.*

table 240 teddy

T

table n mesa f m.
tablecloth n mantel m.
tablespoon n cuchara para comer f.
tablet n tableta f m.
table tennis n ping-pong m.
taboo adj tabu.
tacit adj tacito.
taciturn adj taciturno.
tack n tachuela f.
tact n tacto m.
tactician n tactico m.
tactics npl tactica f.
tadpole n ranilla f.
taffeta n tafetan m.
tag n herrete m.
tail n cola f.
tailor n sastre m.
tailor-made adj hecho a la medida.
taint vt tachar.
take vt tomar, coger.
takeoff n despegue m.
takings npl ingresos mpl.
talc n talco m.
talent n talento m.
talisman n talisman m.
talk vi hablar.
talkative adj locuaz.
tall adj alto.
talon n garra de ave de rapina f.
tambourine n pandereta f.
tame adj amansado.
tamper vi tocar.
tampon n tampon m.
tan vt broncear.
tang n sabor fuerte m.
tangerine n mandarina f.
tangle vt enredar.
tank n cisterna f; aljibe m.
tanned adj bronceado.

tantrum n rabieta f.
tape n cinta f.
tape measure n metro m.
tapestry n tapiz mf.
tar n brea f.
target n blanco m (para tirar).
tariff n tarifa f.
tarmac n pista f.
tarnish vt deslustrar.
tarpaulin n alquitranado m.
tarragon n (bot) estragon m.
tartan n tela escocesa f.
tartar n tartaro m.
task n tarea f.
tassel n borlita f.
taste n gusto m; sabor m.
tasty adj sabroso.
tattoo n tatuaje m.
taunt vt mofar.
Taurus n Tauro m.
tax n impuesto m.
taxi n taxi m.
tea n te m.
teach vt ensenar.
teacher n profesor, ra m/f.
teak n teca f (arbol).
team n equipo m.
teamster n camionero m.
teapot n tetera f.
tear vt despedazar, rasgar.
tear n lagrima f.
tease vt tomar el pelo.
teaspoon n cucharita f.
teat n ubre, teta f.
technical adj tecnico.
technician n tecnico m.
technique n tecnica f.
technology n tecnologia f.
teddy (bear) n osito de felpa m.

tedious adj tedioso.

tedium n tedio m.

tee-shirt n camiseta f.

teeth npl de tooth.

telegraph n telegrafo m.

telegraphic adj telegrafico.

telepathy n telepatia f.

telephone n telefono m.

telescope n telescopio m.

telescopic adj telescopico.

television n television f.

tell vi decir.

teller n cajero m.

temper vt templar:—n mal genio m.

temperament n temperamento m.

temperate adj templado.

temperature n temperatura f.

template n plantilla f.

temple n templo m.

temporary adj temporal.

tempt vt tentar.

temptation n tentacion f.

ten adj, n diez.

tenacity n tenacidad f.

tenancy n tenencia f.

tenant n arrendador m.

tend vt guardar.

tendency n tendencia f.

tender adj tierno, estimar.

tendon n tendon m.

tennis n tenis m.

tense adj tieso, tenso.

tension n tension f.

tent n tienda de campana f.

tentacle n tentaculo m.

tenth adj, n decimo.

tenure n tenencia f.

tepid adj tibio.

term n termino m.

terminal adj mortal.

termination n terminacion f.

terminus n terminal f.

terrace n terraza f.

terrain n terreno m.

terrestrial adj terrestre.

terrible adj terrible.

terrier n terrier m.

terrific adj fantastico.

terrify vt aterrar.

territorial adj territorial.

territory n territorio, distrito m.

terror n terror m.

terrorism n terrorismo m.

test n examen m.

testament n testamento m.

testicles npl testiculos mpl.

testify vt testificar.

testimony n testimonio m.

tetanus n tetano m.

tether vt atar.

text n texto m.

textiles npl textiles mpl.

texture n textura f.

than adv que, de.

thank vt agradecer.

thanks npl gracias fpl.

that pn aquel, aquello, aquella; que; este.

thaw n deshielo m.

the art el, la, lo; los, las.

theater n teatro m.

theft n robo m.

their pn su, suyo, suya; de ellos, de ellas:—~s el suyo, la suya, los suyos, las suyas; de ellos, de ellas.

them pn los, las, les; ellos, ellas.

theme n tema m.

themselves pn pl ellos mismos, ellas mismas; si mismos; se.

then adv entonces, despues.

theology n teologia f.

theory n teoria f.

therapist n terapeuta m.

therapy n terapia f.

there adv alli, alla.

thermal adj termal.

thermometer n termometro m.

thesaurus n tesoro m.

these pn pl estos, estas.

thesis n tesis f.

they pn pl ellos, ellas.

thick adj espeso.

thicken vi espesar.

thief n ladron m.

thigh n muslo m.

thimble n dedal m.

thin adj delgado.

thing n cosa f.

think vi pensar.

third adj tercero.

thirst n sed f.

thirteen adj, n trece.

thirteenth adj, n decimotercio.

thirtieth adj, n trigesimo.

thirty adj, n treinta.

this adj este, esta, esto:—pn este, esta, esto.

thorn n espino m; espina f.

those pn pl esos, esas; aquellos, aquellas:—adj esos, esas; aquellos, aquellas.

thought n pensamiento m.

thousand adj, n mil.

thousandth adj, n milesimo.

thrash vt golpear.

thread n hilo m.

threat n amenaza f.

threaten vt amenazar.

three adj, n tres.

threshold n umbral m.

thrifty adj economico.

thrill vt emocionar.

thrive vi prosperar.

throat n garganta f.

throb vi palpitar.

throne n trono m.

through prep por; durante; mediante.

throw vt echar.

thrush n tordo m (ave).

thrust vt empujar.

thug n gamberro m.

thumb n pulgar m.

thump n golpe m.

thunder n trueno m.

Thursday n jueves m.

thus adv asi, de este modo.

thyme n (bot) tomillo m.

thyroid n tiroides m.

tiara n tiara f.

tic n tic m.

ticket n billete m .

tickle vt hacer cosquillas.

tidal adj (mar) de marea.

tide n marea f.

tidy adj ordenado.

tie vt anudar, atar

tiger n tigre m.

tight adj tirante, apretado/a.

tile n azulejo m.

till n caja f:—vt cultivar.

time n tiempo; epoca f.

timer n interruptor m.

timid adj timido.

timidity n timidez f.

tin n estano m.

tinfoil n papel de estano m.

tinsel n oropel m.

tint n tinte m.

tiny adj pequeno, chico.

tip n punta, extremidad f; propina f.

tire vt cansar, fatigar:—n neumático m.

tissue n tejido m.

title n titulo m.

titular adj titular.

to *prep* a; para; por; de; hasta; en; con; que.

toad *n* sapo *m*.

toadstool *n* (*bot*) hongovejin *m*.

toast *vt* tostar; brindar.

toaster *n* tostadora *f*.

tobacco *n* tabaco *m*.

tobacco shop *n* tabaqueria *f*.

today *adv* hoy.

toe *n* dedo del pie *m*.

together *adv* juntamente.

toilet paper *n* papel higienico *m*.

token *n* senal *f*.

tolerate *vt* tolerar.

tomato *n* tomate *m*.

tomb *n* tumba *f*.

tomboy *n* muchachota *f*.

tombstone *n* piedra sepulcral *f*.

tomcat *n* gato *m*.

tomorrow *adv, n* manana *f*.

ton *n* tonelada *f*.

tongs *npl* tenacillas *fpl*.

tongue *n* lengua *f*.

tonic *n* (*med*) tonico.

tonight *adv, n* esta tarde (*f*).

tonsil *n* amigdala *f*.

too *adv* demasiado; tambien.

tool *n* herramienta *f*.

tooth *n* diente *m*.

toothache *n* dolor de muelas *m*.

top *n* cima.

topaz *n* topacio *m*.

topic *n* tema *m*.

topless *adj* topless.

topographic(al) *adj* topografico.

topography *n* topografia *f*.

torment *vt* atormentar.

tornado *n* tornado *m*.

torrent *n* torrente *m*.

torrid *adj* apasionado.

tortoise *n* tortuga *f*.

tortoiseshell *adj* de carey.

tortuous *adj* tortuoso.

torture *n* tortura *f*.

toss *vt* tirar, lanzar.

total *adj* total.

totalitarian *adj* totalitario.

totality *n* totalidad *f*.

totter *vi* vacilar.

touch *vt* tocar.

touchdown *n* aterrizaje *m*.

touching *adj* patetico, conmovedor.

tough *adj* duro.

toupee *n* tupe *m*.

tour *n* viaje *m*.

touring *n* viajes turisticos *mpl*.

tourism *n* turismo *m*.

tourist *n* turista *m/f*.

tourist office *n* oficina de turismo *f*.

tournament *n* torneo *m*.

tow *n* remolque *m*.

toward(s) *prep, adv* hacia.

towel *n* toalla *f*.

tower *n* torre *m*.

town *n* ciudad *f*.

town hall *n* ayuntamiento *m*.

toy *n* juguete *m*.

toy store *n* jugueteria *f*.

trace *n* huella *f*:—*vt* trazar.

trade *n* comercio *m*; ocupacion *f*.

trade(s) union *n* sindicato *m*.

tradition *n* tradicion *f*.

traditional *adj* tradicional.

traffic *n* trafico *m*.

traffic lights *npl* semaforo *m*.

tragedy *n* tragedia *f*.

tragic *adj* tragico.

trail *vt, vi* rastrear:—*n* senda *f*.

trailer *n* caravana *f*.

train *vt* entrenar * *n* tren *m*.

trainee *n* aprendiz *m*.

trainer *n* entrenador *m*.

trait *n* rasgo *m*.

traitor *n* traidor *m*.

tramp n vagabundo m.

trample vt pisotear.

trampoline n trampolin m.

trance n rapto m.

tranquil adj tranquilo.

tranquillizer n tranquilizante m.

transact vt negociar.

transaction n transaccion f.

transatlantic adj transatlántico.

transcription n traslado m.

transfer vt transferir.

transform vt transformar.

transformation n transformacion f.

transfusion n transfusion f.

transit n transito m.

transition n transito m; transicion f.

translate vt traducir.

translation n traduccion f.

translator n traductor, ra m/f.

transmit vt transmitir.

transparent adj transparente.

transpire vi resultar.

transplant vt trasplantar.

transport vt transportar.

trap n trampa f.

trapeze n trapecio m.

trappings npl adornos mpl.

trash n pacotilla f; basura f.

travel vi viajar.

trawler n pesquero de arrastre m.

tray n bandeja f

treachery n traicion f.

tread vi pisar.

treason n traicion n.

treasure n tesoro m.

treasurer n tesorero m.

treat vt tratar.

treatise n tratado m.

treatment n trato m.

treaty n tratado m.

treble adj triple.

treble clef n clave de sol f.

tree n arbol m.

trellis n enrejado m.

tremble vi temblar.

tremendous adj tremendo.

tremor n temblor m.

trench n foso m.

trend n tendencia f.

trendy adj de moda.

trespass vt transpasar.

tress n trenza f.

trestle n caballete de serrador m.

trial n proceso m.

triangle n triangulo m.

triangular adj triangular.

tribal adj tribal.

tribe n tribu f.

tribunal n tribunal m.

tributary adj, n tributario m.

tribute n tributo m.

trice n momento, tris m.

trick n engano.

trickle vi gotear.

tricky adj dificil.

tricycle n triciclo m.

trifle n bagatela.

trigger n gatillo m.

trigonometry n trigonometria f.

trim adj aseado.

Trinity n Trinidad f.

trinket n joya.

trio n (mus) trio m.

trip vt hacer caer; viaje corto m.

tripe n callos mpl.

triple adj triple.

triplets npl trillizos mpl.

triplicate n triplicado m.

tripod n tripode m.

triumph n triunfo m.

triumphal adj triunfal.

triumphant adj triunfante.

trivia *npl* trivialidades *fpl.*
trivial *adj* trivial.
trolley *n* carrito *m.*
trombone *n* trombon *m.*
trophy *n* trofeo *m.*
tropical *adj* tropico.
trot *n* trote *m.*
trouble *vt* afligir.
trough *n* abrevadero *m.*
trout *n* trucha *f.*
trowel *n* paleta *f.*
truce *n* tregua *f.*
truck *n* camion *m*
true *adj* verdadero.
truffle *n* trufa *f.*
truly *adv* en verdad.
trumpet *n* trompeta *f.*
trunk *n* baul, cofre *m*; trompa *f.*
trust *n* confianza *f.*
truth *n* verdad *f.*
try *vt* examinar, tentar.
tub *n* balde, cubo *m.*
tuba *n* tuba *f.*
tube *n* tubo *m.*
tuberculosis *n* tuberculosis *f.*
Tuesday *n* martes *m.*
tuition *n* enseñanza. *f.*
tulip *n* tulipan *m.*
tumble *vi* caer.
tumbler *n* vaso *m.*
tummy *n* barriga *f.*
tumor *n* tumor *m.*
tumultuous *adj* tumultuoso.
tuna *n* atun *m.*
tune *n* tono *m.*
tunic *n* tunica *f.*
tunnel *n* tunel *m.*
turban *n* turbante *m.*
turbine *n* turbina *f.*
turbulence *n* turbulencia *f.*
tureen *n* sopera *f.*

turf *n* cesped *m.*
turgid *adj* pesado.
turkey *n* pavo *m.*
turmoil *n* disturbio *m.*
turn *vi* volver.
turncoat *n* desertor *m.*
turnip *n* nabo *m.*
turnover *n* facturacion *f.*
turnstile *n* torniquete *m.*
turpentine *n* trementina *f.*
turquoise *n* turquesa *f.*
turret *n* torrecilla *f.*
turtle *n* galapago *m.*
turtledove *n* tortola *f.*
tusk *n* colmillo *m.*
tussle *n* pelea *f.*
tutor *n* tutor *m.*
tuxedo *n* smoking *m.*
twang *n* gangueo *m.*
tweezers *npl* tenacillas *fpl.*
twelfth *adj, n* duodecimo.
twelve *adj, n* doce.
twentieth *adj, n* vigesimo.
twenty *adj, n* veinte.
twice *adv* dos veces.
twig *n* ramita *f:—vi* caer en la cuenta.
twilight *n* crepusculo *m.*
twin *n* gemelo *m.*
twist *vt* torcer.
twit *n* (*col*) tonto *m.*
twitch *vi* moverse nerviosamente.
two *adj, n* dos.
two-faced *adj* falso.
tycoon *n* magnate *m.*
type *n* tipo *m*; letra *f*; modelo *m:—vt* escribir a maquina.
typewriter *n* maquina de escribir *f.*
typical *adj* tipico.
tyrannical *adj* tiranico.
tyranny *n* tirania *f.*
tyrant *n* tirano *m.*

U

ubiquitous *adj* ubicuo.
udder *n* ubre f.
ugh *excl* iuf!
ugliness *n* fealdad f.
ugly *adj* feo; peligroso.
ulcer *n* ulcera f.
ulterior *adj* ulterior.
ultimate *adj* ultimo.
ultimatum *n* ultimatum m.
umbrella *n* paraguas m *invar*.
umpire *n* arbitro m.
unable *adj* incapaz.
unaccompanied *adj* solo.
unaccustomed *adj* desacostumbrado.
unanimity *n* unanimidad f.
unanimous *adj* unanime.
unanswerable *adj* incontrovertible.
unapproachable *adj* inaccesible.
unbearable *adj* intolerable.
unbecoming *adj* indecente.
unbutton *vt* desabotonar.
uncanny *adj* extraordinario.
unchanged *adj* no alterado.
uncharitable *adj* nada caritativo.
uncle *n* tio.
uncomfortable *adj* incomodo.
uncommon *adj* raro.
uncompromising *adj* irreconciliable.
unconscious *adj* inconsciente.
unconventional *adj* poco convencional.
uncork *vt* destapar.
uncouth *adj* grosero.
uncover *vt* descubrir.
undaunted *adj* intrepido.
under *prep* debajo de.
under-age *adj* menor de edad.
underclothing *n* ropa intima f.
underdeveloped *adj* subdesarrollado.
underdog *n* desvalido m.

underestimate *vt* subestimar.
undergo *vt* sufrir.
undergraduate *n* estudiante m.
underground *n* movimiento clandestino m.
underline *vt* subrayar.
underpaid *adj* mal pagado.
undershirt *n* camiseta f.
understand *vt* entender, comprender.
understatement *n* subestimacion f.
underwear *n* ropa intima f.
underworld *n* hampa f.
undetermined *adj* indeterminado, indeciso.
undigested *adj* indigesto.
undisciplined *adj* indisciplinado.
undismayed *adj* intrepido.
undisputed *adj* incontestable.
undisturbed *adj* quieto, tranquilo.
undivided *adj* indiviso, entero.
undo *vt* deshacer, destar.
undoubted *adj* indudable.
undress *vi* desnudarse.
undue *adj* indebido.
undulating *adj* ondulante.
unduly *adv* indebidamente.
undying *adj* inmortal.
unearth *vt* desenterrar.
uneasy *adj* inquieto.
uneducated *adj* ignorante.
unemployed *adj* parado.
unemployment *n* paro m.
unenlightened *adj* no iluminado.
unenviable *adj* poco envidiable.
unequal *adj* desigual.
unequaled *adj* incomparable.
uneven *adj* desigual.
unexpected *adj* inesperado.
unexplored *adj* inexplorado.
unfair *adj* injusto.

unfaithful *adj* infiel.

unfamiliar *adj* desacostumbrado.

unfashionable *adj* pasado de moda.

unfasten *vt* desatar.

unfavorable *adj* desfavorable.

unfeeling *adj* insensible.

unfit *adj* indispuesto.

unfold *vt* desplegar.

unforeseen *adj* imprevisto.

unforgettable *adj* inolvidable.

unforgivable *adj* imperdonable.

unforgiving *adj* implacable.

unfortunate *adj* desafortunado.

unfounded *adj* sin fundamento.

unfriendly *adj* antipatico.

unfruitful *adj* esteril; infructuoso.

unfurnished *adj* sin muebles.

ungrateful *adj* ingrato.

unhappily *adv* infelizmente.

unhappy *adj* infeliz.

unhealthy *adj* malsano.

unhook *vt* desenganchar; descolgar; desabrochar.

unhoped(-for) *adj* inesperado.

unhurt *adj* ileso.

unicorn *n* unicornio *m*.

uniform *adj* uniforme:—*n* uniforme *m*.

uniformity *adj* uniformidad *f*.

unify *vt* unificar.

unimaginable *adj* inimaginable.

unimportant *adj* nada importante.

uninformed *adj* ignorante.

uninhabitable *adj* inhabitable.

uninhabited *adj* inhabitado, desierto.

uninjured *adj* ileso, no danado.

unintelligible *adj* ininteligible.

unintentional *adj* involuntario.

uninterested *adj* desinteresado.

uninteresting *adj* poco interesante.

uninvited *adj* no convivado.

union *n* union *f*; sindicato *m*.

unionist *n* unitario *m*.

unique *adj* unico, uno, singular.

unit *n* unidad *f*.

unite *vt vi* unir(se), juntarse.

United States (of America) *npl* Estados Unidos (de América) *mpl*.

unity *n* unidad *f*.

universal *adj* universal.

universe *n* universo *m*.

university *n* universidad *f*.

unjust *adj* injusto.

unkind *adj* poco amable.

unknown *adj* incognito.

unlawful *adj* ilícito/a.

unless *conj* a menos que, si no.

unload *vt* descargar.

unluckily *adv* desafortunadamente.

unlucky *adj* desafortunado.

unmarried *adj* soltero; soltera.

unmerited *adj* desmerecido.

unmistakable *adj* evidente.

unmoved *adj* inmoto, firme.

unnatural *adj* antinatural.

unnecessary *adj* inutil, innecesario.

unnoticed *adj* no observado.

unobserved *adj* invertido/a.

unobtainable *adj* inconseguible.

unobtrusive *adj* modesto.

unoccupied *adj* desocupado.

unofficial *adj* no oficial.

unpack *vt* desempacar; desenvolver.

unpaid *adj* no pagado.

unpleasant *adj* desagradable.

unpopular *adj* no popular.

unpracticed *adj* inexperto.

unprecedented *adj* sin ejemplo.

unpredictable *adj* imprevisible.

unprepared *adj* no preparado.

unprofitable *adj* inútil, vano; poco lucrativo.

unpunished *adj* impune.

unqualified *adj* sin titulos; total.

unquestionable *adj* indubitable.

unravel *vt* desenredar.

unrealistic *adj* poco realista.

unreasonable *adv* irracionalmente.

unrelated *adj* sin relacion; inconexo.

unrelenting *adj* incompasivo, inflexible.

unreliable *adj* poco fiable.

unrestrained *adj* desenfrenado; ilimitado.

unripe *adj* inmaduro.

unrivaled *adj* sin rival.

unroll *vt* desenrollar.

unsafe *adj* inseguro.

unsatisfactory *adj* insatisfactorio.

unscrew *vt* destornillar.

unscrupulous *adj* sin escrupulos.

unseemly *adj* indecente.

unseen *adj* invisible.

unselfish *adj* desinteresado.

unsettle *vt* perturbar.

unshaken *adj* firme, estable.

unskilled *adj* inhabil.

unsociable *adj* insociable.

unspeakable *adj* inefable.

unstable *adj* instable, inconstante.

unsteady *adj* inestable.

unsuccessful *adj* infeliz, desafortunado.

unsuitable *adj* inapropiado; inoportuno.

unsure *adj* inseguro.

unsympathetic *adj* inompasivo.

untapped *adj* sin explotar.

untenable *adj* insostenible.

unthinkable *adj* inconcebible.

unthinking *adj* desatento, irreflexivo.

untidiness *n* desalino *m*.

untidy *adj* desordenado; sucio.

untie *vt* desatar, deshacer, soltar.

until *prep* hasta:—*conj* hasta que.

untimely *adj* intempestivo.

untiring *adj* incansable.

untold *adj* nunca dicho; indecible; incalculable.

untouched *adj* intacto.

untoward *adj* impropio; adverso.

untried *adj* no ensayado o probado.

untroubled *adj* no perturbado, tranquilo.

untrue *adj* falso.

untrustworthy *adj* indigno de confianza.

untruth *n* falsedad, mentira *f*.

unused *adj* isin usar, no usado.

unusual *adj* inusitado, raro:—~ly *adv* inusitadamente, raramente.

unveil *vt* quitar el velo, descubrir.

unwavering *adj* inquebrantable.

unwelcome *adj* desagradable, inoportuno.

unwell *adj* enfermizo, malo.

unwieldy *adj* pesado.

unwilling *adj* desinclinado:—~ly *adv* de mala gana.

unwillingness *n* mala gana, repugnancia *f*.

unwind *vt* desenredar, desenmaranar:—*vi* relajarse.

unwise *adj* imprudente.

unwitting *adj* inconsciente.

unworkable *adj* poco practico.

unworthy *adj* indigno.

unwrap *vt* desenvolver.

unwritten *adj* no escrito.

up *adv* arriba, en lo alto; levantado:—*prep* hacia; hasta.

upbringing *n* educacion *f*.

update *vt* poner al dia.

upheaval *n* agitacion *f*.

uphill *adj* dificil, penoso:—*adv* cuesta arriba.

uphold *vt* sos tener, apoyar.

upholstery *n* tapiceria *f*.

upkeep n manteniniento m.
uplift vt levantar.
upon prep sobre, encima.
upper adj superior; mas elevado.
upper-class adj de la clase alta.
upper-hand n (fig) superioridad f.
uppermost adj mas alto, supremo:—
to be ~ predominar.
upright adj derecho, perpendicular, recto; puesto en pie; hon rado.
uprising n sublevacion f.
uproar n tumulto, alboroto m.
uproot vt desarraigar.
upset vt trastornar; derramar, volcar:—n reves m; trastorno m:—adj molesto; revuelto.
upshot n remate m; fin m; conclusion f.
upside-down adv de arriba abajo.
upstairs adv de arriba.
upstart n advenedizo m.
uptight adj nervioso.
up-to-date adj al dia.
upturn n mejora f.
upward adj ascendente:—~s adv hacia arriba.
urban adj urbano.
urbane adj cortes.
urchin n golfillo m.
urge vt animar:—n impulso m; deseo m.
urgency n urgencia f.

urgent adj urgente.
urinal n orinal m.
urinate vi orinar.
urine n orina f.
urn n urna f.
us pn nos; nosotros.
usage n tratamiento m; uso m.
use n uso m; utilidad, practica f:—vt usar, emplear.
used adj usado.
useful adj , ~ly adv util(mente).
usefulness n utilidad f.
useless adj inútil:—~ly adv inútilmente.
uselessness n inutilidad f.
user-friendly adj amistoso.
usher n ujier m; acomodador m.
usherette n acomodadora f.
usual adj usual, comun, normal:—
~ly adv normalmente.
usurer n usurero m.
usurp vt usurpar.
usury n usura f.
utensil n utensilio m.
uterus n utero m.
utilize vt utilizar.
utility n utilidad f.
utmost adj extremo, sumo; ultimo.
utter adj total; todo; entero:—vt proferir; expresar; publicar.
utterance n expresion f.
utterly adv enteramente, del todo.

V

vacancy n cuarto libre m.
vacant adj vacio; desocupado.
vacate vt desocupar.
vacation n vacaciones fpl.

vaccinate vt vacunar.
vaccination n vacunacion f.
vaccine n vacuna f.
vacuous adj necio/a, bobo/a.

vacuum n vacio m.
vagina n vagina f.
vagrant n vagabundo.
vague adj vago.
vain adj vano.
valet n criado m.
valiant adj valiente.
valid adj valido.
valley n valle m.
valor n valor m.
valuable adj precioso.
valuation n tasa, valuacion f.
value n valor.
valued adj apreciado.
valve n valvula f.
vampire n vampiro m.
vandal n gamberro m.
vandalize vt danar.
vandalism n vandalismo m.
vanguard n vanguardia f.
vanilla n vainilla f.
vanish vi desvanecerse.
vanity n vanidad f.
vanquish vt vencer.
vantage point n punto panoramico m.
vapor n vapor m.
variable adj variable.
variance n discordia f.
variation n variacion f.
varicose vein n variz f.
varied adj variado.
variety n variedad f.
various adj vario.
varnish n barniz m.
vary vt, vi variar.
vase n florero m.
vast adj vasto.
vat n tina f.
vault n boveda f.
veal n ternera f.
veer vi (mar) virar.

vegetable adj vegetal, n ~s pl legumbres fpl.
vegetable garden n huerta f.
vegetarian n vegetariano, na m/f.
vegetate vi vegetar.
vegetation n vegetacion f.
vehemence n vehemencia f.
vehement adj vehemente.
vehicle n vehiculo m.
veil n velo m.
vein n vena f.
velocity n velocidad f.
velvet n terciopelo m.
vendor n vendedor m.
veneer n chapa f.
venerable adj venerable.
venerate vt venerar.
veneration n veneracion f.
venereal adj venereo.
vengeance n venganza f.
venial adj venial.
venison n (carne de) venado f.
venom n veneno m.
venomous adj venenoso.
vent n respiradero m; salida f.
ventilate vt ventilar.
ventilation n ventilacion f.
ventilator n ventilador m.
ventriloquist n ventrilocuo m.
venture n empresa f:—vi aventurarse.
venue n lugar de reunion m.
veranda(h) n terraza f. *
verb n (gr) verbo m.
verbal adj verbal.
verdict n (law) veredicto m.
verification n verificacion f.
verify vt verificar.
veritable adj verdadero.
vermin n bichos mpl.
vermouth n vermut m.
versatile adj versatil.
verse n verso m.

versed *adj* versado.
version *n* version *f.*
versus *prep* contra.
vertebra *n* vertebra *f.*
vertebral, vertebrate *adj* vertebral.
vertical *adj*, **~ly** *adv* vertical (mente).
vertigo *n* vertigo *m.*
very *adj adv* muy, mucho.
vessel *n* vasija *f.*
vest *n* chaleco *m.*
vestibule *n* vestibulo *m.*
vestige *n* vestigio *m.*
vestry *n* sacristia *f.*
veteran *adj, n* veterano (*m*).
veterinary *adj* veterinario.
veto *n* veto *m.*
vex *vt* molestar.
via *prep* por.
viaduct *n* viaducto *m.*
vial *n* redoma *f.*
vibrate *vi* vibrar.
vibration *n* vibracion *f.*
vicarious *adj* sustituto.
vice *n* vicio *m.*
vice versa *adv* viceversa.
vicinity *n* vecindad *f.*
vicious *adj* vicioso.
victim *n* victima *f.*
victimize *vt* victimizar.
victor *n* vencedor *m.*
victorious *adj* victorioso.
victory *n* victoria *f.*
video *n* videofilm *m*; video cassette *f*; videograbadora *f.*
video tape *n* cinta de video *f.*
vie *vi* competir.
view *n* vista *f.*
viewpoint *n* punto de vista *m.*
vigilance *n* vigilancia *f.*
vigilant *adj* vigilante.
vigorous *adj* vigoroso.
vigor *n* vigor *m.*

vile *adj* vil.
vilify *vt* envilecer.
villa *n* chalet *m.*
village *n* aldea *f.*
villain *n* malvado *m.*
vindicate *vt* vindicar.
vindication *n* vindicacion *f.*
vindictive *adj* vengativo.
vine *n* vid *f.*
vinegar *n* vinagre *m.*
vineyard *n* vina *f.*
vintage *n* vendimia *f.*
vinyl *n* vinilo *m.*
viola *n* (*mus*) viola *f.*
violate *vt* violar.
violation *n* violacion *f.*
violence *n* violencia *f.*
violent *adj* violento.
violet *n* (*bot*) violeta *f.*
violin *n* (*mus*) violin *m.*
viper *n* vibora *f.*
virgin *n* virgen *f.*
virginity *n* virginidad *f.*
Virgo *n* Virgo *f* (signo del zodiaco).
virile *adj* viril.
virility *n* virilidad *f.*
virtual *adj* , **~ly** *adv* virtual(mente).
virtue *n* virtud *f.*
virtuous *adj* virtuoso.
virulent *adj* virulento.
virus *n* virus *m.*
visa *n* visado *m*, visa *f.*
vis-a-vis *prep* con respecto a.
visibility *n* visibilidad *f.*
visible *adj* visible.
vision *n* vista *f.*
visit *vt* visitar:—*n* visita *f.*
visitor *n* visitante *m/f.*
visor *n* visera *f.*
vista *n* vista, perspectiva *f.*
visual *adj* visual.
visualize *vt* imaginarse.

vital adj vital.
vitality n vitalidad f.
vitamin n vitamina f.
vitiate vt viciar.
vivacious adj vivaz.
vivid adj vivo.
vivisection n viviseccion f.
vocabulary n vocabulario m.
vocal adj vocal.
vocation n vocacion f.
vociferous adj vocinglero.
vodka n vodka m.
vogue n moda f; boga f.
voice n voz f:—vt expresar.
void adj nulo:—n vacio m.
volatile adj volatil; voluble.
volcanic adj volcanico.
volcano n volcan m.
volition n voluntad f.
volley n descarga f; salva f; rociada f; volea f.
volleyball n voleibol m.

volt n voltio m.
voltage n voltaje m.
voluble adj locuaz.
volume n volumen m.
voluntarily adv voluntariamente.
voluntary adj voluntario.
volunteer n voluntario m.
voluptuous adj voluptuoso.
vomit vt, vi vomitar.
vortex n remolino m.
vote n voto.
voter n votante m/f.
voting n votacion f.
voucher n vale m.
vow n voto m.
vowel n vocal f.
voyage n viaje m.
vulgar adj ordinario.
vulgarity n groseria.
vulnerable adj vulnerable.
vulture n buitre m.

W

wad n fajo m.
waddle vi anadear.
wade vi vadear.
wafer n galleta f.
waffle n gofre m.
wag vt menear.
wage n salario m.
waggon n carro m.
wail n lamento m.
waist n cintura f.
wait vi esperar.
waiter n camarero m.
waiting list n lista de espera f.
waiting room n sala de espera f.
waive vt suspender.

wake vi despertarse.
waken vt, (vi) despertar(se).
walk vt, vi pasear; andar.
walking stick n baston m.
wall n pared f; muralla f; muro m.
wallflower n (bot) aleli m.
wallpaper n papel pintado m.
walnut n nogal m; nuez f.
walrus n morsa f.
waltz n vals m (baile).
wan adj palido.
wand n varita magica f.
wane vi menguar.
want vt querer.
wanton adj lascivo.

war *n* guerra f.
ward *n* sala f
wardrobe *n* guardarropa f.
warehouse *n* almacen m.
warm *adj* calido; caliente.
warm-hearted *adj* afectuoso.
warmth *n* calor m.
warn *vt* avisar.
warning *n* aviso m.
warp *vi* torcerse.
warrant *n* orden judicial f.
warranty *n* garantia f.
warren *n* conejero m.
warrior *n* guerrero m.
wart *n* verruga f.
wary *adj* cauto.
wash *vt* lavar.
washbowl *n* lavabo m.
washing machine *n* lavadora f.
washing-up *n* fregado m.
washroom *n* servicios mpl.
wasp *n* avispa f.
waste *vt* malgastar.
watch *n* reloj m; vigilar.
watchdog *n* perro guardian m.
water *n* agua f.
watercolor *n* acuarela f.
waterfall *n* cascada f.
watering-can *n* regadera f.
waterlily *n* ninfea f.
water melon *n* sandia f.
watertight *adj* impermeable.
watt *n* vatio m.
wave *n* ola, onda f.
waver *vi* vacilar.
wax *n* cera f.
way *n* camino m; via f.
we *pn* nosotros, nosotras.
weak *adj* , **~ly** *adv* debil(mente).
wealth *n* riqueza f.
wealthy *adj* rico.

weapon *n* arma f.
wear *vt* gastar, consumir; usar, llevar.
weary *adj* cansado.
weasel *n* comadreja f.
weather *n* tiempo m.
weave *vt* tejer; trenzar.
weaving *n* tejido m.
web *n* telarana f.
wed *vt, vi* casar(se).
wedge *n* cuna f.
Wednesday *n* miercoles m.
wee *adj* pequenito.
weed *n* mala hierba f.
week *n* semana f.
weekend *n* fin de semana m.
weekly *adj* semanal.
weep *vt, vi* llorar.
weeping willow *n* sauce lloron m.
weigh *vt, vi* pesar.
weight *n* peso m.
welcome *adj* recibido con agrado:—
    ~! ¡bienvenido!.
weld *vt* soldar.
welfare *n* prosperidad f
well *n* fuente f *adv* bien.
wench *n* mozuela f.
west *n* oeste, occidente m.
wet *adj* humedo, mojado.
whale *n* ballena f.
wharf *n* muelle m.
what *pn* que, qué?, el que, la que, lo
    que.
whatever *pn* cualquier o cualquiera
    cosa que.
wheat *n* trigo m.
wheel *n* rueda f.
wheelbarrow *n* carretilla f.
wheelchair *n* sillita de ruedas f.
wheeze *vi* jadear.
when *adv* cuando.
whenever *adv* cuando; cada vez que.

where *adv* dónde? *conj* donde.

whether *conj* si.

which *pn* que; lo que; el que, el cual; cual:—*adj* qué?; cuyo.

while *n* rato *m*; vez *f*:—*conj* durante; mientras; aunque.

whim *n* antojo *m*.

whine *vi* llorar, lamentar

whinny *vi* relinchar.

whip *n* azote *m*; latigo *m*.

whirlpool *n* vortice *m*.

whirlwind *n* torbellino *m*.

whiskey *n* whisky *m*.

whisper *vi* cuchichear.

whistle *vi* silbar.

white *adj* blanco.

who *pn* quién?, que.

whoever *pn* quienquiera, cualquiera.

whole *adj* todo.

wholemeal *adj* integral.

wholly *adv* enteramente.

whom *pn* quién? que.

whooping cough *n* tos ferina *f*.

whore *n* puta *f*.

why *n* por qué?

wick *n* mecha *f*.

wicked *adj* malvado.

wide *adj* ancho.

widen *vt* ensanchar.

widow *n* viuda *f*.

widower *n* viudo *m*.

width *n* anchura *f*.

wield *vt* manejar.

wife *n* esposa *f*.

wig *n* peluca *f*.

wild *adj* silvestre.

wilderness *n* desierto *m*.

wild life *n* fauna *f*.

will *n* voluntad *f*.

willful *adj* deliberado; testarudo.

willow *n* sauce *m* (arbol).

willpower *n* fuerza de voluntad *f*.

wilt *vi* marchitarse.

wily *adj* astuto.

win *vt* ganar.

wince *vi* encogerse, estremecerse.

winch *n* torno *m*.

wind *n* viento *m*.

wind *vt* enrollar.

windfall *n* golpe de suerte *m*.

winding *adj* tortuoso.

windmill *n* molino de viento *m*.

window *n* ventana *f*.

window box *n* jardinera de ventana *f*.

window ledge *n* repisa *f*.

window pane *n* cristal *m*.

window sill *n* repisa *f*.

windpipe *n* traquea *f*.

windshield *n* parabrisas *m* invar.

windy *adj* de mucho viento.

wine *n* vino *m*.

wine cellar *n* bodega *f*.

wine glass *n* copa *f*.

wing *n* ala *f*.

winged *adj* alado.

wink *vi* guinar.

winner *n* ganador.

winter *n* invierno *m*.

wintry *adj* invernal.

wipe *vt* limpiar.

wire *n* telegrama *m*.

wisdom *n* sabiduria *f*.

wisdom teeth *npl* muelas de juicio *fpl*.

wise *adj* sabio.

wisecrack *n* broma *f*.

wish *vt* querer.

wishful *adj* deseoso.

wit *n* entendimiento *m*.

witch *n* bruja *f*.

witchcraft *n* brujeria *f*.

with *prep* con; por, de, a.

withdraw *vt* quitar.

withdrawal *n* retirada *f*.

withdrawn *adj* reservado.

withhold vt detener.

within prep dentro de.

without prep sin.

withstand vt resistir.

witless adj necio.

witness n testigo m.

witticism n ocurrencia f.

wittily adv ingeniosamente.

witty adj ingenioso.

wizard n brujo m.

woe n dolor m; miseria f.

woeful adj triste.

wolf n lobo m.

woman n mujer f.

womb n utero m.

wonder n milagro m.

wonderful adj maravilloso.

won't abrev de will not.

woo vt cortejar.

wood n bosque m; selva f; madera f; lena f.

woodland n arbolado m.

woodlouse n cochinilla f.

woodpecker n picamaderos m invar.

woodworm n carcoma f.

wool n lana f.

woolen adj de lana.

word n palabra f.

wordy adj verboso.

work vi trabajar; obrar.

world n mundo m.

worm n gusano m.

worn-out adj gastado.

worried adj preocupado.

worry vt preocupar.

worse adj, adv peor.

worship n culto m; adoracion f.

worst adj el/la peor.

worth n valor m.

worthwhile adj que vale la pena; valioso.

worthy adj digno.

wound n herida f.

wrangle vi renir f.

wrap vt envolver.

wrath n ira f.

wreath n corona f.

wreck n naufragio m; ruina f.

wreckage n restos mpl.

wren n reyezuelo m (avecilla).

wrestle vi luchar; disputar.

wrestling n lucha f.

wretched adj infeliz, miserable.

wring vt torcer.

wrinkle n arruga f.

wrist n muneca f.

wristband n puno de camisa m.

wristwatch n reloj de pulsera m.

writ n escrito m; escritura f.

write vt escribir.

write-off n perdida total f.

writer n escritor, ra, m/f; autor, ra m/f.

writhe vi retorcerse.

writing n escritura f

writing desk n escritorio m.

writing paper n papel para escribir m.

wrong n injuria f; injusticia f.

wrongful adj injusto.

wrongly adv injustamente.

wry adj ironico.

XYZ

Xmas n Navidad f.

X-ray n radiografia f.

xylophone n xilofano m.

yacht n yate m.

yachting n balandrismo m.

Yankee n yanqui m.

yard n corral m; yarda f.

yardstick n criterio m.

yarn n estambre m; hilo de lino m.

yawn vi bostezar

yeah adv si.

year n ano m.

yearling n primal m, ala f.

yearly adj anual.

yearn vi anorar.

yearning n anoranza f.

yeast n levadura f.

yell vi aullar.

yellow adj amarillo.

yelp vi latir, ganir.

yes adv, n si (m).

yesterday adv, n ayer (m).

yet conj sin embargo; pero:—adv todavia.

yew n tejo m.

yield vt dar, producir.

yoga n yoga m.

yog(h)urt n yogur m.

yoke n yugo m.

yolk n yema de huevo f.

yonder adv alla.

you pn vosotros, tu, usted, ustedes.

young adj joven.

youngster n jovencito, ta m/f.

your(s) pn tuyo, vuestro, suyo:—**sincerely ~s** su seguro ser vidor.

yourself pn tu mismo, usted mismo, vosotros mismos, ustedes mismos.

youth n juventud f.

youthful adj juvenil.

youthfulness n juventud f.

yuppie adj, n yuppie m/f.

zany adj estrafalario.

zap vt borrar.

zeal n celo m; ardor m.

zealous adj celoso.

zebra n cebra f.

zenith n cenit m.

zero n zero, cero m.

zest n animo m.

zigzag n zigzag m.

zinc n zinc m.

zip, zipper n cremallera f.

zodiac n zodiaco m.

zone n banda, faja f; zona f.

zoo n zoo m.

zoological adj zoologico.

zoologist n zoologo, ga m/f.

zoology n zoologia f.

zoom vi zumbar.

zoom lens n zoom m.